D0931388

Endorsements

"The US Park Service hadn't let a news camera into my grandparents' home for 30 years. Bulky equipment and bric-a-brac are not compatible. Then along came Andrew. He made promises about caution and hand-held recorders, which he kept. But more than that, it was his enthusiasm. It was infectious. Once in the house, he really enjoyed himself. Yes, he's accurate and thorough. But the fun is what really comes through in his work."

- Clifton Truman Daniel
Truman Grandson, Author, Historian

"Andy's hard work, research and passion come through in his words and this book. I applaud his enthusiasm and appreciation for our First Ladies. The First Ladies Man is bringing these great women into the spotlight and getting them the recognition they so well deserve."

- Anita B. McBride
Former Chief of Staff to Laura Bush
Executive Chief-in-Residence, Center for Congressional and Presidential Studies
American University, School of Public Affairs

"Och doesn't just tell a good story. He's read the documents, touched the artifacts and met the characters. His enthusiasm for and devotion to his topic are infectious. For anyone doing research that involves First Ladies, his books are a must-read."

- Jay L. Gordon, PhD
Youngstown State University
Youngstown, OH

"This book is a delightful mix of biography, history, and personal storytelling. Little-known details about our presidents' wives are revealed, as well as particulars of Andrew Och's journey to uncover their stories. Unusual for their Time: On the Road with America's First Ladies II is informative, creatively imagined, and a good read."

- Nancy K. Loane,
author of Following the Drum: Women at the Valley Forge Encampment

"Highly recommending Unusual for Their Time: On the Road with America's First Ladies Volume 2 is the easy part. Matching up to author Andrew Och's engaging writing, well, that's a tough challenge. He's traveled airways, highways, big city streets, back roads and country meadows to bring us up close and personal with these amazing women. As a C-SPAN producer he did a lot of research, talked with professional historians and visited well-known and little-known places. He also had one-of-a-kind moments with First Ladies' family members. (You'll never forget your visit to the Truman home with their grandson). Good history with humanity. I'm already planning my first road trip ..."

- Linda Evans
Greensboro Historical Museum
Greensboro, NC

"Without the enthusiasm and passion for his subject matter, the author could never have made this whirlwind journey into the lives of America's First Ladies. I find it an excellent example of the more you are aware, the more you want to learn; thus, your life is richer. Volume One gave me a new perspective on this sorority of unusual, but historically obscured, women. It made me stop, think and appreciate their contributions, comforts and additions to the culture of American life. Now, for Volume Two, it's goodbye to Ida McKinley, the many in between, and hello to Edith Roosevelt and the First Ladies of the twentieth and twenty-first centuries! What is your guess?"

- Jennine Hedler
Jailhouse Antiques
Galesville, MD

"I had the pleasure of meeting Andrew Och while I was an archivist at the Hoover Institution Library and Archives at Stanford University. He was filming an episode for C-SPAN's "First Ladies" series focusing on Lou Henry Hoover. Andrew is a consummate professional who has delved deep into the history of America's First Ladies and is almost certainly the most knowledgeable person in the world on the subject. After half a decade focusing on the intricate stories of the women who have loved and supported their husbands in the most difficult job in the world, Andrew Och has truly earned the title of First Ladies Man."

- Nick Siekierski
Hoover Institution Library and Archives
Stanford University

"The journey continues in Volume 2 of Unusual For Their Time [On The Road With America's First Ladies] and like Volume I, it is a sheer delight that does not disappoint! The stories, the travel log and the First Lady's themselves are all a fascinating read. Once again, Mr. Och takes you on an informative and entertaining odyssey into the lives of the women who not only shaped the White House but history itself. Through his inquisitive eyes, assortment of observations, ability to retain details and willingness to share personal antidotes, you are literally transported every step of this excursion, without ever having to leave the comfort of your environment."

- Jacqueline Berger
National Speaker and Author on America's First Ladies
"The First Ladies Lady"

Unusual For Their Time

On The Road With America's First Ladies

VOLUME TWO

Andrew Och

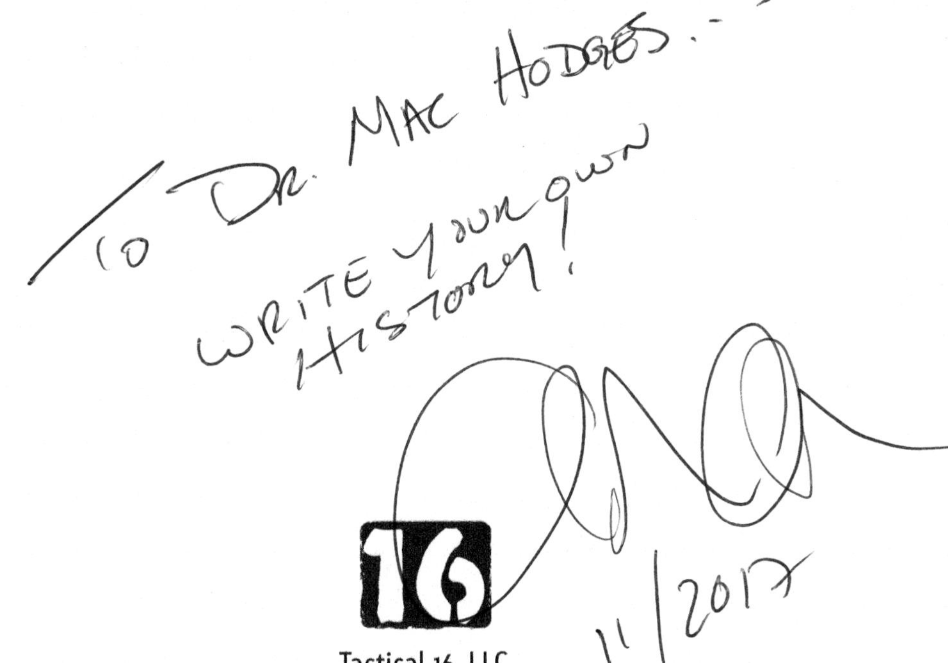

To Dr. Mac Hodges...
Write your own history!
11/2017
16

Tactical 16, LLC

Unusual For Their Time:
On The Road With America's First Ladies
Volume Two

First Edition

Published by Tactical 16, LLC

Colorado Springs, CO

eISBN: 978-1-943226-29-0
ISBN: 978-1-943226-28-3 (hc)
ISBN: 978-1-943226-27-6 (sc)

Printed in the United States of America

This book is dedicated to my mom

JULIE CARROLL OCH
December 5, 1943 – November 17, 2010

She would have loved this project

And my uncles

Tiffany Blake Carroll
February 11, 1934 – July 1, 2017

He showed me the importance of putting other people first

David C. Carroll
March 11, 1929 – June 29, 2014

He taught me to be an individual

Volume 2 is further dedicated to

Arabella & Remington

be unusual for your time

Thank You

Erik and Kristen Shaw at Tactical 16, Andrea Lea Samari, Stacy Hickman, Harriet Handler, Jay Gordon, Joe Wilk, Frank P. Och, The Zeus Man, and all of the family, friends and fans that followed this amazing journey

Special Thanks

Brian Lamb, Susan Swain, Terry Murphy, Mark Farkas, Peter Slen, Michele Remillard and everyone at C-SPAN, Anita McBride and the White House Historical Association, Clifton Truman Daniel, and all of the consulting historians, live guests, authors and experts who contributed to the "FIRST LADIES: Influence and Image" series

Very Special Thanks

Heather York thompson for being my heart and my fire, for believing in me and getting in on the "Ground Floor" …I'm so glad we found each other…we fit…and #hashtagsDOcometrue

Table of Contents

INTRODUCTION 1

CHAPTER 1 27
Edith Roosevelt

CHAPTER 2 49
Helen Taft

CHAPTER 3 63
Ellen Wilson

CHAPTER 4 77
Edith Wilson

CHAPTER 5 95
Florence Harding

CHAPTER 6 107
Grace Coolidge

CHAPTER 7 131
Lou Hoover

CHAPTER 8 155
Eleanor Roosevelt

CHAPTER 9 179
Bess Truman

CHAPTER 10 199
Mamie Eisenhower

PHOTO ALBUM 215

CHAPTER 11 235
Jacqueline Kennedy

CHAPTER 12 251
Lady Bird Johnson

CHAPTER 13 267
Pat Nixon

CHAPTER 14 279
Betty Ford

CHAPTER 15 291
Rosalynn Carter

CHAPTER 16 305
Nancy Reagan

CHAPTER 17 323
Barbara Bush

CHAPTER 18 333
Hillary Clinton

CHAPTER 19 347
Laura Bush

CHAPTER 20 359
Michelle Obama

CHAPTER 21 369
Melania Trump

CONCLUSION 383

ADDENDUM 387

LIST OF LOCATIONS 391

LIST OF RESOURCES 395

PREFACE: INTRODUCTION FROM VOLUME ONE

Behind every great man is an even greater woman...or in this case...lady.

If George Washington had never met and married Martha Dandridge Custis, this book would be called something quite different. It may have been written in a different language, or perhaps never written at all.

If George and Martha Washington had never married, America would be a very different place... or quite possibly... not America at all.

Martha Washington was unusual for her time.

My name is Andrew Och and I am the "THE FIRST LADIES MAN." I have completed an unusual journey. This journey gave me the opportunity to learn about every First Lady of the United States from Martha Washington to Michelle Obama (at the time). I have traveled to nearly every city, town, village, home, school, church, birthplace, cemetery, train station, farm, plantation, library, museum, general store, town center and cottage that relates to these women, these ladies. I wanted to find out what type of woman grows up to become married to a President of the United States. What I discovered was that many of our Presidents married up. Most of these men would not have made it to the White House without the help, influence, and support of their wives. Nearly all our Presidents married a woman who was unusual for her time. I have traveled tens of thousands of miles in the lives, footsteps and shoes of these First Ladies, and in this book, you will get to travel in mine.

In early October 2012, I signed on with a team at C-SPAN, the American cable and satellite television network, to be a series producer for their special television project called "FIRST LADIES: Influence and Image." Little did I know this project would become an adventure, and a journey that would change my life forever.

When I interviewed for the job, I was asked if I was a television producer that specialized in historical subjects. I said that I was not. They asked me if I had taken a lot of history classes in school, or if I had a special interest in political history or the First Ladies specifically. I said that I did not—nothing out of the ordinary anyway. I was then asked why I should be hired for this position or why I even wanted it. The answer to that question was very simple.

I thrive in the field—"on assignment"—and I like a good story. I like to tell good stories, and I like to listen to good stories. These women…these First Ladies…are full of amazing stories. Stories, I feel, not many people have ever heard. That alone intrigued me. I was curious and wanted to know more about these women. More than "her husband was…" or "when she was First Lady she…" I wanted to get to know the women behind the title. This project and this series did just that.

Women have been part of America's history from the very beginning, and yet, their contributions are often under-documented and under-credited. Women have long risen to the challenges before them, often without a vote or voice in matters that directly affected them. Even though, as a result of their hard work and efforts, they have achieved victories in both social and legal circles. Still, history relegates many of their achievements and contributions to the back of storage facilities and the bottoms of closets. I wanted to lift the dust cloths and empty out the historical closets. These First Ladies were, and continue to be, an example of how each of us—man, woman and child—can be unusual for our time and make the world around us a better place.

What we typically know best about each of these women (if we know anything at all in some cases) is what they accomplished during their time in the White House as America's First Lady. Serving as First Lady put each of these women directly into the public eye, and on the world's stage, but before they served as First Lady, they were women. They were daughters, sisters, teenagers, cousins, young women, students, successful working women, wives and mothers, and later, after leaving the White House, they often went on to become ambassadors, grandmothers, widows, and countless other great things. These are the women I wanted to get to know. I wanted to tell the stories of these women.

I have been in the room where Edith Wilson was born, and the room where

Lucy Hayes died. I've seen the cradles in which First Ladies have rocked their children to sleep, and the sewing machines used to mend their husband's military uniforms. I have been in the room where Martha Washington said goodbye to her husband, our first President, George Washington. I have stood at the bed-side in the room where Dolley Madison nursed her ailing husband, President James Madison, and helped him transcribe the notes of the Continental Congress during his dying days.

I have seen Lady Bird Johnson's swimsuits hanging in her walk-in closet at the LBJ ranch outside of Austin, Texas. In Marion, Ohio I saw a lucky four-leaf clover charm given to Florence Harding by a war veteran. It remains in the jewelry box given to her by her father. I have seen Harriet Lane's music book. It was still sitting on the piano in her presidential uncle's parlor at Wheatland, the James Buchanan House, in Lancaster, Pennsylvania. I have held earrings woven from Elizabeth Monroe's hair. I have held a letter that Martha Washington wrote to Abigail Adams wishing Mrs. Adams well in her new role as the wife of the second President of the United States, John Adams. I have climbed back staircases to private sitting rooms and special places where some of these women chose to be alone with their thoughts.

I have examined Lou Hoover's unique and vast weapons collection in West Branch, Iowa. I ventured out to the Roosevelt's Pine Knot cabin in Keene, Virginia. I have gone down into the Adams' crypt beneath the United First Parish Church in Quincy, Massachusetts, and I stood on the steps of the Plains United Methodist Church in Plains, Georgia where a young Jimmy Carter asked a teen-age Rosalynn Smith out on their first date.

I have learned about the gifts of state that First Ladies receive. I have seen those gifts from foreign lands, and the more personal gifts from their presidential husbands. I learned that even as frugal as President Calvin Coolidge was, he spared no expense when it came to his wife Grace's wardrobe. I learned that Mary Todd had a rather happy childhood with rare access to her influential father and his political discussions, in the Todd family home in Lexington, Kentucky. I have looked out of the window where Julia Dent watched a young Ulysses S. Grant walk up to her parents' White Haven plantation house to ask for her hand in marriage.

In 2013, I interviewed Harrison Tyler, the living Grandson of President James Tyler—the tenth President of the United States (It's true…I've done the math and traced the history). He lives in his grandparents' Sherwood Forest Estate in Charles City, Virginia. Clifton Truman Daniel gave me a private tour of his grandparents' home (President and Mrs. Truman) in Independence, Missouri. He spent a significant amount of time there as a boy. Due to a clumsy television crew, including a nearly disastrous incident involving an elbow and a teacup, my C-SPAN camera was the first allowed in the home in over 30 years. I have seen Mamie Eisenhower's extensive wardrobe, including her shoe and hat collections. Each pair of shoes has a label in them stating the shoes were made exclusively for First Lady Mamie Eisenhower.

I have been in private parlors, sitting rooms and libraries, each of which hold personal and professional writings of these women, as well as those of their Presidential husbands. I read letters that I probably wasn't supposed to read. I read letters that only the intended recipient was to have read. I have seen journals and photo albums of these women and their families showing some of the most private and personal moments in a person's life.

I have walked the hallways of privately owned homes, glided my hands along the handrails and physically followed the footsteps of American History. These are the stories that I wish to share with you. I want you to get to know and understand these First Ladies as I have. I want their stories to be told.

I was so very fortunate to have been given an all access, backstage, VIP pass to many of the nation's most treasured collections and historical landmarks. There were very few doors that were closed to me, and even fewer vaults that remained locked. This was not something I took lightly or for granted. I felt a great responsibility to use this access to share the most complete and accurate accounting of these women, and the amazing lives they led that I could.

Traveling to the many places, seeing all the wonderful collections and getting this unrestricted look at the lives of these women, I could not help but feel a personal connection to all the First Ladies. I think it's impossible to see and read so much about a person's life and not feel a closeness to them.

When I was hired by C-SPAN as a contracted producer and began my work, I was handed a large red book—about the size of a 1980's phone book—it became one of my main resources for historical and regional information about these women. I was told to start reading, outlining and planning, because I would most likely start traveling within a month.

I knew right away this series was going to be a massive project. I knew it was going to be important, but I didn't know what my exact role was going to be, and I had no idea how quickly, or how much, I was going to have to learn about these women. Perhaps most significantly, I had no clue how much I was going to enjoy the subject matter and research.

What I also didn't know—what none of us on the show knew, I don't think—was that I was not going to stop traveling for over a year. We could not have guessed that by the end of the series, we would be responsible for having collected one of the largest and most comprehensive collections of video, interviews, B-roll (supplemental footage of places and things to use over voices, interviews and narrations) and information on the collective group of American First Ladies that exists in the world today.

The research, planning and studying for this endeavor was so intense, it almost didn't leave me time to think about the big picture or long term implications of the work. I didn't realize its scope until people started to tell me—friends, family, strangers I met along the way—how interested in this project they were.

Looking back, I think I didn't have time to grasp the overall end game, because I was too caught up understanding the material, or the First Lady or the trip that was right in front of me during whatever day, week, show or month I was involved in at that exact moment. I couldn't see the forest for the trees. At its most hectic, my schedule was:

Mon.....edit location pieces and research – live show – guest relations/booking

Tues.....travel and shoot for upcoming shows

Wed.....travel and shoot for upcoming shows

Thurs.....travel – edit – book guests – research next trip/lady

Fri.....edit – book guests – research next trip/lady

Sat/Sun.....more editing and research

REPEAT

This was a pretty consistent schedule for the entire series. It was like that for six weeks straight during the summer of 2013 between Seasons One and Two of "FIRST LADIES: Influence and Image." At one point, I was sitting in a hotel room in Plains, Georgia, having just shot material for the Rosalynn Carter show, while I was watching the Pat Nixon show live on TV. At a certain point during Season Two, gate attendants and TSA agents began to recognize me—and my gear—at Baltimore Washington International (BWI) Airport.

There were many challenges to my work. I was traveling to places that I had never been to before, and at each location I worked with new people who I had not previously met. I had to carry and set up all my gear (video, audio and lighting equipment), scout the location based on information from a phone call or two, maybe a few e-mails, and conduct interviews with experts and historians. All while I filmed the interviews, toured houses and museums, shot B-roll and scenery (as well as any other material that might come in handy for the show). All of this in an eight-hour (or often more) work day. This would be challenging for a crew of five or more. I was a crew of one.

I must acknowledge the people I met along the way, who were helpful in gathering information and footage of related locations. Without them, their knowledge and collections, the series and these books would not have been possible. There is a unique and hard working group of people out there preserving our nation's history. We should be grateful for them, and take full advantage of the work they are doing. We should strive to teach it to our younger generations, and not to leave a single stone unturned, as we seek additional information. We should be relentless in our desire to discover new things about historical subject matter, even that which we think has been fully researched. There is almost always more to the story.

People always notice you when you travel with a camera. So, as I went around the country to these various locations, historical sites, museums, homes and libraries I attracted a lot of attention. People approached me and asked me things like "what are you doing?" or "who do you work for?" and "what show will this be on?" My answer was usually the same or similar. I said that I was "working on a show about the First Ladies." The response was almost always the same."Which one(s)?" And I would say, "all of them!" Invariably, this would prompt a follow up like "Well, sure…but no…which one SPECIFICALLY are you focusing on?" And to this my answer was always the same."EVERYONE. MARTHA TO (at the time) MICHELLE." The more people were amazed by the thought of this, the more I began to understand there was something bigger than I realized to all this. There was a hunger for this material, and a broad desire to know more about these women.

Another interesting and frequent occurrence was running into people with direct or indirect ties to the First Ladies. A woman came up to me in the gardens of Monticello while I was there researching and filming for the Jefferson women (Martha and Patsy). In our conversation, she told me that her mother had worked for Lady Bird Johnson. While I was filming for the Hoover show, a man in West Branch, Iowa told me about land his family owned that was once owned by President and Mrs. Garfield. In Virginia, I crossed paths multiple times with a couple tracing their family heritage. We spent the better half of a week trading stories about what each of us had learned at several different locations.

I would also run into colleagues and other TV folks both at home in Washington, DC and on the road. When TV people see other TV people they know—there's an unspoken word or look—the dead giveaway "PortaBrace" camera cases and gear bags. We would talk about projects: current, past or future. When they heard what I was doing for the series, the time frame in which I was doing it, and the fact that I was traveling by myself with no local hired crews, assistants, or built in extra days for site surveys or scouting…they all had similar reactions, they'd say "YOU'RE NUTS!"

While researching and filming the series, I found myself in a lot of airports, train stations, rental car offices, lounges, restaurants, hotels, bars and cabs. The more I talked to people, the more I was convinced there was interest and excitement about this information. There was a thirst for knowledge about these women that further fascinated me. In most conversations, people would bring up the subject of me writing a book, keeping a journal, or starting a blog or travelogue. To this I would say I was flattered by their interest and that those were all great suggestions. Maybe I would get to something like that down the road. However, for the time being, I had my hands full with the television series.

I remember during Season Two, being on a plane to Kansas City sitting across from a very nice woman who noticed my odd shaped camera bag as I stowed it above my seat. She asked if it was a dog carrier (you would be surprised by the number of people who thought my camera bag was a dog). I laughed and told her that A) my dog wouldn't fit in such a small carrier and B) even if he did, I wouldn't put him in the overhead storage. We both laughed, and then I explained that it was a video camera. Her reaction was like the reactions I described earlier: "What show? What's it about? Who do you work for?"

So, I told her about the C-SPAN project and my role. She took an immediate interest. We talked the entire flight (apologies to anyone around us on that flight who may have been trying to sleep or had no interest in the First Ladies). Throughout our discussion, I suggested she could—and should—stop me anytime the conversation got dry or she'd had enough. She never stopped me. We chatted all the way up to the baggage claim where she was meeting her estranged half-brother for some family business surrounding a sick relative. We exchanged information, because she said she wanted to watch the series and read my book, if I ever wrote one. I hope she's reading this now, and recognizes herself here.

She was one of many significant encounters I had during my travels, leading me to further believe there was an audience out there for these First Ladies and me, beyond the C-SPAN series. Every trip I took I would find myself sitting on a plane or train, in a bar or hotel, standing in line to pay for a soda at a convenience store, talking to someone about the series. The reaction was usually the same. First, they seemed very interested in the project, and second, they wanted to know when I would be writing a book.

Right about the time I started working on season two of the series, it hit me. All this time, I'd been talking to people across America about the series and my work. They showed interest in what I had to say and the untold stories of these women. The information had implanted itself so deeply in my brain; I had no other choice but to continue talking about them, and telling their stories.

So, I started to put together a speaking program and began writing my first speech. At first, the plan was to introduce the C-SPAN series and myself. Then, I would talk about Martha Washington because…she was the first. I mean, I had to, right? After that, I would explain what the series had done for the field of study, and what the journey had meant to me. I would then talk about and discuss every first lady from Martha to Michelle (again, at the time). Then, I did the math. That speech would end up being over four hours long. I have no doubt I could speak to a crowd for over four hours, and not run out of things to say. However, I would never put an audience through such an ordeal. After some re-thinking—and more than a few edits—the speaking program came in just under an hour (not including the question and answer portion at the end).

That's when I started to consider a book. A book? A book could be as long or as short as I wanted. A book could—and should—cover every First Lady, all the related locations I'd visited, and all my adventures along the way. A book could be that initial speech I wanted to write. It could be a travel guide, with things like "where to eat when you're in Abilene, Kansas." It could be written in first person. It could be informative, a narrative, a collection of short stories, even a textbook. It could be informal. It could be anything I wanted it to be.

Author's Note - Unusual For Their Time

The title and phrase "UNUSUAL FOR THEIR TIME" started out as something I was told about the women I was studying at most of the places I visited. One First Lady was unusual for her time, because she was highly educated or well-read— another, because she triumphed over great loss or adversity – and, yet another, because of her musical ability or tastes or a European adventure as a young woman. These women and the people who studied them and kept their collections were all amazing people. But, I started thinking, these women can't be unusual if they are all so similar, and have so much in common. Could they? Of course, the people at each location thought their First Lady was something special, that's their job. And they all were and are special, of course. But how were they so unusual for their time? It was said so many times that when I came back to DC, I would say to my colleagues, "You're not gonna believe this... BUT...First Lady X, Y or Z was UNUSUAL FOR HER TIME!" Then my co-workers began to ask me, "Hey, man, is "so and so" UNUSUAL FOR HER TIME?" We even had an "olde tyme" voice that we used which required the person saying it to hook their thumbs into their armpits and rock back and forth on their feet in exaggerated pontification. The bit was always met with good-natured laughter. But then, I started to think. These women weren't necessarily unusual when you put them in a group together as First Ladies.

Their uniqueness came when compared to other women of their time (which, I knew, was what the historians and curators meant all along). Even other men of their time. They were unusual when compared to just about anyone; man, woman or child—and in many cases this uniqueness spanned decades, lifetimes and centuries. These women were indeed, UNUSUAL FOR THEIR TIME. The phrase took on a whole new meaning, and now is the title of this book and my speaking program.

Which brings us to this. This is the travelogue of my adventures…the sharing of the information I gathered during my contributions as a producer for the C-SPAN series "FIRST LADIES: Influence and Image." It is a recalling of my journey, which lasted from October 2012 through February 2014 (and, now beyond), as experienced, documented and chronicled by me. Andrew Och. THE FIRST LADIES MAN. Enjoy.

The chapters in this book go in chronological order of First Ladies – there have been more First Ladies and Hostesses than there have been Presidents – therefore the chapter number does not alway coincide with the related President's number in Presidential order and history.

INTRODUCTION TO VOLUME TWO

Author's Note – Unusual For Their Time

I am starting Volume Two over Memorial Day weekend of 2016 in the rustic and peaceful surrounds of my family's Deep Creek Lake, Maryland cottage. It is where much of Volume One was written. It's a quiet place (if you want it to be), and I have family and friends up here for when a distraction or break is needed. I am grateful for many things in life, and this place is one of them.

SEASON ONE ended with Ida McKinley on Monday June 10, 2013, and the entire "FIRST LADIES: Influence and Image" crew and staff breathed a sigh of relief. It was a true milestone. We had covered the history of America through the eyes of the First Ladies from its very humble beginnings in the late 1700's through 1902 when President William McKinley was assassinated, and his Vice President, Theodore Roosevelt, took over as President. C-SPAN's technical team had set out a nice dessert table complete with a congratulations sign. We were all very pleased with what we had accomplished with our relatively small team. We celebrated that night, but got to work on Season Two the very next day.

There were no new live shows during the summer between Seasons One and Two. Like Season One, this would give me a three-month head start to travel, collect video and edit final pieces before the new shows began again in September. There were a couple staff shifts, changes and additions, but the core group remained basically the same. At first, I wasn't sure if my travel would continue as it had in Season One. There was talk (as there had been during Season One) of adding another traveling producer. At first, I thought this would be a much-needed addition. The travel for Washington through McKinley had been exhausting and brutal at times. It would be helpful to lighten to load a bit when it came to the location shoots. However, I had also started to realize the scope and long-term implications of this project. People outside of the project were telling me how interesting this work was, friends were asking me questions about this work—more so than any other of my past projects or shows. Personally, and professionally, I was on a roll. The whole team was on a roll. We hit a stride during Season One as all the pieces fell into place, and we had a real rhythm going. Then I thought, "No, no, no…I got this." I had a conversation with Executive Producer, Mark Farkas, and assured him I could keep up the pace, and I could continue to bring home strong pieces on my own. Something big was forming in my mind. I wasn't sure what it was, but it was on the horizon.

I had learned a lot during Season One, and I don't just mean about the First Ladies. Professionally, I learned how to edit video on Final Cut 7. Personally, I learned how to pack efficiently for a week's worth of travel to multiple locations with completely different climates. Late night battery charging issues, laptop media transfer and gear management mishaps were all but gone. I had refined my whole operation, and was a well-oiled production machine. I had become a warhorse, and I liked it. A lot of blood, sweat, tears and back pain had gone into Season One…on everyone's part. For me specifically, I had unofficially accepted the challenge to do what so many of my TV friends and colleagues had said was crazy or altogether impossible. As I mentioned in Volume One, this project was huge. It was significant. It meant something. I didn't consciously know it yet, but I was becoming the FIRST LADIES MAN.

As well as I had come to know my seven bags of gear, and the employees and TSA Agents at BWI Airport, there was always more to learn. There would always be new challenges. Light bulbs would still burn out in the middle of an interview. Gear would still malfunction. Planes would still be late. Meals would be missed. Travel would be difficult. Days would be long, and I was still on the road by myself. But I liked it that way. When things went wrong, I had only myself to blame, and went things went well, I could congratulate myself on a job well done (right before having to drive myself to the next town).

As it was in Season One, so it was in Season Two. Couples got married, women got pregnant, families welcomed babies, we celebrated birthdays, and unfortunately, some people left for other projects and other endeavors. Life went on around us. However, life for me was the First Ladies. At one point, I was in DC preparing for the live Lucy Hayes show, and I mentioned that Peggy Eaton (you'll remember her from the Andrew Jackson Administration and the Petticoat Affair scandal which caused nearly the entire Executive Cabinet to retire) had a loose tie to Mrs. Hayes. Mrs. Hayes had sent flowers to Eaton's funeral on behalf of her and President Hayes. She got a bit of public grief for it. As I mentioned this, our show host, Susan Swain, looked across the table and laughed as she said, "it's possible you know way too much about these women, Andy!" She said something very similar during the show prep for the Caroline Harrison show when I asked if we were going to get into anything about Mrs. Harrison's pet goat (Whiskers) or her horse (John).

The research and travel for Season Two began as it had for Season One. I had my big red book (along with a few new ones), my U. S. map with color-coded pushpins, and my dry erase board. My DC desk/cubicle at C-SPAN was still my command and planning center. I was still conducting phone and email pre-interviews with people I had neither met nor worked with in places I had never been. The books taught me about the locations and told me where I needed to go. The map and push pins let me visualize where in the U. S. I would be traveling. The dry erase board (and my desk blotter calendar—which I still have) kept track of when I would be going to these various places, and how many women I would be covering for each trip. Like I said, I had become a well-oiled production machine. However, like every machine there were break downs, and the occasional monkey wrench.

The first woman I would be covering for show number one of Season Two was Edith Roosevelt. She was the first First Lady of the 20th Century, and a significant influence on the modern day White House. She moved the role of First Lady into the 1900's. She is often lost in history, because of her husband. Theodore Roosevelt was a striking and memorable figure. She also gets cast aside a bit in popular culture and mainstream recollection because of Eleanor Roosevelt. It seems that the public—and much of history—only has room for one First Lady when it comes to the Roosevelts…and that's Eleanor. I will get into the specifics of the two Roosevelt women in their respective chapters, but suffice to say that BOTH are quite unusual for their time. So, what was the Edith

Roosevelt "monkey wrench?"

When I traveled to the Roosevelt's Oyster Bay Long Island estate, Sagamore Hill, it was covered in scaffolding, and the house was completely empty. The entire house was undergoing a massive renovation project. The collection was spread out in storage facilities across the United States. This is not the way I wanted to start Season Two. Especially, after I had heard so many amazing things, and seen so many incredible pictures of the home. But time, and the series, marched on. We had to get some kind of footage. Fortunately, some of the collection was stored in a building on the property. The staff there was top notch, and we captured some wonderful stories and artifacts. There will be more on this in the Edith Roosevelt chapter.

Another monkey wrench (and it was not a small one) was the Federal Government shutdown which started on October 1, 2013, and lasted until October 16, 2013. Regular Federal Government operations resumed on October 17 after an interim bill was signed into law. I will get into exactly how difficult it was, what we did to work around it, and just how amazing Samantha Kenner and her staff were at the Dwight D. Eisenhower Presidential Library, Museum and Boyhood Home in Abilene, Kansas in the Mamie Eisenhower chapter. To the world outside of Washington, DC and Government work, this two-week plus period was but a blip on the radar screen, if that. A DC political "stunt." However, for our show, and my travel schedule, it was crippling. Once again, there were no extra days or wiggle room for delays like this, and we needed work-arounds and back-up plans. We put safety nets in place, and waited for the Federal Government to get their act together. It all worked out in the end, as viewers saw, and as you will read later in this book.

A welcome addition to Season Two was more existing audio and video recordings. The 20th Century brought with it new technological advances in communications and multimedia. We saw our first First Lady appear in a moving picture with sound. This also made my job a little easier. As the season progressed, we discovered there was more and more video in existence of these women, so I didn't have to fill in as many of the gaps with new and original video. If you remember all the way back to Martha Washington, I had to go to five different locations to tell her story with my videos. We still wanted to get as many places on camera that related to these women, but each live show was only 90 minutes. The in-studio guests, and live calls from viewers still played a significant part in each show. By the second half of the 20th Century there was a plethora of solid interviews, speeches and other videos of First Ladies. We used the women in their own words every chance we got. However, my location shoots and videos still provided a valuable historical tone, a sense of discovery and took the viewer out of the studio and Washington, DC for a sense of adventure. The access I was afforded remained remarkable and the collections and places were just as amazing in the second season as they had been in the first.

Another thing that was different about Season Two was the fact that every President from Herbert Hoover through George W. Bush had a Federally-operated Presidential Library and Museum. Many of the Presidential Libraries and Museums libraries have foundations that also collect and archive valuable material, all of which helped tell the stories of these women. In Season Two there was almost too much to work with. This made narrowing down the subject matter for my videos more difficult. These facilities were truly amazing and each one gets more modern and more advanced than the one before it. The George W. Bush Presidential Library and Museum in Dallas, Texas was the newest in the fleet at the time of the series. It was impressive, to say the least, and I'm sure when President Obama completes his facility in Chicago, that one will be the flagship.

I completed my work on the C-SPAN series on February 17, 2014. Since then, I have continued my travels and my research. I put my speaking program and Power Point presentation together pretty quickly, and used the contacts I had made to book speeches at the Hoover, Eisenhower and Truman Libraries in May 2014. It was really nice to revisit these locations from the series. When I returned to speak, I didn't have my camera, and I wasn't working like I had been during the series. I got to spend time with people who I now considered to be friends, and I got to examine the collections and exhibits in different ways.

In some cases, these locations invited me to return and speak because of a new or different—sometimes traveling—exhibit or featured item(s). When I spoke at the Hoover Library in West Branch, Iowa, they were featuring a special collection of Lou Hoover's items which included one of her cars. They also had a special exhibit of First Ladies' dresses that was traveling the country. It was great to see these things that weren't there on my first trip. I also got another private tour to see some of the things I didn't get to see the first time.

My trip back to the Rutherford B. Hayes Presidential Center in Fremont, Ohio gave me time to tour parts of the Spiegel Grove Estate that had been under renovation while I was there in 2013. They were also hosting a special "Red Dress" exhibit, aimed at raising awareness for women's heart health. The exhibit included many First Lady's red gowns and dresses. This exhibit was making its way through various museums and historical locations across the country that year. They had dresses as far back as Lucy Hayes, and as recent as Laura Bush. These return visits were helpful to continue my research, and update my speaking programs.

When I return to speak at the places that also happen to be the final resting places for these Presidential couples, I take some time before the speech to visit their graves for reflection and a moment of meditation. I feel it's important to remember these people were real. They had private lives, which are no longer very private, and our access to their lives must be respected and acknowledged. I am grateful for their service to our country, and I feel honored I can continue to explore and discover them, their belongings and their homes. Expressing that in my own way allows me to set my mind straight before I go into their museums, or libraries, or homes to talk about them, their families, and their impact on our Nation and the world.

I have spoken at several Presidential Libraries and Museums, state universities, town halls, local historical societies and groups, local libraries and museums, private parties and functions, Daughters of the American Revolution groups, Colonial Williamsburg and at the Smithsonian Institute in Washington, DC since the series finished. It has been a great honor and privilege to speak in front of all these groups and audiences. It is very thrilling to bring these women's stories to new audiences and new places. It is equally rewarding to entertain repeat crowds and locations. Every time I speak something new is revealed, or discussed. The question and answer session at the end of the program is one of my favorite elements of any live event. It's a time for me to find out and answer what you—the people—are interested in knowing. Many times, the Q & A lasts longer than the speech. This was definitely the case at the Hoover Library in 2014. I even had people following me out to my car to continue their questions and comments. It was more than flattering, and I stuck around to make sure everyone got the answers and information they were looking for.

In August 2016, I spoke at the Smithsonian Associates in Washington, DC. I will do my best to explain what this meant to this punk kid from Rockville, Maryland, but suffice it to say it meant the world. This, for me, was a sort of homecoming. I had family members there. My girlfriend was seeing me speak for the first time. There were colleagues and former classmates in the audience. Friends had driven great distances to see the speech. And, HELLO…it's THE SMITHSONIAN! One friend in particular had been telling me for quite some time how impressed he was with the whole First Ladies Man project. He had mentioned several times how much he wanted to see one of my speeches. He sent me an interesting text the week BEFORE the actual speech. The text started off by saying how sorry he was that he and his wife had missed my speech. He went on to explain the various conflicts and obligations that had kept them from attending the speech. I laughed out loud as I texted my response, which was something like, "GOOD NEWS, MAN!! The speech is NEXT WEEK so you didn't miss it!! SEE YOU THERE!!" I obviously thought he was trying to politely back out attending, and I get it…people are busy. Believe me…no one is more flattered and humbled than me by people's interest and support of this whole First Ladies Man project. But, he is a long-time great friend and any chance to call him out and poke a little fun is welcomed. In any event, I was floored when Eric "Solo" and Jennifer Solomon walked into the Smithsonian Associates theater. He and I were both laughing as they sat down in the front row, because we both knew how his original text and my response sounded. We still laugh about it every time we're together. He always says, "you didn't think we were gonna post, did you, Ochster!" I'm laughing writing this now. It's just another amazing part of this whole adventure. I get to share moments like these with friends, family, loved ones and new friends all across America, and hopefully one day around the world.

Something else I've been doing since February of 2014 is going to completely new historical places. The series schedule was tight. So, was the budget. Like

I've mentioned—more than a couple times—I was the only traveling producer. We only had so much time and money to get to places. It was impossible to go to every single place that related to each of these women. Hard decisions were made and some locations got left out of the series. However, now that I'm on my own schedule (and dime), I can go anywhere I want, any time I want. So, I do.

I recently went to speak in Greensboro, North Carolina on my Volume One book tour. Greensboro used to be Guilford County in the British Colonies. This was where Dolley Madison (then Dolley Payne) was born on May 20, 1768. What's left of her birthplace is a marker in front of a Real Estate office on a busy road next to a gas station. It ain't much, but it's there. The Greensboro Historical Museum has some remarkably rare Dolley items on display. Some of the items in their collection are so rare they are kept in a secure storage area and rotated into museum exhibits (and traveling collections) to limit their exposure to the destructive elements of regular public display. Among those artifacts that they don't just break out for anybody, were the original daguerreotype plates from what is most likely the first photograph of a First Lady (although she was not a sitting First Lady at the time). Mrs. Madison was invited to be a special guest at the Washington Monument cornerstone ceremony. Her picture was taken at the event. She was wearing one of her trademark turbans. The Greensboro Historical Museum has the turban from the event. It was thrilling to see these pieces right in front of me after having seen them in the photograph in so many different books.

These and other Dolley Madison artifacts were found in an attic in outside of Philadelphia. A family descendant or ancestor lived in the house. It had perhaps been written in their Will, or mentioned repeatedly to family members, not to forget about the "treasure chest in the attic." When the woman died the executor of the Will was going through the house, and found a hidden panel in a wall in the attic and opened it up. There was a trunk inside full of Dolley Madison items and documentation. A historically minded philanthropist in Greensboro heard about the items and purchased the trunk for the museum in Dolley's hometown.

In October 2016, I visited the Lucy Webb Hayes House in Chillicothe, Ohio. I gave five different speeches in one day—a new personal record (four school groups during the day in the house, and one open to the public in the evening at the Historical Society building). It was the home in which she was born, and unfortunately there had not been time to get there during the filming of the series. The two-story, clapboard house was built in 1825, and had a staircase that ran up the middle of the home. This divided the four-room house in half. Most of the interior woodwork is original. One bedroom upstairs to the right contained museum style Lucy and Rutherford exhibits filled with photographs, newspapers and other documents and memorabilia. They had incredible photographs from their early courtship that I had never seen before. The room across the hall was set up as an actual bedroom with some original pieces, including a childhood bed. The parlor downstairs had pictures of Lucy's parents, and other period pieces to give an accurate feel of the home from when Lucy had lived there. It was an important place in the life of one of my favorite First Ladies. I have been to many birthplaces, and I feel they are crucial locations in understanding where these women's stories began. Local historians had recently done substantial renovations to the property, and it was a productive trip all around.

All these places—big and small, near and far—are important parts of these American First Ladies' lives. It is my goal to continue to visit, study, research and write about all of them. It's fun to think that this adventure I started with C-SPAN will continue. There are still so many places to go and things to see. So much more research to be done. I enjoy these women and the travel so much, and I appreciate the interest people have in them and my FIRST LADIES MAN project. Give the people what they want, I say.

I followed the 2016 Presidential election very closely. However, not in the way most people did. I was interested in what was arguably the most unusual possibility of potential First Spouses in our country's history. People really took an interest in those possibilities. So much so, that I did several national and international television and radio interviews on the subject. I also wrote several articles about the different outcomes and what they would mean for the office of the First Lady, their spouse, their families and the country.

From my first speech in May 2014, people began asking me what would have happened in a Hillary Clinton White House with Bill Clinton as the first male Presidential spouse. They asked if I would have to change my name to the First Man's Man or something crazy like that. The answer to that was simple. NO. I will always be the FIRST LADIES MAN. What people didn't think about in this case is that Bill Clinton is a former President, and his title will always be President Clinton. So, if Hillary had won the election, we would have had President Clinton and President Clinton. In all likelihood, the future male spouse of a President will be called the First Gentleman. However, it wasn't until Harriet Lane and the 15th Presidency (James Buchanan) that the term First Lady was usesd. So, you never know what we'll settle on, or when we'll settle on it. A day will come when a man is the one married to a President (hopefully, sooner than later). Had Carly Fiorina done better, her husband Frank (who has never been an elected official) would have been a clearer cut case.

There were also two chances in 2016 for the country to have its second foreign-born First Lady. Jeb Bush's wife, Columbia, was born in Mexico, and Melania Trump was born in Slovenia (former Yugoslavia). The first and only foreign-born First Lady, before Melania Trump, was Louisa Catherine Adams (born in London on February 12, 1775). The second only Catholic First Lady was a chance with Bernie Sanders's wife, Jane O'Meara, and we now know that Melania Trump is Catholic. Although it was not publicized during the campaign, Mrs. Trump's Catholicism was recently revealed during the Trump's 2017 trip to Italy. President and Mrs. Trump had an audience with the Pope, and Mrs. Trump had her rosary blessed. A spokesperson for the First Lady verified her faith after the trip. Until now, Jacqueline Kennedy had been the only Catholic First Lady. So, in Melania Trump America got its second foreign born and second Catholic First Lady.

Yes, 2016 had a lot of very interesting potential outcomes right from the start. Here in Volume Two's Hillary Clinton chapter I have included a "WHAT IF" side note. Here I examine what a Hillary Clinton Presidency might look like with Bill as the first First Gentleman. There is, of course, a Melania Trump chapter with my thoughts and research from her brief time as First Lady (as of August 2017). We must give her a chance to mold and craft the role as she sees fit, just as every First Lady before her has had.

So, here is VOLUME TWO. The continuing stories of our First Ladies. All of the ladies from the 1900's and 2000's. This is the next travelogue of my adventures; the sharing of information, research and stories I gathered during my contributions as a producer for the C-SPAN series "FIRST LADIES: Influence and Image." It is a recalling of my journey, which lasted from October 2012 through February 2014 as a producer for C-SPAN, and now continues, on my own, as THE FIRST LADIES MAN…as experienced, documented and chronicled by me. Andrew Och. Enjoy.

Travelogue Food Tip

So much of this book was written in Deep Creek Lake, Maryland, I would be remiss if I didn't make mention of one of my favorite places to eat up there. My family has been going to Deep Creek Lake since the late 1970's, and one place that has always been there, and keeps the lights on and the doors open to this day, is Little Sandy's. Over the years, it has had only two owners (both of whom I've met). They've had gas pumps and a car wash (both now gone). They serve breakfast, lunch and (now) dinner with daily specials and friendly servers. They've always had a down-home diner atmosphere, not to mention the BEST breakfast on the lake. They have everything you would expect from a diner breakfast menu, but during the whole writing process I have ordered the same thing every time—a soda and an omelet.

I start with a Coke Zero. Although the last time I was there, they were out of Coke Zero, so I got a Diet Coke. My waitress, Peggy, set it down in front of me, and it had "ANDY" on it. I yelled, "Hey, I got my name…that NEVER happens!" The owner, Tina said, "That one's on the house then!" I then ordered my usual sausage, bacon, tomato and cheese omelet with an English muffin. The muffin comes buttered, and I add grape jelly. This breakfast has fueled many chapters in both books, and I can't thank the Little Sandy's gang enough. During the week days, Hannah was my waitress, and she always asked which First Lady I was on, or how the book was coming. She should get a proper "thank you" here, too. Also, as of June 2017, and another well-attended and fun speech at the Garrett County Historical Society, my book can now be purchased at Little Sandy's. Tina has a very nice little gift shop set up in the diner that features local arts and crafts, and she was kind enough to clear some space on the shelf for my books. If you're in the area stop in for a bite, and as always…tell 'em THE FIRST LADIES MAN sent ya!

Author's Note – In The Beginning

For those of you who didn't read the first book, or need a refresher course, here is Chapter One from Volume One—Martha Washington.

CHAPTER 1
Martha Washington

New Kent County, Virginia – Williamsburg, Virginia – Valley Forge, Pennsylvania – Philadelphia, Pennsylvania – Mount Vernon, Virginia

Martha Washington was born Martha Dandridge on June 2, 1731 on her family's Chestnut grove plantation in New Kent County, Virginia. Her parents were John Dandridge and Frances Jones Dandridge. Martha and George Washington were married on January 6, 1759. They had no children together. Martha had four children with her first husband, Daniel Parke Custis. Martha Washington died in Mount Vernon, Virginia on May 22, 1802 at the age of 71.

NEW KENT COUNTY, VIRGINIA

Martha Dandridge Custis Washington and her first husband, Daniel Parke Custis, lived in New Kent County, Virginia on what was known as the White House Plantation. So, perhaps it's fitting that she should end up marrying a second time, to a man who would become the first President of the United States of America. And even though the title "FIRST LADY" wasn't coined until after her death, but Martha Washington is considered to be the first First Lady of the United States of America.

Historical Note – Build It, They Will Come

The actual White House wasn't built nor was Washington, D. C. the Nation's capital until the Adams Administration.

The Custis family owned the White House Plantation, and while it no longer exists, New Kent County, Virginia does. It was a clear and chilly November morning on the day I drove into New Kent County. The low, rolling hills were frequent as I drove the winding roads. The trees were stripped bare by fall, and there was a distinct smell of water in the air from the local creeks and rivers.

I pulled over to the side of the road and assembled my camera and tripod. With no house or specific location to shoot, this would have to do. We needed some kind of visual to characterize the childhood of the first First Lady.

As I stood there in the middle of a field, waiting to hear someone shouting from a distant farmhouse, "GET OFF MY LAND!" I pictured a young Martha Dandridge growing up and spending her childhood here. We see Martha today in paintings like her official portrait – older, heavy set, grandmotherly – in her bonnet and apron. But, what was she like as a little girl? Where did she run and play? What did her house and room look like?

Looking at these fields and creeks and farms and waterways took on new meaning. An image of a young girl and her friends laughing and playing came to mind. Maybe she was sitting on a rock by a creek in the sun learning how to read or splashing in the water? Maybe she was wandering through the fields and woods? Maybe she was sitting on the front porch of her parent's house, as she liked to do later in life on the promenade of Mount Vernon?

As my camera rolled and I panned and zoomed, this was the scene that played out in my mind when suddenly, a crow cawed overhead and a tractor trailer roared by, bringing me back to modern times. This would be the footage we would use to set the scene for the discussion of Martha's childhood.

Martha was definitely better educated than most young women of her day. Being home schooled by her mother definitely put her at an advantage later in life, however, it wasn't initially enough to impress her first husband's father when the two met in Williamsburg, Virginia. There was more to look at and less left to the imagination about Martha Washington in Williamsburg than there had been in New Kent County.

WILLIAMSBURG, VIRGINIA

Duke of Gloucester Street was bustling with holiday shoppers and tourists when I visited, the day before Thanksgiving. In fact, it was a race to beat the workers installing all of the Christmas decorations around town. I needed to keep the decorations out of my footage to preserve the shelf life of the show, and not have it tied to any specific day, time or season. This was just another added challenge to my daily list of obstacles.

The day started off by conducting sit down interviews with "Martha" and the lead historian for Colonial Williamsburg, Dr. Taylor Stoermer. My hosts had arranged for a small, recreated house to be the set for the interviews. The house had electricity, heat, plenty of space and a bathroom. This would not be the case at many locations during my journey.

The woman who reenacted Martha for visitors was Lee Ann Rose. During my conversation with her, I was amazed by a story that she told about a young Martha Dandridge's conversation with her future Father-in-Law. George Washington was not Martha's first husband. She was first married to, and widowed by Daniel Parke Custis. And, it would seem that Martha was not of the same social standing as the Custis family and John Custis did not approve of his son marrying Martha.

A closed-door meeting between Custis's father, John, and young Martha Dandridge was arranged. Custis went into the meeting with every intention of denying Martha permission to marry his son. When the meeting was over, Custis was said to have completely changed his mind saying something to the effect that he could see his son marrying no one other than Martha Dandridge. No one knows exactly what was said in the meeting, but clearly Martha had the wit and wherewithal to impress John Custis enough that he consented to the marriage.

This is so important in the life of Martha Washington, and so crucial to the story of America, because it is her marriage to Custis, and the wealth she inherited from him, that elevated Martha into a social position that would later become very appealing to a young military man named George, who was, not only looking for a bride, but also, to improve his social standing. Just think if Martha had never married Daniel Custis (which was extremely close to happening), she would have never met and married George Washington. The ripple effect on what we now know as the United States of America is almost unimaginable.

Custis's untimely death left Martha a widow in her early twenties, a mother of two (Martha and Daniel had four children, two died in childhood), and extremely wealthy. Upon her first husband's death, Martha found herself in charge of over 8,000 acres of profitable tobacco fields, the owner of very valuable real estate in Williamsburg and the surrounding area, and in possession of more than three times the Virginia Governor's salary in silver. She had the silver on hand, in the house. Also, contrary to our common perception of Martha based on her portraits as an older woman, recent DNA reconstructive computer imaging shows that Martha, in her early 20's, had been quite attractive. In short, she was young, rich, attractive and one of Williamsburg's most desirable bachelorettes.

Dr. Taylor Stoermer, Williamsburg's leading historian at the time, was the next interview. He was so knowledgeable about not only Martha Washington, but also Martha Jefferson, Martha Jefferson Randolph and Letitia Tyler that he will appear in future chapters of this book as well.

It was Taylor who really brought into perspective the pre-Washington life of Martha Custis for me. Martha's marriage to Custis produced two surviving children who later gave her two grandchildren. These grandchildren would be raised by George and Martha Washington as their own; neither child of Martha and Daniel Custis lived beyond early adulthood. Martha's first marriage produced something else that would endure. Wealth.

Production Note - Live Guest

Dr. Stoermer was also a two time live guest on the series, appearing on the Letitia Tyler and Frances Cleveland episodes.

When Daniel Parke Custis died, Martha became a widow at the age of 26. This left her with land, money, and property in excess, which was especially rare for a woman of her age in the 1700's. One of the first things she did was to contact the principal tobacco purchaser in England. She let him know of Custis's death, and more importantly, she informed the purchaser that she intended to continue growing and shipping tobacco to him at the same price, with the same deal, that he'd had with her husband. This is an important part of the story. Society was not set up for women to be business owners and land operators. Women were not legally allowed to own land. A mother could oversee and take care of land and financial inheritance, but only to keep it intact for their sons or to provide for their families. Many women of the day did not succeed in doing so. Not only did Martha succeed, she thrived.

It would seem Martha had everything. Everything that is, but a husband and a father for her children. Enter George Washington.

George Washington was a young, up and coming military man. He was tall and good-looking, a perfect match for the young and attractive Martha. As the story goes, Martha wasn't terribly interested in George at first. It was his attention to her children that attracted her to him. They began a courtship, and the rest – as they say – is history. So, this is why I say consider what might have happened had Martha NOT married George.

She is the one that brought the social status and significant wealth to the relationship. She is the one that had the tobacco fields and real estate in Williamsburg. She had her financial affairs in order, not that George was a financial wreck, nor was he lazy, however, if Martha had not had her affairs well in order at the beginning of their relationship, George might not have found himself in the enviable position as Martha's husband. George would've had to become a more productive tobacco grower and acquire higher social standing on his own merits. What I'm trying to say is, George Washington married up by taking Martha Custis as a bride. This made it logistically possible for him to initiate and command a revolution that would form a new country.

Historical Note – Custis Graves

You can visit the gravesites of Daniel Parke Custis as well as their children, in Williamsburg. Visitors can trace the lives of the people connected to her first marriage that really launched Martha into the high social circle of Williamsburg and its budding new surrounding territories.

VALLEY FORGE, PENNSYLVANIA

Author and Historian Nancy Loane taught me a very valuable lesson within our first 2 minutes together at Valley Forge. DON'T BELIEVE EVERYTHING YOU READ.

Martha Washington – at great personal risk to her life and safety – came to stay with General George Washington at nearly every winter encampment during the Revolutionary War. Most famously, she stayed at the house in Valley Forge, Pennsylvania. It took Martha 10 days to travel from Mount Vernon in Northern Virginia to Valley Forge. This is a testament to the love George and Martha had for each other, and the need for Washington to have his wife by his side. By all accounts, Martha and George were a love match. She was his closest consult and kept him focused and on task.

I arrived early for our interview to get some footage of Washington's Headquarters and the surrounding area. It was a very cold and windy day in January. I remember I was bundled up in my new wool peacoat thinking how cold I was in my Thinsulate™ lined jacket, wool hat, leather gloves, proper shoes and wool socks (with no holes in them). How in the world did the soldiers of the Revolutionary War do it? Sure, it was cold when I was there, but there wasn't even snow on the ground.

Now for Nancy's history lesson about not believing everything you read. I was very much looking forward to hearing the stories of Martha Washington mending uniforms, tending to the wounds and sicknesses of young soldiers and doing her part for the cause during the war. And that's exactly what I asked Nancy about. Her response took me by surprise. She smiled. She even chuckled. She said something like, "please tell me you don't think that's what happened here". She went on to explain that Martha Washington was the wife of the man that led the revolution against Great Britain. She was not out on the battlefield mopping bloody brows and stitching up flesh wounds. Nor was she sitting by the campfire with needle and thread darning the socks and patching the worn elbows of soldiers' jackets.

The "romaticization" of history has become fairly common in modern day story telling. Nancy told me in very precise words how the story of a nurse's letter made its way through family members and the ages into the hands of an all-too-eager-to-believe person who later authored a fantastical telling of Martha's activities at Valley Forge. Only none of these activities were based in truth. In fact, the dates on the letters were so off that it could only be made up. This is what has been ingrained into public opinion, however historically inaccurate.

I said, "Fair enough. What did she do here?" Nancy knew and she told me.

Martha Washington was very busy at Valley Forge and at all of the winter encampments she visited. Her travels from Mount Vernon, just to get to her husband's side, were difficult in and of themselves. Surely she would need time to recover from the journey each time, and to get things in order in camp and prepare for her time there.

At these encampments, she did what any proper lady of the house, farm, estate or plantation would do. She ran the house and entertained guests. She was the lady of Valley Forge just as she was the lady of Mount Vernon. There were meals and events to run and daily tasks and preparations to tend to, to make sure camp ran as smoothly as possible.

While at Valley Forge, Martha threw elegant dinner parties for visiting

Generals, other military officials, and foreign dignitaries. When I think of Valley Forge the word elegant does not come to mind, but the primary documentation supports it. To support these events, a log hut – that no longer exists – was built off of the kitchen for these dinner parties which Martha said, "made our conditions much more tolerable than they were at first".

She talked with and entertained visitors. Martha went to several worship services there at camp. She once held a celebration of the French alliance on May 6th; over a thousand people were in attendance. We know from written records that the food stock and consumption was something quite different than what the soldiers were eating. During the six-month winter encampment, Martha brought in 2,000 eggs, 750 pounds of butter, at least 1,600 pounds of veal. She commissioned paintings of General Washington and arranged for theatrical performances, including General Washington's favorite play (Addison's 1713 tragedy, *Cato*), to be performed on his birthday.

And as surely as Martha Washington was running the encampment and hosting, she was foremost there as a wife to General Washington. Visitors from Philadelphia were frequent. They had friends and important figures come and stay with them at camp. The British were occupying Philadelphia at the time, and there was always news from the city described to Martha in detail during conversations with female friends who would've brought the latest news.

An original banister exists in Washington's Headquarters at Valley Forge. This was the first time during my travels that I got to run my hand along a piece of furniture, a piece of history that also knew the hand of a significant historical figure. It would not be the last. This trip also taught me to look for accuracy in the romanticized versions, stories and legends. Some would end up being true, as you will read about later. But others, like Martha's supposed activities at Valley Forge, needed to be set right in my work and the C-SPAN series.

PHILADELPHIA, PENNSYLVANIA

The second executive mansion of the President of the United States can be seen though Plexiglas viewing panels in the ground at Independence Park in Philadelphia, Pennsylvania. Martha Washington was the first First Lady. There was no one before her. This entire country was new and so were the roles of its leaders. It's here, in Philadelphia, where Martha developed the role of the wife of the President. At this point and time, she wasn't even called the First Lady. She was referred to as Lady Washington or the President's wife.

As the new country began to take shape and people and places were defined, it's here, at the executive mansion, that Martha and the President would host weekly State dinners on Thursdays. On Friday evenings, Martha organized and held Drawing Room receptions. These weekly Drawing Room Receptions were open to the public and anyone of social standing was welcome to attend. It's here in Philadelphia at these more informal Drawing Room Receptions that we again see evidence of Martha and George's relationship. People would often write or remark that President Washington was always more at ease with Martha by his side.

The story of slavery in the President's home is covered at Independence Park. There were as many as 30 paid, indentured and enslaved people serving in the mansion. One story of particular interest is that of Oney Judge, a female slave and personal maid who had come with Martha from Mount Vernon. Oney ran away to gain her freedom, which upset Martha greatly. It is thought that Oney escaped to avoid being given to Martha's granddaughter once she married. Reports tell that Oney liked working for Mrs. Washington, but was not looking forward to becoming the granddaughter's property. Although not a pleasant part of our history or aspect of some of our founding father's lives, it is necessary and well told in Philadelphia.

Author's Note – Happy Birthday, Jim

It was so good to spend the evening just outside Philly with my good friend Jim Deorio on his birthday. This was the first time I had met his son Jimmy. We ate pizza, had cake and played with Batman action figures. You have to take these opportunities to visit with friends and family when work travel allows.

MOUNT VERNON, VIRGINIA

Mount Vernon is the most visited house and home in the United States. It is rarely closed and the visitor always comes first. So much so, that I was only permitted access before they opened to the public. I loaded up my gear and headed out before the sun came up. My hosts there were very gracious to open the house to me, providing me with a behind-the-scenes look at one of the most well known homes in the world. The Washingtons didn't spend much time together here at Mount Vernon. George was often off on a battlefield or living as the President in New York or Philadelphia. So, even though the property itself belonged to George's family's, to me it seemed as though Martha's story is better told here.

Mount Vernon Curator, Susan Schoelwer, knows a great deal about the life and times of Martha Washington at Mount Vernon and the collection of artifacts at the facility. Martha arrived at Mount Vernon in April of 1759, and there was much to do as she brought 12 house slaves with her from Williamsburg to help manage and run the household. She had the financial resources and managerial skills necessary to oversee the estate, much of which, as I mentioned previously, were gained and developed in Williamsburg. Again, Martha's unique abilities enabled President Washington to carry on with his missions away from home for long periods of time. Schoelwer describes Martha as a "take charge woman" a phrase gleaned from the existing letters, research and what we know about Martha's time at Mount Vernon.

The second most visited home in the U. S. is Elvis's Graceland in Memphis, Tennessee and I have been there, too – TWICE.

Martha enjoyed gardens and gardening. She liked to grow vegetables and flowers. She had both gardens off of the kitchen and could easily walk right out to see and choose fresh flowers to be cut for the house or vegetables for any of the daily meals. Mount Vernon was a big operation. It was the center of her life and she was in charge of running the show.

Martha outlived George by less than three years. It was amazing to see the couple's bedroom in such quiet privacy. This was one of the most humanizing moments of the series for me. It is well known that Martha would take daily morning meditations in this room while she and George were living there together. She would sit at her desk surrounded by paintings, etchings, and images of her family. She read her bible, wrote letters or just sat in her chair by the fireplace to quietly think. While Martha took this time to herself, George would be down on the main level, in his office.

We have images of George and Martha Washington. They are old, white haired, powdered wig and wooden toothed grandparent-like figures that do not possess any sense of normalcy or regular life. George may be sitting on a white horse with a sword in his hand, and Martha is usually wearing a bonnet and an apron. At least that's how they appear in my mind.

However, now I imagined a real couple. They were husband and wife. They were parents. They lived together in a house going about their daily routine in the most normal of ways. It was an instant realization and acknowledgement that all of these First Ladies, had similar stories, and I would have an unbridled glimpse into that part of their world. I was sure that the whole story wouldn't just be of their time in the White House as First Lady. Make no mistake, of course that was an important part of their story, no doubt; they did amazing things during that time in their lives. It's why we want to learn about them. But before they were First Ladies, they were the actual people. They were the women. They were the young women that would become the ladies that would marry Presidents.

SUMMARY

What I take away from my travels and research for Martha Washington is that she set the tone. She had to. She was the first. Her traits, characteristics, intelligence, influence and image set the standard against which all who would follow would be judged. Martha Washington was unusual for her time.

She was smarter and better educated than most women of her day. She married a man in a higher social bracket than herself – a man whose father was initially against the union until he met her and she changed his mind. She was widowed at a very early age. She lost two of her four children very early, and the other two in young adulthood. She picked up after her first husband's death and learned how to run and manage the family properties, businesses and fortune.

She then re-married and improved the financial and social standing of her new husband, who later organized and choreographed a revolution, and became the first President of the United States of America. She ran his house and businesses in his absence during times of war and politics. To say that this woman was unusual for her time may be the greatest understatement of this book. This part of my journey taught me not only to not believe everything I read, but also to look for the truth and the facts that tell the stories of our country's history.

The most important thing this first First Lady taught me was that without her, there would be no book to write. There could be no history for a country that doesn't exist. This is a distinct possibility if Martha and George Washington had never gotten married. And quite possibly most amazing of all, is the fact that had young Martha Dandridge not impressed Daniel Parke Custis's father, she would not have been in a position to meet young George Washington. If none of this had happened, the rest (of us) might NOT have been history.

Travelogue Food Tip

Eat at The Cheese Shop on Duke of Gloucester Street in Williamsburg, VA. Their house dressing and fresh sub rolls make any sandwich something special. The roast beef was excellent. I should add here that any and all of these food tips came from friends, family, co-workers, locals or my own exploration and discovery. I did not receive any free food, endorsements or favors for these recommendations. If you go to these places and say my name, I doubt anyone will throw you out. Nor do I think they will give you anything for free. I am expecting you will just get the same fine food and wonderful treatment that I received. ENJOY!

Unusual For Their Time

On The Road With America's First Ladies

VOLUME TWO

CHAPTER 1

Edith Roosevelt

Oyster Bay, New York – Keene, Virginia

Edith Roosevelt was born Edith Kermit Carow on August 6, 1861 in Norwich, Connecticut. Her parents were Charles Carow and Gertrude Tyler. Edith and Theodore Roosevelt were married on December 2, 1886. They had five children together. They raised Theodore's daughter (Alice) from his first marriage to Alice Lee who died giving birth to daughter Alice in 1884. Edith Roosevelt died in Oyster Bay, New York on September 30, 1948 at the age of 87.

OYSTER BAY, NEW YORK – LONG ISLAND

Edith Roosevelt was a beginning. She was actually many beginnings. She was the first new First Lady of the 20th Century. You may recall, Ida McKinley came into the White House in 1897, and after only eight months into his second term, her husband died on September 6, 1901. President McKinley was shot in Buffalo, New York, and died eight days later from his injuries. As the wife of the Vice President, Edith Roosevelt packed up her six children and moved to Washington, DC. Even though her husband had already been the Vice President, McKinley's death left Mrs. Roosevelt uncertain about the fate of her husband and of her family. She and her young family were a welcome breath of fresh air, and a lively contrast to the McKinley Administration. She was also the beginning of a new season for the C-SPAN's "FIRST LADIES: Influence and Image," and has come to represent the beginning of new adventures for the FIRST LADIES MAN.

When I set up my travel plans for Oyster Bay, I realized that I was living a "Planes, Trains and Automobiles" lifestyle. Originally, when I was putting together my July 2013 schedule, I was going to expand that and add a boat to the list. A ferry to be specific. I couldn't make all the dates fit into that second week in July. The ferry ride from Long Island to Massachusetts never happened. I had to split up my New York, Massachusetts and Vermont travel. I guess I will have to add a boat to the mix somewhere on a trip soon. The Edith Roosevelt portion of my journey ended up being different than all the others. The first part was easy enough. I had to pack up my gear, trek across Capitol Hill, and board an Amtrak train at Union Station in DC. I've taken several trains to New York, and my gear was like an appendage by this point. So, no problem there. However, on this trip, my travels did not stop in Manhattan. Once I got into the city, I had to lug my gear on foot through the crowded sidewalks of New York City. I was looking for the Avis rental car office. I had to drive out of the city to Long Island. This was the part that had me a little nervous. But, a FIRST LADIES MAN's gotta do… what a FIRST LADIES MAN's gotta do!

I put my seven-bag traveling road show together, got off the train, found the rental car office on W 31st Street, loaded my gear into the car, plugged the hotel address into the Google Maps app on my iPhone (no Waze yet), and headed out of town to Garden City, NY. The toughest part was pulling that gear along the crowed sidewalks. Every direction I went I seemed to be going against the flow of people. The whole thing was actually a lot easier than I thought—not that I want to do it again in any time soon. Coming back to the city after the shoot was the hard part (that story a bit later). I checked into my hotel, and started my ritual. I looked over my gear, charged my batteries, formatted my media cards, laid out my clothes, double checked times and places, went over my research, and headed off to the nearest Harley Davidson dealer (Nassau Harley Davidson, if you're curious) for a t-shirt. It was good to be back on the road.

When I played drums, and toured in the band—Who is God?—in the 90's, I usually sat in the back of a windowless van with my drums when we traveled. Our guitar player—Veen—was a wildman, and did most of the driving (especially, in NYC), and I liked it that way. I always knew when we got out of Delaware and well into New Jersey, because we would get a great Princeton radio station. I also knew when we were getting close to the city, because I would smell Elizabeth, NJ (sorry, Jake). The guys would also usually wake me up or call me up front when the Statue of Liberty came into view. That and the Empire State Building are my two favorite NYC landmarks. In any event, back then, I didn't drive in New York City.

My day in Oyster Bay got started like most. Early. It was July, and it was hot. The earlier I could get my outside footage, the better. The Roosevelt estate, Sagamore Hill—as I explained in the introduction—was under extreme renovation. Fortunately, the house was built on a hill (funny how that works with a place called Sagamore Hill), and the structure and its contents were not damaged in Hurricane Sandy the previous year. However, full renovation of Sagamore Hill was well underway. The house was all but eclipsed with scaffolding, and much of the Roosevelt collection was scattered all over the country in other museums and storage facilities. Fortunately, a good number of artifacts and historically relevant items were being kept in another building on the property. That's where I was headed, and I was eager to see and hear what these items would tell me about the life of Edith Roosevelt. Theodore Roosevelt bought the land in

1880, and had intended to build a house on it for him and his first wife. Sadly, she died before construction was even underway (we will touch on Roosevelt's first marriage when we discuss the children).

I began by capturing some scenery footage, and what I could get of the house (around and in between the scaffolding) and grounds before the sun got too high in the sky and the temperatures became unbearable. I had seen photos of the house fully furnished. It was a place as remarkable as its former inhabitants, and every wall, nook and cranny had been filled with an artifact, each item more interesting than the next. The Roosevelts were a well-traveled family and their belongings reflected that. I look forward to visiting again soon, now that Sagamore Hill has been restored to its original splendor.

With the exterior and surrounding area footage complete, it was time to settle in at the other building and put together the video pieces that would tell the stories of Edith Roosevelt and her family both here at Sagamore Hill and at the White House. The building I would be working in was the former house of a relative that has been converted into offices for the National Park staff. The hallways and conference rooms were filled with special shelving, cabinets and storage for the artifacts that did not get shipped out to other facilities and locations. It was hard to believe this was only a fraction of the collection, given the volume of artifacts there on site. Curator, Amy Verone, and her staff were set up and ready to get started.

Theodore Roosevelt never went by Teddy. The only name he really used was Theodore. Teddy is a modern nickname used by the public and pop culture, or people who didn't know him personally. Sound familiar?If you recall, Mary Lincoln never using her maiden name (Todd) after she was married. Historians use TR when referring to Theodore Roosevelt, like saying JQA when talking about John Quincy Adams. Here in my book, I will always use Theodore, as he would have preferred.

Edith Roosevelt used Sagamore Hill as her primary residence for most of her married and adult life from 1887 until her death in 1948. There were wonderful sketches, paintings and images in the collection that showed Mrs. Roosevelt at various stages of her life. A prime example of this was a beautiful charcoal sketch of her done by John Sergeant Singer in the 1920's. Singer was a well-known American artist of the day. Sagamore Hill was originally designed as a summer home for the family. However, the Roosevelts turned it into their primary residence and Edith ran the household. She organized dinners, hosted events and personally handled the guests who came to visit, much as she did in the White House as First Lady. She also handled the daily household operations of her large family. Edith was extremely efficient, and she wanted Sagamore Hill to be as self-sustaining as possible. She tried to avoid the need of having to get too many things shipped in from the city.

Stacks and stacks of accounting books and ledgers showed that Edith kept track of the finances and investments down to the penny. Each family member had his or her own line items and expenditures. She diligently kept track of clothes, food, household items, livestock, crops and groceries with clear accuracy. There were entries for butcher receipts, plumber's bills and other house repairs. Reviewing these items, I realized it was that moment or "realness" that I had experienced at every other location, for every other First Lady. Edith Roosevelt was more than a woman in a painting or a picture in a history book. She kept a house and had a family to feed. She did every day chores just like you and me. This kind of bookkeeping was something that I had seen as far back as Martha Washington. This was a common thread among many First Ladies. It's how their husbands had time to go out and campaign and get themselves into the White House. When their affairs were in order at home because of women like Edith Roosevelt, they were free to travel and be politicians. Without their wives, these men would more than likely not have been Presidents.

The Roosevelts grew hay, alfalfa and rye to feed the horses, offsetting the high cost of maintaining livestock at Sagamore Hill. She had an arbor and a garden where she grew eight different kinds of grapes. She had strawberry and blueberry fields, and grew corn and other food for her family and the staff. She didn't have the estate set up to make money, but she did have it functional enough to break even or supplement income whenever and wherever possible. She knew how to manage a household.

There were also more personal items that related to the house and the people that lived and stayed there. The Roosevelts kept a guestbook with pages full of signatures from the guests who came to visit them. Many politicians and Government officials, along with friends and family have entries in the book. Theodore Roosevelt's older sister Anna signed the book during a visit in 1904 with some other family members. One guest even took the time to draw a landscape scene with a bearded man in the clouds that he called "Hope at Sunset" inspired by his stay there. There are even entries in Edith's handwriting that make note of guests who visited and didn't sign the book themselves (this is something my mother would have done, too). This guestbook was perhaps even more endearing and real to me than any other as it related to their Sagamore Hill home. It was something I could easily relate to.

Author's Note – Maryland is for crabs

My good friend Andy Head has a family retreat on the Rhode River off the Chesapeake Bay in Mayo, MD. I have been going there with him and his family since Elementary School. A large group of friends and I still gather there every June for a crab feast. In this house, there is a guest book like the one at Sagamore Hill. Andy's mom still keeps up with the guest book. It's fun to go back and read the entries from over the years. Ten-year-old AndyO was a funny little dude!

Family was everything to Edith Roosevelt. Edith and Theodore had five children together; Theodore, Jr. , Kermit, Ethel, Archibald and Quentin. They also raised Theodore's daughter, Alice. Alice was a product of Theodore's first marriage to Alice Lee; they had married 1880. Theodore Roosevelt and Edith Carow grew up together in New York City. Edith was good friends with Roosevelt's sister Corinne. Edith and Theodore were also very close as children and teenagers.

Friends and family had them pegged to get married one day. During Roosevelt's second year at Harvard, something happened. Edith and Theodore stopped speaking. Theodore met Alice during his junior year. This came as a surprise to people who knew Roosevelt, given his history with Edith. Roosevelt married Alice in 1880, and she became pregnant a few years later.

Roosevelt was in Albany as a member of the New York State Assembly when Alice Lee gave birth to their daughter (Alice Lee Roosevelt) on February 12, 1884. He was informed of her birth by telegram. He was also informed that his wife was gravely ill and semi-comatose. She died two days later from Bright's Disease, a kidney failure that went undetected because of her pregnancy. I haven't read anywhere that suggests Theodore was able to say goodbye to his wife. To make a long story short—or a long story longer—Theodore immediately turned his newborn daughter over to his sister Anna while he grieved. Effectively, he erased all memories of his life with Alice Lee. He and Edith would later take custody of Alice when she was three years old.

Historical Note – A picture is worth a thousand words

There is a famous picture of Lincoln's funeral procession going through New York City on April 25, 1865. When you zoom in on a window in an apartment high above the street and the procession, you can see what appears to be two faces watching the events unfold below. Some suggest these faces are those of young Theodore and Edith. I've seen the photograph. I've studied the photograph. You can Google it and do the same. It could be them. The time and place add up. I'm told, even the window matches up. What I cannot confirm or deny is, whether or not it's actually them. I can't find anyone to confirm this with 100% certainty. But, it could be them. So, look it up, and you be the judge. It certainly makes for a good story.

Edith and Theodore Roosevelt's house was full of children, activity and life.

The collection at Sagamore Hill reflects this. They have a beautiful copper relief piece that has the profiles of Kermit, Ethel and Archie. It's uncertain why only these three children were recreated in this medium, but it hung on the wall outside the nursery on the second floor. It is an exquisite and unusual piece, and I relate it to a fancy and more detailed version of the black and white construction paper silhouettes that I remember from my own childhood.

We know from letters President Roosevelt wrote to his daughter Ethel, that all the Roosevelt children wore little red slippers when they were babies. I was shown both the letters and the slippers during my visit. Edith kept several pairs and they were in remarkably good condition. They look like little, red, leather ballet slippers and they are all very well worn in by the active children who wore them. Most of the childhood items in the collection belonged to, or were saved by their daughter, Ethel. She was a driving force in preserving Oyster Bay and the family items after her mother died. Ethel was known as the Queen of Oyster Bay and the First Lady of Oyster Bay. One of Ethel's items on hand at Sagamore Hill was a piggy bank. Ethel took after her mother and was very detail oriented when it came to her own money, expenditures and bookkeeping. There was also Peter Rabbit book in the collection of Ethel's belongings. This copy was written in French; it exemplified the importance the Roosevelt household held for education, language, reading and an awareness of the world outside of the United States.

Another piece which really spoke to me was the needlepoint sampler Mrs. Roosevelt made that represented her life and her family. Growing up, my brother and I had needlepoint made by our mother in our bedrooms. This piece was very similar one to a piece that hung in my family's front hallway. This item really made the big house at Sagamore Hill a home for me. Mrs. Roosevelt's creation traced her and Theodore's life together with a focus on his career and accomplishments. The six children were included, but the highlights were a Cuban flag, the White House, a pelican (I'm told for conservation) an ink well, and their three sons in uniform. I found this to be a surprisingly "normal" item among a mish mash of unique oddities found in the Roosevelts' home.

When the Roosevelts got to the White House the country was ready to celebrate. The death of President McKinley was shocking and depressing enough, but the McKinley White House had not been a very lively one. William and Ida McKinley (you may remember from Volume One) had two daughters, both of whom died at a very young age–long before they got to the White House. As First Lady, Mrs. McKinley was not in the best of health, suffering from what was most likely epilepsy. While she was as public a First Lady as she could be, the disease did come with its limitations. The point being, a young President and his family were very appealing to the American people. Nothing said this better than the print of a Thomas Nast cartoon of Santa Claus at the fireplace in the White House titled, "There's Life in the Old House Yet." Nast was a well-known newspaper man and cartoonist in New York City, and he captured the mood of the country perfectly in this festive and cheerful piece.

With all the excitement and popularity came problems for a young mother who tried to protect and raise her family in the public eye. Remember from Volume One the problems that the Clevelands faced having young children in the White House. Americans get very excited—some would argue overly so—when there are children in the executive mansion. The Roosevelts had six of them, and they were active, rambunctious and attractive. Mrs. Roosevelt had her very public husband to worry about, too. This caused Edith to be nervous and take precautions, especially given the recent assassination of President McKinley still on everyone's mind. Edith was clever though, and had a very effective way of feeding the public's appetite for her young family. Mrs. Roosevelt hired Washington society photographer, Frances Johnson, to take two different batches of photographs of the family. The pictures from these arranged photo sessions allowed Edith to control their images and their access to the press.

These pictures were given to reputable news outlets and magazines by Mrs. Roosevelt. The Ladies' Home Journal wrote an entire article on the family and used these photographs. There were pictures of the whole family together on the lawn which were fantastic. However, the ones of more value to the public were the individual shots of the children. The most well-known of which, might be Quentin sitting on Algonquin the pony next to a White House police officer in the driveway. Algonquin was the only pony known to have ridden the elevator in the White House. He was taken to visit Archie when he was sick. There are pictures of Alice leaned against a tree, Archie on a bicycle, Theodore, Jr. holding a Blue Macaw named Eli Yale, Ethel is pictured on an outside staircase, and Kermit with their dog Jack. Most of the pictures were taken outside, and many of them included various pets. There were plenty of pictures taken with different combinations of children, pets, backgrounds and activities. Mrs. Roosevelt made sure to have enough pictures of the children to keep the press and the public happy for a long time. This strategy gave the American people the access to the children they wanted, and provided Edith the privacy and security for them she needed.

When it came to White House pets, the Roosevelt's probably had the most… and, the most unusual. The long list included a small bear named Jonathan Edwards, numerous Guinea pigs, Josiah the badger, a lizard named Bill, Maude the pig, hens, roosters, dogs, horses and ponies, a barn owl, a hyena and many, many others. Between the children, the President and the animals, Edith had a real zoo on her hands. Like I said earlier, she was raising seven children there, if you count President Roosevelt. One story that stands out about the pets in the White House was about a Guinea pig. The boys were teasing Ethel one afternoon, and said they were going to take her Guinea pig or let it go in the yard, maybe feed it to the hyena or some such nonsense. Ethel took the animal from her brothers and ran into her father's office crying. President Roosevelt was about to have an important meeting with a foreign dignitary. He took the Guinea pig from Ethel, told her it would be safe from the boys with him, and put it in his pocket. The Guinea pig stayed in President Roosevelt's pocket and slept through the entire meeting. Not only are many of the pets in the family photographs that Mrs. Roosevelt had taken, but they are also represented in the collection at Sagamore Hill.

Many of the dog bowls and collars were saved by the family. There was a sizable pet cemetery on the property. Mrs. Roosevelt kept water and food bowls in her personal office. The dogs were the only ones, besides Mrs. Roosevelt, allowed entrance to her private space without appointment or invitation. One of the hallways was outfitted with huge metal, climate controlled cabinets with glass front doors. They held all the items that related to the pets. There were many pictures of Jack "the wonder dog", and things that belonged to him. He was one of the favorites of the entire family. These cases also stored many personal items of Mr. and Mrs. Roosevelt's. Some of the artifacts were from their parents and families. These items included candle sticks, salt and pepper shakers, lamps, statues and figurines. Many of these things were from Edith's personal office at Sagamore Hill. They were sentimental things kept near and dear to her heart. This is how we know how special the pets were to her and the family. She kept them with her personal items and things she had collected from her world travels. This relationship with their pets is just one more thing that made the Roosevelts more human and real to me. I still have collars, leashes, tags and wonderful items to remember the special animals that have come and gone in my life. This is something we will see in quite a few First Ladies and Presidential families moving forward.

Mrs. Roosevelt's time in Washington was well spent, and she was well received. There were many items from this period at Sagamore Hill. A newspaper article was written about the Roosevelts in the Boston Brown Book while they were in the White House about their new china service. Mrs. Roosevelt ordered the 1,125-piece set to replace the "scraps, bits and broken pieces" from past administrations which she found being used when she got there. The new service was white with gold accent lines and the Presidential seal. Like Mrs. Roosevelt, it was simple and elegant. Edith Roosevelt threw excellent dinners and parties. A beautiful and well-preserved invitation to a garden party held on January 4, 1906 shows both a specific time to arrive and an exact time when the party was over and guests were expected to go home. This was a similar tactic used by Martha Washington. Washington always indicated when an event or meal was over. Guests at the White House have an understandable tendency to linger. It has always been a remarkable place, and it wasn't every day that a person got to hang out there. However, it was also a home and the people that live there did like to go to sleep at some point or relax and live as close to a private life as possible. Putting a specific end time allowed women like Martha and Edith to put their house back to normal.

Mrs. Roosevelt used a gold-plated vanity set while she lived in the White House. Her initials were beautifully etched into each piece. She had crystal beakers for rouges, other makeup, lotions and perfumes. There were matching combs, brushes, button hooks and other beauty tools and containers. She took her role as First Lady very seriously and items like this were a status symbol, indicative of a woman in her position and social standing. The pieces were beautifully crafted, and very personal. It was easy to imagine Mrs. Roosevelt getting ready for any number of State dinners, events or garden parties like the invitation I mentioned.

She kept a beautiful silver glove box on her dresser. It was lined with velvet and had very ornate filigree designs embossed on all sides. The box opened from the top and would have held about twelve pairs of Mrs. Roosevelt's dress gloves. There was a long, white silk pair that showed the small size of her hands. She also loved fans, as many women of that time did. They were unique forms of art and fashion, and they had some wonderful examples of them in the collection. Edith loved to stand in receiving lines with her husband, but she did not enjoy shaking hands with so many strangers. By holding fans or flowers and bouquets she avoided all the glad-handing that her husband enjoyed so much, but was still able greet people and support her husband. Ida McKinley, Caroline Harrison, Julia Grant and Sarah Polk were some other First Ladies who used similar tactics.

Like all First Ladies, Mrs. Roosevelt received many gifts while she was First Lady. The rules were not as strict as they are now about keeping gifts of State, and she was able to take many items with her when she left the White House. There was a beautiful set of silver bracelets given to her by the Emperor of Abyssinia (now Ethiopia), and she kept them in a small white box with careful notation as to what they were, where they came from, when she got them and who gave them to her. There was also a beautiful set of medium sized Sevres figurines given to her by the French government displayed in a nice cabinet with glass shelves and lights. The cabinets were opened for me to eliminate the glare of my camera lights. This also allowed me an intensely close-up view of the remarkable pieces. The figurines were made of French porcelain and there were originally fourteen in the set. Mrs. Roosevelt used them as centerpieces at State dinners. There were six on display. In a letter, she made it very clear that they were given directly to her, how much she liked them and the fact that she was taking them with her when the Roosevelts left the White House.

The Roosevelts also brought their everyday china with them to the Washington. It was a classic English made set outlined in cobalt blue some gold pin striping with a blue TR in the middle. This was what the family would have used on a regular basis. They brought this set back to Sagamore Hill with them after the White House. I was told that Mrs. Roosevelt took most of their official White House china out back and smashed it to keep people from selling it for profit. Clearly, she saved some for historical purposes as they have some on hand at Sagamore Hill, and I have seen settings in the Smithsonian and other museums.

Perhaps Mrs. Roosevelt's biggest and most lasting impression on the White House was on the physical structure itself. In 1902, she oversaw one of the most significant reconstructions of the White House in history. The White House wasn't designed to accommodate her large family, and she was going to fix that. The architectural firm of McKim, Meade and White was called in from New York for the job. The old wooden framework and structure were weak and the whole place was showing signs of age. She also declared that the building was, in fact, a home for the family and the offices really needed their own space. This was how and why the West Wing was created. She also created the East Wing. She expanded the structure beyond the living quarters. This made it more functional as a House of State and created the necessary office space. Edith Roosevelt also understood the importance of First Ladies and the unofficial power they had. I have often said in my public speeches that First Ladies are arguably the most powerful unelected women in the world, and I don't think that's a stretch. Mrs. Roosevelt collected portraits of all the previous First Ladies and created a First Ladies Gallery in the entrance hallway of the East Wing. She also had a buzzer system installed to call carriages from the valet. An overhang portico was also put in to protect her guests from the elements while they waited for their rides. Inside and out, there was a dramatic overall change in style and décor. Edith took out all the Victorian influence that had built up over the 19th Century, and brought back a Federalist feel. Some historians say John and Abigail Adams would have felt right at home in the Roosevelt's White House. Elements that were personal to President Roosevelt were added as well. Buffalo head sconces were added to the mantels in the State Dining Room, along with other outdoor and wildlife themes throughout. They got a little good natured ribbing in the press and political cartoons about these additions. When the renovations and construction was done, the architects gave Mrs. Roosevelt a commemorative photo album. That album was kept at Sagamore Hill and made a page by page appearance in my video.

In the days after her husband's death, Mrs. Roosevelt did a lot of traveling. There were several of her passports on hand, each with country stamps from her vast travels. She went to Egypt, France, Portugal, South America and had many other worldwide adventures. When she was in France, she visited the grave of her youngest son, Quentin, who died there while he was a pilot in World War I (there was also a marker and flag pole on the grounds at Sagamore Hill memorializing Quentin). There was a fantastic picture of an older Mrs. Roosevelt on a camel in a desert in Egypt from one of her adventures. It seems she shared some of her husband's adventurous nature. The many documents and photographs were all amazing to look at and study. It was fun to imagine travel back then for Mrs. Roosevelt, and how she would've presented her documents at various customs offices around the world—not unlike you or I would today when we travel abroad. Somehow, I imagine she was not one to be trifled with when it came to looking through her luggage or claiming souvenirs she was bringing back from a trip.

I must be honest, I was initially bummed out a bit when I learned about the renovations and reconstruction going on at the Roosevelt's home. When you're going to a place to look at these people's artifacts and learn as much as you can about their lives, the last thing you want to hear is, "it's all packed up, shipped out and boarded up." But, my visit to Sagamore Hill was a huge success. All the cabinets were opened for me, and the access they gave me was amazing. They really pulled out some great stuff and bent over backwards for me, given the fact that their collection, exhibits and entire location were all in such a state of organized chaos. It was as good a shoot as any on the whole project.

I packed up my gear, loaded up my rental car, and started to head out. On my way, out the scenery looked different to me, and not just because of the time of day or the way the sun was hitting the property. I had learned so much about this woman and her family that it all meant something different to me now. I had to stop numerous times on the way out to get a certain field, garden, or landmark. It was neat to see and realize how different everything looked now that I knew

Edith Roosevelt. I silently promised I would return as I passed the main house ensconced in tarps and scaffolding. I continued down the winding Oyster Bay roads and the water appeared on my right, and another story Amy had told me popped into my head. Theodore had an old beat up row boat. It was his favorite, and he named it Edith. His wife was less than pleased at the condition of her namesake, but I suspect she was used to both his sense of humor and his expressions of affection. Edith would row alongside her husband as he swam in the bay. I had to stop. I popped the trunk and took out my camera and tripod once again and got some pretty footage of the bay. The sun was well into the early evening, and the colors and reflections on the water were breathtaking. More importantly, I got a very clear image in my mind of the Roosevelts. The couple. Not the President and First Lady and not the parents or the public figures. The people. They were two people in love who enjoyed each other's company. They shared a love for nature and adventure and took every chance they could to spend time together with a life style that sometimes catered to separation. It was as humanizing a scene as I could image to isolate a lasting image of Edith and Theodore Roosevelt.

Travel Note — New York's finest

On the way back into New York City I was using my iPhone as a GPS, just as I had on the way out the previous day. Everything was going fine, and it was looking like I would have plenty of time to get to the rental car office before it closed. My train was leaving late enough that there wasn't any immediate concern. I would probably even have time for dinner. Then, I went through a tunnel. My GPS wouldn't reset on the other side of the tunnel. The map on the screen was just kind of spinning and read "RECALCULATING" over and over again. I came to a stoplight, and thought, "good, here's my chance... come on, RESET!" I looked to my right and saw a police officer stopped at the light, too. I nodded and smiled, as I always do in these situations. The light turned green, and off I went—STILL RECALCULATING. I'm driving along, yelling at my phone, "COME ON, COME ON, PLEASE CALCULATE!" And then my yelling was drowned out by sirens and a booming saying, "PULL OVER" like the voices of the gods. So, I pulled over. Not just one, but three police cars had somehow surrounded me. You seriously would have thought I was driving a white panel van with TNT printed on the side and a giant fuse sticking out of the top wearing a coyote costume. I turned off the car, rolled down the window and watched the officers approach and surround my car. The lead guy said, "Do you know why I pulled you over?" I very honestly answered, "No, sir. I do not." He didn't like that answer. He got in my face and yelled, 'YOU LOOKED RIGHT AT ME. ON YOUR PHONE! YOU CAN'T DO THAT! NEW YORK IS HANDS FREE! THERE'S A SIGN AND EVERYTHING! YOU PASSED THE SIGN! YOU LOOKED RIGHT AT ME! I KNOW YOU SAW ME!" I smiled and said, "Oh, no, no, sir. I was not ON my phone. I was using it for a GPS. This is a rental car. I am from DC, and I'm trying to make it to the rental car office before it closes, so I can make my train. The tunnel caused the GPS to recalculate, so, I'm kinda lost and was getting worried. I'm very sorry, and I didn't see the sign. But I did see you at the light. That's why I smiled at you." The officer liked this response even less than my first one. And now that he knew I was trying to make it to the rental office before they closed, he was going to do everything he could to make that not happen. Fortunately, he called off the "back up" officers, as I was hardly a threat. He went back to his car—but not before stopping to chat up some good-looking chick who was walking by on the sidewalk. What a jerk. He came back after what seemed like a lifetime with a bunch more insults, admonishments.... and a ticket. And it was not a small one. I thought at least after all this time and foolishness, I would only be getting a warning. Again, what a jerk. It was nothing short of a miracle that I made it to the rental car place before it closed. I did have time to eat and make my train. When I went to board the train, the Amtrak conductor said, "You can't board with that many bags." I replied, "Sir, this is how I got here two days ago, and I've had a day. What do you suggest I do?" He shrugged and motioned me onto the train. Luckily, he did not attend the same "charm school" as the police officer who pulled me over. I was ready to go home. A word to the wise—if you must drive in New York City, do not even think about touching your phone.

KEENE, VIRGINIA

My trip to the Roosevelt's Pine Knot cottage in Keene, VA was what I called a bonus trip. Location and proximity are king when you travel like this for a television series. Some of the places were too far out of the way, and didn't get included in the series. Pine Knot could have been one of those locations. However, a trip through Virginia for Ellen and Edith Wilson allowed me to pick up the Roosevelt's summer retreat. I was also able to visit the Hoover's Rapidan Camp in the Shenandoah Valley (more on that in the Lou Hoover chapter). I'm really glad I could get to these two locations, because I thought it was important to see how these women and their families relaxed. Most of what we know about these folks was from their time in the White House. The private locations, letters and artifacts gave us that window into their private lives a bit more.

Driving to Pine Knot was no easy task. This place was so remote that GPS, satellite, and cell phone service was almost non-existent. The house was 14 miles south of Charlottesville in Albemarle County, VA. And I was lost. Fortunately, I hit a spot with a good signal by a general store, and could reach my host—Pine Knot Foundation President, Paula Beazley—by phone. She knew exactly where I was and how I had gone wrong, and was able to guide me the rest of the way in once I was close. This was a real "over the river, and through the woods" experience. I had to drive my rental car over a narrow wooden bridge and along a dirt path to get to the cabin. It was easy to see why the Roosevelts enjoyed remoteness. Even in modern times there wasn't anything but trees for miles.

Edith Roosevelt purchased the structure and surrounding 15 acres from a local farmer named William Wilmer in May 1905 for $280. Edith's name was the only one on the deed. She bought it so her husband wouldn't have to travel so far away to "get away from it all." Theodore went on many adventures during his life, and he would always write back about missing his family. Mrs. Roosevelt saw this cabin as a solution to Theodore's need to travel and feel isolated while still being able to have his family with him. The Roosevelts didn't allow Secret Service or the press to accompany them to Pine Knot. The lack of security made Edith somewhat nervous, so young Kermit eased his mother's mind by keeping a small gun under his pillow. The family would board a special car attached to a mail train and head out from Washington, DC on a four-hour train ride. The last 10-mile leg of the journey was usually done on horseback or by carriage. Sometimes they included a stop and a meal with the people from whom Edith bought the property. The Roosevelts made eight recorded visits to Pine Knot between 1905 and 1909.

The structure was an existing farm hand's house when Mrs. Roosevelt purchased it, but she quickly specified changes before she showed it to her husband. She had the staircase moved to the back wall and opened the original two room first floor to one big lodge room. The walls were intentionally unfinished to give the place a more rustic feel. There were fireplaces on both ends of the house. One was for cooking, and Edith designed all the mantels with rocks and stones from the property. She also had stone shelves installed in corners near the mantel for functionality that also added a little flair. Theodore did most of the cooking here and the children would have gathered firewood and water for cooking and preparing the meals, along with other chores.

The upstairs was divided into three rooms. Directly in front of the stairs was where Ethel stayed. Alice was 21 by this time and never visited Pine Knot (that we know of). This smaller room with a dormer window gave the girls a small amount of privacy. The boys room was to the left complete with another fireplace and mantel, and Mr. and Mrs. Roosevelt's bedroom was to the right. The bedroom walls were also unfinished. Light streamed through some of the wall boards just as it had when the family stayed here. Mrs. Roosevelt also specified that a sitting porch—she called it her piazza–be put on the front of the house and the roof of the porch was to be supported by untrimmed cedar posts gathered from the surrounding woods. The posts currently on the house are original, as is the color of the exterior and most of its construction. Photographs from when the Roosevelts used the cottage show a typical rustic cabin in the woods. Mrs. Roosevelt did some minor decorating with local plants and wildflowers, and had things around the fireplace for cooking and daily household needs, as you would expect. The furniture was all fairly basic and functional. A large farm style dining table was the only original piece of furniture that remained. It was easy to imagine the large family gathered at the table for meals, games or socializing. Surely, the family would have gathered by firelight to read in the evenings, as well.

Mr. Roosevelt's main and favorite activity at Pine Knot was bird watching. He even discovered a few new varieties here. Mrs. Roosevelt enjoyed bird watching, too, but did most of hers from the front porch. The children, no doubt, enjoyed playing in the woods and nearby streams. The only non-family visitor on record at Pine Knot was the famous naturalist, John Burroughs. He and the President spent three days in the woods and identified no fewer than 75 different species of birds. Roosevelt said in a letter to one of his sons that "Mother is a great deal more pleased with it than any child with any toy I ever saw." It was clear that Edith enjoyed the Pine Knot cottage as much, if not more, than any of the Roosevelts. It was the only place where the family could truly be by themselves.

SUMMARY

Edith Roosevelt was a transformational woman. She was a modern woman who straddled centuries. She was born in the 1800's, but blossomed in the 20th Century. She was the spouse and partner of one of our country's biggest and most colorful figures. She shined and thrived despite his gigantic shadow. That, in itself, is no small feat. At the beginning of this chapter, I said that Edith was not typically the first Roosevelt that comes to most people's mind. And I stand behind that statement. Franklin Delano Roosevelt was the longest sitting President in history. He was elected to an unprecedented four terms (a record that will never be broken – unless the laws change). Eleanor Roosevelt typically ranks number one on historian's lists, and is considered by many to be the greatest and most influential First Lady of all time. That makes sense, since she had the most time to accomplish things and be First Lady. Theodore Roosevelt... well, he's Theodore Roosevelt. The man survived a trip down the Amazon in the early 1900's, and discovered a whole new part of the river doing it.

Book Note – River of doubt

I read a lot of books during my travels for this series. Some I wanted to read. Some I didn't. Most I enjoyed. However, one of my favorite books that came across my desk (that ended up having very little to do with Edith) was "The River of Doubt" by Candice Millard. It's the story of Theodore and Kermit Roosevelt's exploration voyage down the Amazon. I am borderline obsessed with the Amazon, and I will go there one day (another adventure for another book). Anyway, I was booking guests for the Edith Roosevelt show over the Summer between seasons. I contacted Candice about being a guest (she also wrote a great book about President Garfield called "Destiny of the Republic") on the Edith show. Her schedule didn't fit ours, so she didn't end up being on the show, but she did send me a copy of her book (thank you, Candice). The book is excellent, and I now give it to friends as a gift.

The point is, Edith is just as fascinating as the other Roosevelts when you get to know her. She oversaw some of the most dramatic and long-lasting White House renovations in history. She was the matriarch of one of the most interesting and lively families ever to live in the White House. She was an intelligent and politically savvy woman who was unusual for her time. We see her sense of adventure come alive once her job as wife and mother were complete as she traveled the globe. She was the perfect partner for Theodore. It takes a special kind of woman to be married to a man like that. She understood him, and complimented him in every aspect of his life. She enjoyed the zoo-like household that the family created together.

It was also very easy to tell that she was a real person. She understood the role she had. She could dress up for a State dinner or dress down for a Pine Knot get away. She knew her place in the world and was confident about it. She saw her children go off to war, and even lost one son in that arena. It's interesting to think what would have happened had Alice Lee not died, and Theodore's first marriage not ended so abruptly and tragically. No one knows why Edith and

Theodore stopped talking while he was at Harvard. Edith even had the social graces and fortitude to attend his first wedding. But, what happened…happened. Theodore and Edith did end up together, and the world is a more interesting place because of it.

Travelogue Food Tip

When I stayed in Garden City the night before my full day at Sagamore Hill, I was fortunate enough to meet up with a college friend I hadn't seen in over 20 years. Craig Mauro and (his then lovely girlfriend, now even lovelier wife) Jaimie lived nearby and asked if I like mussels. Those who know me, know I grew up on seafood, and can just about eat my weight in shrimp, crab and oysters. Mussels? Yeah, I can do mussels. So, we met at the Waterzooi Belgian Bistro, and had a feast. Such a great meal, and even better to catch up with an old friend and meet someone so special in his life. This adventure I was on just kept getting better and better. So, if you're on Long Island and near Garden City, stop by Waterzooi and tell 'em the First Ladies Man and "Vic" Mauro sent ya! I have recently learned that another friend, Peggy, likes this joint, too!

CHAPTER 2

Helen Taft

Cincinatti, Ohio – Washington, DC – Arlington, Virginia

Helen Taft was born Helen Herron on June 2, 1861 in Cincinnati, Ohio. Her parents were John Williamson Herron and Harriet Collins Herron. Helen and William Howard Taft were married on June 19, 1886. They had three children together. Helen Taft died in Washington, DC on May 22, 1943 at the age of 81.

CINCINNATI, OHIO

From a young age, Helen Taft wanted to marry a man who would become President of the United States. Like Mary Lincoln before her, she had dreams of living in the White House one day. Her dreams were fueled by a vacation when she was seventeen. When you were a kid, did your parents ever send you to stay with a family friend or relative? Maybe they sent you to camp? You know, for the summer or maybe a Thanksgiving or Spring Break? Well, that's exactly what Helen's parents did. Only their family friend was President Rutherford B. Hayes. Helen's father, John Herron, and Rutherford Hayes were former law partners back in Ohio. In 1878, Helen was invited to be a guest of the First Family at 1600 Pennsylvania Avenue. The White House. She described the stay as the "climax of human bliss," and vowed to return one day to live there as First Lady. This was part of the reason many people say it was Helen, and not her husband, who wanted him to be President. Well, Theodore Roosevelt wanted Taft as President for a while, too, before he changed his mind and decided to run again. We'll get to that story in a bit.

Helen Taft was not a woman that topped my list of First Ladies before I started this project. That's not because she hid from the public, or didn't do anything while in the White House. She just wasn't on my radar, and I think that's true for many people. However, she can be credited with many accomplishments, including First Lady firsts that continue to influence us, our First Ladies and Washington, DC today and the entire country in modern times.

Pro Tip Note – Helloooooooo, Fremont!

Helen Taft is often part of my public speaking program. She was a very influential First Lady with many notable accomplishments. Her husband was the only President to become a Supreme Court Justice. They were a couple that was unusual for their time. In my remarks I ask the crowd, "How many of you would list Helen Taft if you were naming five, ten, twenty First Ladies? Not many, right?" In most places this gets nods and my point is well-taken. I asked this question of the crowd in Fremont, Ohio at the Rutherford B. Hayes Presidential Center, and a woman called out, "You are in Ohio, you know!" We all got a chuckle, and I said, "You know that works in every other state but this one!" More laughs, and we moved on. So, here's your PRO TIP...know your audience!

During my travels and research for Helen Taft, not much was mentioned about her childhood (other than the White House vacation and her father's relationship with President Hayes). She had 10 other brothers and sisters, so I would image it was an active and exciting one. There was also not much mention of the three children she had with Taft. The William Howard Taft National Historic Site in Cincinnati is in Taft's childhood home, and most of the exhibits there focus on Taft, not his wife or children. Helen never lived or spent much time there. She was mentioned and represented there, but you don't really get the whole story. So much of what we know or seem to care about Helen Herron Taft relates directly to her husband or things she accomplished while First Lady.

We do know that she was highly educated. Mrs. Taft was even quoted as saying, "I had always had the satisfaction of knowing almost as much as he about the politics and the intricacies of any situation" (referring to her husband). Like many First Ladies before her (Julia Tyler and Sarah Polk come to mind), she sat in the Congressional Galleries and listened to the political process. Mrs. Taft was well read, and not shy about giving her opinion to her husband. She went to college at Miami of Ohio University. She was interested in German, literature, science, history and music. She continued her education after college at the Cincinnati College of Music. She remained involved with music, the symphony and the theater her entire life. She was directly involved with the Cincinnati Symphony Orchestra. I hope to return to Cincinnati to explore this musical and theatrical side of Mrs. Taft.

It was a rainy day in July when I pulled into the William Howard Taft National Historic Site to meet up with Superintendent Ray Henderson, and his staff. The rain didn't cool things off that day, and their air conditioning unit was down. I think Ray and I both sweated through multiple shirts that day running around the house, and trucking gear up and down stairs. Ray was a trooper and stuck it out to the very end. We covered a lot of ground that day, and I learned a lot about Helen Taft in a relatively short amount of time compared to some of the other locations. We were very efficient.

Given the fact that it was Helen who wanted to occupy the White House more than her husband, it is only fitting that to tell her story, we started with the inauguration on March 4, 1909. This is exactly what I mean when I say President

Taft's achievements were Helen's achievements, in many instances. Now, of course, Taft had to want to be President, even if only a little bit. A person doesn't just become President, because his wife wants him to be. However, the fact remains, she was the driving force behind many of his political accomplishments.

In the collection and on display in Cincinnati, was the Bible used to swear Taft in as the 27th President of the United States of America. His inauguration was the crowning moment of Helen's life and when she realized her childhood dream and moved into the White House. There was a snow storm that day but Helen made sure all the festivities went on as scheduled, even though they had to move part of the ceremony inside the Capitol Building. This was also when Helen achieved her inaugural First Lady first. Helen Taft was the first First Lady to ride with her husband in the Presidential carriage. This seat was previously reserved for the outgoing President. You can Google pictures of Helen Taft in the carriage with her newly elected husband, and the smile on her face speaks volumes.

Historical Note – Theodore takes his balls and goes home

So, here's the story of how Helen Taft got to ride in the carriage. Theodore Roosevelt had decided not to run for a third term as President. Roosevelt inherited one term after the assassination of McKinley, and was elected to another. The Republican Party, Theodore Roosevelt and Helen Taft had all been grooming Taft for the Presidency. Everything was going according to plan, and then Roosevelt changed his mind. When the GOP didn't change theirs, too, Roosevelt formed the Bullmoose Party, and lost. Taft won the election. Roosevelt wasn't happy. So, when it came time to ride in the carriage from the White House to the Capitol, Roosevelt passed. This left an empty seat. Who do you think was right there to say something like, "Well, if no one's going to sit there I'll gladly take the spot!" That's right. Helen Taft. So, the precedent was changed and a new tradition was born. Thank you, Helen. Now, I always imagine William Taft's reaction to this. I figure at least some part of him had to be thinking, "I didn't even want this damn job, and now my friend won't talk to me or ride in my carriage, and half the party is mad at me...BUT...my wife couldn't be happier!"

The Bible in Cincinnati is also the same Bible used to swear Taft in as the tenth Supreme Court Justice. Some say being a judge is the only thing Taft wanted to do in life. No matter what the case was, Helen Taft would have been right at his side. She was his biggest fan and supporter.

There were also numerous Inauguration souvenirs on hand at the Taft site. There were beautifully preserved programs. They had a classic formal look with black writing on white paper that listed the day's events. They also had numerous invitations to private events and celebrations. The most interesting piece—one I had never seen before—was a dance card from the Inaugural Ball. The little booklet had the date and the event with places to write the names of all the people the individual danced with that evening. The booklet even came with its own pen. This was one of the more unique inaugural souvenirs I saw during the entire series. We'll get to Mrs. Taft's dress when we get to the Smithsonian in Washington, DC.

Shortly after the Tafts got into the White House Mrs. Taft suffered a stroke in May 1909. This rendered her physically incapable of performing some of her First Lady duties, but she remained an intellectual resource and confidant to her husband. She was very visible for their anniversary party in June 1911. The Tafts celebrated their 25th wedding Anniversary in the White House, and it was a celebration to end all celebrations. Thousands of guests attended the party and sent well wishes to the Presidential couple. The Taft Site was overflowing with countless silver objects that were given to President and Mrs. Taft for the occasion.

I was taken downstairs into a storage and work area to see some of the larger and more rare pieces that were not on display in the museum. Ray opened every cabinet and pulled out every drawer for me. He could not have been more accommodating and happy to show off the collection. By the time we were done, every surface in the large room was covered with protective cloth bags and countless silver pieces. The room was incredibly shiny with light reflecting off all the items. It was very dramatic and looked fantastic on camera. It was like stumbling upon a pirate's treasure.

You name it, and the Tafts got one (or ten) in silver for their anniversary. Almost every piece was intricately engraved with the Tafts' initials (WHHHT), dates, patterns and designs. There were all sizes of items, too. They received trays, cups, trophies, urns, bowls, platters, plates, goblets, plaques and some things neither Ray nor I even could even identify. But they were all silver. The gifts came from friends, supporters, cabinet members, officials, foreign leaders, and the general public. Write ups of the event noted an "embarrassing number of items." I'm sure Mrs. Taft wasn't too embarrassed. This was her big celebration as First Lady and her time to shine. The party was a strengthening affair for her.

Another unique and interesting item associated with their wedding anniversary was a scrapbook collection of telegrams they received. It was a large, rectangular, navy blue book with gold writing and detailing that resembled a photo album. Instead of photos, this album contained telegrams displayed in the same way one would display pictures. On the spine of the album it read, "Telegrams of Our Silver Wedding." The book was full of pages upon pages of well-wishes from across the country and around the world. There was no doubt that Mrs. Taft would have enjoyed sitting and reading them while she reminisced about the party and her marriage. By all accounts the Tafts were a very happy couple and very much in love.

President of the United States wasn't the only job William Taft had that Helen enjoyed. In April 1900, almost a decade before he would become President, Taft was assigned by President McKinley to be the Chairman of the Philippines Commission. By 1901, he was the Governor General. He had to resign from the bench of the U. S. Court of Appeals to take this position. He did so only with the promise from McKinley that he would get the next Supreme Court seat when he returned to the States. The Tafts moved their whole family there. The Tafts loved the Philippines, and the people of the Philippines loved the Tafts.

Mrs. Taft loved to travel, and was excited about giving her children the experience of living overseas. She understood and included the local people in her banquets. The Tafts joined in their celebrations and embraced the language and the culture entirely. There were full dinner menus and exquisite invitations on display at the museum. Each meal was more delicious and involved than the previous. The invitations were decorated with flowers, pretty ladies and wonderful text. Helen Taft knew how to throw a party. These intricately designed menus and invitations were some of the best examples of her hostessing skills. Who knows what she might have done in the White House, had she not suffered a stroke in 1909.

Mrs. Taft also loved the furniture, style and art of the Filipino people. She brought back many pieces of large hardwood furniture. There were beds, dressers, and chairs. All the pieces had detailed carvings and artwork in them. One piece that caught my eye, was a large chest of drawers with heavy brass hardware. The chest was magnificent and very typical of Mrs. Taft's taste and the style of the Philippines in the early 1900's. Much of their children's bedroom furniture was this style, too.

When they left to come back to the United States, Mrs. Taft received several formal studio photographs as gifts from local women. The women were all individually photographed in their best dresses and ceremonial gowns. They all signed the backs with personal messages to Mrs. Taft. One photograph read, "My Dear Mrs. Taft – Best Wishes From Adella Paterno Dec 12, 1903 Manila, PI." The photographs were all beautifully done and kept in a big album with other keepsakes, articles and mementos from their travels through Asia. The albums were kept locked up in large metal cabinets with trays that slid out. Mrs. Taft went above and beyond when it came to helping the Filipino people. She got involved with their education, parties, musical performances and plays. The photographs were a wonderful gesture of appreciation and admiration from the women of the Philippines. Clearly, it was a special part of Mrs. Taft's life, too.

Ray and I did a lot of on camera walking and talking, along with door opening sequences, and he nailed them all like a pro. It really gave the pieces that sense of discovery and element of being there that we were looking for out of these location pieces. It brought the viewer out of the studio, and gave the shows movement. It was very effective.

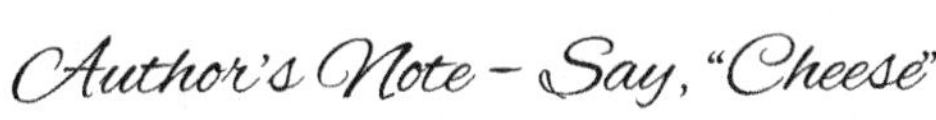

Author's Note – Say, "Cheese"

How many of you know of or went to an Olan Mills photography studio? Show of hands? I'm guessing a lot of you. Well, growing up we had one in the Del Marcado shopping center—which also had a great McDonald's and a Baskin-Robbins. Later in life the mall would be the home of Joe's Record Paradise. Someone told me they had seen one of my band's albums in the "bargain bin" there…but that's another note for another book. About the time I was in 7th or 8th grade, my mom bought a coupon book from Olan Mills. It gave her all kinds of discounts on photo sessions and print packages. Well, I guess they were about to expire, because one Summer I remember a mad dash to get my brother, me, our pets (anyone and anything really) into Olan Mills. One day I came rolling into the driveway on my Torker BMX bike after a gnarly session on our half pipe. Ahhhh, the 80's!! (Jeff Tremaine, Joey Cavanaugh, Nick Rigopolus, and Greg Barbera will remember these days and that ramp we built together fondly) My mom was already halfway out the door yelling at me, "YOU'RE LATE! YOU'RE LATE!" To which I responded, "For what?" "OLAN MILLS!" she replied. I complained that my hair was all messed up from riding and sweating. She didn't care. Missing the appointment and losing the coupon savings were way more important. I added that I didn't have time to change and would have to go in my Levi's 501's, Vans and Torker jersey. My mom was used to my nonsense, plus she was quick on her feet and creative. She told me to throw my bike in the car and we were off. I reluctantly tossed my bike in the back of the car and off we went. The result was one of the greatest pictures I've been a part of to this date (and will be included in the pictures in the middle of this book), and not because I look good in it. It's a great picture because it's a great story and a great memory. That coupon book produced a lot of unusual family portraits and good times. My mom was unusual for her time.

WASHINGTON, DC – NATIONAL MUSEUM OF AMERICAN HISTORY

Whenever I studied a First Lady that didn't have her own museum or birthplace home, I always turned to the wonderful people at the National Museum of American History in Washington, DC. They are a part of the Smithsonian Institution, and there are no better museums and collections in the world (I say with a fair percentage of home town pride). Lisa-Kathleen Graddy and her staff were a huge help filling in some gaps and adding valuable content during Season One (Frances Cleveland comes to mind), and I knew they would be able to do the same during Season Two.

I was born just outside of Washington, DC at Suburban Hospital in Bethesda, MD. I grew up in Rockville, MD. I have traveled the world, but have always kept my "home base" in or around the Nation's Capital. The Smithsonian was the location for nearly every school field trip from kindergarten through my senior year of high school. Now, as an adult, I have realized how spoiled we were to have these museums and collections at our finger tips. When I went there for the C-SPAN series, it was a real treat to use special elevators, walk down hallways and get behind electronically coded and locked doors. This really was the epitome of the VIP Pass and Backstage Access I loved so much.

In the video we did together, Lisa-Kathleen explained that they didn't have many Helen Taft pieces, but the piece they did have was one of the most significant in the entire First Ladies collection. They had Helen Taft's inauguration gown. Initially, this didn't seem that unusual. The Smithsonian has ALL of the inauguration gowns. Then she explained that it was the first inauguration gown ever given to the Smithsonian. It started the exhibit. Mind blown. How did I not know this? How had I not read this or been told this on one of my ten thousand visits to the museum over the years? It turns out Helen Taft was First Lady when the two founders of the First Ladies exhibit—Cassie Mason Myers Julian-James and Rose Gouverneur Hoes—were putting the collection together in 1912. The two women met Mrs. Taft at a luncheon in DC commemorating Dolley Madison (DRINK!! That's a joke from Volume One. If you haven't read it, you should. It's a pretty good read).

The Inauguration was not only her husband's entrance to the White House as President, but hers as First Lady. And she knew it. It stands to reason that this dress may be the most important dress she ever wore. It was a big deal. She had the gown embroidered in the Philippines. It was a long, slightly off-white gown with a flowing train. She wore it with matching elbow length, evening gloves and a neck piece that was not connected to the low-cut bodice. The embroidery was pearl beads and sequins that took on a purplish gray hue. It was beautiful. She loaned it to the exhibit, and later donated it to the collection. She started the tradition. She was the first. Every First Lady since, whose husband had and Inauguration Ball, has donated their dress to the collection.

So, there I stood, in the Smithsonian, in front of Mrs. Taft's Inaugural gown, in the National Museum of American History at The Smithsonian Institution in Washington, DC with my jaw on the floor. They took it out of storage for me. They laid it out on a work table and carefully unwrapped it for me. I balanced on stools to get high enough above the dress to capture its full grandeur on camera. I was in awe. I had just been told the reason we had the gowns on display, if at all, was because of Helen Taft. And even though it was not currently on display (dresses are rotated to avoid wear and tear) the dress was now in front of me. I had not read this in any book. I had not seen it on any show or heard it at any lecture. I had no previous knowledge of this dress being the first. I didn't even know this was the piece I would be filming for Helen Taft when I planned the visit. This all happened on the fly. When I ask audiences across the country, "What is the first item or image that comes to mind when you hear the term First Lady?" there is always—without fail—multiple people that call out "dresses" or "gowns." The number one thing that we picture when we hear the term First Lady is what it is all because of Helen Taft. A woman most people won't name if they're naming five, ten, fifteen or twenty First Ladies. This may sound repetitive...but...mind...blown.

WASHINGTON, DC – TIDAL BASIN

Another question I ask audiences across the country at my live speaking programs is, "How many of you have ever been to Washington, DC to see the Cherry Blossoms?" I have never been in a place where no one has raised their hand or called out. In fact, it's probably been more than one person at every speech. I say, "Good. Do you know who you have to thank for those trees?" Yup, you guessed it. Helen Taft. Mrs. Taft first discovered the trees during her travels through Asia, and she loved the river side parks she saw there. There was no one better to walk around and learn about the trees with than author and historian Ann McClellan.

I learned that the Tidal Basin was a mess at the beginning of the 20th Century. The only thing there was a dirt roadway where people cruised along in their new motorcars at a roaring 15 mph. There was nothing else there to attract visitors. Mrs. Taft took it upon herself to inspire a beautification project inspired by the parks she had seen in Asia. Asian culture, style and art were very popular in the

United States at the time. She was initially going to get the cherry blossom trees from nurseries in Pennsylvania. The Japanese government heard about her plans, and insisted on giving the United States the trees. Two thousand trees were sent to Washington, DC as a gift from the city of Tokyo in Mrs. Taft's honor. This was also in appreciation for America's support during the Russo-Japanese War.

The initial batch of 2,000 trees were delivered in January of 1910, and they were not saplings. They were quite large, and to our surprise—and Japan's embarrassment—the trees were bug infested. President Taft and the Secretary of the Interior ordered the trees to be burned. And they did just that. Right on the National Mall. The Japanese government quickly had a new shipment of 3,000 trees delivered. The new batch of trees were much smaller, bug-free and arrived in 1912. Some of those original trees from 1912 were planted by Mrs. Taft and the wife of the Japanese Foreign Minister to the United States, and they are still there today around the north corridor of the Tidal Basin closest to the Washington Monument. You can tell the older trees by the significantly wider trunks and gnarled twisting branches that hang over the water.

This was, again, brand new information for me. I have walked under, past and around these trees for my entire life. I have been to countless Cherry Blossom Festivals. I was never taught this in school—not that I heard or remembered anyway. Now, I'm no MENSA candidate, but I'm not the village idiot either. I was further amazed by yet another Helen Taft accomplishment and First Lady first. The cherry blossoms and inaugural gown videos have remained among my favorites from the series to this day.

ARLINGTON, VIRGINIA

My final location for my Helen Taft travels was her final destination on Earth. Arlington National Cemetery. Mrs. Taft outlived her husband by about thirteen years. Not much was written about the specifics of Helen's death. It was surprising, given her stroke in 1909, that she lived as long as she did. In the New York Times, her obituary said she played "an important part in planning the career of her distinguished husband." This, to me, was an understatement of her role, her influence and her lasting imprint on the country. Even in her final resting place, she was the first. She was the first First Lady to be buried in Arlington

National Cemetery. She was laid next to her husband under a very impressive memorial marker.

It was a beautiful clear day in September, and I barely got the footage submitted in time to make the live show. It was a personal mission of mine to recognize the grave of a woman who had made such a quiet, but lasting impression on America. I gathered my gear, took a cab across the Memorial Bridge and the Potomac River into Northern Virginia. It was a poetic and fitting way to close the books on a First Lady that wanted so badly to live in Washington… to be First Lady in the White House…that here is where she would remain, on such honored and hallowed ground, next to the man she loved and supported for most of her life. I was given more than enough time to get more than enough footage for the show. I got close ups, pans, pulls, pushes…everything. I just kept shooting. Maybe I felt badly for not knowing more about her before I started this project. Maybe I was embarrassed that she hadn't been on my radar all these years. Whatever the reason, I kept filming. Then, it struck me. Even though I didn't know before, I knew now, and I could tell people about her. So, I do… every chance I get.

SUMMARY

This is a hard summary to write. I've said it all. Helen Taft was the First Lady of First Lady firsts. I'm not sure how else to say it. She wanted something out of life and she got it. I respect that. She improved the country and influenced traditions that extended way beyond the walls of the White House. Hers is a very remarkable story. She was smart. She loved to travel. She celebrated the performing arts. She was politically astute, and her Presidential husband's biggest fan and supporter. She was attractive. She overcame the great adversity of having had a stroke just months after her husband was elected and she achieved her goal—for both herself and her husband. She understood her role as First Lady. She was another First Lady who outlived her husband. She was a truly remarkable woman and undoubtedly unusual for her time. She was a text book First Lady, and before I started this project with C-SPAN, I'm not sure I could have told you her name.

Travelogue Food Tip

Many times during the series and my travels, I would land in a friend or co-worker's hometown or state. This was the case with Cincinnati. My friend and C-SPAN colleague, Rachel Katz, was stoked I was going to Cincinnati to study Helen Taft. I'm not sure if she was more excited about Mrs. Taft or that she would be able to send me to Skyline for some chili. Rachel worked with the traveling C-SPAN Bus and the education department, and besides doing a lot of leg work on and off the road for the series...she's hilarious. She was one of my first buddies at C-SPAN. In a sea of friendly people there, her smile is one of the biggest (she also may have wet her pants a little laughing when I gave her a ride on my Harley to meet some of her college friends at a happy hour in DC... but, that's a different story for a different book). ANYWHO...she told me I had to HAD TO go to Skyline Chili before I left town. So, I Googled the Harley dealer, and headed in that direction. As I pulled into the Harley dealer I noticed a Gold Star restaurant. Was that what Rachel told me? They served chili. Had to be! How many chili places were there in Cincinnati. So, I got my Harley shirt and went to Gold Star. I ordered two chili cheese dogs and a side of chili with all the trimmings (I'm writing this at 11:01pm and haven't had dinner yet. This sounds so daggone good right now). I ate up, headed out of town, and emailed Rachel back in DC."MISSION ACCOMPLISHED!! GOLD STAR CHILI WAS AWESOME!! THANKS FOR THE TIP!!" I cannot publish her response. When in Cincinnati...PLEASE go to Skyline Chili. Tell 'em Rachel sent you!

CHAPTER THREE

Ellen Wilson

Princeton, New Jersey – Staunton, Virginia – Washington, DC

Ellen Wilson was born Ellen Louise Axson on May 15, 1860 in Savannah, Georgia. Her parents were Reverend Samuel Axson and Margaret Jane Hoyt Axson. Ellen and Woodrow Wilson were married on June 24, 1885. They had three children together. Ellen Wilson died in Washington, DC on August 6, 1914 at the age of 54.

PRINCETON, NEW JERSEY

Ellen Wilson was President Woodrow Wilson's first wife. She was the third, and hopefully last, First Lady to die in the White House (Letitia Tyler was first, and Caroline Harrison followed after her). Her funeral was a quiet and private ceremony that was held in the East Room. Her body was returned to Rome,

Georgia, where she was buried in Myrtle Hill Cemetery. Ellen was the lesser known and lesser talked about Mrs. Wilson for reasons we will get into in Edith Wilson's chapter. However, Ellen Wilson was Woodrow's first love. It is difficult to know what kind of First Lady Ellen might have been, because she was in the role for such a short period of time. She was only First Lady for slightly more than a year before she died of Bright's Disease (the same kidney ailment that killed Theodore Roosevelt's first wife). During her brief tenure, she did a lot of work with poor African American neighborhoods in Washington, DC. Her family had been slave owners in Georgia, but she spent a lot of time trying to improve the slums and living conditions for minorities in and around the Nation's Capital. She pleaded with her husband from her death bed to continue this work. After her death, Congress passed a slum clearance bill that cleaned up Washington's alleyways, and sought better housing—particularly for black laborers—called the Ellen Wilson Bill.

There isn't much more than signage around her Savannah, Georgia birthplace or in Rome, Georgia where she grew up. She and Woodrow met in church in Georgia. At the time, both of their fathers were Presbyterian ministers. They fell quickly in love, but their marriage was postponed until Woodrow could finish graduate school. Ellen was an accomplished landscape painter. She gave up a promising career as an artist to be with Wilson. Their love story was well documented in their letters, and one of the greatest in White House history. The best place to learn about Ellen Wilson was Princeton, New Jersey, where Ellen Wilson was "First Lady" when Woodrow was the university's president and they lived in the Prospect House with their three daughters.

I took the train to Princeton out of Union Station in DC on a sunny day in early July 2013. I was beginning to like train travel, because it was easier to navigate my bags and gear when I didn't have to check most of them. I arrived in New Jersey without incident, took a cab to the rental car place and checked into my hotel. I have friends that went to Princeton who had given me several recommendations for restaurants, and I was looking forward to a calm evening before my real work began the next day.

Travel Note - Out Of Order

With such a big break in between Season One and Season Two, I had more time to play with as far as scheduling my travel. The country was much larger by the 1900's, and Presidents and their wives were spreading out geographically speaking. The largest concentrations of locations related to Presidents—and thus First Ladies—were in Virginia, Ohio, New York, California and Texas. The locations didn't necessarily go in order of Presidencies. For example, my first trip for Season Two was to Princeton, NJ, Northampton, MA, and Plymouth Notch, VT to cover Ellen Wilson and Grace Coolidge. I circled back (because of scheduling conflict) to pick up Oyster Bay, NY on a one-off for Edith Roosevelt. The next trip had me in Cincinnati, OH for Taft, Marion, OH for Harding, and West Branch, IA and Palo Alto, CA for Hoover. It was fun, but it was nuts. A lot of flying and driving. It wasn't until the second half (and after the Government shutdown) that I started going in order at break neck speed to hit my deadlines. Basically, I did whatever it took and went wherever I needed to go to get the stories. There is a fun interactive map on the JOURNEY page of my website www. firstladiesman. com that lays out all my travel. It's fun to go back and watch the series unfold before my eyes.

I checked in at the Public Relations and Communications office for Princeton University early in the morning to get my passes and credentials. I drove through campus with my paperwork, and found the Prospect House and my contact—Author and Historian, Barksdale Maynard. He welcomed me to the Wilson's former residence and we got started in my usual fashion. I set my gear in a central location in Wilson's old office, which was beautiful. The whole house was beautiful. It had been converted to part Historical Landmark, because of Wilson, and part catered conference center for the school and its officials. The house has a large castle-like exterior with grand rooms and a stunning staircase. Barksdale and I toured the house, as he gave me the rundown on each room and the Wilsons' lives while they lived there. This house was where Ellen Wilson spent the most time running a household. It's where Wilson and the GOP crafted his Presidential campaign. This was where I would get the best vision of what she might have done as First Lady, had she lived longer. It's also where I would see what kind of mother she was. She raised three daughters here in the middle of a campus full of would-be suitors. They also entertained many high level political figures and leaders here.

On the first floor as I passed through the grand foyer, to the right was the study. This was Wilson's office when they lived here. The layout was like it had been in the days of the Wilsons. Large built-in bookcases surrounded the room. Two sitting chairs and a coffee table were in front of the fireplace, and Wilson's desk (which was not there) would have been to the back of the room with a larger window behind it. This room was important to Ellen Wilson, because she was highly involved in her husband's professional career. It was Ellen Wilson who steered her husband away from a job in Arkansas and towards Princeton. Wilson had a successful run for New Jersey State Governor before his presidential campaign and election. Woodrow and Ellen Wilson both transformed from academic people to a political couple in this office. This was where Wilson would have met with officials from the school and the Republican Party to transform him into a political candidate, and Ellen Wilson would have been right at his side. There were, no doubt, late night fireside strategy meetings that took place in this room, and speeches would have been written and practiced here, too. When I walked around the room I felt the electricity of political power and planning.

The formal dining room was directly through the main foyer and Mrs. Wilson had space to feed and entertain twenty to thirty people in the room. She was also responsible for a redecorating of the interior of this house. She had most of the Victorian era items and décor removed as she modernized the home. The fireplace mantels were some of the more significant renovations in the dining room. Ellen had the ornate figures removed and stone work with more classic lines and symmetry replaced them. Mrs. Wilson hosted many important people and dinners here at the Prospect House. Most notably, President Theodore Roosevelt. I was taken to the top of the wide, stone staircase to look down on the foyer from the second floor, as the Wilson daughters would have when important guests like the Roosevelts arrived. One of the biggest features of the home was a huge stained glass window that remained from the earlier Victorian era. There was also a large domed skylight directly above the open foyer that could be seen from all floors of the house. The craftsmanship on both pieces was fantastic. It was nice to see so many features that remained from the Wilsons' days there, even though it was still a fully functioning and modernized building. This allowed me to see what the Wilsons would have seen and imagine them living there and using the same fireplaces, rooms and staircases, as they looked through the same wonderful skylight and stained glass window. All the bedrooms have been converted to smaller meeting rooms, but the views from their windows were similar as the gardens and grounds were restored and kept to most of their original glory from the days of Ellen Wilson.

At the time, the garden at the Prospect House was Ellen Wilson's pride and joy. I like gardens, in general, but when a First Lady has designed them or taken special interest in them, they become that much more interesting to me. This garden of Mrs. Wilson's had an extra tidbit of historical significance that made it the most interesting garden I saw during the entire adventure. This was the garden that became the blueprint for the Rose Garden at the White House. The same Rose Garden which is still very much in use today. Barely a week goes by that some event is not held there, and broadcast all over the world on network and cable news channels. I think Mrs. Wilson would be happy to know that her beautiful garden is still enjoyed by so many people here in America and all over the world.

The Prospect House garden was designed by Ellen when she lived there from 1902 to 1910. Before she was married, Ellen was a very accomplished landscape painter. She was creative and had an eye for aesthetics. So, it was easy to see how she converted this perspective into gardening and created such a beautiful space. She surrounded the garden with cedar trees and planted all kinds of bushes, shrubs, roses and other flowers. Later, when she was in the White House, she brought the White House gardener to the Prospect House and asked him to recreate the rose section of her garden at the White House. Mrs. Wilson could see her garden from her bedroom window in New Jersey, and she wanted the same for her new home in Washington, DC. Sadly, Ellen Wilson never got to see the Rose Garden completed. She was wheeled out in her wheelchair to watch the gardeners work, but she didn't live long enough to see her vision in full bloom.

After lunch, Barksdale and I made our way over the Seeley G. Mudd Manuscript Library at Princeton University. This facility housed one of the largest and most significant collections of love letters between a future President and First Lady. The letters were kept sealed in a trunk by the Wilsons when they moved to Princeton in 1902, and they weren't opened again until the 1960's. It was letters like these that gave me the clearest vision into the hearts of these Presidential couples. Historians all agree that the Wilson letters are among the most romantic of any Presidential partnership. If you have read any book on Ellen Wilson, these letters were highlighted there.

We walked the long corridors of shelves with box after box after box of letters. So many of them were quoted in the books I had already read in preparation for my visit. However, nothing compared to seeing the actual letters, and having them read to me while I filmed and hung on every word. There was something so personal about an individual's handwriting. It supersedes any and all text I read in books or emails. It made the authors of the letters—in this case, Ellen and Woodrow Wilson—come alive and speak directly to me. These are exactly the kinds of letters I'm talking about when I say' "I have read letters that I probably wasn't supposed to read." It always gave me a funny feeling to invade these people's personal lives in such a way. I understand that they chose to live the lives they did, and to run public office and for President. I'm just not sure all of them—especially the earlier ones—knew it would mean this kind of access to their inner most personal lives and feelings.

Rather than quote line after line after line, I have chosen to repeat the passages shared in the final video that appeared in the show (the full letters are published and readily accessible, if you are interested…I highly recommend reading them). I feel it encapsulates what the Wilsons meant to each other. This first piece was from Woodrow to Ellen, when he was living in Baltimore and taking graduate classes at Johns Hopkins University. He writes to her in January 1894:

> "My own darling, when you come into my study, and kiss me as I sit at my desk, it is odd how this attachment of yours to me seems part of the force of my mind. Ah, darling, I trust it is not wrong to

> worship you as I do. You are presiding genius of both my mind and my heart. And in that fact, consists the happiness and the strength of your own, Woodrow."

That's powerful stuff right there. Wow. And Ellen responds:

> "How happy it makes me that you think such things of me, even when I feel with a heartache how sadly unworthy I am of it all. I too trust it is not wrong to worship you as I do. I had as well question if it is wrong to breathe. Both are inevitable if I am to live at all. For I am in every breath altogether your own, Ellen."

Again. Wow. This exchange exemplifies how each of them felt completely at the mercy of the other's love. They each gave for the other. Woodrow confessed that Ellen was his mental and physical inspiration, and Ellen feels unworthy of his affection and high praises. This was heavy (and mushy) stuff. We don't know much about Ellen's public perception, image or reputation. We do know that history viewed Woodrow as stiff and stodgy. Clearly behind closed doors and left to their own emotions and words, the two had no problem "letting their hair down, and expressing their love for each other. This perhaps was one of the greatest examples of a man and woman who had only been statues or paintings in a museum, pages in a book, or names on a bridge. Here at Princeton, the Wilsons just came alive. They walked right into the room, picked me up and shook me. It was if they were speaking directly to me and saying, "I lived. I breathed. I was real." To this day reading and writing these words gives me goosebumps.

Author's Note – Seven Degree Of The First Ladies Man

I'm no Kevin Bacon, but I've been around. I try not to burn bridges, and I like to think that most people I've worked with would like to do so again. I have traveled all over the world, but kept my home base or headquarters primarily in Maryland or the DC Metropolitan area. One of my closest friends is Scott Stonesifer. He and I went to Preschool, Elementary, Jr. Highland High School together. We went to different colleges, but stayed in close touch, and I know as I write this, I will see him two days from now. The point is, I know a lot of people, have been a lot of places, and I don't lose touch with folks. So, I'm not terribly surprised when people say, "Hey, aren't you…or don't you know…or didn't we meet at…" and that sort of stuff. However, when Barksdale and I were shooting stand up sequences in front of the library, I was completely caught off guard when he said, "Oh, my gosh, my wife wanted me to ask you if you know Norm Veenstra from DC?" First of all, it had been some time since Norm and I had crossed paths, but I know him well, and the name immediately conjured great stories and fond memories. Norm and I know each other through music in DC, and it's a friendship, like many, that was formed by, surrounded, and involved the 930 Club. Norm gave me a nickname that has only been used by him. He calls me "DUFF" (bassist from Guns 'N Roses), because of some silly, curly blonde wig I wore to a Halloween party or show at the club one year. It's been many years since that night, but every time he sees me he calls me "DUFF" through his big, warm grin. Norm is one of the good guys, and it was great to now have that connection with Barksdale.

I said goodbye to my new friend and the Princeton campus, and headed off to my next stop. I was off to Northampton, Massachusetts to learn about Grace Coolidge. It's difficult to have all these ladies running around in my head. But, I keep them straight most of the time. That's why I'm the FIRST LADIES MAN!

STAUNTON, VIRGINIA

President Woodrow Wilson was born in Staunton (pronounced STAN-ton), Virginia. When it came time to pick a location for the Woodrow Wilson Presidential Library and Museum, his second wife, Edith Wilson, chose his birthplace (which is not uncommon). At the time of the series and when I was traveling for Season Two, we got a tip from a colleague that they had an Ellen Wilson art exhibit on display at the museum there in Staunton. Wilson was the last President to have two wives, because of Ellen's death, and I jumped at the opportunity to delve into the lives of both women at one facility. I had to go to Staunton anyway, for research on Edith Wilson, and while I was there, I would pick up some valuable footage and stories about one of the most significant parts of Ellen's life. Her art. So, in early August 2013, I packed up the car, and headed off to Virginia. Again. This trip also afforded me the chance to visit the Roosevelt cottage in Keene, VA, the Hoover cottage in the Shenandoah Valley, Edith Wilson's Birthplace Museum in Wytheville, and I really got to know both of Wilson's wives very well in Staunton. This was an extremely productive leg of my journey, and brought back several video pieces from off the beaten path.

If Ellen Wilson had been born in more modern times, she might have had an art career of her own. It has been said—I know, because I've said it—that many of these women might not have married the men they did if they were living in today's world. Most of these women were independent thinkers and extremely talented in their own right. They were unusual for their time. However, as a circumstance of their times, they needed to hitch their wagons to powerful men to showcase their talents, and get their opinions and views heard. I feel this was the case with Ellen Wilson. Ellen and Woodrow were both aware of the role she played in the development of his career. In one letter, she wrote that her life's mission was to "embolden her husband's confidence in his abilities and vision." Woodrow once wrote to her, with great appreciation of her subtle yet vital role in his professional successes, "you are all-powerful in my development." So, Ellen was another First Lady who played a crucial role in her husband's life which led to his becoming President. So much so, that he recognized it openly to her. And while her role was significant, she never fully let go of her own identity and passion for art.

Peggy Dillard was Director of Library Archives when I rolled through on my second (or third or fourth) tour of Virginia, and she was all too happy to show me around the museum and the exhibits. The most striking and personal pieces I saw were surprisingly not her paintings, but her painting supplies. I'm a writer, a producer and a musician. I'm all about the creative process. For me, it was very cool to be able to see Ellen Wilson's easel, palette, and art studio stool. This was where Ellen sat, and viewed the world around her in an attempt to create her interpretation of life. This was a very personal space in her mental and physical world. I took extra time here to get the lighting right, so I could capture the tones of the wood, the paint stains on the pieces, and the overall vibes that were coming off the artifacts.

Mrs. Wilson's art was all over the walls in the gallery. They had a whole room set up exclusively for her work. Ellen primarily painted landscapes of fields and flowers. I had seen her garden in Princeton, and she had painted it here on canvas. The same cedar trees, fountain and bushes came alive once again in front of me. The flowers were different, but the overall feel was the same. The museum housed paintings that won awards, paintings that were featured in magazines, and paintings that hung in the White House. When Mr. and Mrs. Wilson were engaged, she studied at the Art Students League in New York. She had shows that featured and sold her art. Many of her pieces and shows were listed under her maiden name after she was married. She didn't want her husband's fame to taint her original art. I found this to be in stark contrast of what I had read in many books about her putting her own needs second, and committing to a life serving her husband's priorities and needs. It showed me she had her own needs, too. She had her own dreams, and she didn't completely give them up for Woodrow. This exhibit made it very clear that Mrs. Wilson didn't just paint as a hobby. The sheer volume of works she created indicated how seriously she took her artwork.

Not all the pieces were landscapes. I saw some earlier examples of still life work—bowls of fruit and such. Her color palette was tasteful and her work was very clean and professional. The piece that struck me the most was not on display. Peggy took me upstairs in the museum, and into a cluttered back room. The back room had what looked like a closet, but it was just a door to another room. In that room were a lot of clothes, shelves, racks and a standard file cabinet (like you would expect to see in any office). In the bottom drawer of that filing cabinet was—what was likely—the last piece Ellen Wilson painted while on this earth. She painted it while she was in the White House. From the date—which I do not recall, have on tape or in my notes—forward, there were no more paintings that anyone has or can find that she completed after this one. It was not framed. Just bare canvas edges. It was a landscape. A simple field with grass, and trees and flowers. There was nothing that stood out about this painting. Other than the fact that it was likely her last. What this did tell me was, she never gave it up. She didn't throw away her paints and brushes when her husband graduated from Johns Hopkins, or when he was at Princeton. She didn't ditch it all when he went into politics. She was an artist. That's something you carry with you for life, and she did.

WASHINGTON, DC

The live Wilson show was done a little differently that the other shows in the series. The show covered both Edith and Ellen Wilson. This wasn't terribly irregular for the series, especially given the short amount of time that Ellen spent in the White House. We had two guests in studio for the conversation and live calls. We had the location pieces that I had done, as always. The unique part of the Wilson show was that Edith and Woodrow Wilson moved out of the White House and directly into a beautiful home in Northwest Washington, DC in 1921. We did live location pieces from this house throughout the show. The house cost $150,000 and they paid for it with President Wilson's Nobel Peace Prize money, as well as from contributions from ten of his wealthy supporters. Woodrow Wilson died in the home in 1924, and Edith Wilson died there, too, in 1961.

While Ellen never lived in the Northwest, DC home, Executive Director, Robert Enholm, and his staff at the President Woodrow Wilson House, noted that Ellen Wilson was represented in this home. Among President Wilson's last wishes, he asked that during his funeral, a particular painting done by his first wife, Ellen, be hung over his casket at the National Cathedral. Edith Wilson fulfilled this request, and the painting now hangs in the parlor of the Wilsons' Northwest, DC home, along with some other pieces of Ellen's. They represent the significant role she played in Woodrow Wilson's life. The painting was unusual for Ellen. It's a large portrait of a woman, perhaps a nun or religious figure. She was painted wearing a maroon robe with a white head scarf, sitting in front of a dark brown wall with a faint halo around her head. It was a beautiful painting and with the religious tone to it, no wonder Wilson chose it to be displayed at his funeral.

The C-SPAN crew and I, along with location host for the evening, Peter Slen, had a wonderful time at the house. Enholm was a perfect host, and it was great to include Ellen and some of her work from this live location. I'll have more about the live location set up in the next chapter on Edith.

SUMMARY

From the early examples of Ellen's work and interests, both at Princeton and in the White House, we can see that Ellen could have continued to be a successful First Lady. She knew how to host dinners, guests and events from her time as First Lady of both Princeton and the State of New Jersey. She was a good mother. She raised three proper daughters (one of whom, Margaret, filled in as First Lady after her mother died, and before her father married Edith). She carried out important work in the slums of Washington, DC, and she left her mark on the White House in the form of the Rose Garden. We know she was smart and counseled her husband in personal, professional and political matters.

The big thing for me with Ellen Wilson was that she was an amazingly passionate woman. Some may argue that her letters were not always as passionate as Woodrow's or that she was melancholy at times, and perhaps not a fan of her husband's political ambitions. I saw evidence to the contrary. I read letters in the Mudd Library that were full of exuberant language and love. She was there to offer advice to Wilson when he needed it in academics and in politics. The two spent much of their time together reading poetry to each other. Her paintings alone—the sheer numbers of them —show a woman driven by creativity. She was still painting in the final months of her life. Her husband wanted one of her paintings over his casket at his funeral, and his second wife did not object (this says a lot about both women). She touched people with her art, but more importantly, she painted for herself. This was a woman at peace with herself, her husband, her family and her role as First Lady. She wasn't in the White House very long, but she made her short stay count. Mrs. Ellen Wilson was an accomplished and independent woman who was definitely unusual for her time.

Travelogue Food Tip

I don't usually give you more than one food tip for each location. However, here, I will because the eternal college student in me loves a good college dive hot spot. So, let's start there. We all have hometown or college town favorites. At University of Maryland it would be Cluck U chicken or Hungry Herman's. My friend and sometime bandmate, Noah Silverman actually went to school at Princeton (I can still say I went to Princeton – as in I visited the campus. I can also say that for Harvard and Stanford – hahaha). Noah told me to go to Hoagie Haven and get a steak and cheese sub. So, I did. Barksdale got a chicken cheese steak. Both subs were excellent and I recommend them highly (especially after last call, if you know what I mean…and I know you do). Now, if you're in the mood for something a little less college-y, go to the Blue Point Grill. I had a crabmeat guacamole martini with tortilla chips to start, which was top notch. I really could've just stopped there and been perfectly fine. It was very filling. I also had a Caesar salad (of course) which was light and delicious, and an order of calamari. The calamari had a sweet chili Thai sauce and a tangy aioli sauce. It's a toss-up between the sauces. I think I dipped the salad bread in both to finish them off. The meal was great, the service was fantastic, and everything I saw come out of the kitchen looked incredible. Two enthusiastic FIRST LADIES MAN thumbs up for the Blue Point Grill.

CHAPTER FOUR

Edith Wilson

Staunton, Virginia – Wytheville, Virginia - Washington, DC

Edith Wilson was born Edith Bolling on October 15, 1872 in Wytheville, Virginia. Her parents were William Holcombe Bolling and Sallie White Bolling. Edith and Woodrow Wilson were married on December 18, 1915. They had no children together. Edith Wilson died in Washington, DC on December 28, 1961 at the age of 89.

WYTHEVILLE, VIRGINIA

Edith Wilson was the first unofficial female President of the United States. There. I said it. People had told me this. I had read a few vague stories about the possibility of it. It had been proposed to me as loose concepts in a kind of joking manor, as well. As always, I took things I heard or read like this with a grain of salt. Let's remember the lesson I leaned from Nancy Loane, at Valley Forge, from Volume One. Do NOT believe everything you read. Then, I went to the Woodrow Wilson Library and Museum in Staunton, Virginia. Now, I am a believer. But, for that part of the Edith Wilson story…you'll have to wait, because we're starting from the beginning, in Wytheville, Virginia…the birthplace of Edith Bolling Wilson (remember, I'm a television producer, and that's a classic example of a teaser).

It was a rainy August evening when I drove into Wytheville on US 81 S. Let me correct that. It was a "monsoony" evening in August when I floated into Wytheville. I had just finished a long week looping through Virginia. During which, I had been through one of the prettiest parts of the United States—in my, and the Hoovers' opinions—when I visited the Hoovers' Rapidan Camp in the Shenandoah Valley. I was lured to Staunton by the letters between President Wilson's doctor and other White House staffers that they had in their collection. I was amazed at the isolated beauty of the Roosevelts' Pine Knot cottage. And when I pulled off the interstate in Wytheville, I realized, "I've been here before." I even recall saying that out loud to myself in the car. I recognized the town by their Harley dealer. I had stopped here a few years prior on a trip to Lake Norris outside of Knoxville, Tennessee. That was one less thing I had to do while I was there—I already had a shirt. So, I checked in, and began my ritual. I laid out my clothes, checked my gear and did my final research and preparation for the morning. I looked forward to meeting Farron Smith the next morning. She and her husband along with some historians in town, had purchased, and were in the process of restoring, the Edith Bolling Wilson Birthplace Museum.

Edith Bolling's father was a very successful southern man, who ended up on the losing side of the Civil War. He moved his family to Wytheville to rebuild and realign with the new world around them. They lived upstairs, on the second floor, over a store front on a main street in town from 1866 to 1899. It was a large family. Edith was the seventh born of eleven children. As many as twenty family members lived there at one time, including Edith's grandmother.

The rain had passed, but it was already heating up by the time I got to the museum. The strip of buildings and much of the street looked almost unchanged from the days when Edith and her family lived there. I got a very cool and historical vibe from the whole town. I got some really nice footage of the main street, the museum and the other shops and surrounding town.

Farron greeted me at the front door of what used to be the Bolling family store. Now, it was the main entrance to the museum and gift shop. They had a marvelous collection of books and information about Mrs. Wilson and her family. They also had several pictures from when the family lived there and period pieces. Farron and her group were just getting started there and didn't have much funding, at the time, to improve upon the structure or construct fancy exhibits. The stories here would have to speak to me from the structure itself and come directly out of the unfinished walls and scuffed floors. We walked back out onto the street so I could get shots and introduction stand ups of Farron walking through the original front door and up the stairs to the second floor living quarters.

Production Note – Knock, Knock!

Any time I got the chance to open an original door, or run my hand along an original banister, or walk up an original staircase or on original floors at one of these locations, I jumped at it. Filming these types of pieces gave the viewer the perspective of the women I was studying. This was the door that Edith walked through every day to go to school or wherever she was headed that day. It's as personal as walking through the door of the front house or bedroom where you grew up. If you've had the chance to do this and walk through history for yourself, you know exactly what I'm talking about. It's a very powerful feeling.

I lugged my gear up the stairs and set it down in the main open living room, or parlor, and had a look around. It was not a large space. I could not image twenty people living here, but I guess they made it work. The front room to the right was Edith's parent's bedroom, and the room where Edith was most likely born. The room—like the rest of the house—had not been restored, and I didn't mind it. Not even one bit. Don't get me wrong, the polished museums and historical locations with big budgets and high dollar exhibits and artifacts are fantastic and necessary. However, so are locations like this. This was raw. This building had a historical tone that gave me a distinct feeling that something or someone important had been here. In this situation, it was better that it was still in the "as is" condition in which Farron and her group had purchased it. I was also able to get some artsy shots out of the front bedroom window. An American flag on the front of the museum was waving in the breeze over the street. I was already imagining the opening shots of some of the video piece from here.

Here was where they had the two oldest pieces in their collection. They were also the most significant pieces when it came to Edith. The Bolling family cradle was in this room. It was a small, delicate wooden cradle without much to it. It was simple, but functional, and what you would expect from a family of Edith's size. I'm sure Edith wasn't the only Bolling child to sleep in it over the years. They also had a small child's chair. This piece was a bit more ornate than the cradle. It had nicely carved legs and armrests. It was covered in crushed red velvet, and had large, brass tacks to hold the fabric in place. It was a well-worn, but well-made chair, as I was told it was the original covering. This was something that Edith would have used here as a small girl. There was no better place to get a feeling for a person's start in life than the room in which they were born. I had many opportunities to stand in these rooms, and this was just another great way to get a visual feel for the life of this First Lady.

Series Note – May We Ask You A Few Questions?

Farron was really on top of things for my visit. She had a sign in the window of the museum with images and written materials from the C-SPAN series. She also arranged for the Mayor to stop by and have a very welcoming chat with me. If that wasn't enough, a photographer and reporter stopped by from the local paper to do a story on the series, my visit and my travels. It was all very flattering and a nice way to end a long week.

The next most significant room in the house was a back bedroom. It belonged to Edith's grandmother. Edith was the favorite grandchild and slept in this room with her grandmother. The semi-private room (which I would imagine was a valuable commodity in the Bolling house), came with a price. Edith served as her grandmother's caretaker. Her grandmother was an invalid with back trouble. She spoiled Edith however and whenever she could. It was in the silence of this room, I got a sense of where Edith learned the skills that would come to be so useful later in life, after President Wilson would suffer a debilitating stroke in the White House.

Edith and her grandmother were close and shared a love of birds. Her grandmother had what I would call and unusual number of birdcages full of small birds. She kept them in her room and on the sleeping porch on the back of the building. The sleeping porch looked very much the same as it had nearly 150 years earlier. This was validated by an old photograph of Edith when she was thirteen. She was pictured sitting on a stool with her school books, surrounded by bird cages on the same porch. This picture really gave me an idea of exactly how Edith looked to her grandmother when they were spending so much time together. This and similar photographs had been made into displays in many of the rooms and they helped tell the stories of Edith and her family. As I explained in Volume One, pictures like this were a fantastic resource in the final edits of my video pieces to show the rooms then and now, and to complete the story and the visual effectiveness of my footage.

Production Note – Right Angles

It's always fun to shoot rooms at these locations knowing you have original photographs to use in the final piece. It lets me set up my tripod and camera in exactly the same place to get exactly the same perspective on the room, house, street or artifact as appears in the picture. The end result is a morph-like dissolve that takes the viewer back in time.

The formal parlor to the right of the stairs was where Edith would have seen her parents entertain guest and friends. This was also where she would have learned proper hostessing skills which would certainly come in handy later in life. This was very typical of the training most of these would-be First Ladies received in their homes from their mothers and grandmothers. It was important to know, not all women got this kind of training—especially in a big family like Edith's. Given the number of children and the limited resources, Edith was fortunate to have this element during her childhood.

There was also a back bedroom for the other children. There was no doubt that Edith would have spent time in here, too. For one, it was a small house with a lot of people. There weren't many places to go. She also, most likely didn't spend every night in her grandmother's room. She probably played in here with her brothers and sisters, maybe even did schoolwork or other activities in there, as well. It was another piece to the puzzle of Edith's childhood, and I was happy to have seen it and gotten the footage.

The last room we looked at in the house was her father's office. This was where I got the most remarkable story of my visit. This room told the story of her upbringing, and more specifically, her father. This was where her father's desk would have been. It was easy to see Edith or any number of her brothers and sisters on one side of the desk, and her father on the other. He—like any father or parent—would be dolling out rewards for good behavior and punishments for the opposite. We've all been there. This was where I was told the story of how and why young Edith Bolling went to Washington, DC.

An older, and not entirely desirable, man was interested in courting young Edith there in Wytheville. Edith seemed to have feelings for him, too. Mr. and Mrs. Bolling didn't like this man. In an attempt to make her forget about him, they sent her to visit one of her older sisters who was married and lived in Washington, DC. Edith went to DC, where she met and fell in love with a prominent jeweler named Norman Galt. The two were married on April 30, 1896. He died very unexpectedly in January 1908 at the age of 43. Galt didn't leave Edith a rich widow, but she did stay in Washington and remained in the social circles where she would later meet President Woodrow Wilson.

We have seen these kinds of situations many times before (Julia Tyler, Mary

Lincoln and Angelica Singleton Van Buren come to mind). It was very common for families to send their younger daughters to visit older siblings—especially sisters—in big cities. The purpose of these visits was to find a husband. What if the older man had been more suitable for Edith in her parents' eyes? She might not have gone to DC at all. Then she wouldn't have married Galt. What if Ellen Wilson or Edith's first husband hadn't died? Or whatever other scenario might be conjured up to prevent Edith from meeting and marrying President Wilson. Things would have been very different, that's for sure.

Historical Note - Back To The Future

I'm fairly certain everyone reading this has seen or knows the premise of the "Back to the Future" movies. If Marty McFly changed–as he sometime did—it always had a significant effect on the present day. We could play this game with any of these women, and predict or assume different scenarios on what America and the world around us would look like. I do it during all my speeches and it usually gets laughs from the audience. But, seriously, let's think about this. It's how I started Volume One, and I liked it so, much, it's how I started Volume Two. If Martha had not met George, we would not be here together reading this book. The circumstances that surrounded their meeting were so precarious, so delicate, so potentially changeable, it's a wonder it happened at all. Honestly, we can say this about any and everything that happens to us every day. But, not all of us are Martha or George Washington. Without Martha Washington, George Washington doesn't do what he did to start America. Without America, the world is a very different place. That's just a fact. To think that one woman changed the face of planet Earth as we know it blows my mind. It should blow yours, too. The "Back to the Future" game. Mindbomb. BOOM.

STAUNTON, VIRGINIA

Okay. The moment we've all be waiting for. The first unofficial female President of the United States. Edith Bolling Galt Wilson. The Wilson Museum in Staunton was full of amazing exhibits, artifacts, information and documentation that surrounded the lives of President Woodrow Wilson and his two wives, Ellen and Edith. It was a really neat little town, too. I actually took time to sit down, have lunch at a nice street side café, and walk around the town a bit. I very much enjoyed my day there. The most remarkable part of my visit and my day came after lunch.

Archivist, Peggy Dillard, took me way back into the Wilson Library to look at the Dr. Cary Grayson letters. We went deep into archives where there were file cabinets, shelves and gray archival boxes were stored. We took down boxes and boxes, and folders upon folders, and went over a massive number of notes and letters. A family member had donated the entire collection of Grayson letters to the library, and it was the absolute best way to get a look inside what was going on in the White House when President Woodrow Wilson had his stroke in 1919.

President Wilson, Edith Wilson and the White House staff told the American people that the President was suffering from exhaustion, and needed to rest. They even told this to Congress. Only the closest of confidants and staff knew the truth about Wilson's stroke. It was even suspected that Mrs. Wilson and a White House aide produced a false interview with President Wilson with a local Washington, DC journalist to support the cover up.

Can you imagine if the current President, or any President in the last forty plus years had tried to pull off this kind of stunt? If we—the people—don't see our President on TV almost daily, we get nervous. It doesn't even matter what he does or says. We just need to see him get lunch, play golf, walk to his helicopter...ANYTHING... we just need proof of life. To think that a President could disappear from public life is mind boggling.

It was well-known that the President was out of commission. However, it was not well-known, at the time, that Edith Wilson was the gatekeeper for all access to her husband. No letters, no information, no business and no questions got to President Wilson without Mrs. Wilson's approval. This alone was more than a bit remarkable given it was 1919, but those were her rules. She was very protective of her husband and wanted to vet all incoming material to determine the importance and stress level attached. She also wanted to predict the impact or effect the issue at hand would have on her husband's health and recovery. People had no concept of the degree to which President Wilson was incapacitated. The administration and staff didn't know how much or how little Mrs. Wilson was telling her husband. To this day no one knows really knows how much or how many of the decisions that came back "from the President" were actually his. This was reflected in letters and documents I saw that were signed by Edith Wilson. One such document was a telegram from a U. S. foreign dignitary in Turkey. The man was asking permission to speak at a public forum in Turkey on a matter of international security involving the Turkish occupation of Constantinople. At the bottom of the telegram was Mrs. Wilson's handwriting that advised not to get involved with this matter at that time.

It could be argued Mrs. Wilson consulted her husband on all matters, and even if she didn't, it wasn't the biggest of deals in some unimportant cases. He could have easily told her to sign and approve things after he had seen and weighed in on them. President Wilson could have also instructed Mrs. Wilson to sign his name on any number of documents during this time. She could have consulted with various cabinet members or staff on her own, or at the instruction of her husband. A lot could have happened. No matter how you slice it, Mrs. Wilson controlled anything and everything intended for the eyes of her husband, the President of the United States, during this time. If that doesn't make her the acting President, I don't know what does.

There were also letters that went back and forth between Dr. Grayson and various Wilson Administration and White House staff members. These letters were very telling. The most remarkable letters were between a Wilson Administration member and Dr. Grayson. The man was asking Dr. Grayson's permission to use a story Grayson had told him in a book he was writing. The story was about the planned resignation of President Wilson. Dr. Grayson and President Wilson had determined it would best for Wilson to go to Congress and resign. They planned every detail. Then they told Mrs. Wilson. Mrs. Wilson disagreed. She thought it would be best for her husband to stay in office to keep his mind active, and improve his condition. The original plan was changed, because of Mrs. Wilson. Woodrow remained in the White House, and finished his term. This woman had an unprecedented amount of influence over the highest office and position in America, and quite possibly the world. Mrs. Wilson effectively reversed the decision of her husband—the President of the United States—and his doctor to keep him in office.

Historical Note - In Her Own Words

Mrs. Edith Wilson on the possibility of her taking on the role of President while her husband was sick:

> "I studied every paper, sent from different Secretaries or Senators, and tried to digest and present in tabloid form the things that, despite my vigilance, had to go to the President. I, myself, never made a single decision regarding the disposition of public affairs. The only decision that was mine was what was important and what was not, and the very important decision of when to present matters to my husband."

I have a tendency not to entirely believe her. Nearly every First Lady protects her husband and his reputation with appropriate and unrelenting vigor. Mrs. Wilson long outlived her husband, and made sure his legacy was intact to the best of her ability. Any recognition of her own authority, or decisions she made during her husband's illness could undermine his reputation and legacy.

The Wilson Library and Museum had more than just letters to tell the story of Edith Wilson. Mrs. Wilson had a statuesque frame, and the museum had the dresses to prove it. She had been a tall and sturdy woman described by many as buxom. Her gowns, dresses and clothes showed this to have been true. She was older by the time she was in the White House, and dressed respectably for her role. She had been in Washington society for several years, and knew the scene well. Her hats, coats, dresses and outfits all represented a woman of class and prominence. Woodrow Wilson remains the last President to have had two wives. Therefore, he is also the last President to get married while in office. She and Wilson did not have a very big wedding. In fact, I would describe it as low key.

A big deal was never made over Edith and Woodrow Wilson's actual wedding ceremony. They didn't get married in the White House, like Mr. and Mrs. Cleveland had done. They were not a young or particularly scandalous couple, as had been the case with President and Julia Tyler. Whatever the case, no detailed written history could be found. There were not many artifacts or mementos from the wedding, either. The museum had invitations, and a few other items to represent the wedding, but nothing extensive. It just kind of happened. One day President Wilson wasn't married, and the next he was, with little or no fanfare.

There was always more emphasis on Edith Wilson when she was already First Lady or on her life after the White House. The museum had a place setting from Edith Wilson's White House china. It was a subtle, and effective way for Edith to make a statement and register her claim as First Lady. The settings were made by Lenox in 1918. It was a classic design of white china with gold pin-striping borders, and grand, but tasteful Presidential eagles. Some of the plates had an additional cobalt blue band between the gold leaf rings. It was elegant and appropriate, which was exactly what I would have expected from Mrs. Wilson.

Travel Note – Home Plate

If you're not up for an EXTENSIVE road trip to all of the Presidential Museums, there are two central locations in Washington, DC where you can get a fantastic look at most of the White House china patterns from all the different administrations. The National Museum of American History and the White House both have excellent collections. The White House collection is more complete, but it's is a little more difficult to get in on a scheduled tour day. The Smithsonian collection has more than enough pieces to give you an idea of all the different settings. They even have examples of Washington, Adams and Madison china. These early leaders brought their best personal china from home. Mrs. Monroe was the first First Lady to have official White House china. The National Museum of American History has pieces from the Monroe collection as well.

Edith Wilson was an independent woman and an independent thinker. This should come as no surprise given the other things I have told you about her here. President Wilson's prized 1919 Pierce-Arrow automobile was in Staunton, and I was assured that a local car club kept it in working order (sadly, they did not start it for me, nor did I get to ride in it). Even though the car had more to do with President Wilson than Mrs. Wilson, I got plenty of footage of that beautiful machine—just in case. The car was massive and very impressive. President Wilson was a huge fan of driving, and he was the first President to be a member of the AAA. The museum wasn't even sure if he had a driver's license (but, seriously, who was going to give the President of the United States a ticket for driving without a license in 1919). Mrs. Wilson was a fan of driving, too. There was no record of Mrs. Wilson driving the Pierce-Arrow, but she did have her driver's license, and one of the first electric cars. There was a fantastic picture of Edith driving her car through Washington, DC hanging up in the museum next to the President's car. She enjoyed and asserted herself in the role of First Lady and in the modern world around her, and it was showcased perfectly in these pictures and artifacts.

WASHINGTON, DC

The Wilsons moved from the White House directly into their new Washington, DC home, as I told you about briefly in the previous Ellen Wilson chapter. It was paid for by Wilson's Nobel Peace Prize money, and wealthy supporters. President Wilson only lived there about three years before he died on February 3, 1924, at the age of 67. He wasn't in good health when they moved in March 1921, so his death wasn't a huge surprise. The house is located near the embassy section of Massachusetts Avenue in Northwest, DC just past DuPont Circle, on the way towards Wisconsin Avenue and the National Cathedral (where both he and Edith are buried). This Washington home would tell the story of Edith as soon as I walked through the front door (just another cool original door to pass through as the many historical figures before me).

The plan was to go and take a look at the Wilson House, and talk with Director Robert Enholm about the possibility of doing something completely different for the Wilson show than we had done for any other show in the series, so far. We wanted to do live remote hits from the home during the live show. This would entail a lot more crew, a satellite truck, a location guest and crew, and me as a live shot producer to keep things on track at the house, and stay in constant communication with the control room on Capitol Hill. Enholm and his team were up for the task, so, he showed me around and I started taking notes.

As soon as I walked in, Edith's formidable presence was felt. Mrs. Wilson had given her husband a grandfather clock as a housewarming gift. Not only does the clock still work, but it was still on the landing where it had been when the Wilsons lived there. In fact, most the house was accurate to when they lived there. The Wilsons would feel right at home if they were to walk through the front door today. This was another reason why doing live remotes from here during the live show would be so effective. Some of the ground floor that was office space for President Wilson's staff was converted to museum office space, so even that remained relatively true to form.

The second floor was mainly taken up by the dining room, the parlor and President Wilson's office. Edith used these rooms, and the objects on site supported those claims. The main focus of the dining room was Edith Wilson's official White House portrait, which hung over the fireplace mantel. For the portrait sitting, Mrs. Wilson wore a very fashion-forward and modern dress. It was designed with a long, blue skirt and a suspender-like shoulder strap. With it she wore a waist brooch that had been a gift from the French during the Paris Peace Conference in 1919, which she attended with President Wilson.

The original dining room table was set with Wilson Lenox china settings (as described earlier in this chapter). This was the room where Edith Wilson very famously entertained sitting First Lady Jacqueline Kennedy in 1961. Mrs. Wilson was a big fan of the Kennedy White House, and Mrs. Kennedy was very interested in going to the Wilson House. She heard that Mrs. Wilson had a very special chair there. It seems that Mrs. Wilson and Mrs. Kennedy were both fans of First Lady Elizabeth Monroe's style and White House decor Mrs. Monroe had established. Mrs. Kennedy was restoring the White House as a museum and National Historical Landmark, and heard that Mrs. Wilson might have had at least one of Mrs. Monroe's chairs. As the story was told to me, Mrs. Kennedy asked Mrs. Wilson about the chairs, and she acknowledged that she did have the items in question. In fact, the two women were sitting in the Monroe chairs at the brunch. Mrs. Kennedy politely asked if she could bring the chairs back to the White House, and Mrs. Wilson politely refused to give them to her. That was that. They finished brunch and Mrs. Kennedy went home. The beautiful blue Monroe chairs are still in the Wilson House. There was no doubt the two women spent some time in the parlor before brunch, as well, but, when I visited, the parlor was set up to also include some of Ellen Wilson's art (as I described in the previous chapter).

President Wilson's office looked as Presidential as any office I saw on the entire journey. It was a large room with high ceilings, huge, heavily curtained windows and built-in bookshelves. To the left, as I entered the room, there was a massive desk positioned on a gorgeous area rug. There were bookshelves with countless mementos of a war-time President. The walls were covered in dark paneled wood. Paintings, certificates and photographs occupied every inch of wall space. On a wooden stand, next to the impressive desk, was a metal box with a lock. This was called the President's drawer. During the White House years, this box was filled with the President's official documents, papers and daily briefings. In the evenings, President and Mrs. Wilson would take the box into the private residence and go over all the papers together. Mrs. Wilson would sort them, and give them to her husband to read. She would read them after he was done with them, and then they discussed their contents. They even deciphered top secret and coded material together. Enholm explained this as being very significant to the type of modern First Lady Mrs. Wilson was, and the role she played in her husband's life and administration. I followed up with the fact that it further supported what her role was during his illness.

In December 1917, when it came time came to sign the official documents declaring America's role in World War I, the papers were brought to the President at the White House by the Secretary of Defense. When Wilson went to sign them, he didn't have a pen handy. Edith gave him one of hers. This pen was now on the desk in the President Woodrow Wilson House. I looked at that pen, now knowing what it was used for. It was a very heavy moment. With his signature, President Wilson entered the United States into the first World War, and Edith's pen sealed that fate. Her involvement and influence were omnipresent. The pen set was also quite beautiful. It had a base made from ivory that was carved to look like a walrus with the head and tusks on the end that held the glass ink well. The base and the ink well were enhanced by brass inlay details. The tip of the pen and pen holder were also brass.

The bedrooms on the third floor were carefully designed to replicate those of the White House. By the time the Wilsons lived here, President Wilson wasn't doing very well, and Mrs. Wilson thought any and all familiarity would be good for the President. President Wilson's nurse had a small room between Mr. and Mrs. Wilson's bedrooms. Edith even had the Lincoln bed that Mr. Wilson had used in the White House duplicated for his room here. President Wilson's bedroom looked as though he might walk in and get into bed at any moment. Mrs. Wilson's room looked more like a museum, with her closets converted into display cases and exhibits. The clothes and furniture around the room and in the cases, were all very nice and what you might expect from such a dignified, elderly woman. The furniture was well crafted, medium toned wood, and the clothes matched the styles of the other pieces I had seen through my Edith Wilson journey.

My new friends at the Wilson House in Washington, DC and those from the Edith Wilson Birthplace Museum in Wytheville connected me with Edith Wilson's Great Nephew, Cary Fuller. Cary spent time at the Wilson House as a child and young man, and agreed to be a part of the live show. He walked us through the house, and told us what rooms and what stories related to him and how he spent his time there with Edith—which was what she preferred people to call her. He said she didn't talk about the past much. When she did, it was usually in reference to her husband, who she always called the President. Cary only spent two nights there. He stayed in what used to be the nurse's room, on the third floor in between the Wilsons' bedrooms. Mrs. Wilson took in, and cared for, many family members over the years after her husband died, and the primary use of the house and her time was for family. A lot of card games were played in the office and parlor. Canasta was Edith's game of choice and the cards were always out on the table when Cary arrived for a visit. His mother told him to let his Great Aunt win a few games here and there, if need be, as she was a fierce competitor. Cary said this was easy to accomplish given the rules of the game, and he would just hold cards instead of playing them.

Location Note - Game Night

Many of these historical locations host a lot of special and regular events. Their staffs work very hard to preserve history and make it come alive in very creative ways. Bob Enholm and his staff are no different. They have a regular game night and break out vintage and retro board and card games, and visitors can sit in Edith and Woodrow's DC home and play games. If you live in or around Washington, or you happen to be in town on game night, I suggest you go. Look them up and get on their email list.

Cary Fuller was there the day Mrs. Kennedy visited, but only to pick up his mother and Edith to go somewhere after the brunch. He described his Great Aunt as being very excited about the visit. Cary spent a lot of special and quality time with Edith here in her Washington home. It is also where she would die, in her bedroom, on the third floor on December 28, 1961, what would have been her husband's 105th birthday. Her cause of death was congestive heart failure, she was 89.

Historical Note - The Problem

The problem with history is few—if any—of us were there. We producers, documentarians, historians and researchers do our best to tell you what happened based on our research and our travels. Nothing is a substitute for someone who was actually there and saw it unfold with their own eyes. I had the chance to talk to direct relatives more than once during this series and throughout my travels. We always jumped at the chance to include them in the series. One of the best parts of this particular show was when I got the opportunity to stand out in front of the street with Cary on the sidewalk. The cameras were packed up, and we stood under the stars and the street lights and talked more candidly about Edith. He didn't share anything unusual or remarkably different than what he had said during the live show, but the way he said things showed me just how special this woman was to him on a personal and familial level. He didn't know her as First Lady. He only knew her as Edith. This was a new level of bringing in that human element. Edith Wilson was Cary Fuller's Great Aunt. He played cards with her. He ate meals with her. She was part of his childhood and held a special place in his heart. Everyone can relate to this. Edith Wilson was no longer that oil painting over the fireplace. She was real.

SUMMARY

I made a bold statement at the beginning of this chapter. I get asked about Edith Wilson and her role during her husband's illness at nearly every speech. Historically speaking, many women—almost all of them—have had a significant influence on their husband's administrations. Many of them have had a direct influence over his policies and his thinking. This has been my assertion from the beginning of Volume One. It is why C-SPAN created the series, "FIRST LADIES: Influence and Image." However, no First Lady has had to step in and take over or control access to her husband the way Edith Wilson did. It was unprecedented and thus far unrepeated. Mrs. Wilson controlled the access to one of the most powerful and influential men in the world—the President of the United States of America—in a way that no other First Lady has before or since. This—even at face value—makes her one of, if not the most unusual First Ladies of all.

Travelogue Food Tip

I love hot dogs. I eat them wherever and whenever I can. I make—what I call—gourmet hot dogs at home (loaded with ketchup, mustard, mayonnaise, pickles, onions and cheese). I requested bacon cheddar dogs as my special birthday meal from my mom almost every year growing up (along with her homemade key lime pie). On the trip to Memphis that saw the completion to Volume One, and a very special trip to Graceland, I ate two hot dogs at two separate meals on two separate days (much to the surprise of my local tour guide). In Wytheville, Virginia, they serve the World Famous Skeeter Dog. My host, Farron, and her husband not only joined me, but treated me to two Skeeter dogs—one with slaw and one with chili. The diner setting—which happens to be in the same strip of buildings as Edith's birthplace home—was a fantastic way to finish up our day together. The hot dogs were excellent and the service was friendly. I cannot recommend this place highly enough. I will definitely be going back. You can't miss it, there's a giant Skeeter Dog mural on the side of the building.

CHAPTER FIVE
Florence Harding

Marion, Ohio

Florence Harding was born Florence Mable Kling on August 15, 1860 in Marion, Ohio. Her parents were Amos Hall Kling and Louise Mabel Bouton Kling. Florence and Warren Harding were married on July 8, 1891. They had no children together. She had one child with her first husband. Florence Harding died in Marion, Ohio on December 28, 1924 at the age of 64.

MARION, OHIO

Florence Harding was another example of a First Lady who I didn't know much about, but can be credited with much of her husband's success. She had a lot of influence over President Harding's professional life, even before he entered politics. She was the oldest child of a successful business man who not only wanted a son, but was disappointed that his first-born child was a daughter. He treated, taught and talked to Florence as though she were a son. This was an unusual relationship for a girl to have with her father, especially in the late 1800's. I found this interesting given what I knew about Ida McKinley and her with her father. The training Ida received as a young woman in her father's bank helped her later in life. While Florence's relationship with her father was more difficult than Ida's, it still gave her the skills to help her husband into the highest office in the land (like Ida). I was seeing a pattern. Many First Ladies (unbeknownst to them, or maybe even their fathers) were getting very "male" training and education. They had a relationship with their fathers more like that of a son. In a male dominated world, this gave these young women an edge over other females of their time. I was beginning to see the reasons why some of these women were attracted to (and married) the men who would later become President.

Marion, Ohio is a small town north of Columbus, and I drove there on a cool summer evening in July from the Taft site in Cincinnati. I found it to be charming and quaint. In certain aspects, it seemed as though time had stood still from the days of Florence and Warren Harding. The homes looked as if they were right out of a John Cougar Mellencamp video. I had no idea what was in store for me inside the Harding home when I pulled into the driveway. The only thing I was told during the phone interview before my visit was that the Hardings had a lot of really cool stuff that told a lot of stories about their life together. I was greeted by my host, Sherry Hall, the Harding Home Site Manager, and got we started.

As soon as I walked into the home, I knew this was going to be something special. By this point in the series, I had seen a lot of homes, and a lot of artifacts. But, I had never seen this many artifacts in a single home. They all looked so natural, too. Everything looked like it was in the right place. I know I have said this a hundred times (or more) in these books, but...IT LOOKED LIKE THE HARDINGS STILL LIVED THERE! I mean it really looked as though there should be food cooking on the stove or on plates at the table. I kept turning around to look for Florence and Warren to walk in the door. The other locations were great—fantastic, even. However, this was remarkable, and creepy—in a cool way, if that makes any sense. It was like I was in my grandparent's house. We even walked in the back door through the kitchen, as if we were family members or lived there ourselves, I felt right at home. Sherry had me come in on a day when the home was closed to the public. This made the experience that much more special, and allowed us to really get some good footage and work done.

We took a quick walk around the house, but the rooms literally told their own stories and Sherry was so good on camera. Her knowledge of the house, stories and collections was extensive. We basically powered up and rolled camera without doing my usual walk through the house.

We started off in the dining room. It seriously reminded me of my grandparents' dining room in their Baltimore, Maryland row house. There was a table under the modest chandelier in the center of the room with a beautiful rug under it. The room was surrounded by cabinets, wooden shelves, buffets, servers and chairs. The first piece I noticed was a medium sized curio cabinet full of elephant figurines. Mrs. Harding was somewhat superstitious—not uncommon for the people born and raised in the Victorian era—she thought elephants were good luck (especially the ones with the turned-up trunks). This worked out well later when her husband rose to fame in the Republican Party. She kept this cabinet and collection in the private quarters in the White House. The figurines came in all sizes and were made from all kinds of things like; jade, ivory, wood, marble and stone. This was an immediately humanizing collection. My mom collected cows. I had a fifth-grade teacher (Ed Ragan – if he's reading this) who collected pigs on his desk at Barnsley Elementary School. For some people it's stamps or coins. People collect things. This was real. I could see it and easily related to it.

Author's Note – Skulls, Skulls And More Skulls

I collect skulls. I even have a human skull in the collection (it's my grandfather's—more on that in a minute). I have always liked skulls. I think they're cool. Growing up, my Uncle Dave was always around, and he was into Harley Davidsons, tattoos and all forms of "badassery" like that. I was the only kid at the fouth grade Book Fair who got a subscription to "CYCLE" magazine, instead of a book. At Rockville High School, I took Advanced Placement Anatomy and Physiology with Mr. Hagy and got an "A." I have always loved the skeletal structure and functionality of the human body as a machine. So, in my travels along the many paths of life, my collection has continued to grow. I have shirts, shoes, hats, scarves, coffee mugs, tea steepers, coasters, playing cards, statues, figurines, plates, pictures, paintings, pottery, lawn ornaments, belt buckles, pens, pins, ice cube molds, stickers, refrigerator magnets, sculptures, toys, x-rays, window boxes, chess sets, lights, rings, tattoos, and yes...a human skull that belonged to my grandfather. It's not his actual skull, but he owned it. I got it after he died. I guess I wasn't surprised when no one else in the family wanted it. I am told by my father it was the skull of a WWI fighter pilot. I think, my grandfather got it at a medical school or supply facility. Whatever the case, it sits in my house, on a set of bookshelves built by my grandfather (along with other oddities), in a room I refer to as the "Jungle Room" (more Elvis). I call the shelves my "Smithsonian," because that's what my grandmother called the cabinet where the skull (and other oddities) was kept in their house.

The Hardings came into the White House right after World War I, in the middle of a recession. They chose not to select a new, official White House china pattern. There was plenty of services from other administrations to use, and the Hardings had numerous collections of their own. Their own sets included some wonderful crystal which was on display here in their Marion home in a beautiful, large, wooden cabinet with mirrored shelf backings. The crystal pieces consisted of decanters, vases, wine glasses and remarkable plates with gold leaf detailing and accents. Any of these pieces would have complemented any former administration's china without a problem. Mrs. Harding also had several china sets herself. Examples from at least six different services were on display in the dining room. She and Warren were very well traveled, and they had gorgeous plates and services from Italy, France and all over the world. Their blue and white collection was exquisite, and the other sets had stunning greens and other bright colors. The shelves around the room were full of plates, keepsakes and functional items. Mrs. Harding also collected toasters. She had them in all shapes and sizes; old, new and in between.

I mentioned Mrs. Harding was superstitious, and she was. She also enjoyed symbolism. Examples of this could be seen all over the house in its contents and its design. Here in the dining room there was a medium sized stained glass window. It was high up, close to the ceiling, on the far wall. The main focus of its design was three black rings surrounded by branches, leaves and nuts of a buckeye tree (Ohio state tree). The three rings had two meanings. The first was the Holy Trinity and the life cycle of life, death and afterlife. The other meaning for her was that there were three members of her family – her husband, her son (from her first marriage) and herself. The whole combination in the window meant health, happiness and good fortune for Mrs. Harding and her whole family.

In the dining room the Hardings had one of the most stunning art pieces I saw during my entire journey. It was a Capodimonte porcelain vase they had purchased in Italy during a trip through Europe. Not only was the piece beautiful, and in perfect condition, but the story of how they got it back to Ohio was almost as amazing as the piece itself. First of all, it was huge. It stood at least 3 feet tall, and was a foot and a half wide. It was delicately adorned with over twenty hand crafted flower blossoms in four different sizes, shapes, colors and varieties. A long porcelain branch curved around under the blossoms and ran the height of the vase from base to rim. I examined the vase very carefully for any dings, chips or damages. There were none. It was in perfect condition. I asked how it was shipped to the Hardings. I thought it couldn't even be carried it across the room without damaging it, let alone be shipped from overseas. The vase was shipped on a boat from Italy in a giant wooden barrel, packed and surrounded with saw dust. I'm not kidding when I say, I've had sturdier stuff come from within the U. S. to me recently that was broken or damaged. How this porcelain vase went from Italy to Ohio in a barrel full of sawdust in the early 1900's is beyond me. But there it was right in front of me, so, I had to believe the story.

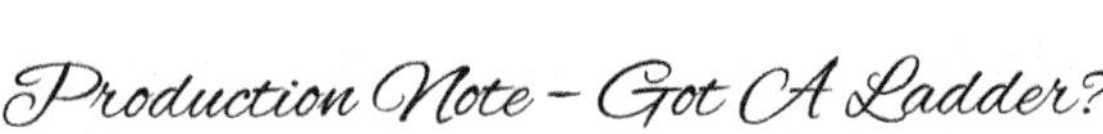

Production Note – Got A Ladder?

As Sherry and I got set up to shoot the piece about the vase, I couldn't get the right angle on it. The vase was covered—understandably so—with a giant, protective, clear, plastic, box. There was a window behind the vase, and I couldn't do anything to cut down on the glare. As soon as I turned on my lights and camera, it lost all its intensity and "wow factor" from the lights bouncing off the plastic case. What Sherry suggested next is what sets good museum folks aside from incredible museum folks. This was the stuff champions are made of. Sherry said, "Let's take the case off!" I couldn't believe my ears. I was actually thinking about telling her "no," because I didn't want to be a part of a monumental catastrophe like damaging this vase in any way, shape or form. But, I manned up, steadied my hand, and put on my game face. She got a ladder and we carefully—and I mean carefully—climbed up and took the case off. She made this shot possible.

We moved past the dining room and into the front foyer. This was the room in which Florence and Warren Harding were married. Evidence of Mrs. Hardings superstitions were in here, too. The Hardings built this house while they were engaged, and scheduled it to be finished in time for the wedding. They were also scheduled to be married during the upswing of an hour at 8:30pm. Mrs. Harding told the minister, if they were not married by 9pm, he would have to wait unit 9:30pm to pronounce them man and wife. This, too, was for good luck. There was a clock hanging on the landing of the stairs that was also there when the Hardings were alive. The clock was a wedding gift from a local jeweler. Warren Harding died in San Francisco at 7:30pm on August 2, 1923. At that exact time on that exact day, the clock in their Marion home stopped. The banister of the staircase was a beautifully crafted and stylized owl. This was for wisdom and good fortune for the Hardings. Symbolism and evidence of her superstitions were all over the home.

To the right of the foyer was the living room or parlor. It ws the one part of the house that Mrs. Harding modernized in order to support her husband's Presidential campaign. She and her husband would entertain town folk, neighbors, supporters and party leaders in this room, and she wanted its decor to reflect a modern woman of the 20th Century. They updated the paint and wallpaper. They got new furniture and rugs. They even updated the art and overall decor around the room. Mrs. Harding was her husband's biggest supporter in business, and it continued through to his political career.

In 1920, she played a crucial role in what ended up being the last successful front porch campaign for a U. S. Presidential candidate. We walked out the front door for the first time during my visit, got set up, and imagined Florence and Warren standing on the porch waving to the crowds out on Mount Vernon Avenue and making speeches. It was a spacious porch. A swing, suspended on a chain, hung from the ceiling of the porch. The flooring was done in a pattern of small, black and white tiles that you would expect to see on a bathroom floor. In fact, it was the same kind of tiles that were used in my grandparents' bathroom back in Baltimore. The modest house in what was, even then, middle America, created a perfect backdrop to present Harding as the everyday man. He even said that his campaign was taking Main Street to the White House.

Florence was a highly visible figure during the campaign. She stood at her husband's side during speeches and parades, and even gave one on one interviews to newspapers and magazines—especially women's magazines. She knew how politics worked and danced back and forth effortlessly between the role of caretaker, candidate's wife and savvy politician. She stepped right into the crowds to shake hands and talk to people face to face. This hands-on approach was very different from other First Ladies who were involved with their husband's campaigns, those who chose to hold flowers or fancy fans in order to avoid physical contact with strangers. We used old black and white footage of the Hardings standing on their porch waving to the masses in the final edit of this video piece. It was even more effective than the old photographs we had been using in the videos up till now.

Florence Harding was also a friend to the press corps. She and Warren were both newspaper people (we will cover this when we get to his office) and they knew how to handle the press. They converted their shed into a news filing center with wire communication set up and desks for reporters to cover the campaign. Florence would make her famous waffles for members of the press on a regular basis to keep them well fed and happy. Clearly the Hardings' strategy worked, and he was elected President.

Television Note – Feed Me, Seymour

A well-fed journalist is a happy journalist. A happy journalist writes positive stories. I have never seen people eat like TV people eat. When you are covering a campaign, you rarely stay in the same town or same bed two nights in a row. The road is a grueling place to work. Food is king and a home cooked meal is worth its weight in gold.

We went back into the house, upstairs to the bedrooms, and continued our tour and work inside. The first bedroom we entered belonged to Marshall De Wolfe. He was Florence's son from her first marriage. Florence had been known as a rebellious and headstrong young woman around town. Men in Marion were attracted to her and her family's wealth. Her father was Amos Kling, a successful business man. He tried to teach his daughter his knack for business and finance. Florence fell in love with Henry De Wolfe. They ran off together, and she became pregnant. Florence married Henry De Wolfe in 1880, and their son, Marshall, was born six months later. Neither family approved of the marriage.

De Wolfe was a drinker and ended up running out on Florence and Marshall. Florence and her son returned to Marion. They were eventually taken back in by her family. Florence and De Wolfe divorced in 1886. This was another element in the difficult relationship Florence had with her father. At this point, I asked what the country might have collectively thought about a potential First Lady who had previously been divorced (remember how well it worked out for Rachel Jackson back in the early 1800's). Sherry told me that Harding's opponent—James Cox—was divorced, too. So, it was a non-issue. I just shrugged, and filed that bit of information in "asked and answered," and we moved on.

In Marshall's bedroom were modest furnishings like the rest of the house. There were period toys in the room that any child from the late 1800's would have enjoyed. I had read that Florence turned Marshall over to her father to raise, and she didn't have much of a relationship with him. However, he definitely had a room in the Harding house. Marshall had a closer relationship with Warren Harding than he did with his mother. Marshall even worked for his stepfather at the Marion Star (the newspaper story is coming, I promise), and later bought a newspaper company of his own in Colorado. The paper, and life in general, did not go well for Marshall in Colorado. Marshall Eugene De Wolfe died there in 1915 at the age of 35 from alcoholism and tuberculosis.

I packed up my gear and walked across the hall to Florence and Warren's bedroom. There were two single beds in their room (once again I was taken back to my grandparents' house). The headboards and furniture were all nicely-crafted bird's eye maple and had been purchased in 1910. It was right about this time that Mrs. Harding developed a chronic kidney ailment that kept her in bed for months at a time. While in the White House in 1922, her kidney problems came back. Her condition was made public, and many people feared she would die from it. I didn't find out any specifics about her sickness, only that when she was well, she was a very public First lady who liked to entertain, and was the life of the party.

There was a purple shawl on a chair in the bedroom that Mrs. Harding used during the times she wasn't feeling well. More clothes were laid out on the beds, the drawers were full of items, there were shoes and hats and dresses in the closets, and the tops of dressers were littered with brushes and jewelry. Florence was on top of all the latest styles for a woman of her age and status. Many of her gowns and dresses were a precursor to the flapper style. After King Tut's tomb was discovered in 1922, the Egyptian style became all the rage, heavily influencing fashion. She had more than a few dresses that showed this Egyptian flair. It was easy to get a very good sense of Mrs. Hardin and her style here in the bedroom

There was a jewelry box on Mrs. Harding's dresser. It was a gift from her father. Given the troubled nature of their relationship, the fact that she kept and used this jewelry box was very telling. Her father still had a place in her life and in her heart. I know many people with difficult relationships with their parents. No matter how hard things are, or get, they always seem to hold on to an item or a hope that the relationship will get better. I'm sure it has something to do with the psychology of needing approval from our parents in life. This jewelry box seemed to be Florence's item. It was made of fine grained wood and lined with velvet. In the jewelry box were several unique and elegant pieces. The most unusual of which was a four-leaf clover charm. The clover was given to her by a veteran who attended an event on the lawn at the White House. She took the clover to a jeweler in DC, and had it encased in a glass locket and wore it on a chain.

Now, for the office and the newspaper story (FINALLY). I didn't save it until the end for any reason other than it was the room we went to last and the story we covered at the end of my visit. It was, however, a great way to close the books—for now—on Florence Harding. This aspect of her life brought her story full circle for me. I started this chapter by saying Mrs. Harding was a perfect example of a First Lady who could be credited with a lot of her husband's success, and here's the proof. When Florence met Warren, he owned and operated the Marion Star newspaper. People liked Warren. He was a young, good looking man who liked to shake hands and talk to people. However, he wasn't a good business man. His paper was losing money and needed a facelift. He needed new ideas and someone with a business mind. Florence Kling came along at just the right time. She had picked up some of her father's business acumen, and had learned about book keeping, mortgages, bill collecting, banking and finance. Florence and Warren turned out to be a newspaper business power couple. He was editorial, and she was business.

There were several artifacts and items that spoke to Florence's influence on her husband's newspaper and its eventual success. A success that put him in a position to run for President. Florence gave Warren a large, silver metal key that hinged and folded into his pocket. This was the key to front door of the Marion Star newspaper building. He kept it in his pocket for over 40 years. It turned into a kind of totemistic good luck charm for him. It was clearly representative of a special part and time in his life. A large, leather bound, ledger book—all in Florence's handwriting—showed her attention to the smallest of details and figures. Every penny was accounted for and kept in careful order (I thought of Martha Jefferson and Edith Roosevelt's account books when I saw this. Again, I was reminded of Ida McKinley, working in her father's bank, and overseeing the finances for her trip through Europe). There was an old-time card stamp from the newspaper that was very industrial and cool looking. Florence also expanded business at the newspaper and developed the first home delivery. She recruited newsboys to sell the paper, she ran the circulation department, and kept things moving forward at the paper. It is impossible to talk about the Marion Star or its success without talking about Mrs. Harding.

SUMMARY

If the Marion Star newspaper had failed, Warren Harding would have failed as a businessman. If Warren Harding's business had failed, there would be no President Warren Harding. Florence Harding was a huge influence in the innovation of home delivery and circulation of the paper and its financial success. Therefore, she was both directly and indirectly responsible for his professional and political success. It's not a stretch to say that she helped him get elected President in more ways than one. She was even unusual as a political spouse. She got more directly involved in his campaign than many wives before her. She was a "hands-on" political asset. She was right there in the trenches, shaking hands and talking to people. Behind every great man is an even greater woman. There isn't much written about her life as a young woman—her rebellious years. However, she seemed to triumph over them, and move on with her life and new husband. Her personal and political victories and successes make Florence Harding more than unusual for her time.

Travelogue Food Tip

Sherry and I were cruising along on the pieces at the house. Sometimes, I didn't even get to eat lunch when things were really moving along, and when that happened it wasn't the end of the world. However, Subway was close, and I like Subway. So, that's where we took a break for lunch. It was always nice to sit and get to know the people I was working with at these locations. Life on the road can be lonely, and company is always welcomed. I always get the same thing – 6-inch wheat, double meat BMT with everything—make it a meal with a large drink and a bag of regular Doritos. If it ain't broke don't fix it. I also knew that I would be flying out of Columbus to West Branch, Iowa, and probably wouldn't get to eat dinner until late, if at all, in Iowa. This seemed like a safe and tasty bet. Sometimes it's just best to go with what you know when you're eating on the road.

CHAPTER SIX

Grace Coolidge

Northampton, Massachusetts – Plymouth Notch, Vermont

Grace Coolidge was born Grace Anna Goodhue on January 3, 1879 in Burlington, Vermont. Her parents were Andrew Issachar Goodhue and Lemira Barrett Goodhue. Grace and Calvin Coolidge were married on October 4, 1905. They had two children together. Grace Coolidge died in Northampton, Massachusetts on July 8, 1957 at the age of 78.

NORTHAMPTON, MASSACHUSETTS

Grace and Calvin Coolidge's story is a good one. It's a well told one. It's a love story for the ages. Like Martha and George Washington or Dolley and James Madison, had one or two things been different, the two may never have met. Some historians—including this one—have said that the Coolidges are very much like the Madisons. This was because both James Madison and Calvin Coolidge were all business. Some people even called them "stuffy." President Coolidge's nickname was "Silent Cal," and some described him as monosyllabic when he spoke. One guest at a White House dinner party sat next to the President, and challenged him to a bet. The person (I believe it was a woman) said they could get him to say more than three words in under a minute. President Coolidge only replied, "You lose." Grace Coolidge was so full of life, she made her husband more affable by association. Like Dolley Madison, she softened her husband's gruff public persona. It was a definite "opposites attract" situation, and it worked out well for them personally and professionally. Grace was one of the few things that made him smile. She was his light.

As I have mentioned in this book, history is a funny subject. As historians and documentarians, we try our best to accurately research, define, explain, and recreate the past, but none of us—in most cases—were there. Much of what we learn and discover has come from stories that have been passed down. Sometimes those stories have been romanticized or embellished. The story of how Grace and Calvin met has been well documented. It was told in almost every book I read about them. According to all the versions I read, Grace and Calvin were living across a courtyard from each other at the Clarke School for the Deaf in Northampton, Massachusetts. She saw him shaving in an upstairs window. He was wearing a t-shirt, and Grace was really taken with him even though she didn't know who he was. Again, I go back to my experience in Valley Forge with Martha Washington and the Revolutionary War. So, here with the Coolidges, I was cautious to jump in with both feet. This story sounded nice, but how could I verify it?

The Forbes Library in Northampton is also the home of the Calvin Coolidge Presidential Library and Museum. Mrs. Coolidge helped design and create the Coolidge section of the library. My contact there was Julie Bartlett, and I asked her about the story of their meeting. She not only confirmed it, but said she could probably arrange a visit to the school and show me where it all went down. I was thrilled, and jumped at the chance. She went on to explain that the school wasn't a school anymore, and had been bought by a local real estate developer. She wasn't sure what the plans were, or how much longer the original building would be there, but we should be fine to get in and have a look around. Julie made all the necessary arrangements (another bit of luck and good timing on my part). My day started in Northampton before the Forbes Library opened, on a rainy July morning, with Julie at the Clarke School for the Deaf.

The Coolidges had Vermont in common. Grace was born and raised in Burlington, and Calvin was born and raised in Plymouth Notch. Grace came to Northampton right out of college, to teach at the Clarke School for the Deaf. She lived in a room at the school. Calvin rented a room in the dormitory there, on the second floor. He was a young lawyer and worked at a relative's law firm in town. So, they both came to the same town and lived at the school. Good. This put them in the same place at the same time. Now, for the whole "window… shaving…courtyard" part of the story.

Julie and I set up in the middle of an outdoor, blacktop, basketball court. There were buildings on three sides of us. Julie told me the story, as she pointed in all directions to support her words. The courtyard was once a garden, and Grace liked to work in that garden. Without much effort, I was directed to look behind us and up to a third-story window of a dormitory building. This room had been Calvin's. We know this from school records. This was where Grace looked up and saw Calvin shaving. This was where Calvin looked down from his window, and saw a pretty, dark haired girl tending to a flower garden. I panned my camera back and forth between the two spots. I didn't even have to move my feet to see history unfold before my eyes. It was incredible. And then it got even better.

Julie told me to look up to the window, above the garden area, directly in front of us. That was Grace's bedroom window. Her dorm room was facing Calvin's room, up and across the courtyard. We went inside to see Grace's old room. I filmed through her window…inside the room…across the courtyard…to his window. This was now very real. I was standing there, as Grace had, looking across the courtyard to Calvin's room. This story was no longer a few paragraphs in a book, or an urban legend shared among historians. I could see it.

Grace would light a candle in the window to let Calvin know that the parlor room downstairs, and a chaperone available, so they could spend time together. Even though she was in her 20's, and he was in his 30's, they needed to abide by the rules of school and the appropriateness of the times during their courtship here. Even back then, it was obvious the two were opposites, but she was attracted to his shyness and quiet sense of humor, and he was attracted to her outgoing personality and beauty. The parlor room was small, with a fireplace. It was an empty room when I was there. In Grace and Calvin's time, when there was furniture and a third person in there with them, it would have been tight, with no room for privacy. Clearly, they made it work.

This was a rare opportunity for me, and just plain dumb luck that I got to the Clarke School before it was torn down or changed in any way. This story couldn't have been told like it was without seeing all this. This was one of the coolest ways to prove a fantastic story was true. It was another chance to walk the footsteps of history, and bring that reality to the series and the viewers.

Our next stop was a small white house across town that had been converted into the Northampton Historical Society. They had some Coolidge artifacts I wanted to see. We had to really dodge the rain at this point, which was difficult with all the gear. However, it wasn't as difficult as getting up the narrow stairs, and into the storage area where all the Coolidge artifacts were kept. This facility had some unique wooden storage drawers that kept dresses, purses and other articles of clothing. It was said that President Coolidge knew the value of a penny (that's putting it politely). The only thing he splurged on was Grace's wardrobe, and man, did he ever splurge. Every place I went to study Grace Coolidge had fantastic clothes, and Northampton Historical Society was no exception.

There are two well-known portraits of Grace Coolidge. Her official White House portrait, in which she wore a red dress with her dog, Rob Roy (we will get to this one when I get us back to the Forbes Library later in this chapter). In the other, she was seated, and wore a white gown. Both paintings were done by Howard Chandler Christy. This white dress was carefully stored in one of the drawers at the Northampton Historical Society. As the drawer was pulled open, and the tissue paper folded back, I could see that the dress was in pristine condition. It was sleeveless, in the empire style with a jagged bottom, and had a flapper "flair" to it, without being too outrageous. Mrs. Coolidge was older by the time she got into the White House, and had impeccable fashion sense; not to mention that she knew the importance of her title. There was something different about seeing an actual dress from a painting. This was only the second actual dress from a formal portrait painting I had seen in person, in my travels (the other was Lucy Hayes's dress form her official White House portrait). It was very cool, and hard to explain. Somehow, it made both the person and the painting more real.

Author's Note - High School Reunion

I post daily First Lady facts on social media (Facebook, Instagram & Twitter), and people seem to enjoy them. I know I do. They're fun. Along with the fact, I post a picture, painting or image of the related First Lady. A friend who I hadn't seen since High School, took an active interest in the portrait images I posted. His name is Jim Head, and he and I reconnected because of these images and my First Ladies Man project. We had lunch together at the University Club in Washington, DC (which has strong ties to President Taft). I was finishing Volume One of "Unusual for Their Time," and Jim was working on book one of a trilogy series about the life and works of Howard Chandler Christy. Jim has taught me a lot about Christy, his relationship with every President from Theodore Roosevelt through Harry S. Truman, and writing in general. It's just a wonderful side effect of the series and this project to be reconnected with him after all these years. I highly recommend his book, "An Affair with Beauty: The Mystique of Howard Chandler Christy – The Magic of Youth," and look forward to his next two in the series.

There were three houses in Northampton that related to Grace Coolidge. They told stories about her life with Calvin and after his death. There was a break in the weather, so Julie and I decided to take advantage of it, and visited each of them. The houses were all privately owned, and access to them was limited, but we managed to get the story behind each.

The first was a gray duplex with white trim and a nice front porch at 19-21 Massasoit Street. The house was non-descript and fairly similar to those around it. I set up my camera on the sidewalk across the street and got a good angle on the house to avoid parked cars and traffic. The Coolidges lived here while Calvin was Governor, Vice President and President. It was their home for most of his political career. When they left the White House, and returned to Northampton they lived here at first. It didn't take long for the crowds to gather on this modest street. Security and privacy became an issue. Even in Northampton, the Coolidges had become too well-known and gained, as could be expected, national interest. They packed up and moved across town to The Beeches.

Their new home was called The Beeches, because of all the beech trees on the property. This new home afforded the Coolidges the privacy and security they were looking for in their post-White House life together. It was a large house with many rooms for guests and entertaining. The grounds were spacious and beautiful. Mrs. Coolidge kept a sizable garden there to the left of the main house. She also spent a lot of time walking in the beech tree grove and along the stream.

In present day, this property was privately owned, but Julie knew the owners. They were out of town, so we didn't get access to the inside, but we were free to walk the grounds and get the footage I needed. I wasn't worried about not getting inside, as it had changed so much over the years, and didn't look anything like it must have when the Coolidges lived there. I used existing black and white footage of the Coolidges at the Beeches, combined with my new material, in the final video piece that made air. In the early footage, Mrs. Coolidge stood with her husband and was presented with the new 1930 Christmas Seals, by a man dressed as Santa Claus. President Coolidge looked as though he has just bitten into a lemon in the video, and Grace was smiling and having a good time, as usual. They were surrounded by local children and their afghan hound, Rob Roy (also in her official White House portrait). Their time in this home was cut short when Calvin Coolidge suffered a fatal heart attack in 1933. Mrs. Coolidge didn't want to live in what was supposed to be their retirement home alone. She sold the house and property in 1937.

Production Note - Men At Work

There were three guys working on the roof at the Beeches when we came by. They were very nice and accommodating. They were already working in between the rain clouds, and high up on ladders. The last thing they needed was my me and my camera further interrupting their day and work flow. Sometimes it wasn't easy to avoid their tools, gear and supplies in my shots. I would get set up and begin recording and an extension cord would come swinging through the shot. But, we moved around each other, refocused and got what we needed. Julie was a trooper through all this, as well. She knew her information and was great with coming up with lines on the fly and repeating them when necessary. She was also pregnant at the time, and didn't complain once about being on her feet all day or the multiple takes. People like Julie made my work much easier and more fun. Thank you, Julie!

After selling The Beeches, Mrs. Coolidge began building her new home in Northampton, which she named Road Forks. During the build, she rented the house across the street to keep an eye on things and monitor the progress. She was very involved in its design and construction. I had to be a little more careful with my filming here, because the owner had not returned any calls about filming for the series. The two-story house was unique in design and surrounded by thick trees and foliage. I set up across the street to get the shots and view of the home I needed. This had to be a similar view to the one Grace had from her rented house across the street.

Grace said she wanted to be close to the treetops in her new home, so the living room and much of the public areas were on the second floor. She had always enjoyed the outdoors and nature. This was a pleasant surrounding for her as she continued her work with the deaf, children, and veterans well into her later years. She wanted to have red toilets and sinks in her new home. She needed special permits from the city for bathroom fixtures that were not white. I got a kick out of this, knowing that Grace always had a certain flair and unique style. It even showed in her bathroom décor.

This was the house where Grace Coolidge lived out her final days. She was hospitalized in 1957 and died of heart failure at the age of 78. In the days before her death she lived with a childhood friend, a nurse, and man named John Bukowsky. He had also been the Coolidge's chauffeur for years. He was the same man Mrs. Coolidge sent to buy her first car after her husband's death. She didn't want to be recognized and taken advantage of on the price of the vehicle. Mrs. Coolidge was a frugal woman (like her husband) and learned to live and travel very well on her annual widow's pension of $5,000 a year. I'm glad I got to visit all three of these homes, even if I never made it inside any of them. This was a poignant way to tell Grace's story in Northampton from before, during and after her time in the White House.

Historical Note - Growing Up Grace

Grace Goodhue's childhood home still stands at 312 Maple Street in Burlington, VT. I figure I need to go there, as it is preserved with Coolidge era furniture and artifacts. Having seen so many other of the homes important to Grace Coolidge's life, I need to see this one, too. I will make arrangements to see and study this building for future editions of this book. Plus, Vermont is a beautiful place, and I've never been to Burlington.

With the homes filmed and the stories told, we headed back to the Forbes Library and got set up for the rest of the afternoon. Grace was very instrumental in donating items and designing the Calvin Coolidge Presidential Museum there. The display cases at the facility were all her idea and design. Not only were there wall cabinets and displays, but there were freestanding cases in the middle of the rooms which allowed a close-up look at the items that showcased her husband's life and legacy. As expected, there were more items for President Coolidge than Mrs. Coolidge, but one giant piece could not be avoided. Grace's First Lady portrait by Howard Chandler Christy was right next to her husband's on the far wall in the main room of museum. It was a stunning piece of work with Grace in beautiful long, red gown with her white dog, Rob Roy. It was quite unusual in comparison to other First Lady portraits because of its vibrant colors and the dog. It was also quite unusual to get that close and have that kind of access to original White House portraits, outside of the White House.

Research Note – President Reagan Calling

I called the Forbes Library while writing this chapter to double check the color of Grace's sinks in her Road Forks home. We got to talking about the Christy portraits, and I was told something new I had not heard during my visit. When Ronald Reagan was President, he contacted the Northampton folks wanting to get the Coolidge portraits back in the White House. The Forbes Library respectfully declined Reagan's request, saying that the American people needed to have access to them there at the Forbes Library, in the Coolidge collection. I was told Mr. Reagan was very gracious and understanding about it, and to this day, the paintings remain in the Coolidge collection, at the Forbes Library in Northampton.

As is the case in many Presidential Libraries and Museums, Mrs. Coolidge was not extensively represented in the public displays. Given the fact that Grace was so involved (as most First Ladies are) in protecting, preserving and promoting her husband's legacy, this was not particularly surprising in her case. However, I wasn't there to learn about Calvin, and Julie knew that. So, once again, I went into the back rooms and storage areas to get to know this First Lady a little bit better.

As I mentioned, Calvin Coolidge spared no expense when it came to his wife's wardrobe. I have even gone so far as to say that Grace Coolidge was the best dressed First Lady in history. I understand that is a matter of personal taste, but I am not alone in my opinion. Mrs. Coolidge was well-known for her fashion. They had dresses and gowns full of sequins and shiny beads. There were boxes of empire style clutch purses. Grace had an eye for jewelry, too – both costume and expensive. The late 20's and early 30's were such a classic period for these items, it made it easy for a woman with Grace's flair and zest for life to be a fashion plate for her time. One thing that was noticeably absent from the museum were examples of President Coolidge's clothes. So, I asked about them. This was because Mrs. Coolidge very intentionally cut her husband's name out of them and donated them after he died. Mr. Coolidge didn't spend the kind of money he did on his wife's clothes as he did on himself, but he was still a President and dressed the part. In fact, he had very nice clothes, and Grace didn't want people profiting from selling a former President's wardrobe.

The Coolidge's spent so much time in Northampton, it was crucial that I visited there. Their story, as a couple, both started and ended there. It was a small town, very proud of its history and heritage when it comes to their ties to Calvin and Grace Coolidge. Northampton gave me a knowledge and closeness to Grace that I couldn't have gotten anywhere else.

PLYMOUTH NOTCH, VERMONT

Vermont is beautiful any time of the year. It was particularly nice the day I drove into Ludlow and the area surrounding Plymouth Notch. I had an extra day off on the work week, because of a scheduling conflict at Sagamore Hill. So, I got to spend two nights in the same place. This was rare. I got to my hotel only to find out that my room wasn't ready and they would have to upgrade me to a suite. The day just kept getting better and better.

The cell phone reception was less than ideal out there, and I was a little nervous about finding the President Calvin Coolidge State Historical Site, after I had a bit of trouble locating my hotel. I had time, so I went out to look around and do a dry run of my commute for the next day. I drove through town and passed a lot of people enjoying the nice weather and their yards. One older, white-haired guy was up on a step ladder carving a sculpture—of what, I have no idea—out of a giant freestanding tree trunk with a chain saw. He was wearing only shorts, sneakers and safety glasses. He was a blur in the midst of a flurry of wood chips and sawdust. I remember thinking to myself… "you go, dude!" … and that maybe I should move to Vermont and take advantage of the fresh air and country living. I continued my drive through town and marveled at the mountainside community. I was pretty convinced I knew my way around and had my bearings for the next day. Instead of going back to my room, I found a cool hippie dippy, tie dye themed, brick oven pizza joint called Goodman's American Pie (more on that later in my food tip). After dinner, I went back to my spacious suite and prepared to get to know Grace even better here in Plymouth Notch.

The next day, all the driving and "bearing getting" I had done the night before didn't amount to squat when I turned off the main road and my cell service went completely dark – as in zero. Non-existent. None. So, I followed my nose and the small signs until I stumbled upon the Coolidge Historic Site. I even got there a little early, before they opened their doors.

Travel Note – You Snooze You Lose

During this whole adventure, my time and schedule were tight. Tighter than tight even. I didn't have enough time at most of the locations to see everything in their collections. I barely had enough time to get what I needed for the series. Every location was a race against time, and a dash for the airport or next town. Every hour I worked was an hour I didn't sleep. I had to be organized right down to the minute, to maximize my time. I learned early on that my success in this project would stem from my punctuality and preparedness. It was much better to be very early than a minute late. Sometimes, even such a small increment meant the difference between making or missing a flight.

My host and guide at the President Calvin Coolidge State Historic Site was William Jenny. He was the Site Administrator there, and had spent much of his professional career preserving and promoting the legacy and history of President and Mrs. Coolidge. This was where Calvin Coolidge was born, in a little wooden clapboard house attached to his father's shop, right in the center of town. When Calvin was four, the family moved into the bigger house across the street (which was more of a path). This was the house where—at 2:47AM on August 3, 1923—he would be sworn in as the 30th President of the United States. President Harding had died, and word reached Plymouth Notch via telegram. Once again, a Vice-President became a President. We have Grace to thank for turning the whole town into a museum-like historic site. This was where my day in Plymouth Notch started.

I set up in the middle of the street in the little town of Plymouth Notch. Bill gave me the lay of the land, and told me about all the buildings that surrounded the Coolidge home. Calvin's father's shop and birth home were still there along with the General Store and Post Office. There was a church and an artisan cheese shop. Various barns and outbuildings peppered the little valley town, as well. I got my beauty shots (it was a gorgeous clear blue sky that day) and close-ups of the surroundings and the buildings before we headed inside the Coolidge homestead, across from his father's shop.

As I mentioned, the Coolidges moved into this larger house when Calvin was four years old. He grew up here. It was a one-story building without many (if any) modern conveniences. Like Andrew Jackson's home, the Hermitage in Nashville, this home had floor-to-ceiling Plexiglas barriers to preserve the rooms, but give visitors unobstructed views. I was taken in the "EMPLOYEE ONLY" side doors to go behind the glass and into the rooms. You all know how much I loved this type of special access. It was fantastic. C-SPAN's good name got me into these places like this, and I was always extra careful in these "backstage access" situations to get my stories but leave that good reputation intact. It was not easy to carry all that gear around with all those wires and cords dangling behind me. I also had to stay focused on operating all the equipment while I maintained the editorial theme and guided the interviews and story lines for each of the pieces. Once again, I worked with a pro who knew his subject matter, the facility, and its collection, like the back of his hand. Bill was a joy to work with.

We started out in the most significant room in the house. The sitting room—now known as the Oath of Office Room. This was where the group gathered in the early hours of the morning when word came via telegram that President Harding had died. Grace stood by her husband's side, by the light of a lamp, as Coolidge's father swore him into office. John Calvin Coolidge, Sr. was a State Notary Public, and therefore qualified for the task. Everything in the sitting room was as it was on that night. Mrs. Coolidge made sure of it. She saved all of the original furniture. She kept the lamp that lit the room for the ceremony, and the pen used to sign the documents. The original Bible was still on the table, too. Vermont State Law didn't require the Bible to be used during the swearing-in, but the group assembled thought it should be included in the ceremony. The entire scene was captured in a well-known painting by artist, Arthur Keller.

Political Note - Hurry, Hurry!

Whenever a President dies and a Vice President is "promoted" it seems that the new President is sworn in almost immediately...no matter where or what the circumstances. We will get into this a little more with Jacqueline Kennedy during the swearing in of Lyndon Johnson, but it is typically a very urgent matter. I'm told the reason behind this is to give the impression of being in control of the situation to the outside world, particularly our enemies. It is important to have a seamless transfer of power whether planned—as in an election, or unscheduled—in the event of a death. Therefore, when it might seem like a "can't this wait until morning" kind of thing to the public, the answer is, "no, it can't."

We then shifted and set up in the kitchen. There was no formal dining room, so this was where the family would eat most of their meals. This was also where the only running water in the house was. A single spigot ran from a spring outside into the kitchen sink, and it had to be kept dripping during the winter to keep the pipe from freezing. There was a two-hole privy in the back of the house, which was the only sanitary facility in the home. Grace was raised in Burlington. Burlington was the biggest city in Vermont at the time and very modern. She grew up in a house with running water and electricity. Plymouth Notch was a stark contrast to her life as a young girl, and even more removed from her life in Washington, DC and the White House. Even in the 1920's, Plymouth Notch was a bit behind the times.

The bedroom furniture used by the Coolidges when they visited was still in the house. It was a typical wooden farm style set from the late 1800's. Like the rest of the house and the furnishings, it was quaint, but nothing too fancy or outlandish. None of the rooms were very big. Again, this would have been quite different from what the Coolidges were used to in Washington, DC and Massachusetts. Grace enjoyed her time here with her husband's family and rolled with the punches. She was known to be very a good-natured and usually had a smile on her face. Grace enjoyed sitting on the front porch knitting while she was here. She also loved the outdoors and went on long hikes through the mountains. Occasionally, she would walk down the hill to the family cemetery.

As I walked back over to the modern building that housed the museum, I ducked into the church. I didn't expect to do a whole piece on it, but it was cool to go inside and look around. Since I had my camera with me, I got footage that would be available to the live show if needed. It was fun to imagine Grace and Calvin Coolidge walking right across the street from the front porch of their home, into the church for Sunday services. The press would have been there, too, capturing their every move in written word and picture. I have covered more than a few Presidents in Washington, DC and across the country doing exactly the same thing, so this was a neat experience for me. It was also interesting to see inside the beautiful little New England church. The Presidential pew was clearly marked, and it took me back to the days of studying Ellen Arthur and the Church of the Presidents in DC.

In yet another lucky coincidence, the museum featured an exhibit specifically on Grace Coolidge at the time of my visit called "Grace Coolidge: The First Lady of Baseball when I was there. Ever since Grace was young she loved baseball. In college, she was the official score keeper for the baseball team at the University of Vermont. There was a team jersey, as well as a ball and glove in the exhibit. In her adult life, Grace's favorite team was the Boston Red Sox. She even attended the World Series in 1946 with some of her girlfriends. She wrote in a letter that even though the Red Sox had lost it was still a great game and fun to meet some of the players. When she and President Coolidge lived in Washington, DC, she rooted for the Washington Senators (she was a true President's wife). The exhibit also had many pictures of Grace and Calvin at games. She stood right by her husband's side as he threw out first pitches on opening day, and her smile could not have been bigger. There was also video of Grace at games where she jumped, clapped and cheered like the true fan she was. The Red Sox and Senators even issued her a certificate in 1955 that named her the "First Lady of Baseball." A baseball signed by both Babe Ruth and Lou Gehrig was given to her son, John, and also part of the exhibit. I was told it is likely to be the only ball in existence with both of their signatures.

As we worked our way around the room, we came to a case that had several purses similar in style and design to those I had seen in the Northampton collections. These purses were each unique and special. They were given to her over the years by the American Baseball League and contained season passes to all American League games. President Coolidge received little gold charms that served as his pass. President Coolidge was a fan, too, but Grace had the lifelong passion for the game.

The museum also served as a social hall and gathering place for public events. A grand piano that Grace had kept in the White House was in the main room. She hosted many concertos while she was in Washington. Grace played the piano and this one was a gift from the Baldwin Piano Company. Even the piano bench was original with an embroidered seat cushion hand made by Mrs. Coolidge. This was another "real" moment for me in my journey as it related to Grace Coolidge. She made things. Practical things. She enjoyed needlepoint, and the items she made for her and her family were still around and in use. This was just like my family or anyone's family. The only difference here was her handcrafted things had been in the White House.

Then came the moment I hoped for at every stop in my adventure. Bill said something like, "let's go upstairs to the attic, and I'll show you the items that aren't currently, or too fragile to be on display!" Many items were kept in storage to avoid damage from light, air, gravity, or any one of the many factors that can destroy an artifact. They were kept there for their own good and preservation. Sometimes, a particular item was given limited exposure to help keep it intact. So, I lugged all my gear up the stairs, down the hallway and waited for Bill to unlock another "Indiana Jones" moment of discovery.

There were boxes and shelves, wardrobes and trunks, and all sorts of storage and artifacts up in the attic. Bill had several things already out on tables for us to examine. He even had them in groups of related items for easy access and the work we needed to do. One table of great interest was full of jewelry and accessories owned by Mrs. Coolidge. I have spent a lot of time talking about Grace's style and her clothes, but her jewelry collection was also quite exquisite. Much of what Mrs. Coolidge wore and preferred—because of the trends of the day—was costume jewelry, but the museum also had some wonderful examples of her more legitimate pieces. There was a jade pendant with a small clock surrounded by sapphires and diamonds. It was very indicative of the time (no pun intended) and people's fascination with clocks and machines. Some of the pieces, clearly influenced by Asian trends, were a holdover from the decade before—a trend Mrs. Taft had been so incredibly fond of. There was still a fascination with Asian art and style that continued into the 1920's. An interesting little pocket-watch fit the clock theme, as well. It was about the size of a lighter, or a Matchbox car, and even looked like a little blue and white, striped race car. When you pulled it apart from the ends, a small clock was exposed in the middle. The blue and white part was the case that surrounded the clock. It was a clever and attractive piece that would have fit into any purse or pocket. The most remarkable piece of jewelry was a brooch pin of an eagle, set in platinum. It was made up of diamonds, sapphires and rubies which gave an overall patriotic red, white and blue effect. The beautiful pin was about the size of a quarter, and there are newspaper reports of Mrs. Coolidge wearing the pin at public events and gatherings.

Like many fashion conscious First Ladies, Mrs. Coolidge liked fans, and there were many in the collection. One, in particular, was a beautiful fan given to her by the President of Cuba. Cuba was the only foreign country President and Mrs. Coolidge visited during their White House years. The fan had a hand painted landscape scene with trees held together by a mother of pearl handle with shiny, gold inlays. Again, this would have complemented any of her ensembles and been a welcome accessory at any formal event or casual garden party.

In my humble, yet qualified, opinion, the crowning jewel of the collection was gorgeous silver gown that was sadly destroying itself under its own weight. It was stitched top to bottom with what had to be millions of tiny beads and sequins which shone in every particle of light they could grab from the room.

It was a 1920's style with a ragged hemline and low waist, but it wasn't a traditional flapper dress, as Grace would have been a bit more modest. It was truly amazing. The style, craftsmanship and overall appearance of the dress was spectacular. The dress was so heavy that it could only be displayed spread out and flat. And that happened very infrequently. Bill left it in its box on a bed of tissue paper. Even when he gently moved it—tilting it ever so slightly—the sound of beads rolling through the tissue paper made me cringe. It was all silver and no doubt lit up the entire room when Grace wore it.

All of the items and artifacts Bill had shown me, so far, were prime examples of things that belonged to a woman who knew her role and place in American History. She understood the nature of her husband's political position and her role as First Lady. They were also what I had grown to expect from Grace Coolidge. The next set of items—once again—humanized her. We moved to a table filled with items from all the Coolidge's pets. As a lifelong pet owner and animal lover, these artifacts and items always hit home. We know how important Grace's animals were to her. She has one with her in her official White House portrait. This collection represented so much and so many more. There were collars, bowls, statues, tags, pictures, etchings, paintings and every type of memento you could associate with an animal that was clearly considered one of the family. It takes a special kind of person to love an animal this much, and an even more special person to save all these items. This part of the collection was a great way to finish up in the attic and confirm Grace as one of the most human and special First Ladies of my travels.

Historical Note - No Balls

Calvin Coolidge was a president like Pierce, Wilson, Harding, Hoover and Franklin Roosevelt, in that he had no inaugural ball. Whether it was a death in the family, a time of war or state of the economy, these Presidents were inaugurated, but did not celebrate with a public gala. Therefore, their wives and First Ladies did not have gowns. Women like Grace are still represented in the First Ladies' dress exhibit at the National

Museum of American History in Washington, DC. Every time I go there, I make a remark about the fantastic dresses on display that belonged to both Grace Coolidge and Lou Hoover – neither of whom had inauguration gowns.

Although my primary interest was the ladies on this adventure, it was impossible to ignore some of the cool stuff all these places had that belonged to the men. The Presidents. In the attic at Plymouth Notch they had several Calvin Coolidge's fly fishing reels and flies that he tied himself. Many of the reels had engravings on them of fishing scenes and men fishing and even had his name and presidency noted on them. These items were especially interesting to reflect upon, as I drove back to my hotel and passed several people fly fishing on the rivers along the roadside. I was so taken by the scene and the scenery I got out and took some pictures (see the photo section in the middle of this book). It was a peaceful place to imagine Silent Cal, out here by himself on the river solving the world's problems, or contemplating the issues of his position and office. I don't fish or golf with any consistency or passion, but somehow fishing seemed more thought provoking an activity for a President of the United States. I'm sure all you golfers reading this are closing the book and shaking your heads now, but that's just me. I will say this...I love a rousing game of mini-golf (or putt-putt, as we call it in Maryland)! FORE!

Bill reminded me that the Calvin Coolidge Memorial Foundation had their offices in the building. So, I gathered my gear once again, and we headed to the basement floor to meet up with Kate Bradley and had a look at some of Grace Coolidge's letters. As always, these letters were a fantastic way to get to know this First Lady. It always made me feel a little funny reading someone else's private thoughts and words, but it really was a true window into their soul. Mrs. Coolidge was not a fan of her own handwriting, so most her letters were typed. This served two purposes. It made them easier to read (remember Julia Tyler's hand writing was that which only a mother could love and read), and it also made me feel like I was being a little less intrusive reading them.

The offices and common rooms of the Calvin Coolidge Memorial Foundation were about what you would expect of any office. However, most offices didn't have a giant bank vault built into their back rooms. Visually, this was my dream shoot. The door to the vault was over four inches thick with giant knobs and a combination lock. It had all kinds of wheels and handles (just like in the movies). When you opened the primary outer door, you were greeted with a secondary tinted glass door that dramatically showed off the shelves, boxes and contents of the small fortress. Once inside, I saw all the familiar gray archival boxes that held letters and documents from the Coolidges' life—even things from before Grace married Calvin.

The Coolidges' had two sons. John Calvin Coolidge III was the first born and Calvin, Jr. was the younger son. Both boys attended Mercersburg Academy in Pennsylvania (you'll remember Mercersburg from the Harriet Lane chapter in Volume One). Some of the letters in the collection revealed a considerable amount about Grace's relationship with her sons, her role as a mother, and one of the darkest times in the Coolidge's lives when Calvin, Jr. died suddenly, from blood poisoning which was the result of a staph infection from a blister on his foot.

In a letter dated January 16, 1922, Mrs. Coolidge wrote to the head master of her son's boarding school, Dr. William M. Irvine. She was concerned about Calvin, Jr. after a minor medical procedure, and she wanted to make sure he was eating well. She asked if it could be arranged "without great inconvenience" that her son be given soft boiled eggs for extra nourishment as he recovered. She went on to compliment Dr. Irvine on the fine job he was doing, grateful for the impression he was having on her boys. She also mentioned a trip to visit the school after the winter and the roads were cleared. This shows us that she was a concerned parent that was involved in her children's education Even though the letter was typed, her words and her sentiments were genuine and heartfelt.

On June 12, 1924, young Calvin, Jr. wrote his mother a letter from school. In the letter, he explained that he wasn't doing as well as he had hoped that semester, but he was looking forward to coming to stay with his parents in the White House for the summer. He closed the letter with "I hope you are well and happy.

I know you are happy. With love, Calvin." He then wrote an afterthought up the side of the letter that read, "send more socks." On June 30, 1924, Calvin Jr. and his older brother, John, played a game of tennis at the White House. Calvin, Jr. played in his tennis shoes with no socks. This resulted in a blister. The blister developed into a staph infection. A week later, Calvin, Jr. was dead at the age of 16. I had read the stories of his death and all the circumstances that surrounded it. When Kate read the last part of the letter with the note that said, "send more socks" my jaw dropped. What an odd thing to write given the tragic outcome. He was going to be at the White House in a couple weeks' time. He asked his mother for socks while he was still at school. He ended up playing tennis without socks, which gave him a blister that got infected and killed him. If I were Grace Coolidge and went back to read that last letter from her son, I would not be able to ignore the fact that a pair of socks could have saved Calvin, Jr. 's life. For a mother who obviously loved and cared for her children, this connection or coincidence would be devastating, and haunt the rest of my days. I expressed my thoughts out loud. The group assembled in the room all had an "ah ha" moment. My guess was that no one had considered this correlation. I found the letters, the dates and the information and circumstances around Calvin, Jr. 's death remarkable, and so did the folks in Plymouth Notch.

After the death of their son, the Coolidges received countless letters of condolence from family members and the general public. Each one was as heartfelt and warm as the next and said what you can imagine people would tell someone in the instance of such a sad event. The Coolidges' responses were always on black bordered stationery to symbolize their state of mourning.

Mrs. Coolidge was close to both of her boys, and her son, John, lived until the age of 94 (he died in 2000). He remained close with his mother for the rest of her life, but neither he nor the family spoke much publicly about Calvin, Jr. 's death. The best example of John's relationship with his mother was in a birthday letter he wrote to her in 1929. He opened the letter with "Dearest Mother" and he continued "thinking of you on your birthday and loving you as no boy has ever loved his mother." There are also many pictures of Grace and John together later in life when it was just the two of them. There was no doubt of the close bond they shared after the passing of both Calvin, Jr. and President Coolidge.

Grace's college life was well represented here, too. She was a founding member of the Pi Beta Phi sorority chapter at the University of Vermont. This was an organization in which she stayed active for most of her life. There were school yearbooks and class photos to support the fact that Grace had been a good natured and popular person throughout her entire life. There was a fantastic, large, black and white, horizontal, panoramic photograph of a sorority gathering Grace hosted on the on the grounds of the White House. It was booked as the largest gathering of Pi Beta Phi's ever. Grace was front and center in a snappy dress and stylish hat with a big toothy grin on her face. This was a positive note and image on which to end my research and filming at the historical site. I thanked my hosts for their time and information, packed up my rental car and took a stab at finding my way out of Plymouth Notch with no GPS. As I drove out of the parking lot, it dawned on me that the Coolidges' were all buried nearby. Bill had even mentioned Grace used to take walks through the cemetery, especially after Calvin, Jr. was laid to rest there. I wasn't done with Plymouth Notch yet.

The cemetery was on the side of a hill and beyond a retaining wall that made way for the road to pass by. It was very similar to some of the other cemeteries I had encountered (Letitia Tyler and Jane Pierce came to mind), in that there was nothing fancy or ceremonial about it. It was very "Calvin and Grace," if that doesn't sound too odd. It was understated and classic. Four thin headstones stood at waist height and clearly marked who was buried there and when they got there. I had to take a second glance as President Coolidge died on the same day (not year) as my own birth—January 5. So, that was a little odd, but other than that it was a beautiful, quiet evening and I could get all kinds of angles, dramatic lighting and footage of the final resting place of all four Coolidges. As always—Cemetery Gates by The Smiths—was the soundtrack in my head "all those people all those lives where are they now? With loves and hates and passion just like mine, they were born, and then they lived, and then they died."

Author's Note – On The Road Again

I had done so much traveling up to this point, and had so much more ahead of me, you would think the last thing I would want to do after I got home was hit the road. But, you would be wrong. I felt like I hadn't been on my motorcycle in months, because I hadn't. So, I called my buddy Brian Filler and we packed light and hit the open road on our Harleys. We drove through the mountains of Western Maryland and met up with our friends Tim and Tori Michael, and their kids Alex and Zach. We had a great ride up, hit all the good restaurants and did a ton of water sports—including paddleboard surfing, wave runner riding and a bunch of runs on the Sumo Tube. The Sumo Tube really must be seen to be believed. It's a giant inflatable bell that you wear like overalls and get dragged behind a boat. You have to see it to believe it. At any rate, it was a great way to blow off some steam and enjoy the outdoors after so many miles in the confines of a plane or a car.

SUMMARY

Grace Coolidge is one of my favorites, and I'm sure that comes as no surprise to anyone who just read this chapter. She had everything—style and grace (pun intended there). In all seriousness, she was smart and pretty. She recognized her role and played it well. She softened her husband's hard exterior in the public's eye, and she tirelessly preserved and promoted his political career and legacy. She supported causes that helped humanity and she loved baseball. She taught deaf students and was a loving mother. She considered pets to be part of the family, and even had a raccoon named Rebecca when she lived in the White House. During my research and travels she showed herself as a human being to me as much if not more times than any other First Lady. I can see why the country loved her so much. Historically, she didn't do anything terribly monumental or lasting like some of the other First Ladies had done, however, she did carry on where others have not had the fortitude to do so. She lost a son, mourned him, and then got back to her role and life as First Lady. She remained extremely active with her causes in her life after the White House. She could've gone into seclusion like some First Ladies who lost their husbands shortly after leaving (or during) the White House years, but she didn't. She helped establish Plymouth Notch and the Coolidge Museum in Northampton. Both places are how and why we know so much about her and her husband. My research found her to be very down-to-earth while embedded in a world of politics. That makes her unusual for any time.

Travelogue Food Tip

Goodman's American Pie brick oven pizza parlor was a great little find in the mountainside town of Ludlow, Vermont. The employees were tie died and friendly, and the hippie vibe came through in the VW bus converted counter top. I had a clear view into the brick pizza oven and watched my pepperoni and onion pie cook to perfection as I ate a delicious Caesar salad. I hope to go back to Plymouth Notch for work or pleasure someday sooner than later, and when I do…I'm stopping in for another pizza.

CHAPTER SEVEN

Lou Hoover

West Branch, Iowa – Stanford, California – Shenandoah, Virginia – Washington, DC

Lou Hoover was born Lou Henry on March 29, 1874 in Waterloo, Iowa. Her parents were Charles Delano Henry and Florence Ida Ward Henry. Lou and Henry Hoover were married on February 10, 1899. They had two children together. Lou Hoover died in New York, New York on July 7, 1944 at the age of 70.

WEST BRANCH, IOWA

To say that Lou Henry Hoover was unusual for her time would be the understatement of this book and the entire C-SPAN series. She was the elder of two daughters by eight years. Her mother was not always in good health, and her father raised her like the boy he always wanted. Even her name. Lou. In

West Branch, they will tell you, Lou is not a nickname. It isn't short for Louise. When I speak about her publicly, instead of Johnny Cash's "Boy Named Sue," I say she's a "Girl Named Lou." Her grave reads, "Lou Henry Hoover," and her college diploma from Stanford was awarded to, "Lou Henry." Every historical reference from the White House Historical Association and the Smithsonian Institute refer to her as "Lou", and the National First Ladies' Library in Canton also lists her as "Lou Hoover." I could find two instances online that refer to her as "Louise." They are incorrect.

Lou traveled the world with her husband and two sons. She collected amazing things from her travels. She appreciated art and culture. She spoke seven different languages, and was the only First Lady to speak Chinese (or any Asian language). She had a flair for architecture, and designed two of their houses. She was committed to causes like the Red Cross, and supported groups like the Girl Scouts. She embraced technology. She built schools and promoted education. She assisted with international aid efforts during World War I. Much of all this was done with her and her husband's own money. Her humanitarian efforts, both overseas and at home, in times of trouble and depression were virtually unprecedented.

Herbert Hoover was the first of only three Presidents to decline a salary, and Lou was part of this decision (Kennedy, and now Trump are the other Presidents). She was ahead of her time, and beyond her time—a Renaissance women that was unusual for her (or any time). There was nothing Lou couldn't do when she put her mind to it. Lou and Herbert Hoover were two of the most qualified and prepared people to live in the White House and serve as President and First Lady in the history of our country. However, three months into Hoover's term, Wall Street crashed and so began the Great Depression. President and Mrs. Hoover's efforts and accomplishments would be forever overshadowed by this dark time in American History, for which they were not at fault. If the Hoover's were in office today, and could have taken advantage of modern public relations techniques and the 24-hour cyberspace information highway, we would remember them differently. In fact, it might just be safe to say that we would remember them. Lou Hoover was another remarkable woman that was not on my list of top 10 or even 20 First Ladies that I knew about or even looked forward to getting to know on this adventure. She was not on my radar. I can now say that she is quite possibly our smartest, most giving and forward thinking First Lady in History. Yet, she remains one of the least well-known.

Historical Note – The Real Economy

In 2007 & 2008, I had the good fortune of being the Senior Producer for the PBS documentary "The Real Economy with Ben Wattenberg." For this project, I was tasked with interviewing a lot of people much more knowledgeable than I about micro and macroeconomics [Nancy Koehn, Larry Summers, Michael Mandel, Ken Fisher, Michael Gross, Ben Stein, Jared Bernstein, Jerry Bowyer and others]. In studying the history of economics in America, it was easy to see that no new President creates an economy. He inherits one. Sometimes he inherits a good one, and other times he inherits a bad one. The sitting President does, however, take the fall or get the accolades for our economic failures and successes during his term. The bottom line here is, President Hoover couldn't have caused the Great Depression in the three months he had been in office, nor could he have fixed the country's devastating financial woes in one term. He did, however, take a lot of the blame. I should also add here, Ben Wattenberg and the production team at Grace Creek Media under the executive guidance of Andrew Walworth were all a pleasure to work with. Gerald "G Man" Goldman did a particularly fantastic job on the edit.

The Henry family settled in California when Lou was young, and she took to the outdoor life with her father. She enjoyed and excelled at archery, shooting guns, fishing, camping, boating, horseback riding, and pretty much everything else she tried. She was also very intelligent and couldn't seem to learn enough. She was an excellent artist, and drew all that she saw during her adventures with her father. She said that she was a Girl Scout before there were Girl Scouts. She was directly or indirectly advocating for women's rights and the inclusion of women in all aspects of life from the time she could walk. She was the perfect match for a man like Herbert Hoover when the two met at Stanford University in

California. But, I'm getting a little ahead of myself.

I had only driven through Iowa a couple of times before I visited the Herbert Hoover Presidential Library and Museum in West Branch. The director, Tom Schwartz, was the perfect host. He showed me around the facility, and the town, and helped me with my research for the day. He worked at the Abraham Lincoln Historic Site previously, and we now had some mutual friends.

Production Note - It's A Small World After All

The world of History—more specifically, American History—even more specifically, American Presidential History, may be spread out over many miles, but it's very, very close knit. These people talked. They knew and called each other. This will come into play in the Truman chapter BIG TIME. I was checked out within these circles by many directors and curators long before I arrived on their doorsteps. I passed every time!

The Hoover Library was easy to find, and Tom and his team were ready for me. Lou was a fascinating individual and there was a lot of ground to cover. It should also be noted that the house where Herbert Hoover was born was purchased and preserved here in West Branch by Mrs. Hoover. Like many First Ladies before—and after—her, one of Mrs. Hoover's priorities was to preserve her husband's legacy. I got there early, before the museum opened to the public, and parked my rental car. I loaded my gear in and set up in a large research room surrounded by artifacts and started going over the collections and the stories to be told. It seemed to make sense to start out with Lou as a girl, since that was when her tom-boy adventurous side first made its appearance.

Lou kept journals during her childhood and throughout most of her life. The library had her old diaries, essay books, sketch pads and school books. The early journals from when she grew up in California fascinated me. They included many of her drawings. She was a talented sketch artist. Curator, Marcus Eckhardt, walked me through the pages and pages of her work. It appears she drew anything and everything she and her father came across. She drew their various campsites, and the activities they did—such as fishing and horseback riding. She drew the scenery and the specific flowers and rocks they found.

There were also photographs of Lou as a young teenager. In one, she was in the mountains, riding on a donkey with a rifle slung over her shoulder. She was a regular Annie Oakley and looked right at home out in the wild. They had one of Lou's old . 22 caliber rifles there in the museum, like the one in the photograph. There were all kinds of pictures of young Lou Henry in all kinds of field dress on archery ranges, and out with her father camping and hiking. Between what she wrote, drew and looked like in the photographs, it was clear that Lou belonged outside. This was something I noticed in every place I went, and in everything I saw and learned about Mrs. Hoover.

In her 1891–92 diary, Lou remembered a hike for her field work in Botany class. She saw lupines, primroses, forget-me-nots, lizards and frogs. She sketched them all in a separate notepad, and listed their Latin names underneath. She wrote about the hike, "Miss Palmer and I were a good match for hiking. We beat the others all to pieces." She also wrote about other classes and life in general, but this entry spoke specifically to her love of the outdoors and spirited sense of competition. She was a driven person, even from an early age.

Lou never really wrote about herself, or got too personal. She wrote more about the things she did, the places she went or the subjects she studied. One essay she wrote in the third person revealed a lot about the way she thought about women and their role in the world. This piece, entitled "Independent Girl," was in an essay book from high school. She wrote it on January 30, 1890. The essay closed with the line, "sooner or later she will meet a spirit equally as independent as her own, and then there is a clash of mortal combat or they unite forces with combined strength to go forth and meet the world." This came from 16-year-old Lou Henry. This kind of thinking and writing was almost unimaginable from a woman of any age at that time in American History. Later, in Geology class at Stanford, she met her equal spirit in Herbert Hoover. It was almost as if she had prophesied it in her essay.

Lou and Herbert Hoover were such a great team, it was difficult to talk about her accomplishments without mentioning him, and vice versa. At all the locations for the series, I always asked people to leave the husbands—the Presidents—out of the story as much as possible. With the Hoovers, it was much harder—nearly impossible—to talk about them as individuals after they met and married. They were a true partnership in every sense of the word.

To say that Lou Hoover was well traveled would be the second biggest understatement of the book and the series. Herbert Hoover even proposed to Lou in a letter. He was working in Australia at the time when he sent the proposal. She accepted. He came back to the States for the ceremony. Lou didn't even wear a wedding dress. They were married at Lou's parents' home in Monterey, and their bags were packed for his next job in China. They left almost directly after the ceremony for Shanghai. They basically, got married, hopped on a boat and never looked back or stopped. They went full steam ahead at everything in life, together.

During her travels, Mrs. Hoover started collecting things. Her love for, and collection of, blue and white Chinese porcelain began right after they were married. She eventually had one of the largest collections the United States with 400 or more pieces. She mainly collected Ming and Kangxi Dynasty pieces. She was an expert at the origins and artists of all the pieces in her collection. She spoke fluent Mandarin, researched everything in her collection, and she went to great lengths to acquire rare pieces and matched sets. The museum in West Branch had several wonderful pieces, including giant vases and platters from their apartment at the Waldorf in New York City.

The Hoovers enjoyed their time in China immensely, even though they were there during some turbulent times, particularly during the Boxer Rebellion. Lou wrote to a friend back in the States about her time there. She had invited her friend to visit and told her about all the excitement. Mrs. Hoover carried a pistol on her during this time and had the tires of her bicycle shot out while she was riding through town. From the letter and her words, it seemed that Lou took it all in stride. Mr. Hoover always brought his wife a gift or token from the places he went without her. The museum had a beautiful jade dragon—about the size of my palm—that he gave her from one of his business trips before they moved to China together. And there it was. The Hoovers both became very real to me. This was something my father did when he traveled for work. It was something

I have done (and continue to do) for friends and significant others during my work travels. My dad used to bring me miniature silverware from the airplanes he took on business trips. China and the Chinese people were always special to the Hoovers. For the rest of their lives together, if the Hoovers wanted to have a private discussion in a public place, they spoke to each other in Chinese.

When the Hoovers lived, and worked in London in the early 1900's, she began collecting pewter. The collection wasn't nearly as extensive as the Chinese porcelain, but the museum had about 50 or 60 pieces. They had pitchers, cups, mugs, platters, candlesticks and all sorts of intricate pewter pieces. Some of the more ornate teapots had ceramic handles and stylized feet and stands. There wasn't any evidence that Mrs. Hoover kept collecting pieces of pewter past 1920. London was also where the Hoovers' humanitarian side first shows through at the beginning of World War I (We'll get to that later in the chapter).

The most unexpected collection that Mrs. Hoover had was her weapon collection. From an early age, Lou had a love for guns, archery and target shooting, but it seems this appreciation extended to all forms of weaponry. She collected pieces from all over the world and everywhere she lived. Just by sheer number in the collection, it seemed that swords were her favorite. She had several ornate Asian swords. She also had Civil War swords, and a large number of bayonets, and daggers. Some looked quite primitive, with wooden handles. She collected several boomerangs from their time in Australia, each were very well crafted and highly decorated. The most unusual piece could not even be clearly identified. It was from Indonesia, and was a large, flat, hand spear or sword-like axe. While it didn't have any particularly sharp, piercing points like a traditional sword, it did have numerous pointed ends that Marcus assured me "would do a lot of damage to somebody." This collection was not only vast and unusual, it was not what I would describe as traditionally feminine for that or any time. Lou Hoover was definitely her own woman, and her collections reinforced that impression.

There were a few other odds and ends that I needed to examine before Tom and I went out into the public part of the museum. One such group of items were a few wooden toys. On Christmas Eve 1929, the White House had the worst fire since the British torched the place in 1814. The Hoovers were hosting a Christmas party for the children of White House staff and friends, and far on the other side of the Executive Mansion, the West Wing was on fire. To make a long story short, Lou continued to host and entertain the children—complete with the Marine Corps Band—while the President and his staff—along with over 120 fire fighters took care of the fire. The folks at the party had no idea, but there were major repairs to be done. Unbelievably, the White House wasn't insured at the time, and they needed a special appropriation of funds from Congress to fix the damage from the fire. The toys at the museum were all made from wood that had been damaged in the fire. Some were given to the children who had attended the party, and others were sold for charity funds. Mrs. Hoover headed up this project.

There was also a vintage Girl Scout leader's uniform on a mannequin. Lou Hoover was extremely active in the Girl Scouts. She was a driving force in the creation of the Girl Scouts of America, and the first First Lady to be President of the organization. She always said she had been a Girl Scout her entire life. She thought all girls should be exposed to those experiences she had always enjoyed from a young age. She modeled the Girl Scouts after a boy's group she had seen during her time in London called the Boy Scouts. She held many positions in its administration, and supported women's groups getting involved in wartime efforts and humanitarian relief. Every First Lady since has held that honorary position of President of the Girl Scouts of America. Most remarkably, Lou was part of the first Girl Scout Cookie drive, and its success. She continued her work with the organization throughout most of her life. She even had leader retreats at the Hoover's "Summer White House," Rapidan Camp, in the Shenandoah Valley in Virginia (which we'll also get to later in the chapter). This uniform was a great symbol that merged Lou's childhood with her adult life.

Tom took me out into the public part of the museum to get set up. The exhibits there had many of the things represented that we had just discussed in the back workroom. They had many of Lou's weapons, pewter pieces and blue and white porcelain pieces on display. The pieces out here for public viewing were the cream of the crop. They had even recreated a room from the Hoover's last residence at the Waldorf Hotel in New York City. The pieces were exquisite. Out here Tom went into greater detail about how much the Hoovers did for Americans in Europe and international relief efforts during World War I.

One of the first things Mrs. Hoover did was to set up safe house for American families who lived and worked in London and Europe. She was concerned for how they would get back to the States. The U. S. State Department could only do so much and get as many people to safety as possible. When gaps and resources needed to be filled in, Lou Hoover stepped in and made things happen. She even paid for people to travel out of Europe with her own money. The Hoovers never hesitated to use their money to help people.

Family Historical Note - Pack Your Bags And Go

Sadly, I never got to meet my mom's father, Donald Llewellyn Carroll. He was a geologist—much like the Hoovers (without the millions and millions of dollars)—who worked for the State Department. He was living and working in Seoul, Korea in and around 1950 when the Korean War began. My mother (Julie), Uncle Tiff, Uncle Max and my grandmother (Catharine Carroll or Nana) were living there with him in South Korea. Because my grandfather was working for the U. S. Government, and specifically the State Department, they got an early heads up to pack their things and get out. A taxi came to pick them up around midnight, with only their suitcases, and took them to a motor pool to join other families being evacuated. The family (minus my grandfather) was packed up and shipped out in the cargo hold of a Norwegian freighter in Inchon. My Uncles have told me they remember my mother reading stories to other younger kids during the trip home. My grandfather stayed behind to shred documents and button up his work and their affairs. These were stories I had heard my entire life. Now, they were stories I was hearing about these First Ladies and their families and friends. I always thought the stories were cool growing up as a kid—especially the one about my grandfather finally getting on a bus to go the airport to fly out of Korea and hanging out the window shooting his pistol at an enemy plane coming right down above the street ahead of him (over the years the gun has gotten bigger and the plane gets completely blown out of the air...but you all know how that goes). All their adventures were documented by my grandfather in journals and letters to other family members.

In 1982, my Uncle Tiff went back to Seoul and visited his old home. He was on a guided tour of the house, and was told about an American family who lived here just before the war. A few of the details were incorrect, so my uncle spoke up. The tour guide asked how he knew about the family, and he told them because he was one of them. Anyone who knows my Uncle Tiff, and knows how great his memory is, will be able to see this whole scene go down. This story made the Hoovers' story in London, at the beginning of World War I, that much more interesting.

Another group of people the Hoovers helped during and right after World War I were the Belgians. Mrs. Hoover headed up efforts to keep their lace industry alive and thriving during the war. Lou helped Belgian lace products get shipped out of the country and sold in America. She also helped filter the money back into the country which kept them stable during the war, and helped them rebuild after the war. I'm told that Belgium is the only foreign country to have a statue of a U. S. President. Clearly, the people of Belgium appreciated the Hoovers and all they did for their country. The museum in West Branch had beautiful examples of Belgian lace on display, and all kinds of articles, posters, signs and artifacts that related to the Hoovers' efforts there.

The Hoovers were well traveled, we've gone over that. Much of their travel was done by ship over many miles of oceans. Once they had children, two sons, Lou Hoover had them to think about during their world travels. If Lou saw a problem she fixed it. She designed and invented (for lack of a better term) a swinging bassinet specifically for ocean travel. It had bars and hinges that allowed the basket holding the baby to sway evenly with the pitch of the ship in rough waters. The bassinet was on display with one of Lou's pistols and an early movie camera used by Lou during one of their voyages. I was constantly being reminded that Lou Hoover was unusual for her time.

She also stood out in the area of Civil Rights. In 1929, Mrs. Hoover caught a lot of grief from the public for inviting the first African American woman to a White House tea. Jessie DePriest was the wife of U. S. Congressman Oscar DePriest from Illinois. The women were greeted in the Green Room, and had tea in the Red Room, and some accounts of the affair mentioned Mrs. DePriest as "the most composed one of the group." President Hoover supported and commended his wife's decision to invite Mrs. DePriest, and criticized the people that took issue with the whole affair. A well-constructed exhibit in the museum had pictures, and articles to represent the event.

STANFORD, CALIFORNIA

I packed up that Wednesday evening and drove to the tiny airport in West Branch. I was on a 7pm flight to Denver and would connect to San Francisco there. I had a noon appointment at the Lou Hoover House at Stanford University the next day. I wouldn't get much sleep, but that was par for the course, and as long as all my planes were on time, I would be fine. I even had time to sit in the airport and enjoy a reasonably good Caesar salad and chicken wings (my travel meal of choice when regional specialties were not available). Everything was going like clockwork. This California trip was going to finish up another long week of work with a huge amount of material collected for multiple women. I may not have said any of this out loud, but I sure was thinking it. Then the announcements began."Plane has not left Denver," "Heavy weather over Denver," "Thunderstorms," "Should be fine," "Only slight delays," "All connecting flights still good." These announcements went on intermittently for a while, and then they stopped altogether. Everyone just sat around looking at their watches. A few people went up to the counter and asked questions. I knew what the answers were. The plane would get there when it got there. Any and all adjustments would be made accordingly. I considered the forced option of staying the night in Denver, and still being able to make my noon appointment. Then something happened that I had never seen before, nor have I seen since.

The incoming plane from Denver finally landed—albeit a few hours late. The pilot was the first person off the plane—which I thought was strange. He grabbed the mic from the gate agent and said something close to this, "This is your Captain speaking and the plane that just landed from Denver will not be going back to Denver tonight. I have been in the air way past the number hours deemed safe by the FAA and I am in no condition to fly." He then gave the mic back to the gate agent and walked off. Everyone sat or stood where they were. Stunned. Then there was a mad dash back to the ticket counter. I stepped aside and let the uproar settle a bit. I called C-SPAN's travel service, the airlines, my contacts in California and made all the proper adjustments. The airline booked me on the first flight out to San Francisco in the morning—which connected through Chicago O'Hare airport, and arranged a room for me with a shuttle close to the airport in Iowa. This may all sound pretty easy and hassle free. It was not. It was also about midnight at this point, and I would get about three hours of sleep once I got to the hotel and made sure everything was on track for the next day. The connection in Chicago was the closest I have ever had due to more storms and delays. I have never sprinted so fast through an airport with a camera bag and a backpack…in flip flops. If the plane to San Francisco had not also been delayed, I would have missed it. Then, I really would've been in trouble. Instead, I just got no sleep for 48 hours, had media cards full of video footage with zero time to get them on a separate hard drive, and was cutting every aspect of the final leg of the week's journey closer than close. Good thing San Francisco is a small city with a little airport and there's never any traffic in California. THAT'S A JOKE, by the by.

Travel Note - I'll Show You To Your Room

Have you ever stayed in a room that is designed for handicapped people? Before this trip, I would have assumed that meant special bathrooms and beds and maybe wider doors to accommodate a wheelchair and someone who may need more room or assistance in certain situations. All of this is true, however, there are other features that I was unaware of that are offered in some hotels. The nice young man (I think his name was Brad) who checked me in at one (something) AM to one of the ritziest hotels I've ever stayed in asked me if a handicapped room was okay with me?

Side Note To The Travel Note - Puttin On The Ritz

Three of the nicest hotels in which I have stayed in my life—Minneapolis, Minnesota, Maputo, Mozambique, and now West Branch, Iowa—I have stayed in for less than nine hours…combined.

ANYWAY...

I answered Brad, "I don't see why there would be a problem. I'm not even going to be in the room very long before my flight. Is there a reason I would or should mind?" Brad then explained to me that the entire room was wired for alerts and emergencies should a handicapped individual require assistance. There was a doorbell that made the bed vibrate. The alarm clock did the same and the whole room was wired to the lights to make them flash for notifications. It was late, and I was very tired. I politely asked Brad," ARE YOU MESSING WITH ME?" [truth be told I used a word other than "messing," but I used it as politely as possible]. With an amazingly straight face, he told me he said, "No, I'm not kidding." I asked if there were any other rooms in which I might be guaranteed an uninterrupted three hours of sleep before my shuttle would be there to pick me up for my flight. Brad explained that this was their only room."There have been a lot of unexpected guests in the hotel that evening, due to cancelled flights." [Thanks, Brad] I asked him [again, very politely] why he had offered me another room if there wasn't one? He said he was trying to be nice. I double checked to see if he was messing with me and asked what would happen if some idiot walking down the hall at two or three in the morning decided to randomly ring my door bell? He said the bed would shake and the lights would flash. I asked for clarification. Shake? Or vibrate, like a cell phone? Brad said it was dramatic. I shook my head, took my key and went to my room. Fortunately, no chuckleheads passed my room or rang my doorbell. I got my three hours of sleep, made my plane and spent a glorious—less than 24 hours—in San Francisco.

Stanford was a special place for the Hoovers. Herbert Hoover was an orphan. As a child, he bounced around between many relatives' homes, all over the country. He finally settled in California and established residency so he could get a tuition free college education, afforded at the time, under state law. Lou Henry and her family had moved quite a bit, too, before settling in California. Both Lou and Herbert ended up at Stanford, in the Geology Department, which is where they met. Lou Henry was the first woman to graduate from Stanford (and most likely any college in the United States) with a Geology degree.

The weather in San Francisco was amazing. There was barely a cloud in the clear, blue sky when I picked up my rental car and headed south towards

Stanford University. I was headed for the Lou Henry Hoover house to meet Nick Siekierski from the Hoover Institution. Mrs. Hoover helped design the home in 1920. The Hoovers lived there as a primarily residence before and after the White House. It now belonged to Stanford University and the school's president lived there with his family. The president was not in town when I visited, so we only had access to the grounds and the outside of the house. That was plenty to get an idea of its structure and design, which matched up with the drawings and plans they had back at the Hoover Institution, on Stanford's main campus. Numerous old photos from when the Hoovers lived there helped fill in the gaps and tell the story of the house and its architecture, too.

The house was a huge, adobe style mansion with multiple terraces, patios and unique design features. It had arches over most of the doorways and exterior staircases that added to its flair. It sat high up on a hill that overlooked the valley and Stanford's campus. There were clear Native American and Southwestern influences in its design. I could also see the international aspects that would have come from many of Mrs. Hoover's travels. Nick and I walked all around the property and tried to get every angle, terrace, staircase, patio and unique element of this fantastic home. We completed a few on camera stand ups to explain the exterior of the house then packed up and headed to the Hoover Institute to look at several papers and drawings that related to the house.

The Hoover Institution was in the same building as the Hoover Tower on Stanford's campus. We went into in the library and archives, Nick spread out pages and pages of letters, plans, correspondence and documentation about the house. Lou Hoover was not a professional architect or designer, but it was clear that she was the driving force behind its design. Many architects that worked with her wrote or remarked about how impressed they were with her skills and knowledge of design. Her handwriting and sketches were all over the plans and blue prints. There were very specific notes on types of cabinets, multiple terraces, and arches over doors that exited to the outside wherever possible. This was all very in step with Lou's love of the outdoors. It was amazing to put all these puzzle pieces together having just seen the finished product.

There were also letters between Mrs. Hoover and contractors about various work and construction of the house. Lou ran a tight ship, watched every penny and wrote very specifically what she was looking for and wanted out of the workers. There was one letter to a plumber that was discussing materials, cost and functionality. Lou was very involved in this build from start to finish.

There was also a small museum in of the lobby at the Hoover Institution. They had more artifacts and items from Lou's various collections, and the Hoovers' travels. They had bows and arrows, pistols and rifles from her weapons collection. They also had more blue and white Chinese porcelain. I was really beginning to see what my friends in Iowa meant. Her collections really were extensive. There seemed to be beautiful examples of them anywhere that had anything to do with the Hoovers. The items of interest to me here were the ones that had to do with Mrs. Hoover's time at Stanford, as the first female to graduate with a Geology degree in 1898. Her actual diploma was on display. It was about the size of a large index card and in a red leather-bound cover. The lettering was a formal, block, old English looking print that read "Lou Henry" in black, "Bachelor of Arts" in red, and "Geology" in black. Beside it in the case, they had some of Lou's field tools. There was a small pick-like hammer and a few rocks and gems which she had collected when she was a student. They had a Geology text book and her yearbook from 1898 alongside her diploma. This display case was also peppered with numerous pictures of Lou when she was a student. The long dress and jacket she wore in the field appeared to be made of heavy flannel, and resembled that of a Civil War uniform (except made for a woman). I was dressed in short pants and a camping shirt all made of modern wicking material and I was hot. I can only imagine how hot it would have been for Lou as she collected rocks and worked out in the mountains and desert. Nick and I completed my work at the University with a trip to the top of the Hoover Tower. It was a landmark of the school and allowed for some fantastic panoramic landscape and scenery footage. I could even see the Hoovers' house up on the hill from my vantage point.

I packed up my things, thanked my host and new friend, and headed to my hotel. I had come straight from the airport to make my appointment with Nick, and hadn't even checked in yet. I still had material, media and footage from Iowa to manage, in addition to the new footage I had gathered there in California. Nick had made a few suggestions for dinner and places to go, but I was running on a few hours of sleep, a lot of travel and a long work week. I passed a nice-looking sushi place that was walking distance from my hotel, so I checked in, started the media cards transferring to my hard drive, and walked over to get some dinner. After dinner, I was exhausted, and knew I had an early flight back home the next morning. I was full of fish, information, new adventures, and I crashed hard in my little ground floor room of the Comfort Inn. Tomorrow would be another day.

SHENANDOAH VALLEY, VIRGINIA

It was a sunny August day when I headed out from my Shady Side, Maryland home for another week in Virginia. This was the trip that would cover both Wilson women in Staunton, Edith Roosevelt in Keene and the Hoovers' Rapidan Camp in the Shenandoah Valley. The Shenandoah Valley was my first stop. The drive was amazing. It took me past the Luray Caverns (anyone from the DC area will remember the television commercials that boasted the world's largest "stalacpipe organ"), and along Skyline Drive. My father always talked, with great fondness, about vacationing here as a kid, with my grandparents. It was easy to see why the Hoovers said it was one of the most beautiful places they had ever seen in all their worldly travels.

As I cruised along Skyline drive, the sky was so clear and the weather so perfect, I vowed to come back and do the drive on my motorcycle (I have yet to do this, but it's on my list). I pulled over to get some footage of the scenery and the valley. I could see for miles and miles (yes, The Who song went through my head, as I surveyed my surroundings). It was some of the most remarkable establishing shots I recorded during the entire series. I kept my camera and tripod out and in the back seat, just in case I came across any more "must have" video opportunities. As I came around a curve just before the main gate at the National Park, traffic came to a standstill. I thought it strange, and my "city brain" took over and thought, "what the hell is wrong with people not being able to just drive and get somewhere?" As the stop and go traffic persisted, I got closer and could see that people were stopping to look at something in the woods beside the road. When I got my turn to stop and see, it turned out to be a mother Black Bear and her three cubs on an afternoon stroll. It was absolutely amazing. I mean, I saw the signs "DO NOT FEED THE BEARS," but growing up watching Yogi Bear, and having done a lot of camping as a kid with my family, I never saw the bears, and didn't take the signs seriously or think I would ever encounter one. Here, right in front of my eyes were four of them. It was here that I had my personal epiphany that I still talk about in my speeches. Two things I had heard all my life were very true. STOP AND SMELL THE ROSES ALONG THE WAY and DO NOT FEED THE BEARS.

I checked into my cabin at Big Meadow campground, and prepared for my local TV news interview with Litsa Pappas from WHSV-TV3 in nearby Harrisonburg, Virginia. She drove up with her camera and gear. She interviewed me overlooking the valley. She did a great job, and it was always fun to discuss the series, the project and my travels with local news folks. I had to do some "acting" for B-roll in the piece. I stared thoughtfully over the valley, and contemplated Lou and Herbert Hoover and the time they spent there. I think I was facing the wrong side of the valley, but it worked for TV. I got some well-deserved ribbing for the "thoughtful stare," but it was fun and Litsa was a real pro. After the interview, I had dinner at the lodge, and went back to my cabin to get rested up for the next day of work.

Travel Note – Where There's Smoke There's Fire

My cabin at Big Meadow campground was the only place I stayed during the whole adventure that had a fireplace. So, even though it was the beginning of August, I lit a fire before going to sleep. Being in the woods and the mountains with the smell of a fire was a wonderful way to drift off to sleep. Lou Hoover shared this love of a campfire smell, which we will get to down at the cabin.

My morning started early—as most mornings did. I drove to the Visitor's Center and met up with my guide, Park Ranger Sally Hurlbert. The first time the Hoovers came into the valley, they came on horseback in 1929. There were no roads into the mountains back then, and the Hoovers had instructed a secretary to find them a spot no more than 100 miles outside of DC, with at least 2,500 feet of elevation and a stream for fishing. Sally and I drove down through the woods as far as we could in my car, and hiked the rest of the way in with my gear to the Hoovers' cabin and Rapidan Camp.

The state of Virginia was so pleased the Hoovers chose this location they offered to give the 164 acres at the top of the Rapidan River to the President and his wife. In true Hoover form, they insisted on paying with their own money for the land and the building supplies. They were even going to pay for the road into camp to be built. The Secretary of Defense convinced them that the Marines needed training and work, so the Hoovers agreed to let the Marines punch the road through and build the main house and surrounding buildings.

Structurally speaking, the house was pretty much all original. The furniture and decorations inside the home were replicas. Once again, Mrs. Hoover was instrumental in the architectural elements and design of their house. She had originally thought it would be more of a large tent than a house, with open screened sides for walls. She thought better of the temperatures and elements and designed screened-in-windows that had fold-down panels to give them the open feeling and fresh air she wanted. Her sunroom and office overlooked a large front deck, and the deck had a great view of the point where two streams connected. The house was put here, because it was a perfect fishing spot for President Hoover. I found further evidence of this from original photographs and letters Mrs. Hoover had written to friends describing what was one of her favorite places in the world.

The cabin had a large living room for entertaining. Mrs. Hoover kept a nice tea set here for just that purpose. They would have friends visit and stay for periods of time, and the room was casually decorated with Native American rugs, rustic couches and chairs, and items from the Hoovers' world travels. This eclectic mix of interior design followed the Hoovers to most of their homes. Mrs. Hoover had a small but adequate bedroom that looked very comfortable, and the President had a separate room of his own. I was told President Hoover spent much of his time on the porch outside of his bedroom. He had the burdens of the Great Depression on his mind, and they had separate bedrooms so he wouldn't keep his wife up late at night. This reminded me of the Lincoln House in Springfield, where Mrs. Lincoln kept a separate bedroom, because of her husband's late night hours as a corporate lawyer.

Mrs. Hoover's favorite room was her front sun room. She kept a desk there, and it was here where she did most of her writing while she was in camp. These writings, whether letters or journals, are where we get most of our information about Rapidan Camp and how the Hoovers spent their time there. The room stuck out from the main part of the cabin onto the deck, and had windows on three sides. These windows let a lot of natural light in, as there were no electric lights in the home. From pictures, we know that Lou kept various trinkets and mementoes on her desk. She had a small set of shelf-like drawers to keep track of papers, and a couple of chairs for guests to join her in the room.

The house and rooms weren't the only thing Mrs. Hoover took interest in designing. She was the driving force behind the layout of the grounds, as well. She had a huge, outdoor stone fireplace built behind the house. When she and the President were there they kept, a fire burning around the clock. Mrs. Hoover loved to have the campfire smell in the air. Lou hosted many Girl Scout leadership meetings and retreats at that fireplace. A couple of black snakes were sunning themselves on the warm stones when I visited. She also was very particular about her gardens. She wanted them to be very different from the ones in California and at the White House. The word she used in describing her gardens there was "wildish." She only wanted plants that were indigenous to the valley and marked her gardens and walkways with rocks she found around the property.

When Mrs. Hoover first assembled her walkways and garden borders with rocks from the area, she was pleased with her work, and returned to Washington, DC. The next time she came back to Rapidan Camp, she found all her rocks painted white. It seems, the Marines that were working on the property wanted to "surprise" her with this new paint job. She was surprised alright, but not in a good way. She explained to the soldiers she appreciated the thought, but she had designed the grounds to have a natural feel that the paint then took away. The Marines took the painted rocks away and replaced them with more natural, unpainted ones like Mrs. Hoover had originally used. There was also an actual rock garden on the property at Rapidan Camp. Lou had gathered a number of larger rocks and made a waterfall fountain out of a natural spring, right next to her rock garden. She referred to the area as her "rockery."

The most amazing story that surrounded Rapidan Camp occurred on one of President Hoover's birthdays. A local boy had wandered into camp with a present for the President. It was an opossum he was supposed to cook for his birthday dinner per local custom. The President graciously accepted the animal, but did not cook it for dinner. Instead, Mrs. Hoover invited the boy to stay for a while and asked him about his life in the valley. She wanted to know about where and what kind of schooling he received. He explained that he had no school or formal education. Mrs. Hoover didn't like that answer, and did what she did in nearly every other similar situation. She fixed the problem. Once again, she did it with her own money. She designed the building and hired a teacher. She even paid for some of the students to continue their education and go to college. After Mrs. Hoover died, a box was discovered in her personal desk. The box was full of uncashed checks from students who tried to pay Mrs. Hoover back for their college educations.

The Hoovers spent a lot of time here during their White House years. They visited all year round. There was even footage of Mrs. Hoover making snowballs on the deck and throwing them at the camera. She even brought one of her sons here to get fresh air during a time of minor illness. I used the rock lined paths and bridges to get every angle and shot of the house and gardens. The natural sounds of running water and wildlife provided an excellent soundtrack to the footage. It was easy to see how a couple of well-traveled geologists could fall in love with a place like this.

WASHINGTON, DC

The Hoovers did not have an inaugural ball. Therefore, Mrs. Hoover does not have an inaugural ball gown on display at the National Museum of American History. However, they do have some of her other dresses. On one of my visits there during Season Two, I got a behind the scenes glimpse at Lou Hoover's style and fashions. The two dresses the Smithsonian had on display showed two different sides of First Lady Lou Hoover. The first was a floral patterned, light summer dress with a low-waist side, cinched by a beautifully jeweled buckle. This would have been worn at one of her daily tea or garden parties. A long flowing silver gown that looked as if it were made from a delicate metal was worn at a formal night time event for the Girl Scouts. She had a well-known association and love for the group, and this would have been a very special event for Mrs. Hoover at the White House. Both dresses showed that Mrs. Hoover definitely knew what was expected from a First Lady, and that despite her outdoorsy, tomboyish reputation, she could dress up for the right occasion.

Behind the scenes, in the work and storage areas, they had the black metallic low-heeled shoes that matched the silver dress on display and the metal glasses on a fashionable chain that appeared in a photograph of Mrs. Hoover in the dress. The shoes had elegant little buckles on the straps that were surrounded by diamond-like stones. Her eyeglasses were also an accessory for this outfit. They had a long neck chain with ornate round ¼ inch balls with filigree patterns. The glasses are also seen in her White House portrait. These were nice additions to the dress and the Girl Scout event, because it completed the ensemble and helped tell the story of the outfit and the evening.

Mrs. Hoover had money and as charitable as she and the President were with their money, they also had nice things for themselves, and this included Mrs. Hoover's clothes. She was known to be very fashionable, and made several best dressed lists even before she was First Lady. She was the first First Lady to be in Vogue magazine. Another dress in the storage area was given to the museum by Lou Hoover to represent her in the First Ladies exhibit. It was an off-white almost pale blue drape style Grecian dress with matching shoes. The dress was on display in the exhibit until 1987. The Smithsonian had a rare piece of Mrs. Hoovers clothes collection, one that they did not have for many First Ladies. It was an average daywear or work dress. It was a simple black dress with a clover pattern, and gave me an idea of what Mrs. Hoover wore on an average day. So much of what we see with regards to clothes for these women were the glitz and glamour of their position. It was nice to see what such a down-to-earth First Lady would have worn when she wasn't in the public eye.

Author's Note - In The Beginning

The Herbert Hoover Presidential Library and Museum was the location of my first public speech as The First Ladies Man, on Saturday May 3, 2014. This speech started my tradition of whenever possible visiting the graves of the First Lady and her husband for a moment of meditation before a speech. This was the beginning of doing something I had never done before. It was a new chapter in my life, and it brought me to where we are today. Smack dab in the middle of Volume Two. That day my speech ran about 50 minutes. The formal question and answer session lasted almost 45 minutes. People came up to me at the stage as I packed my things, and asked questions for about 20 more minutes. I got a tour of a new exhibit that featured one of Mrs. Hoover's cars, and a few other things that weren't on display when I visited in 2013, and people followed us around and asked more questions. I even had two women follow me out to my car. They still had more comments and questions. It seriously could not have gone better. To top things off, Tom Schwartz and his wife took me out for a lovely sushi dinner in West Branch that night. If the First Ladies Man had started and finished on that day, I still would've been very happy. Because of all this and more...Lou Hoover, Tom Schwartz, the Hoover Library and Museum staff and West Branch, Iowa will always hold a special place in my heart. Thank you all.

SUMMARY

Lou Henry Hoover. The girl named Lou. A regular Annie Oakley, and a Girl Scout before there were Girl Scouts, the woman who would help establish the Girl Scouts of America. She was a selfless, self-made woman who, along with her Presidential Geologist husband, traveled the world and spoke seven different languages. She helped Americans overseas in times of war, and helped rebuild countries and their industries after times of war. She was well-dressed and knew how to throw a good party. She built schools and was extremely charitable. She embraced technology, and used her position to promote good causes. She helped preserve her husband's legacy as well as any other First Lady did. She was a First Lady's First Lady. When you look at all the check marks in all the boxes of all the categories of things that make a great First Lady, Lou has them all. The one thing she didn't seem to have, was timing. Her husband's administration came at a dark time in American History. The stock market crash and the Great Depression could not have been caused nor repaired by President and Mrs. Hoover. Yet, they were running the show when it happened. This didn't erase all the good they had done, and continued to do, but it eclipsed it.

The Hoovers were probably the most qualified couple to be President and First Lady in the history of this country. Have there been other greats? Of course. Have there been others as good. Maybe. Better? Doubtful. Now, keep in mind I'm saying better qualified. With the Hoovers, that means on paper and in real life experience. Just because you look good on paper with experience, doesn't mean you will be the best. In the case of the Hoovers it seems they could talk the talk and walk the walk. Their actions spoke as loud as their words. They just couldn't overcome the worst economic years in our country's history. Now, when we look back and take all things into account, we must look at Mrs. Hoover as a First Lady from a different point of view, above all the dust and rubble of the Great Depression. When we do this, we see a woman who is extremely unusual for her, or any other, time.

Travelogue Food Tip

When traveling through the Shenandoah Valley or along Skyline Drive, it is worth a trip to the Big Meadow Lodge. If you don't stop anywhere else along this drive, stop here. Go into the restaurant and have the homemade blueberry ice cream pie. I don't care if you don't like blueberries, don't like ice cream and don't like pie. There is no way on Earth you won't like this pie. You should probably have the homemade fried chicken, too, but I'll leave that up to you. The night I ate there, I enjoyed a beautiful sunset and watched the deer come out to have their evening meal from the deck alongside the dining room. The combination of the food and the surroundings made for a memorable evening.

CHAPTER EIGHT

Eleanor Roosevelt

Hyde Park, New York

Eleanor Roosevelt was born Anna Eleanor Roosevelt on October 11, 1884 in New York, New York. Her parents were Elliott Roosevelt and Anna Rebecca Hall Roosevelt. Eleanor and Franklin Delano Roosevelt were married on March 17, 1905. They had six children together. Eleanor Roosevelt died in Hyde Park, New York on November 7, 1962 at the age of 78.

HYDE PARK, NEW YORK

By the time I got to my travel for Eleanor Roosevelt, Season Two of C-SPAN's "First Ladies: Influence and Image" had started. In fact, I was traveling by train to Poughkeepsie, New York to visit Hyde Park and the FDR Historic Site and Museum when the Edith Roosevelt show aired live. I had made up a lot of time and collected a lot of footage over the summer. I had actually started to feel somewhat comfortable about the lead I had on my travels for the first time of the entire project. That would all change though—which we will get to in the next couple of chapters. I was on my way through New York to Hyde Park, and had a quick train transfer at Penn Station. My travels went smoothly, and I got to my hotel in time for a quick dinner. Then it was back to my hotel to prepare for two full days of shooting in Hyde Park.

Eleanor Roosevelt was so well known, I realized we would have many of the same issues we had with Mary Lincoln. How would we teach the viewers anything new about this woman? Mrs. Roosevelt was in the White House from March 4, 1933 through April 12, 1945. She was First Lady longer than any other woman in history. Her husband was elected to an unprecedented four terms as President of the United States of America. Her post White House career and public service went on for decades. She was a prolific author, and remained active in politics and the Democratic Party her entire life. There have been countless movies, documentaries and books about this woman—maybe more than any other First Lady of the 20th Century (it's got to be her or Jackie, right?). I was up for the challenge, and these locations, museums, collections, curators, park rangers, and historians never disappointed. The Home of Franklin D. Roosevelt National Historic Site and the Franklin D. Roosevelt Presidential Library and Museum were no different.

The Springwood estate was right on the Hudson, clearly marked and easy to get to. Once again, my hosts remarked about my one-man team, and small amount of gear. I explained, as I usually did, they would be surprised how much we would get done in a day. And we did. And they were. They were also impressed and remarked about the ease of the work flow compared to other crews in the past. I only make mention of this again here, because it's important to know that good behavior, respect and professionalism still go a long way in this world. And you don't have to sacrifice a good time or good product for it. I guess it's kind of like the "catch more flies with honey" thing. In any event, it always worked out well for me, and I am welcome back at all of these locations (which I think I may have mentioned before, too).

I was paired up with Park Ranger Victor Pennes. We spent two days together between the house, the museum and Mrs. Roosevelt's Val-Kill home further out on the property. The first thing I learned after I loaded in my gear, and we walked around the house, was that this wasn't Eleanor's house at all. She and Franklin lived there. Their children lived there. The house belonged to Sara Delano Roosevelt, Franklin's mother, and she lived there, as well. One of the first things Victor told me when we walked into the house was that Eleanor didn't even have a regular seat at the family dining room table.

It was a beautiful table, too—as you would imagine. The whole dining room was fantastic. The whole house was amazing. It was the Roosevelt's estate on the Hudson, after all. They made the Bill Murray movie, "Hyde Park on the Hudson," about it. Everything was elegant and first class. Top to bottom. The only problem was…none of it was Eleanor's. It was all FDR's mother's. Back to the dining room. The dining room was straight back and to the right of the main entrance (front door) and foyer. The foyer was complete with statues, busts, paintings and a massive grandfather clock. Most of the first floor had beautiful dark hardwood floors and well preserved area rugs. The dining room table was long and surrounded by tall dark hardwood china cabinets and buffets. The shelves and cabinets were full of wonderful pieces. There were statues, clocks, bowls, platters and other decorative items collected over the years by the family. There were also a few decorative screens with painted floral patterns framed in wood that matched the room. The ceramic center piece, place settings, and flatware out on the table were equally appropriate and in line with the tone of the room.

The dining room chairs themselves really pulled the room together. Their ornate, yet tasteful elegance and craftsmanship was shaped and carved into every back and arm. Franklin sat at the far-left head of the table, and his mother at the far right. Eleanor would just pick a seat anywhere that was vacant. Right off the dining room was a small nook with another table and chairs for the children. The Roosevelts had six children together, and this permanent version of the kid's card table at Thanksgiving would have been very necessary. It was mentioned that Eleanor would have been just as happy to eat here with her children at some meals, too. There was no record or indication of this lack of a designated seat bothering her. However, one conversation that took place at this table did seem to get under her skin.

Eleanor wanted to take her children camping. Sara Roosevelt explained something to the effect that "Roosevelts did not camp." This was just one example of how while under Sara Roosevelt's roof, she was in charge and had the final word in most situations. Even when Eleanor and Franklin were first married, Sara bought them a house in New York City. She also bought the attached brownstone right next door, and had the walls between them taken out, so the two homes could be one. I would see this type of intrusion and influence in many ways during my visit to Hyde Park. FDR's mother even continued this type of behavior in the White House. She often suggested to her son she should hostess certain events or have privileged seat next to her son at dinners. These seem to be some of the only times that FDR stood up to his mother and told her that Eleanor was his wife, and the First Lady, and protocol dictated that she was the one to perform these duties and take on these roles.

During his first term, the Obamas got some public criticism for moving Mrs. Obama's mother into the White House. Some said this was not an appropriate use of tax payer dollars, or the space in the executive mansion. What these critics don't realize is that it's been going on since the beginning of our country. In fact, President Andrew Jackson moved half of Tennessee into the place while he was President. Many Administrations have had countless family members stay there as guests, part or full time residents, and even staff and administration members. In addition to the historical precedent, I would think that Mrs. Obama's mother probably didn't eat very much, and saved us all money babysitting on "Date Nights."

A huge portrait of Sara Roosevelt hung in the dining room of the Hyde Park home. It was impossible to miss her presence, influence, and position as the matriarch of the family. Roosevelt's father, James, had died in 1900, five years before Franklin and Eleanor married and moved into Springwood together. This left FDR—and more so, his mother—in charge of the estate. Eleanor was not in charge of the finances or daily functions of the home. So, we have no records of her as a bookkeeper or accountant like we did with other First Ladies. But, Eleanor's value to her husband and his time in the White House would come in other forms.

One room on the first floor held a lot of significance to Eleanor Roosevelt. She managed to find a way out from under her mother-in-law's wing. That way out was through politics. The strategies for this plan were made largely in the great room at Springwood. It was a huge room that ran the width of the house from front to back. It was also laid out from floor to ceiling in dark wood. There were two different fireplaces with leather chairs and couches with tasteful floral patterned fabric all around. Various tables and lamps were also spread about the room. The walls were covered with built-in bookcases and cabinets that overflowed with books, statues, clocks, and knickknacks. The top border of the room where the walls met the ceilings were surrounded by a large shelf with more items and collectables. Large drape-covered windows, spanning from floor to ceiling provided some light for the dark room. There was also a sizable wooden desk with a custom wheelchair designed to look like a regular chair next to it. This was where both Franklin and Eleanor's political careers were born. Or in the case of Franklin—reborn.

In 1921, FDR contracted Polio. At this point, his mother suggested he end his career in politics and stay at Springwood in the role of gentleman and estate keeper. Certainly, the family had the means to cover this lifestyle. However, this meant Eleanor would be trapped in the house with her husband and his mother in a role that wasn't appealing to her. It was at this point that Eleanor Roosevelt stood up, encouraged FDR to go against his mother's wishes and continue his career in politics. She partnered up with a journalist and political strategist from Bethesda, Maryland named Louis Howe. Not only did Howe reinvigorate FDR, and help craft his successful campaigns, he tutored Eleanor.

Historical Note - March Of Dimes

The March of Dimes was founded by President Franklin Delano Roosevelt in 1938. It was originally called the National Foundation for Infantile Paralysis. It is a non-profit organization created to promote the health of pregnant women and their babies. FDR was the first president of the group.

Eleanor needed FDR as much as FDR needed Eleanor. He was wheelchair bound because of his disease, and Eleanor needed to find her voice, to support her husband, and get herself out of the house, and away from Sara Roosevelt. FDR's political success was her ticket out of there, and would keep her from having to be a fill-in hostess or playing second fiddle to her husband's mother for the rest of her life in Hyde Park. That's exactly what she did, with the help of Howe. They sat at the desk in the great room and crafted political strategies, but more importantly, they worked on Eleanor as a public figure. Howe coached her in public speaking and taught her how to control her sometimes high-pitched voice. He taught how to effectively emphasize certain words to get her point across. He showed her the value of herself as a public figure and instilled in her the confidence she would need for a successful political career of her own. I could see the whole scene unfold in the late night, dim lamp light and warm fires. These were the beginnings of what would turn into the longest Presidential and First Lady careers in the history of our country. There was a heavy historical feeling in this very important room for the Roosevelts.

There wasn't much on Eleanor's childhood at Springwood, however her early years are important to note here. Eleanor Roosevelt and Franklin Roosevelt were distant sixth cousins. Strangely enough, FDR's parents, Sara and James Roosevelt were also sixth cousins. It wasn't terribly uncommon for upper crust and high society families to marry within the family like this. However, it was funny how similar this was to the royal families of England and Europe—the very place Americans struggled so hard to separate themselves from during the Revolutionary War. Eleanor was well educated, but she was shy. She was called an "ugly duckling" by her family. The marriage of her parents joined two very powerful New York families—the Halls and the Roosevelts. Eleanor lost her mother when she was 8 years old, and her father shortly after that. Her father was Elliott Roosevelt, the younger brother of President Theodore Roosevelt. Elliott had substance abuse issues. He jumped out of a window while he was institutionalized in France. The direct fall didn't kill him, but he did die days later from his injuries.

After her parents died, Eleanor's education was scattered and informal for a bit, as was her living situation. She was being raised by an aunt and her Grandmother Hall. She had some interaction with her Uncle Theodore, but the remaining family sides didn't always see eye to eye. Eventually, she was shipped off to private school in England. She thrived at the school called Allenwood and described it as the happiest time in her life. So, although privileged and wealthy, her childhood was anything but easy. These were all interesting puzzle pieces to put in place. They formed the life of one of the most popular, effective and successful First Ladies of all time. It was also interesting to see these contrasts in her early years compared to the different roles she would play in her lifetime. First Lady. Public servant. Activist. Wife. Mother. And daughter-in-law.

I packed my gear up on the first floor and climbed the steps to the family quarters on the second floor. This was where I saw one of the most startling situations of the household. It, once again, contrasted Mrs. Roosevelt's powerful and confident public image to her position under her mother-in-law at Springwood. At the far end of the second-floor hallway there were a series of three rooms. These were added on to the original structure after Eleanor and FDR were married; moved into the home and began having children. One of the rooms belonged to Franklin and Eleanor. They shared the room until infidelity was revealed on Franklin's part in 1918. Eleanor's initial reaction to this news was to ask for a divorce. Sara Roosevelt convinced the couple to stay together, advising that it would be financially and publicly advisable. Eleanor agreed, but also moved out of the bedroom and took a smaller room right next door. Now, here's where things got tricky or interesting.

At this end of the hall there were three rooms. The far right which was now FDR's...the middle which was now Eleanor's...and the far left which had always been Sara's. The rooms were all connected and accessible to each other by doors in the wall like a hotel suite. I pointed out even in her physical living situation, she was always sandwiched between her husband and her mother-in-law. Victor and I both looked at each other, looked at the rooms, and even walked through the doors as I said this. He liked my assessment of situation so much he said it in the video piece. He may even still be using the line during tours to this day. It was remarkable though to think of such a powerful woman having been caught up in this struggle. I didn't intend to overdramatize the situation, but it was right there in front of my face. I had been told what a strong force FDR's mother was, and how she influenced her son's life. It was hard to ignore how much influence she had over Eleanor, as well.

FDR's room was large, well-appointed and functional. It had big, sturdy, wooden furniture. There was a daybed, nightstands, dressers, and many pictures and wall hangings. It had numerous windows and a door that opened to a terrace overlooking the spacious great room below. The most interesting thing I found in the room was the very first direct telephone line to the White House. It was on the wall by the President's bed, and gave him direct access to Washington, DC. My first thought was, this was the first version of the Presidential "Batphone," and that was pretty darn cool.

Sara Roosevelt's room was almost as large as her son's. It was decorated with elegant furniture and soothing blue tones. It was a nice as you would expect for a lady of her status. The most relevant point here was the room stayed like this even after Sara died on September 7, 1941. After her death, Eleanor thought she might be able to decorate Springwood, and make it more of her own. FDR firmly denied her requests. He wanted to leave the house just as his mother had left it. Springwood would always belong to Sara Delano Roosevelt. Even in death.

Eleanor's room was stark to say the least. And it was tiny in comparison to the others in the house. There was a single bed pushed into the far-left corner. There was a desk and a chair, everything was more functional then ornamental. Two large French doors with glass and curtains provided access to the same terrace that was off the President's bedroom. At first, it looked to me like a bit of a jail cell. The fact that it was smack dab in between her husband and her mother-in-law didn't help that image. It seemed as if she was being watched from all sides. However, I looked deeper into the room and contemplated another scenario. This was Mrs. Roosevelt. She was not fancy. She was an appropriate and proper lady, she had good taste, but she was not over the top or outlandish on any level. This was a clean and uncluttered private space where she could be alone with her thoughts. It was comfortable and functional. This was the only place in the huge Springwood estate that was truly hers. I was very pleased with the three parts of the interior of the house that told me so much I didn't know about Eleanor. It was a huge house and we covered a lot of physical and informational ground.

My next stop was in the library and museum at Hyde Park, where I learned more about Mrs. Roosevelt's public career as a First Lady, author and activist. Eleanor Roosevelt was one of the most publicly active and successful First Ladies of all time. When FDR was elected President, their romantic relationship was long over, but their professional and public relationship thrived. She was her husband's eyes, ears and legs. FDR's polio kept him confined to a wheelchair. She often traveled to places and did things her husband couldn't because of his physical limitations. This served two purposes. It gave Mrs. Roosevelt the freedom to spread her wings and become her own woman—like she wanted—and it gave FDR a certain bit of plausible deniability should there be a need for it. If a plan or program didn't work out, he could say that he was going on the best information he was given by his wife. The public liked Eleanor and often accepted this reasoning with less criticism. Today, this doesn't sound acceptable, but it was a different world back then, and worked out for the Roosevelts.

There was a life-sized picture of Mrs. Roosevelt that took up an entire wall in the museum. In the picture, she was walking across an airport tarmac runway, carrying a suitcase. In front of the picture, in the display, was the same suitcase from the photo. The combination of the original picture and the suitcase made for a very effective exhibit. This showed Mrs. Roosevelt's mobility and represented her wide spread travel. She was First Lady for 12 years, and logged a lot of miles during that time. After her husband's death on April 12, 1945, she left the White House, and continued her work as an activist for civil rights and gender equality. She was appointed to many different positions at the United Nations. She was the first Chair of the Presidential Commission on the Status of Women until 1962, the first United States Representative to the United Nations Commission on Human rights from 1947-1953, and the first Chair of the United Nations Commission on Human Rights from 1946-1952. She also continued to work closely with other Presidents and White House administrations and staffs on related issues. If this suitcase could talk it would tell the tales of a hundred thousand miles. Such a simple and uncomplicated item, yet one with which I could relate. My suitcase and I were best friends during this adventure. We were both well-traveled and had seen many miles. This exhibit spoke volumes.

Education Specialist, Jeffery Urbin, showed me around the museum which had numerous rooms and exhibits dedicated to Eleanor Roosevelt, and her work during and after the White House. Another very simple item and exhibit that had a lot to say about Mrs. Roosevelt, was her Smith & Corona typewriter. It was a small, black metal typewriter, with little, white keys and bold, black letters. It was simple. Basic. It was right out of an old black and white movie, in which an author or a detective might sit smoking a cigarette with a bottle of bourbon. It was classic. A clear, square, plastic case surrounded it. Mrs. Roosevelt was a prolific writer. She had a syndicated column called "My Day" that she wrote six days a week, for 26 years. She published nearly 8,000 "My Day" columns and numerous books, most of which were written on this very typewriter.

Author's Note - An Apple A Day

When I first visited the museum at Hyde Park and saw Mrs. Roosevelt's typewriter, I thought it was cool. It was a unique part of history. It was in perfect condition and it looked great on camera. Now I can relate to this artifact even more given the two books I have written on my laptop. A typewriter—or now, computer— is a very personal item to a writer. You get used to the way the keys feel under your fingertips. You know which letters are worn off the keyboard. You get to know its quirks and unique features. As a writer, I have spent a lot of time with my laptop. We have traveled many miles and written many words, notes, pages, and thoughts together. In most cases the laptop hears the stories before anyone else.

The first "My Day" column I read was the first one she wrote. They had all her typed drafts in a huge storage room full of shelves with those familiar gray archival file boxes, and it made sense to start at the beginning. On December 31, 1935, Eleanor Roosevelt wrote from the White House:

> "This is a day for taking up a more or less regular routine again. The house is filled with guests of the children's, but the President and I take up a full schedule today. At 11 am I met with ladies of the press. I always enjoy this hour on Monday mornings."

This was a window into a regular day for Mrs. Roosevelt as First Lady, and it set the tone for future columns. Mrs. Roosevelt was the first First Lady to hold press conferences exclusively for female reporters. This laid the foundation for the female reporters, journalists and news anchors we have today. It opened journalism to women and changed the face of news reporting forever. Much of what my female friends and colleagues have done in their careers can be attributed to this bold move by Eleanor Roosevelt.

The next column was from December 7, 1941. Pearl Harbor Day. It was a first-hand account of exactly what was going on and the mood within the walls of the White House. She wrote:

> "As I stepped out of my room, I knew something had happened. All the secretaries were there, two telephones were in use, the senior military aids were on their way with messages. I said nothing, because the words I overheard on the telephone were quite sufficient to tell me that finally the blow had fallen, and we had been attacked."

Mrs. Roosevelt also delivered the radio address that informed the country about the attack on Pearl Harbor. She was a voice the American people trusted. It was remarkable to think that the First Lady was the one who spoke to the country about the deadliest attack on our soil—up to that point—and not the President, as we might expect today. We used the audio recording of this address in the live Eleanor Roosevelt show in the C-SPAN series. It was very effective, and showed Mrs. Roosevelt's influence in the White House, and on our country.

I was shown the final draft of Mrs. Roosevelt's "My Day" column written after her time in the White House, right after she returned from a Martin Luther King, Jr. speech. On February 6, 1961, she wrote:

> "I have just had the opportunity of hearing Dr. King speak. He is a very moving speaker, because he is simple and direct, and the spiritual quality which has made him the leader of non-violence in this country touches every speech he made."

Mrs. Roosevelt was a civil rights leader in her own right. Ever the student of life, she kept a wide variety of company with an equally wide perspective of the world and options of the day. She met with people that weren't always popular in the eyes of the world and the U. S. government (not speaking of MLK here). The FBI kept a huge file of documents concerning her whereabouts and the people with whom she met. The museum had an entire file cabinet out on display with duplicates of the FBI files. Visitors could thumb through all of them as if they were an FBI agent checking up on Mrs. Roosevelt.

There were also actual examples of the published "My Day" columns on hand in the museum's storage room. They had clippings from the various newspapers that published Mrs. Roosevelt's column. The clipping Jeffrey selected was from November 6th, 1940. The Roosevelts had a tradition of being in Hyde Park on election night. Mrs. Roosevelt writes about her quiet afternoon. She enjoyed a walk and some tea. She mentioned a "larger crowd than usual" with a band and signs for "the President." A picture from that same night showed the Roosevelts all lined up on the front porch of their Springwood estate, dressed to the nines in formal wear. Sadly, Eleanor was in the second row, kind of pushed to the side. FDR's mother was right at his side, as was one of his sons. It seems when they were at Hyde Park, she couldn't catch a break or get credit for the good work and support of her husband's political career—even in pictures.

Author's Note – Mrs. Roosevelt's Girlfriend

After Eleanor discovered FDR was having an affair, she cut off all romantic ties with him. As I explained earlier in this chapter, FDR's mother convinced them to stay married. Eleanor found a way to make that work for her via his political career. This opened the door for her to explore other love interests. Letters have been published that reveal Eleanor had a long standing and serious love relationship with Lorena Hickok. I read that there were over 3,000 letters that went back and forth between the two women. While they acknowledged Hickok and her relationship with Mrs. Roosevelt, it was not something they wanted to highlight in the video pieces we did together for the series. I accepted that. I also accepted the fact that it happened. I do not feel it's right to ignore what is known here in my book. Therefore, I will tell you what I saw, was told and know for myself in a respectful manner. People often ask me about this subject at speeches, and it is a part of Eleanor Roosevelt's life.

A low, two-sided display of books—almost like what you see in public libraries, typically in the children's section—started just behind Mrs. Roosevelt's typewriter and ran almost the entire length of the front room on the lower level of the museum. This was where most of the Eleanor exhibits were. There were over 30 books in the display. They were all books authored or co-authored by Mrs. Roosevelt. These books were written both in and out of the White House, throughout her long and productive life. She wrote about foreign policy, international politics, civil rights, women's rights and other issues and subjects geared towards children. It appeared that she wrote a book about every and any topic that interested her. It was hard to believe she had time to write all these books on top of her "My Day" column and the other work in which she was involved. Not to mention all the travel. She co-authored some of these books with Lorena Hickok.

Lorena Hickok was a reporter for the Associated Press, and regularly attended Mrs. Roosevelt's weekly press conferences for female journalists. She was credited with many firsts for women in journalism, and was very well-known and widely read. When she and Eleanor became an item, it wasn't public knowledge, but she left the AP and the White House press corps, because of the conflict of interest. Hickok went to work for the Federal Emergency Relief Administration. This was an FDR creation during the New Deal. After FERA, she worked as the executive secretary of the Women's Division of the Democratic National Committee. She lived in the White House from 1940 to 1945. Her room was closer to Eleanor's than the President's was. Eleanor called her "Hicks." President Roosevelt knew about her, and called her the "She-Man." People close to the Roosevelts and in the administration had to know what was going on. There were many rumors that surrounded Mrs. Roosevelt and various affairs with various men and women throughout the course of her life. This was the only one I found that was confirmed by her own words.

I saw something at Hyde Park I had not seen for any other First Lady—nor would I see it repeated in any of my adventures that followed. They had an exhibit that contained the items found in Eleanor Roosevelt's wallet only days after she died on November 7, 1962. At first I was amazed and intrigued. Then I got that familiar feeling of trespassing that I felt when I read personal letters, diaries and journals. These were her personal and private items that she kept close to her on a daily basis. Now, they were on display, in a flat glass case on the wall. Each card and item numbered with an explanation of what it was. She kept certain things you would expect anyone to have like credit cards, ID cards and a minimal amount of cash. She also had a permit to carry a pistol. Dated on August 5, 1957, her license to carry permit had her Val-Kill cottage address, and a picture of a little old lady in a fur coat, wearing a hat. It was fantastic, and somewhat comical. Her clothes resembled something I'd seen my grandmother wear when I was a kid. Mrs. Roosevelt was not a fan of the Secret Service that shadowed her in her post-White House life. She compromised with them, and agreed to carry a small pistol in her purse when she traveled alone. I went back and took another look at the giant picture of her carrying the suitcase across the airport runway. Was she packing heat there? I would have to guess the answer was, yes. She had a couple poems typed out and folded up on small pieces of paper. The most poignant of which did not have a title or source. It was most likely typed by Mrs.

Roosevelt on her typewriter in the earlier display. It was only two lines and read:

> "He worked as if he would live forever...He lived as though he would die tomorrow."

This was the perfect way to sum up Mrs. Eleanor Roosevelt and my time at the museum.

Location Note - Almost Famous

As I mentioned in Volume One, when you walk around and travel with a camera, you attract a certain amount of attention. When I was shooting B-roll outside of one of the displays, two ladies (sisters as I recall) asked me the typical questions I received during my adventure."Who are you?" "Where do you work?" "What show is this on?" "Can we be on TV?" That kind of stuff. One woman was very outgoing and followed me around for a while. My host, Jeffrey, told them I was working on the C-SPAN series "First Ladies: Influence and Image." The women erupted with cheers and excitement. They had seen every episode, and thought I was really something after learning what I was working on. They followed me around for the rest of my B-roll filming in the museum. They had been to almost every Presidential Library and Museum (some twice, they were all too eager to point out) and wanted to share their thoughts of each and listen to mine. They were quite envious of my "ALL ACCESS...VIP PASS" and wanted all the details. They said they hoped I was taking good notes and would be writing a book someday about my adventures. I laughed as I did when others made the same suggestion saying, "I'm a TV guy. I don't write books." They were a lot of fun, and I hope they are reading this and recognize themselves here.

Before I packed up for the day, there was still enough light out and the sun was high enough in the sky to get some establishing shots of the house and surrounding property. The Roosevelts were both buried at Hyde Park and their graves were surrounded by a lovely garden. I took note that Mrs. Roosevelt was named as Eleanor Roosevelt Roosevelt on the massive grave marker. It reminded me of her and FDR's distant relations. It gave me pause to review our country's history. Where we came from. Where we had been. And where we were going. This project was becoming more and more interesting with every trip, and it was sinking deeper and deeper into my brain. The rest of the afternoon was lovely, and the deer had started to come out of the woods for their evening meal. It was a very quiet and serene way to wrap up day one in Hyde Park. I went back to my hotel and prepared for day two at Mrs. Roosevelt's Val-Kill cottage, only a few short miles away from the Springwood home.

VAL-KILL

Day two started off a bit rainy, but I was back with park ranger, Victor Pennes, and we picked up right where we left off the day before. The Fall Kill Stream (Valley River in Dutch) ran through the Roosevelt's Hyde Park property about two miles from the Springwood house, that the family always referred to as the "big house." There was a spot along the stream the Roosevelts favored as a location for family picnics. One late summer afternoon in 1924, the family was enjoying one of the last picnics of the season before Sara Roosevelt closed the big house for the Winter (the family moved into the city during the fall and winter). Mrs. Roosevelt thought it was a shame to close the Springwood house. She liked it so much better at Hyde Park. FDR told her she should build a cottage out here in the woods that she and her lady friends could enjoy all year long. That was exactly was Mrs. Roosevelt did. FDR leased his wife the land and drew up the plans for a stone cottage to be built there at their favorite spot. At this point it was difficult for me to imagine the family dynamic after Eleanor and Franklin had reached their new marital agreement, but they continued to function as a somewhat normal family and enjoyed outings like this together.

The stone cottage was built and two of Eleanor's close friends—Nancy Cook and Marion Dickerman—moved in almost immediately. These women were FDR supporters and described as "progressive thinkers." They were also a romantic couple. They shared a room at Val-Kill, and made it their primary residence. Mrs. Roosevelt kept a bedroom in the house for herself when she was in town and stayed at the cottage. When Franklin and Eleanor were in Hyde Park together, they stayed at the big house. By 1926, there was a second building constructed and an in-ground pool. The second building would become the Val-Kill Industries factory (which I'll get to). And I'm told that FDR won a swim race against Winston Churchill in the pool, at one time—even with polio. The compound at Val-Kill was the only home that Mrs. Roosevelt ever called her own. It was where she was referring to when she said, "The greatest thing I have learned is how to come back home."

Victor knew the property like the back of his hand, and was a lot of fun to work with. He was great at walk and talk interviews and did as many takes as I asked, walking through doors and into rooms for potential intros to the video pieces.

Production Note - Walk On The Wild Side

A walk and talk interview is exactly what it sounds like. A person walks along and talks as they get asked questions. Most times there is a reporter walking along with the person getting interviewed, and it provides thoughtful and engaging video that gives motion to a piece or story. In my case, I had no reporter. In a one-man production team, there is exactly that. One man. So, I had to operate the camera, monitor the audio and lighting, conduct the interview, and not trip over anything or fall down any stairs. This was no small feat. But neither is conducting a walk and talk interview. Especially, when the person asking the questions is behind the camera instead of right next to you. So, kudos here to Victor [and all the folks along the way] who provided me with all the information in this fashion. Being on camera is not easy. For some, it is downright difficult and feels very uncomfortable. For these folks to be taken out of their element, and asked unusual questions about their collections and facilities and do it with such proficiency, says a lot about their knowledge of these women and the facilities.

We began in the stone cottage—the original structure. The exterior and the building itself were the same as they had always been, but over the years, the interior had been changed a bit and now served as an open space for luncheons and receptions with some period farm and textile industry artifacts spread about on display. The room structure was the same as when Eleanor and her friends lived there. Nancy and Marion shared the upstairs master bedroom. Mrs. Roosevelt took a smaller room in the back. Even with the lack of original décor and empty rooms, the cottage gave off a homey vibe. It was easy to see how they enjoyed their time out there. The three women, along with their friend, Caroline O'Day (from the Democratic State Committee) came up with the idea for Val-Kill Industries.

This was a plan to revitalize jobs and incomes for local farmers during the harsh Winters. They wanted to build a furniture factory that replicated quality, early American style. The two story second structure was completed in 1926, and did reasonably well for many years. I was told FDR was their best customer, but it helped the local economy and residents for a good chunk of time, and they made quality products. The factory even expanded to accommodate the manufacturing and fabrication of pewter pieces, an area to make linens and textiles. Val-Kill Industries closed shop in 1936, and Mrs. Roosevelt converted the factory into her private home. Her friends Mary and Nancy stayed in the stone cottage until Eleanor's post-White House popularity and frequent guests became a little too much for them to handle. They felt as if their privacy had been infringed upon, and they moved out in 1947. The Val-Kill Industries story was a good one, and an important part of Mrs. Roosevelt's professional life, but there was nothing that told her story like the inside of the only place she called home.

Victor and I walked up the back steps and into Mrs. Roosevelt's private office in her Val-Kill home. This was the main entrance to the house and where all her guests entered and were greeted. Some of her more notable guests were (then) Senator John F. Kennedy, Winston Churchill and Nikita Khrushchev. It was always a treat to walk in the footsteps of history this way. I carried my gear through the narrow hallway and got set up in the office. The first thing I noticed was that none of the furniture matched. It appeared as though no thought had been put into arranging the room. I was quickly corrected when Victor told me that was all intentional. Mrs. Roosevelt had said her chairs represented her guests. They came in all shapes, sizes and colors, and worked well together when grouped. When furniture was delivered to the house Mrs. Roosevelt gave specific instructions not to put it into the rooms. She would take care of all the placement of furniture in all the rooms. Guests who stayed in the house said she could be heard at all hours of the night rearranging the place. I understood this well, her Val-Kill cottage was the only home she ever owned and had the opportunity to decorate.

Her desk was a focal point of the room. This was where she wrote many of her "My Day" columns, other articles, books and regular correspondence with the American people. There was a nameplate on her desk that read "Elinor Roosevelt." It was made by a young man from Hyde Park in his shop class. He had no idea he had spelled her name wrong. Mrs. Roosevelt graciously accepted the gift and kept it on her desk for the rest of her time there. In front of her desk was a large, wooden, Asian chest with intricate designs carved all over it. There was a small black and white TV on a low table and other items around the room from the 1960's, when Mrs. Roosevelt last occupied the house. This room also served as the reception area for parties, and was where the cocktail hour was served. Around the corner and down the hall was the dining room.

The dining room was set to duplicate photos from a 1950's McCall's Magazine article called "How Eleanor Lives at Val-Kill." Mrs. Roosevelt preferred a buffet style setting to accommodate larger gatherings and more guests. Her long dining room table helped enable this kind of entertaining. Around the room were more intentionally mismatched pieces of furniture, china cabinets and other hardwood cupboards and side tables. The china, center pieces and glassware were equally eclectic. Mrs. Roosevelt's wide range of tastes and interests were well represented here in her home. An interesting feature of the dining room were numerous Christmas cards from many different years displayed all year round on one of the walls. These were cards Mrs. Roosevelt received from former White House staff and friends over the years.

We moved through the house to the living room. More chairs of every shape, size and colors were placed in between tables and couches. The room wasn't huge and the ceilings weren't particularly high, but it didn't have a cluttered feel. Unbeknownst to me, I had subconsciously been made to feel right at home. Eleanor's decorating scheme had even worked on me. One feature, not to be missed was the alcove where Mrs. Roosevelt met with Senator John F. Kennedy while he was campaigning for President in 1960. Eleanor Roosevelt was arguably the most powerful woman in the Democratic Party. Her endorsement was worth its weight in gold. Mrs. Roosevelt had purposely chosen a tall chair for herself and a shorter chair for Kennedy. She knew she was the matriarch of her party, and she wanted Kennedy to know it, as well. He would have to earn her vote, which he did.

All around the living room—and the entire house—there were pictures of all sizes in all different kinds of frames. Mrs. Roosevelt said she kept pictures and lists of people who had been inspirational in her life. She had pictures of Gandhi and Louis Howe. There was also a picture of Amelia Earhart in the living room. Earhart gave Mrs. Roosevelt her first flying lesson over the city of Baltimore, Maryland in 1933. She had a picture of her Uncle Theodore in this room. I learned that in his brother's absence, President Theodore Roosevelt walked his niece, Eleanor, down the aisle at her wedding. Eleanor even had a picture of her mother-in-law, Sara Delano Roosevelt, hanging on the wall. She had at least one picture of FDR in every room in the house. I asked Victor, why—in her own private space where she made all the rules—would she have photographs of people who were not always the kindest to her in life? I was specifically thinking about her husband, who cheated on her, and her mother-in-law, who wouldn't even give her a seat at the dining room table—the woman who wanted to raise her children and take her position as First Lady. Her husband, okay, I understood maybe displaying one picture. I mean he was the President of the United States and they figured out a way to make the marriage work—even if only professionally, but multiple pictures in every room? Victor assured me that Mrs. Roosevelt said just because someone was influential in a person's life, it doesn't mean they were a good influence. It just meant they had had some kind of significant impact upon it. This was major food for thought. When Eleanor Roosevelt died in 1962, a private wake and viewing was held in the living room at Val-Kill for family and close friends. This room and this house were both clearly very special places for Eleanor.

I carried my gear up the creaky steps to the second floor only to find more random furnishings in the private bedrooms and an array of framed pictures and images on every wall. I passed modest size guest bedrooms and a bathroom on my way to Eleanor's master bedroom. She still only used a single bed here, but the room was considerably larger than in the big house, and this one included a beautiful sleeping porch. There were towels and linens laid out on the bed that were made at Val-Kill Industries. All of the linens used by Mrs. Roosevelt and her two friends, Nancy and Marion, were monogrammed. There were bath towels with large "R"'s and other smaller items with "Nancy" or "Marion." The things that were used by all three had "EMN" on them. Again—strangely—there was a large photograph of FDR on the wall directly in front of her bed over the fireplace. This was most likely the last thing she saw before she went to bed each night, and the first thing she saw when she woke up in the morning. This room was another reminder of the simple lifestyle she had, even after growing up surrounded by so much wealth.

Her sleeping porch was probably the most personal space of Eleanor's in the entire house. She said it reminded her of a treehouse. There were screened-in windows on all three sides facing the property around the house. From this vantage point she saw and enjoyed the tennis and badminton courts, the garden, the outside fireplace where picnics were held, the stream, and the original stone cottage that started it all. This was her refuge.

Mrs. Roosevelt typically said goodnight to her guests around 11pm and headed upstairs to her room with her Scottish Terrier, Fala. The two liked to sit out on the porch at the long, plain wooden table where she read or wrote any final letters or thoughts on the day. There was another simple, single bed on the porch if she decided to stay out there for the night. It was a stripped down and open version of her already simple lifestyle. It was a very raw and honest place with even less pretense and more acceptability than the rest of the house. This was where I pictured her sitting and contemplating her life and her many interests in their purest forms. This was where I concluded my research on Mrs. Eleanor Roosevelt.

Author's Note - The People You Meet

I recently spoke at the Garrett County Historical Museum in Oakland, Maryland, and a very nice woman came up to me after the speech. She told me when she was a young girl her class visited the United Nations on a field trip. The trip was during the time that Mrs. Roosevelt was the U. S. Representative to the U. N. Commission on Human Rights or maybe the Chair of the U. N. Commission on Human Rights [she didn't mention a year, and I didn't ask]. The woman told me she got separated from her class [I can relate to this, because I'm a "wanderer," but that's another story for another book], and got lost in the U. N. She came around a corner and found herself face to face with Eleanor Roosevelt. Mrs. Roosevelt introduced herself, and helped the woman—then a young school girl—find her class. This story is not unusual for Eleanor Roosevelt. Nor is it unusual for me to hear first-hand stories from people about their run-ins or interactions with First Ladies. It's another thing I love about public speaking and traveling. I get to continue my studies and research and continue to meet interesting people and hear interesting stories. So, if you see me out there in the world or attend one of my speeches, please don't hesitate to come up to me and introduce yourself and share a story or two. It's part of why I do what I do.

SUMMARY

What do you tell the world about a woman about who is so well-known people don't believe there is much left about her to learn? You tell them what I have just told you. You take someone larger than life and make them human and accessible. You make them real and you make them a person. Why? Because just like Mary Lincoln, that's what these houses and places told me about them.

Eleanor Roosevelt was in the role of First Lady longer than any other woman in history. It would take a Constitutional Amendment to break her record. She usually comes in at number one in public opinion and historian's polls for most accomplished, successful and popular First Lady of all time. She was the eyes, ears and legs for her husband's administration in many arenas. She rose to the top of her political party, and continued her work and service to her country nearly to the day she died. She wrote books upon books, countless articles and daily columns. She was the mother of six children, and a faithful wife, despite her husband's philandering. She remained with him and revitalized his political career. She was the voice over the radio airwaves, announcing Pearl Harbor had been bombed. She was largely responsible, and deserves credit, for helping create the man who would be the longest serving President in the history of our country.

No matter what your politics—which I rarely mention or discuss in these stories—she was a remarkable woman that was unusual for her time. It is impossible to deny her contributions and staying power in American politics, world recognition and career accomplishments. Was she the greatest First Lady of all time? That is for others to discuss and decide. For me, I found a woman who through all her power and dominance was still vulnerable. She was the "ugly duckling." She tragically lost both her parents at an early age. Despite wealth and privilege, she suffered great hardships. However, she rose above all of that to make herself the woman she was. She bided her time, and made a long-lasting career for herself, contributing to social and global justice. She even managed to end up with a home she could decorate and truly call her own. She didn't conform to social and political norms. She followed her head and her heart throughout life and blazed her own trails. I had to respect that in her, as I try to achieve and demand that of myself.

Travelogue Food Tip

The Hyde Park Brewing Company has a classic and quaint English Pub atmosphere. It's easy to get to, and has a spacious bar to belly up to. It also has one of the best steak Caesar salads I had during this entire adventure. Yes, I enjoy a good Caesar salad. I enjoy most Caesar salads. This one had a delightful homemade creamy dressing and a wonderfully crafted shaved Parmesan cheese topping that was perfect with the light, but tasty croutons. This is a Caesar lover's Caesar, and the streak was juicy, and cooked to a perfect medium rare. They had a full selection of craft beer on tap and plenty of TVs to watch any number of games and sporting events. All of which added to a pleasant and delicious evening.

CHAPTER NINE

Bess Truman

Independence, Missouri

Bess Truman was born Elizabeth Virginia Wallace on February 13, 1885 in Independence, Missouri. Her parents were David Wilcock Wallace and Margaret Gates Wallace. Bess and Harry Truman were married on June 28, 1919. They had one child together. Bess Truman died in Independence, Missouri on October 18, 1982 at the age of 97.

INDEPENDENCE, MISSOURI

I was at a happy hour with friends, standing around on a patio enjoying a beautiful fall evening when my cell phone rang. I looked down and said, "Excuse me guys. I have to take this call. It's President and Mrs. Truman's grandson calling." One friend said, "You're kidding me, right?" I responded, "Dude. You know what I do for a living!" Everyone laughed. They did know what I did for a living. Most people I knew and ran into knew what project I was working on and asked me about it on a regular basis. Everyone seemed to be into this project, and never got tired of hearing about it. It's part of the reason I wrote these books and became THE FIRST LADIES MAN.

The phone call was very important, because it set up my access to the Truman house that was operated by the National Park Service as a National Historic Site. The problem was, up to this point, I was not going to be granted access. The story I was told goes as follows...

Production Note - Tea Time

Over thirty years ago, when dinosaur cameras ruled the Earth, and cables ran wild, an innocent cameraman just trying to do his job was filming in the Truman house with his giant cinderblock of a camera on his shoulder. He bumped into a tea cup and sent the artifact tumbling to the floor, headed for certain destruction. At great personal risk, a park ranger dove across the room and saved the tea cup (not all heroes wear capes). Even though the cup—and the day—was saved, the curator at the time felt it best to lock down the site, and not to permit any more cameras/TV crews into the house. This was a rule that was still in place when I went to schedule my visit. Fortunately for me—and the series— C-SPAN has an impeccable reputation, and friends in high places. As a favor to the Truman family, the National Park Service opened the house to my camera and me at the request of Truman family representative, Clifton Truman Daniel. He was also my host, tour guide and on-camera personality for the shoot at the house. And really, who better to tell me the stories of the house than someone who spent time there with Mrs. Truman (his grandmother). I brought special battery packs and light kits to reduce my whole footprint and presence there, had to wear special paper booties, and was not allowed in the house without my new best friend, Clifton. All of this was fine by me, as long as we got the stories and the footage. The result was the first new footage of the inside of the Truman house in over 30 years. And that was an honor and a privilege I did not take lightly.

Personal Side Note To The Production Note - My Reputation Preceded Me

Remember earlier in this book, when I said the historical community was very tight? Well, here in Independence I discovered just how tight. When my admittance into the home was in question, and everyone was working out the details of my visit, a call was made by the folks in Missouri. Carol Dage was in charge at the Truman house, and she was friends with Susan Haake from the Lincoln Historical Site in Springfield, Illinois. Carol told me our mutual friend Susan had nothing but nice things to say about our day together in Springfield, and I checked out alright. We both had a good laugh over her running a background check on me, but if it put her mind at ease, it was all fine by me. As I've said before, I am welcome back to all the locations I have visited, and I didn't have to use my insurance once. My reputation—and C-SPAN's even more—was something I valued and protected with everything I had.

Independence, Missouri was one of the more remarkable experiences of my entire journey. I know I have said this, or something similar, about a lot (if not all) of these locations, but it's TRUE! This was like meeting Tyler's grandson in Charles City, Virginia only slightly different because of a few unusual circumstances—not that meeting the living grandson of the tenth President of the United States wasn't unusual enough on its own.

I started my first day in the morning at the Harry S. Truman Presidential Library and Museum. Director, Mike Devine was my host there, and we had already spoken on the phone to set things up—as was my typical modus operandi. He had explained to me that the Trumans had so many items and artifacts they had to store many of them off campus in facilities built into the mountains and caves of Independence (who knew). At 97 years old, Mrs. Truman was the longest-living First Lady, and she had amassed quite a "collection" throughout her life. The collection is so large, and spread out, to the point where the jacket of the suit in which President Truman married Mrs. Truman belongs to the library and the pants belong to the Historical Site. When the suit goes on display or travels with an exhibit, the two facilities must get special permission and fill out forms to allow the suit to travel together as one. This was going to be a long and productive day in Independence.

Author's Note – Pop Pop Was A Collector

It is in this portion of my live speaking program—when I am talking about Mrs. Truman or various collections—I point out that the Trumans had a lot in common with my grandfather (Pop Pop)...they kept EVERYTHING! However, Pop Pop's house in Baltimore wasn't nearly as organized as the Truman Historical Site. He did have anywhere between five and fifty of just about anything you can name. If the television show "American Pickers" had been around when my brother and I cleaned out Pop Pop's house, I'd be a wealthy man.

Along with Devine, I was greeted at the library and museum by archivist, Tammy Williams, and the Trumans' grandson, Clifton Truman Daniel. Tammy did all the on-camera work for the pieces we completed at the museum. We all chatted for a while, got to know each other, outlined our morning together, and got to work. We headed immediately for the basement work rooms and storage facilities. Backstage Access. I know you all know how I feel about the back rooms. The sense of adventure and discovery always had new things to offer and was always exciting.

With so many items in the collection, we had to be selective in our story telling. Bess Truman was a steady and constant partner to her husband. She didn't spend a lot of time in front of the camera, and she never made many public speeches or appearances. In fact, when Eleanor Roosevelt told her about her women only press conferences, Mrs. Truman said something to the effect of that was nice, but she didn't intend to continue them. This and other, subtler, things about Mrs. Truman's time as First Lady made her very interesting to me. Bess

Truman came into the White House directly after Eleanor Roosevelt. Eleanor Roosevelt was one of the most well-known women (and First Ladies) in the world. She was First Lady for an unprecedented four terms. Her's were big shoes to fill. Rather than try to imitate or duplicate Mrs. Roosevelt's role or actions, Mrs. Truman created her own version of a First Lady. This immediately gave me a lot of respect for Mrs. Truman.

Bess Truman was criticized for not spending a lot of time in Washington, DC or in the public eye. Many thought this was because she didn't like Washington or politics. This proved to be only partially true. Harry and Bess Truman are one of the great love stories of the White House (which we will get to), and she was truly her husband's partner in life. His life included politics, therefore, Bess was all in. She was in on, and privy to, some of the most important decisions of her husband's political career and presidency. The key to Mrs. Truman was, she did it behind closed doors and out of the public eye. This was not uncommon among First Ladies. She admired Elizabeth Monroe for—as Truman's daughter, Margaret, put it, "virtually disappearing from the White House during most of her husband's two terms."

It's true, Bess Truman spent a lot of time out of DC at home in Independence (I couldn't help but think of Abigail Adams home in Quincy during much of her husband's time in the new White House). But, why? Was it because she didn't like Washington, DC and its people and politicians? Maybe, a bit. Who could blame her? I'm only half kidding here. Mrs. Truman had an elderly mother at home in Missouri. A mother who had become a virtual recluse after Bess's father committed suicide in 1903. Bess was 18 at the time. Her father, David Wallace, was a well-known and well-liked man with a good family, but he had failed in business, and turned to alcohol. His alcoholism, and the problems associated with it, no doubt, contributed to his suicide. The Wallace's were also very well-known in and around town. David Wallace's funeral was said to be one of the biggest the town had ever seen. He was known to be a kind, generous and helpful man. However, Bess and her family could not escape the stigma of suicide. After his death, Bess's mother moved the family to Colorado, to stay with relatives, while things settled down in Independence. This was a lifelong shadow that hung over Bess and her family, and kept Bess in Independence for much of her time as First Lady. So, once again, with the full story, I viewed the situation a bit differently after my trip and research. The important part was that Mrs. Truman was there for both her husband and her mother when they needed her. She just didn't make a big public spectacle of it. She handled and enjoyed her duties as First Lady in a more private or "behind the scenes" manner than some of the other, more public, First Ladies. She was more like Elizabeth Monroe whom she admired so much.

Bess Truman had a style—as do most woman. Especially, a First Lady. And some of the stories behind her clothes also gave me more perspective on her distaste for public life. Tammy had many significant articles of clothing that belonged to Mrs. Truman out on work tables for us to examine. It was pointed out that the library had so many photographs, letters and even videos, that helped put the entire story together with a number of artifacts and the significant events or locations. This was a technique and resource we had used throughout the entire series, when available, but they really made good use of it here at the Truman Library.

Mrs. Truman's first public event as First Lady was for the christening of two hospital war planes. They were described as "flying hospitals," and one was for the Army and the other was for the Navy. Her daughter, Margaret, was with her on stage at the event. Mrs. Truman gave a nicely prepared speech, and was then handed a bottle of champagne to break over the nose of each plane. This would have all been well and good save for the fact that the bottle had not been etched or scored so it would break easily. The result was Mrs. Truman slamming a champagne bottle on the nose of the first plane over and over and over again, without it breaking. All of this was captured on black and white newsreel. The bottle clunked and clunked on the metal plane and the crowd laughed loudly with each unsuccessful hit. Mrs. Truman smiled and laughed along graciously, but after a while it became uncomfortable. A soldier on stage with Mrs. Truman stepped in to help. He was also unable to break the bottle. They moved to the other plane, and a different soldier attempted to help her with a properly timed hammer. Even this first attempt was unsuccessful. The second try resulted in the champagne exploding all over the plane, the stage and Mrs. Truman. When the First Lady and her daughter got into the car to leave, Mrs. Truman said that was the last time she would agree to anything like that again. In the collection at the Truman museum was the hat she wore during this embarrassing first public event.

This story was brought to life for me by so many elements. First, there was the known factor that Mrs. Truman was not a very public person. Then, the event itself did not go as planned, and resulted in Mrs. Truman feeling foolish and embarrassed. Not only did the bottle not break after multiple tries, but when it did, it sprayed champagne all over her and her clothes. I had seen video and pictures of this very public event. Now I had the clothes she wore that day right in front of me. This was a first. The whole event and scene came alive right before my eyes and on camera. All the puzzle pieces fell into place. It was amazing to see this story unfold this way, and to hold the actual hat she wore. I could almost smell the stale champagne on the small black feather and netted hat. After I saw this hat and heard the details of the story, I can't say I blamed Bess Truman for having stayed out of the public eye as much as she did. Her first real taste of it was tainted by bad champagne.

From an early age her friends remarked how Bess had more style or panache for her age than most other girls in town. Her mother came from money, and they appeared to have good taste. Again, the presence of letters and pictures was of great help in telling the stories of Bess Truman through her clothes and her style. What some say was Mrs. Truman's happiest day in Washington, DC came in 1952 at the Jefferson-Jackson Dinner. President Truman announced he was not running for another term as President. This meant the Trumans were going home to Missouri for good. That night, Mrs. Truman wore a classic black sleeveless dress with a shin-length hemline. It was surprisingly youthful for a woman her age, but it looked very nice on her in the photographs. In fact, if not for the photographs, the dress might have been lost forever. When Mrs. Truman got back to Independence, she gave the dress to her church bazaar. It was sold to a man who discovered the dress had belonged to Bess Truman, and later donated it to the museum. Archivists at the museum scoured pictures and documents until the dress and the event were properly identified. This also gave me a little perspective into Mrs. Truman and the importance she gave to her role as First Lady. I got the sense that her loyalty was with her husband and her country. She took her role as First Lady very seriously, but didn't put too much importance on some of the physical items—particularly a dress—that went along with it.

That's not to say she didn't enjoy a pretty outfit. Bess especially loved hats. In one of the earliest pictures of young Bess Wallace when she was 13 years old, she is wearing a very elaborate straw hat decorated with all kinds of folded and patterned fabric. It had a rather ornate center pin or brooch, and more material that went up in the air in a feather-like fashion. Sadly, this particular hat wasn't in the collection at the library. However, at least 55 other hats (primarily worn during her White House years from 1945 to 1953) were.

There was a very beautiful and detailed white and pastel colored hat with flowers and veil-like netting out on display. Along with this hat was a hand-written draft note in Mrs. Truman's handwriting. The note said:

> "Dear Miss Kelley, I am simply delighted with my new hat! It is the most attractive I have seen all spring, and I am happy it is mine."

She went on to say that she had worn the hat for Queen Juliana of the Netherlands' visit, when the queen had presented the Carillon to the nation.

Historical Note - Ring My Bell

A carillon is a bell tower monument. This particular carillon was presented by the Queen of the Netherlands on April 4, 1952 in Meridian Park in Washington, DC. It was a symbol friendship between the U. S. and the Netherlands. It now resides on a hill in Arlington, Virginia along the George Washington Parkway and is maintained by the National Park Service.

When the archivists first discovered the hat in Mrs. Truman's collection there was no note in the box and no way of knowing where the random hat had come from. When the note was located, it was matched with photographs from the event. From there the hat was combined with the hand-written note and the photograph of Mrs. Truman greeting Queen Juliana, and the story of the flowered hat was completed.

Another hat in the collection was made by one of her favorite designers in Washington, DC, Madam Agasta. It was a simple brown felt hat with a brown egret feather plume. From pictures, I saw it was worn in 1952, when she and President Truman welcomed Prince Philip and Princess Elizabeth to America. This was so cool to put all these events together with the pictures, dates, stories and artifacts in so many cases. It made them all that much more real and tangible to me.

The library and museum were excellent resources with an abundance of artifacts and information, but there was only so much time in the day and the Truman's living grandson was there, ready to take me to his grandparent's house for a private tour. The museum staff understood. Clifton was a favorite among the staff at the Truman Library and Museum. He was the main family member keeping and promoting his grandparents' legacy. He was the reason I was allowed into the house at all. He was about to share personal stories and experiences not only of his grandparents' lives, but his mother's, his brothers', and his own. This was a big deal, and not everyone would extend this kind of offer or take time out of their personal lives to do it. I wanted to give us plenty of time at the house. So, I wrapped up the gear, and headed across town to North Delaware Street where park rangers were waiting for Clifton and me.

Harry and Bess Truman had one child. Margaret Truman Daniel. Clifton Truman Daniel's mother. As soon as I walked in the front door, the Trumans' love for their daughter Margaret was clear. Mrs. Truman suffered two miscarriages before the successful and healthy birth of Margaret in 1924. This made their daughter extra special to the Trumans, and it showed in their relationship. There was a life size portrait of Clifton's mother in the main foyer facing the front door. Margaret died in 2008 at the age of 83. I was in Independence in 2013, and I saw the closeness Clifton still felt for his mother as he looked at the painting and told me about her.

Clifton was a great representative for his family. He was very natural on camera and we enjoyed our time together. We had full run of the house, as long as I stayed with him, kept track of all my gear and cables, and didn't break anything. The first thing I asked him, was what a typical visit was like for him here. I wanted his perspective on everything. I wanted to see this house, and his grandmother, through his eyes. The exterior of the house was nicely done, not over-stated or ornate. The main part of the two-story shaker style house (with finished attic or third floor) had a wraparound porch, and was painted white with black shutters. The first thing he said was that we had come through the wrong door. When he visited, family members came in through the kitchen door in the back of the house. So, that's where we started. We mic'd him up and got rolling. He was so cool about everything I wanted to do, and he was up for anything.

Clifton's tour went something like this. As he mentioned, he always entered through the kitchen door and went to the pantry first. There was always a round tin of brownies on one of the middle shelves that were made by the same cook and housekeeper Mrs. Truman had from the time they left the White House. The kitchen was like any home you would expect to find in the 70's & early 80's—which was the time Mrs. Truman last lived there. The curtains on the door were white with red trim. The walls were a mixture of pale pink paint and red and white patterned wall paper with pale green lower border and cabinets. The appliances were all fairly regular looking. There was a blender and an electric can opener on the counter. They were like the ones I had grown up with during that same time period. This house was so real and full of original items—items I recognized from my childhood—it really looked like Mrs. Truman might walk through the door at any moment. There was even a fly swatter hanging on a nail on the wall. This was like going through a time warp.

After checking the brownie supply, Clifton walked through the back hallway to his grandfather's study. As President Truman got older he would not meet them at the airport and this was Clifton's first official stop when he visited. His grandfather would be sitting in his big, comfy, upholstered chair with his desk to his side and full of books. The room still looked exactly this way. The walls had floor-to-ceiling built-in bookshelves filled with books of every shape, size and subject. Across from the President's chair were two smaller sitting chairs with a small end table and lamp between them. Mrs. Truman and Clifton's mother would often sit in there and read with President Truman.

Then Clifton told me something the tour guides probably didn't know or mention. Mrs. Truman and her daughter would strike up a conversation while they read. This would, at times, cause an argument or disagreement—as happens with parents and children of any age. President Truman would mark his page with his finger as he assessed the situation and decided whether he should continue reading, offer a word or two, stay quiet or leave the room altogether. Clifton said, "sometimes he left…sometimes he stayed." This was the kind of insider information and charming stories that made this location so special.

We moved into the formal dining room. This was perhaps the fanciest room in the house. Breakfast and lunch was eaten in the kitchen, but all the family dinners were served in the dining room. Mrs. Truman sat at the end of the table, closest to the kitchen. The furniture in this room was made from dark wood and the table was long enough to accommodate their large family. With Clifton, his parents, his three brothers and their grandparents, they were eight strong. Beautiful, sheer, white curtains covered the windows, and a detailed cabinet showcased various silver serving pieces and plates. The table was set with a full service of Truman family china, crystal and flatware. The plates and cups were bone white with a delicate inner and outer goldleaf border. The glasses were simple with clean lines, and the flatware matched in class and simplicity. It all shared an elegance with the room, not too flashy or extravagant. Under each place setting was a white lace placemat, and beneath each drinking glass, matching coasters. There was a buffet in the dining room with more interesting serving items. One piece was a silver epergne (center piece) which was quite intricate. It had two cherubs, vases for flowers, a fist size hanging bowls for nuts or other snacks, and a plate size tray on top. In the tray was a handful of colorful marbles. I knew there had to be a good story behind them.

When Clifton was two years old, his grandmother gave him this set of marbles. Clifton said his grandmother always gave the best presents. She gave them stuff their parents didn't always want them to have just like any good grandparent, aunt or uncle should. He said if they wanted a dangerous toy, and their mother had already said no, his grandmother would wait for her daughter to leave the room, and quietly ask, "how many do you want?" A treasure trove of cap guns was among the items Clifton recalled his grandmother buying for all the boys. This did not make their parents very happy. At the time, Margaret felt the marbles were too small and unsafe for a two-year-old. They were initially taken away and put up into the tray or bowl of the silver epergne. However, Clifton distinctly remembered getting ahold of them, at some point, and playing with them there in his grandparents' house. And there they were, the marbles his grandmother gave him as a small boy, still in the serving tray on the buffet at the far end of the dining room. Clifton picked up a few of the marbles to showed them to me. He did so with a white cotton curator's glove. When Mrs. Truman passed away, the house and all its contents became federal property and were designated as historical artifacts. This included all of Clifton's childhood toys that were in the house at the time. His toys no longer belonged to him. Nothing in the house did.

As we walked out of the dining room and into the front foyer, we stopped again at the painting of Margaret Truman Daniel. It was framed in an ornate, gold painted, wooden frame. In the painting, Margaret is wearing an all-white gown with puffy lamb chop short sleeves and a medium neckline. It had a "princess" feel to it. It was easily the largest painting or picture in the house. A focal point. He explained that his grandmother was 39 when she gave birth to his mother. Clifton described his mother as being "very precious" to his grandparents (especially, after two miscarriages). President Truman spoiled his daughter, and Mrs. Truman was the disciplinarian. He further described them as a "close little family unit."

It was also here in the foyer where Clifton told me how he found out his grandfather had been President of the United States, and thus, his grandmother had been a First Lady. He said his parents never told him or his siblings that their Grandfather had been a U. S. President when they were young. They wanted their children to grow up, at least initially, thinking of and knowing their grandparents as just that—their grandparents. However, when Clifton came home from his first day of Kindergarten, he had some news for his mother. His teacher had asked him in school that day, "Wasn't your grandfather President of the United States?" He said something close to, "Mom, did you know that Grandpa used to be the President of the United States?"

To the right of the foyer was the sitting room. This was where Bess Truman spent most of her time in the house after her husband died on December 26,

1972. A few little sculptures and figurines were interspersed between the pictures of Clifton and his brothers on the fireplace mantel. He said they had been gifts from him and his brothers over the years. Books and bookshelves were a constant throughout the house and that included this room. The focal point in this room for me, was the gold, upholstered, sitting chair to the right, just as you entered the room. There was a large floor lamp beside it, and this was where Bess Truman did most her reading. Clifton said she kept a pile of books she was waiting to read on one side of the chair, and a pile of books she had finished or was currently reading on the other. Mrs. Truman liked murder mysteries and thrillers. She shared them with her daughter after she read them. Margaret Truman Daniel was a murder mystery writer, herself, for part of her professional life. This was a special place for Mrs. Truman near the end of her long life.

This room also held another fun story from Clifton's boyhood memories, and involved a plastic toy gun from the 60's called an Okinawa gun. When it was still in working order, it shot plastic bullets the size of shotgun shells about ten or fifteen feet across the room. One afternoon, Clifton and his brother, Will, took the gun into the living room and set up Coke cans as targets on the coffee table without bothering to move any of the plants or other items on the table. Their grandfather was the only other person home at the time, heard the racket caused by the two boys, and walked quietly into the room behind them. Will was supposed to have been lookout as Clifton laid on the ground and fired at the can on the table. His brother saw their grandfather coming and took off. This left Clifton sprawled out on the floor with the gun by himself. Without a word, President Truman snatched the gun from his hands, gave a look of disappointment that hit Clifton harder than words, and the gun disappeared. The next time Clifton saw the toy, he was 36 years old and had to hold it with white gloves. You really couldn't get stories like this from any other source. This was gold.

A quick walk across the foyer and we found ourselves in the living room next to President Truman's study. We had done a complete loop though the house. The living room had another fireplace, a big-screen TV from the 80's, a piano and a portrait of Bess Truman. All of these items had stories attached to them. The story behind the piano was simple. Margaret played the piano and sang. She had a brief career as an actor and opera singer, and she entertained the family here in the living room. The TV was so Mrs. Truman could watch her Kansas City Royals games. Clifton also remembered staying up late and watching "The Tonight Show with Johnny Carson" with the Secret Service agent charged with what Clifton put as "little old lady detail in Independence, Missouri." I got a kick out of this as he further explained he was sure that watching a 90-year-old former First Lady was not what any of these agents had signed up for, but it's what they were stuck with at this point in their career.

The furniture and decor of this room matched the rest of the house. Except for maybe the portrait of Bess Truman over the fireplace. That seemed a little large for the room and out of place, but it wasn't just any portrait. It was her White House portrait. As in her official White House portrait, not a replica. The paintings owned by the Truman Library and the White House were replicas. Mrs. Truman took her portrait with her when she left the White House in 1953, and put it up over her fireplace in Independence. In the 1960's, Lady Bird Johnson—who was First Lady at the time—decided to display all of the First Ladies' official White House portraits. She turned the White House upside down, but couldn't find Mrs. Truman's portrait. She called Mrs. Truman at home, and asked her if she knew where her painting was. Mrs. Truman said that it was on her wall. Mrs. Johnson politely challenged that it should be in the White House. Mrs. Truman disagreed, and said that it was her painting, and it was going to stay where it was in her home. Mrs. Johnson tried a few more times to convince Mrs. Truman to return the painting to the White House with no luck. Therefore, two new paintings were made by the original artist, Greta Kempton. There were two more stories to be told, but for those we had to go outside.

This first was another story of mischief that involved Clifton and his younger brother, Will. Clifton was 12 at the time and Will was 10. They discovered a ladder in the attic that lead to a hatch that opened onto the flat, middle part of the roof. The two boys climbed out onto the roof and looked around. They saw their Aunt May, who lived across the street, and waved. Their aunt waved back, then walked across the street to tell Margaret that two of her boys were up on the roof. Margaret went up to see what her sons were up to and ended up out on the roof with them. Clifton said she told them she hadn't been out on the roof since she was about their age. This was about when the Secret Service agents saw people out on the roof from the two cameras they were using to monitor the house. The head of the Secret Service detail, at the time, was named Mr. Burns. Mr. Burns came out of the house across the street, and walked through the gate and up the front walk. The boys waved to Mr. Burns as he continued up the walk and into the house. The next thing they knew Mrs. Truman was in the backyard with Mr. Burns angrily motioning for them to get down off the roof. Clifton said his mother moved twice as fast as he and his brother, and was already halfway down the ladder and back in the house by this point. After the incident, Mrs. Truman put a lock on the hatch and hid the key so well that the Park Service didn't find the key until three months after she passed away.

Author's Note - Boys Will Be Boys

When I was a kid, I loved to climb trees. We had a huge maple tree in our front yard—the kind with the giant helicopter seeds that clogged up the gutters. It was so tall, I could climb almost to the top, and see over houses, across the creek and into Manor Woods Swim Club on Bauer Drive. I can remember being so high up in that tree, that the branches were still fairly new and I would sway back and forth in the breeze. Some of the lower and larger branches spread out over the roof, and provided easy access onto the roof. This was a no brainer, and I spent a lot of time checking out the chimney, and rescuing stranded Frisbees and lost tennis balls. One day, my mom was taking a nap when I decided to hop over onto the roof and walk around. I heard her bedroom widow come flying open with a crash, and I froze. I knew she couldn't see me. What I didn't know was that she could hear me clomping around up there, and I had woken her up. She yelled out the window, "I can hear you running around up on the roof, Andy, and I've told you I didn't want you up there!" BUSTED!! I climbed back down off the roof, and waited for my father to get home so I could plead my case in hopes for a probation (which were never granted) from whatever punishment my mother had handed out.

The final story Clifton Truman Daniel told was perhaps the most important one I would hear in Independence. It was the story of how his grandfather and his grandmother met and started their courtship. Harry Truman first met—or more accurately saw—Bess when he was 6 and she was 5. It was in the Sunday School at the First Presbyterian Church in Independence. The Trumans were Baptists, but the Presbyterian Church was closer to their house. So, that's where young Harry Truman would go to Sunday School. While Truman's mother was talking to the Reverend about getting her son into the Sunday School, young Harry noticed a little girl he described with "beautiful blue eyes and blonde curls." Many years later, Truman would spend time with his relatives, the Nolans, who lived across the street from the Wallace family. One day Harry's Aunt needed a cake plate returned to the Wallaces, and asked for a volunteer to take the plate across the street. Truman moved with what Clifton's mom once described as "something approaching the speed of light" and grabbed the plate from his aunt and dashed across the street. His hope was that young Bess would answer the door, which she did, and finally give him an excuse to talk to her. Harry was invited inside, and the two were said to have never looked at another person for the rest of their lives.

With these stories on camera and my tour of the house, museum and library complete, I headed back to my hotel to rest. It had been a long day and I had half of the next day to shoot B-roll around town before I had to get out the airport. We had talked about the town and a couple key locations to the Bess Truman story, and I wanted to make sure and get them as well to spice up the final video pieces a bit. I went back to my hotel, and started my routine of managing the media and getting the footage off the video cards and on to the external hard drive. Once this process was started I went to dinner. Sleep came fast and hard after dinner, and my alarm was set for an early rise in the morning.

I woke up to a rainy day. I went to the local Harley Davidson dealer right after breakfast in hopes that the rain would pass, and make for better shooting conditions. It did a bit, and I got my t-shirt, so that killed a couple of birds and bought me some clearer skies. I drove back to town and got some street scenes of local businesses and the clock tower in the center of town. It was windy, so I was able to get great shots of American flags blowing in the breeze outside of local government buildings that really screamed "AMERICA." It was great, and John Cougar Mellencamp's "Small Town" played in my head as the drizzle kept the streets free of people for most of the day. The two places I needed to capture most on camera were the Presbyterian Church where Harry first saw Bess in Sunday School, and the Episcopal Church where they were married on June 28, 1919. I got both, and considered my time in Independence well spent.

Production Note – No Business…Like Show Business

I mentioned in the introductions to both books that TV people know other TV people when they see each other on the road. Even if we are in the same place for different things there are tell-tale signs and the obvious loads of gear and travel cases. As I stood out in front of my hotel after breakfast that last morning, I heard the doors open behind me and another TV crew of about six or eight people came walked out to the other side of the front overhang. We were all looking out at the rain with similar looks on our faces. Without words, we were all saying the same thing, "we gotta work in this crap on a Saturday?" Finally, one of the guys asked me what I was working on. I told him and asked him the same in return. They were there for MTV's "Sixteen and Pregnant" and we all got a chuckle about the stark difference in our two projects. They had been there for a day or so, and had a few more days of shooting for their episode. They couldn't believe I had just gotten there the day before, did most my work in one day and was just picking up some B-roll in another half a day. What really blew them away was my answer to their question about the rest of my crew. I told them they were looking at it. Me. I don't think they truly believed me until they saw me get in my car with my camera by myself and drive off. I'd be lying if I told you I didn't feel like a little bit of a badass. Especially since they told me they had a few months before their show would air, and I told them I had to get back to DC to edit my pieces, because my show was airing in a couple weeks.

Author's Note – Mother's Day

Independence, Missouri and the Harry S. Truman Presidential Library and Museum will always hold a special place in my heart. A lot of great things happened there. I started a new friendship and had a great time with Clifton Truman Daniel. My reputation held its own when I was checked out within the historical community and the National Park Service. And most recently, I returned to Independence and spoke in the library's auditorium on Mother's Day in 2014. This was important to me in so many ways. It was the third speech of my new career, I really felt a comfortable momentum building and I was having a great time. I loved talking and meeting people. I genuinely enjoyed telling these stories and giving these speeches. And the fact that this speech was on Mother's Day was not lost on me. I lost my mother in November 2010. She would have really enjoyed this project, the C-SPAN series, and now this public speaking program as the First Ladies Man. Not a day goes by that I don't think about that and feel grateful for all of it. I only wish she was around to enjoy it all with me. It also gave me a chance to see the final resting place of the Trumans (including Clifton's parents), which I didn't get to do on my first trip there. So, thank you for having me back, Independence. I had a blast and hope to see you again soon.

SUMMARY

Bess Truman was about as behind-the-scenes a First Lady as they come. She most admired another quietly influential First Lady—Elizabeth Monroe. She did all this coming into the White House after one of the most visible First Ladies in the history of our country—Eleanor Roosevelt. She had two choices. Give the country another Eleanor, or be her own First Lady. She chose to be her own. This was one of the reasons Bess Truman has always stood out for me. The love story shared between Bess and President Truman is one for the ages. It lasted almost their entire lives. They were the only ones for each other. That is so rare in everyday life, let alone politics. She was the true partner and confidant to her

Presidential husband during a time of war, in which one of the most serious decisions in the history of the world was been made. The decision to use an atomic bomb to end World War II. She did all this with quiet grace and unfaltering support of her husband. She lived longer than any other First Lady to date, and even though her time in the White House may not have been the favorite time in her life, she kept her White House portrait over a fireplace in her home. This was one way of knowing just how important her White House years were to her. She loved her daughter, her grandsons, and her entire family. She overcame the tragedy of losing her father after he committed suicide when she was only 18. She had a flair for hats, and didn't pay much attention to the prying eye of the public at large. To top this all off, most of these stories were told to me by her grandson, Clifton Truman Daniel in his grandparent's house. A house in which my C-SPAN camera was the first to be allowed access in over 30 years. For all these reasons, Bess Truman was more than unusual for her time...she was unusual for the series...and she was unusual for my personal journey.

In a central part of town, very close to the National Park Service Visitor's Center is a place called Up Dog. A big sign in the form of a smiling hot dog in a bun will greet you. You really can't miss it. They have all kinds of specialty hot dogs—like the Chorizo Dog (chorizo, sautéed onions, mozzarella cheese and mustard), or the BBQ Dog (stadium brat, topped with pulled pork, BBQ sauce and pickles)—and others. You can choose fries or onion rings for a side item. I had two chili cheese dogs with a side of onion rings. I always put a little yellow mustard and chopped onions on my chili cheese dogs, and these did not disappoint. Next to a Caesar salad and wings, hot dogs are my next favorite "go to" on the road. Stop in and see if you agree next time you're in Independence, Missouri.

CHAPTER TEN

Mamie Eisenhower

Washington, DC - Abilene, Kansas – Gettysburg, Pennsylvania – Boone, Iowa

Mamie Eisenhower was born Mamie Geneva Doud on November 14, 1896 in Boone, Iowa. Her parents were John Sheldon Doud and Elivera Mathilda Carlson Doud. Mamie and Dwight Eisenhower were married on July 1, 1916. They had two children together. Mamie Eisenhower died in Washington, DC on November 1, 1979 at the age of 82.

WASHINGTON, DC

When the Federal Government shuts down. It shuts DOWN. My initial trip to the Dwight D. Eisenhower Presidential Library, Museum and Boyhood home was scheduled for late September or early October. We were in the process of working the trip out when Congress and Washington, DC pulled their little "stunt." The Mamie Eisenhower show was scheduled to air on Monday November 4, 2013. It was my preference to air that show with video pieces from the Eisenhower Museum and Library in Abilene, but the show would go on with or without them and the Federal Government. This was a high stress situation for me. I was on a roll, and wanted that roll to continue.

Here is why the shutdown was so crippling. During that time, federal employees were not allowed to use their offices, their work email or their work phones. They could not discuss or deal with any work subjects or projects—past, present or future. None. Zero. Zilch. There was no work-related communication of any kind. All the places I needed to go—most immediately and specifically for Mamie Eisenhower—were run by either the National Park Service or the National Archives and Records Administration. Not only was I unable to schedule my visit as planned, I didn't know how long the shutdown was going to last, and I couldn't put any plans in place for when things got up and running again. Surely, the U. S. Government would reopen, but when? That was the question. I couldn't even work ahead with other facilities, because they were largely all operated by the NPS and NARA, too. I was stuck. And I was not happy about it. Whenever things opened back up, it was going to be a scramble and a mad dash to the finish line.

On a positive note, I caught up on some of the work I had already compiled from past trips while I waited. I edited pieces from the material I had. I read more books, and articles about the upcoming women. I helped book guests for the live show. I could be in the DC on Monday nights, which helped with the live shows. I did laundry. I went to the grocery store. I made and ate meals in my own house. I restored a little bit of my regular life. The women from Mamie Eisenhower on forward, loomed over my head. My research and stalled planning process was spread out across my dining room table. I wanted to get back out on the road and keep the momentum I had built up. So, I did the only thing I could do. I waited.

Congress got their collective act together and reopened the United States Federal Government on October 17, 2013. I picked up where I had left off with Communications Director, Samantha Kenner, at the Eisenhower Library and Museum in Abilene. She was the reason the Eisenhower show had location video pieces. I remember the initial conversation she initiated about not being the only

Presidential Library or Museum to not be represented in the show. She got back in step as if no time had passed, and said, "what do we need to do to get you out here as quickly as possible to make all this happen?" She was as determined as I was to get the work done. I headed to Abilene, Kansas on October 21st with little time to spare. I was back in the hot seat again, with no wiggle room for mistakes.

ABILENE, KANSAS

The Dwight D. Eisenhower Library, Museum and Boyhood Home was in the sleepy Midwest town of Abilene, Kansas. Much of the town was "Ike" themed, and I found that charming. I arrived at the location early and easily as I crossed the railroad tracks that ran through the center of town. It was a warm, fall, day, and the leaves had just started to turn. The parking lot was empty, so I parked as close to the front door of the Visitor Center as possible to unload my gear. The property was huge and spread out. I had no idea exactly where all we would be going throughout the day, but this seemed like as good a place to start as any.

Luckily for me, they didn't mess around at the Eisenhower site. Don't get me wrong, we had fun. But we didn't drag our feet. Samantha teamed me up with Curator, William Snyder. He knew everything there was to know about the museum and the library and their collections. We got set up, did a walk through, and got rolling. The three of us were a production force, and worked seamlessly together. Our work took us through storage rooms, work areas, the public museum, the library and its archives, the exterior buildings, and the Eisenhower's final resting place. The combination of Samantha's pre-interview information and a clear idea about the things I wanted to see, combined with William's knowledge and my well-tuned operation, lead to a very productive day together (I won't get tired of singing the praises of these two in this chapter—they seriously saved the day and the Mamie show).

The first thing William told me about was Mrs. Eisenhower's love for clothes. The collection there was so vast it went on for rooms and rooms, and for what seemed like miles and miles of fabric. This was seriously the largest collection of First Lady's clothes I saw during all my travels. William and I both laughed as we walked on and on among the racks of clothes. He told me the stories and significance of each piece as we walked through the collection. We picked out a good variety of pieces with unusual stories or significance for the video pieces. They had everything—hats, purses, jewelry, shoes, dresses, gowns, casual, formal. You name it, they had it. As William put it, Mamie was a "clothes horse." I've said before, a whole show could be done, not only about each of these women, but each of the locations I visited. However, this was the first time I felt that an entire show could have been done about a specific collection at one of the locations. Seriously, Mamie Eisenhower had a lot of clothes.

Mrs. Eisenhower made the "Top Ten Best Dressed List" every year she was in the White House. As I looked at the numerous items we had laid out in the work room of the museum, I saw why. The first dress we looked at was a beautiful black and white patterned dress with a matching hat that was designed by one of Mamie's favorite designers, Molly Parnis. The modern and intricate black pattern over the white dress and hat was playful, yet sophisticated. It came with a heavy black overcoat. She wore the outfit to the opening ceremony of the Saint Lawrence Waterway. She and President Eisenhower met Queen Elizabeth and Prince Philip at the ceremony. Like the clothes at the Truman Museum, they had photographs which completed the story. In the photo, Mrs. Eisenhower has a black square purse that appeared to be patent leather and white gloves to complete her look. Again, it was fantastic to have all these resources to put into the final videos. William told the stories, I captured the dresses and outfits as they existed today, and the pictures gave them historical context.

The Eisenhower toile dress was one of the more unusual patterns of any dress I had seen. It was a casual day dress that had the cut and design of something you would expect June Cleaver to wear on "Leave It to Beaver." The pale red pattern over the white base of the dress showed a mix of flowers and all the houses and places the Eisenhower's lived over the years and their many travels. There was also a five-star design mixed in to symbolize President Eisenhower having been a Five Star General. This same fabric was used to make curtains at the Eisenhower's retirement farm in Gettysburg, Pennsylvania.

Mrs. Eisenhower loved the color pink. There was even a certain shade called "Mamie Pink." The museum had racks and racks of any and all type of clothing and accessory in every shade, size and style of pink. One pink dress was a cocktail style dress with an intricate beaded top, complete with a sewn in beaded belt or waistline and a simple veiled bottom half that balanced out the busy top. There is no doubt that Mamie was at the height of fashion and the focal point of any event she hostessed or attended. They had ball gowns, casual wear, coats, shoes, hats purses, gloves and jewelry. All in pink.

Many of Mrs. Eisenhower's dresses and gowns were sleeveless. She said her arms were one of her husband's favorite features and she wanted to show them off. They had a fairly plain, handmade, every day dress with a light gray with darker gray patterned polka dots on one of the racks. William explained the hem line of this dress was such that it could be altered up or down to match the style of the day. This was a good representation of Mamie's attention to budget. I had seen this with many first ladies. Especially, the ones with a love for clothes. Many of their dresses were changed or altered over the years to get as much use out of them as possible. This would fall right in line with Mamie having been a frugal military wife, before she became First Lady.

Jacqueline Kennedy was well known for wearing little black dresses, but Mamie wore them in the White House first. She had countless little, black, sleeveless cocktail dresses. Mrs. Eisenhower loved to entertain and have parties. This went way back to the military days, as well. The Eisenhowers often entertained other military families and couples, and had all kinds of parties—big and small—wherever they lived, were stationed or stayed.

Mamie once said she would "never dress like an old lady." She kept her word. She loved fun and vibrant colors and patterns. William put together a special rack of outfits that showcased this. A long pale, green and pink, sleeveless dress could have been worn at any spring or summer garden party or casual evening event. The pattern was thin lines or bars that looked almost out of focus. It was very late 50's or early 60's in terms of style. A wild red, black, maroon and white dress with a matching belt would have been the talk of any event. She had a tropical looking floral print floor length dress of a similar cut on this rack, too. One dress on this rack really caught my eye. The purple top actually had sleeves, and a plunging neckline—both of which were rare for Mamie. The skirt—which was attached—was quilted and had big, bright flowers all over. She wore all of these outfits well into her 70's and 80's. They all kind of reminded me of outfits Mrs. Partridge would wear, or even some of the tamer outfits that

Cher would wear at the beginning or end of the "Sonny and Cher Show." They were definitely not "old lady" clothes or stuffy in any way. Mrs. Eisenhower was a bubbly person who enjoyed being around other people in social settings. She was a strong and confident woman and it showed in her clothes. It was easy to imagine her in any one of these outfits as she cruised around a party and made sure everyone had a good time, as she laughed her way through the room.

Another table in the work room had at least fifteen hats on it. Mamie loved hats, and one of her favorite hat designers was Sally Victor. Mamie had every shape, size and variety of hat. They went from simple to intricate in design. From the pillbox to the wide-brimmed and everything in between. Some had patterns, and others were plain. Some had feathers and ribbons, while others had pins or jewels. Two hats really stood out to me among the ones assembled on the long table. The first had an understated leopard print that banded the head with a white felt beanie-like top that was four squares of fabric coming together. It also had a long pheasant feather and a jeweled pin on one side. This represented the pinnacle of elegance. It was remarkably simple in design, calm in color (even with the leopard print), but spoke volumes about the level of Mrs. Eisenhower's position and title. She knew the importance of her role in her husband's career—both in and out of the military. Not all her clothes were flashy and fun. This hat showed she knew that, and could play any part she needed to as First Lady. The other hat was one that looked more like it belonged to Queen Elizabeth. It was light blue and had a wide brim. It looked like a perfect hat for the Kentucky Derby. It had big, yellow and white daisies that sat on the brim and circled the hat. It also had two blue ribbons that matched and trailed off the back. Pink was well represented in her hats, of course. There were two other hats that were similar in style and design to the blue one with daisies, but they were pink and the flowers were roses and carnations. The variety of all these hats was interesting, because many were different from the style and design she normally wore.

Mamie was a fashionista for sure. All her outfits were well thought out and planned from head to toe. This, of course, included shoes. She had boxes and boxes of them. One table in the room looked like a shoe store with all her shoes and shoeboxes lined up. They, too, came in every shape, size, color and style. Beyond the fact that she had so many pairs of shoes, it amazed me that she kept so many pairs of shoes, and that the museum had them on hand. It shouldn't have amazed me, given the overall amount of clothes in the collection, but the shoes seemed to go on forever. The really unique thing about her shoes were the labels. Many of the shoes said, "Made expressly for Mrs. Dwight D. Eisenhower" in them. This was impressive.

Mamie's style and clothes collection started way before the White House years. One dress from the mid 1920's showed this. She would've been too old to be considered a flapper, but it was in that style, and consistent with trends of the day. It was an off white, sleeveless top with shiny beads and rhinestones that glimmered in the light brilliantly. The attached skirt was black and full of beads and sequins. There were lacey mesh features in the skirt, as well. An off-white slip that went with the dress was on the table, and added a bit of modesty to the look. I'm sure Mamie would've looked great in it and attracted a fair amount of attention at any party she and Ike would've attended on some military base in their 30's.

Style for Mrs. Eisenhower wasn't always about her clothes. She had a very distinct hairstyle that she was known for. It involved her signature bangs and was called the "Mamie look." Women could purchase clip-on bangs in most drug stores to duplicate it. It was pointed out during the live show that Mrs. Obama had recently gone with a new hairstyle that featured bangs, and had received a lot attention from the press and the public. The attention and popularity should come as no surprise, as First Ladies always influence hair and fashion styles of the day.

Mamie's bangs have an interesting story and origin. The Eisenhowers lost their first son, Doud "Icky" Eisenhower when he was three in 1921. They were living at Fort Meade in Severn, Maryland at the time and had hired a nanny. The nanny had Scarlet Fever, and Doud caught it from the girl. Every effort to save their young son failed. The Eisenhowers blamed themselves for not checking into the nanny's background more—as any grieving parent would. Mr. Eisenhower described it as "the most shattering moment of their lives, one that almost destroyed their marriage." It was soon after this tragedy Ike and Mamie focused on their relationship to save the marriage, and her new hair style was part of those efforts.

Mamie's new look was perfected by the Elizabeth Arden Salon in Paris. She needed to ensure she would get the same exact style at any of Miss Arden's salons around the world, and especially at home in the states. This was achieved when Arden had her stylists make instructional, step-by-step drawings that Mrs. Eisenhower took with her when she traveled. These drawing were on display at the Eisenhower Museum. Mamie took her hair and her style very seriously.

Mamie Eisenhower's style and popularity carried over into the political arena. She proved to be quite an asset to her husband, especially in the campaign of 1952. This was the first time in history that women outnumbered men in the electorate, and it showed in the way the candidates campaigned. There were many photographs of Dwight D. Eisenhower surrounded by women at campaign rallies across the country. There were also many pictures of Mamie Eisenhower surrounded by women at campaign rallies and whistle stop cross country train trips. I was able to examine some of the campaign memorabilia up close. Many of the smaller items were kept in tiny boxes, made of the same sturdy cardboard I had seen dresses and documents stored in at most of the other facilities. There seemed to be an endless supply of examples of this material, as well.

There were rhinestone pins that said "IKE" and "I LIKE IKE." One was even in the shape of a heart. More traditional red, white and blue pins not only said "I LIKE IKE," but also "I LIKE MAMIE." One button said, "WE WANT MAMIE." Some buttons had her picture only on them without any mention of her husband."I LIKE IKE" buttons were fashioned into clip on earrings for women to wear. A "MAMIE AND IKE" charm bracelet had Mamie's name first. An "I LIKE IKE" corsage was an item I hadn't seen at any other museum. It said, "You're in HIGH STYLE when you wear an I LIKE IKE corsage" right on the package. A "Mamie Pink" comb had Mamie Eisenhower in gold lettering along the spine. There was a white dress—similar in cut to the "June Cleaver" dress I mentioned earlier—that had "IKE" in big, bold, red letters. There was a fantastic black and white picture that went along with this dress that showed eight women all wearing the dress standing around a giant picture of General Eisenhower. There was even an "Eisenhower Official Campaign Hat" for women to wear at rallies and conventions. The hat was made by Mamie's favorite hat designer, Sally Victor. It was a stylish take on a sailor cap, made from light blue felt with bold, red piping. It came complete with a red, white and blue "I LIKE IKE" button on the side accented by a red ribbon.

Just when I thought I had seen enough and we were moving on, I was taken into the public area of the museum where they had actual drawers full of more campaign items under protective clear plastic. Many of these items were geared towards the ladies and female voters, too. The drawers were full of more buttons and jeweled pins. One red, white and blue button in the drawer featured Mamie Eisenhower and Pat Nixon as potential First and Second Ladies with each of their pictures and simply said, "MAMIE AND PAT." There were "I LIKE IKE" gloves that matched the "I LIKE IKE" dress. Shear white stockings with "I LIKE IKE" in black cursive writing down the side of the calf were also part of the display. It appears the Eisenhower campaign had woman voters covered—head to toe.

Their efforts were rewarded by a victory and Dwight D. Eisenhower was elected the 34th President of the United States. The dress suit Mrs. Eisenhower wore to the swearing in ceremony was on display in the museum. It was a simple, business-like gray dress and button-up suit jacket made by Hattie Carnegie. Given the rest of Mrs. Eisenhower's clothes, it was surprisingly understated and dull in color. There was a matching hat by Sally Victor (of course). The hat was a flat, layered and louvered design that added some panache to an otherwise elegant, but plain outfit. A rhinestone eagle pin also added some flair to the ensemble and the whole outfit was very well put together. Once again, Mamie showed she understood the seriousness of her role, and the part she played in her husband's career. A November 1955 Family Circle issue featured Mrs. Eisenhower on the cover and read, "First Lady—But Wife First."

When Mrs. Eisenhower was a little girl, she was diagnosed with a heart condition that carried over into her adult life. Heart disease was what ultimately ended her and President Eisenhower's lives. Her doctor even told her she should stay in bed three days a week while she was in the White House. This wouldn't do for an active and involved First Lady like Mrs. Eisenhower. She stayed in bed each day until noon as a compromise. Even though she stayed in bed through the morning, it didn't mean she wasn't working. She held daily staff meetings from her bed. The museum had many of Mamie's bed jackets in their collection.

These were light garments that were more like wraps or shawls to cover her nightgowns and bed clothes, so she could have her staff in her bedroom in the mornings. Each morning she woke up, did her hair and makeup, and put on one of her many bed jackets for her morning staff meetings.

Most of these bed jackets were pink (no surprise there). Some were very plain, and others were more elaborate. One had a pink feather-like boa as a collar that also ran down the front. Another had beads and sequins. A third, also pink, had large, ornate buttons. Each of these bed jackets were very "Mamie"—both color and style. There was a great picture of President and Mrs. Eisenhower in bed one morning with their grandchildren in the White House. They are all in their pajamas and surrounded by pink satin sheets and pillows. Given Mamie's public image and her love of pink and fine fashion, President Eisenhower was probably the only President in history who could get away with being in such a picture. It was easy to imagine the same bed surrounded by staffers as Mamie conducted her daily meetings in any one of the many bed jackets I had just seen.

In the library, I could see actual notes, letters and papers from these meetings. There were schedules and documents from every year Mrs. Eisenhower was in the White House. Her schedules were blocked out in very strict increments of time. Some meetings or tasks were even narrowed down to 5 minute intervals. The day I looked at was Tuesday November 9th. She had a diplomatic dinner to attend that night and a ribbon cutting at the National Presbyterian Church Bazaar early the next morning. Each of these schedules had hand written notes from Mamie where she made changes or suggestions to the prepared schedule she had been given. One entry had a reminder to see her Social Secretary, Mrs. McAffrey.

Not all of Mrs. Eisenhower's morning business was work or White House related. One folder held Christmas catalogues, and newspaper inserts from department stores. She had made several hand-written notes about gifts for her grandchildren. The year I looked at, her granddaughter, Susan, was getting a doll and baby carriage. Mrs. Eisenhower had always kept track of the family finances and budget, and this was no different when they were in the White House. Along with the Christmas list and notes were figures and calculations written by Mamie on White House Stationary. This was a clear moment when Mrs.

Eisenhower became that real person I always looked for. I had done the same type of Christmas shopping in W. Bell & Co. catalogues (for those who grew up around Washington, DC who may remember). I had circled things, made notes, clipped toys out and included them in notes to Santa. I passed them around to my parents, and sent them to grandparents and other family members. This was a very endearing moment to see Mamie Eisenhower in that light.

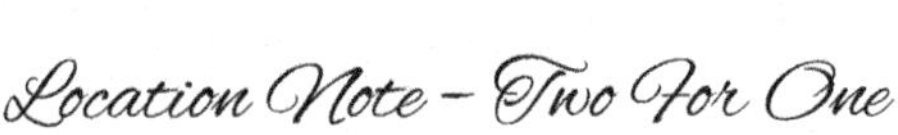

Location Note – Two For One

In one of the offices in the library I happened to see a life-size cut out of President and Mrs. Eisenhower standing in the corner. Not only was this the first cutout like this I had seen with both a President and First Lady together, it was the first one I had seen in full color. I jumped at the chance to get my picture taken with the Eisenhowers (look for this picture and many others from my journey in the center photo section of this book).

While she was in the White House and long after, Mrs. Eisenhower was active in the American Heart Association and other heart health related organizations. Heart disease was what ultimately caused her death, and the death of her husband. In 1970, she was named the American Heart Association's Volunteer of the Year. While she was involved with the organization, donations and membership increased dramatically. The award was given to her by, then First Lady, Pat Nixon, and was on display in the museum. It was a gatefold style dark wood plaque with a dark gold medallion with the AHA emblem and a nice inscription. There were many other ceremonial plates, plaques, ribbons, certificates and awards in the exhibit to show Mamie's lifelong commitment to the cause.

Mrs. Eisenhower loved a party and a fanfare. While some First Ladies shied away from the spotlight, Mamie blossomed in it. One such event that was well represented and documented at the museum, was the christening of the USS Nautilus. This was the first operational nuclear powered submarine in the world, and it was a big deal. Mrs. Eisenhower shined during the entire ceremony. A beautiful wooden box that holds the sterling silver champagne bottle shroud was a beautiful memento from the event. I had to believe this shroud and all the circumstances that surrounded the event went better than Mrs. Truman's war plane christening. They also had a silver whistle, a paper program and a few other random items from the event that added to its significance.

I mentioned her attention to detail, budget and finances a few times during this chapter. It was made even more clear when we looked at the Eisenhower White House china—or lack thereof. Mrs. Eisenhower didn't feel the need to order a brand new full set of china. She thought the Truman china was complete and in good enough condition to use. The Truman's china was a beautiful Williamsburg green. Mamie did, however, personalize and spruce it up a bit. She added gold chargers for under the dinner plates and a few other gold accent pieces to make it her own version of what the Trumans had used before them.

Historical Note - Dinner Is Served

The Monroes' were the first President and First Lady to have official White House china. It was an elaborate set, and Mrs. Monroe caught a lot of grief for it not only being made in France, but having a French style design. The service was various forms of the same eagle with a red, white and blue shield coming through a cloud in the center of the plates. The dinner plates were bordered in red with goldleaf pin striping and the dessert plates had a blue border with the gold. Administrations prior to the Monroes' simply brought and used their best china from home.

In between lunch and working my way from the museum to the library, I took advantage of the daylight and the beautiful weather and got my exterior shots. There were great, big flags in front of each building and nice signage. The blue sky with a few scattered clouds made a nice backdrop for the buildings. The boyhood home didn't apply as much to Mrs. Eisenhower as it did to Ike, but many times these women were so involved in preserving their husband's legacy, I got footage of it. Plus, it was part of the facility and looked great on the property and on camera. The Eisenhowers are both buried there in Abilene in the Place of Meditation there on the grounds. It was a decent walk down a sidewalk and into a tall, narrow, rectangular building to see the graves. It was quiet and cool inside when I respectfully lugged in my gear. Visitors can walk around a granite, oval walkway that circles, and looks down at the graves. There are also benches around the intimate room to sit upon and reflect. So, I did. Once again, "Cemetery Gates" by The Smiths played in my head.

"All those people. All those lives. Where are they now?"

After I captured the footage, I sat and thought about the project, and life. It was funny how everything had worked out with the series…in general…and the Eisenhower shoot specifically. I was happy about the work we accomplished here, and the First Ladies Man concept was really taking shape in my head.

Author's Note – The First Ladies Man

When I got to Abilene, the First Ladies Man concept was firmly in my head. Since trip one through Virginia, I had been saying," It's all about the ladies," and I was really wrapping my mind around the project and the speech. However, I still didn't know what to do or how to do it. I hadn't come up with my title FIRST LADIES MAN, yet either, but I was close. I was walking through the library part of the Eisenhower facility, on our way upstairs to look at papers and documents, when I looked through a window into a large conference room, and saw a promotional sign for an upcoming speech. It hit me like a bolt of lightning. I can start HERE!! I can start with all the places I had visited for the series. After all, that was the adventure and the audience. I casually asked Samantha if what I was thinking about was the type of programs in which this and other historical museums, libraries and locations were interested. She said, depending on what I put together and the angle I took, yes. I had no idea that I would be speaking in the same room in which I saw that first promotional sign in less than a year.

I returned to Abilene on Saturday May 10, 2014, to speak at a Mother's Day weekend tea and luncheon. This was only my second public appearance as THE FIRST LADIES MAN, and it was great to be back with my friends in Abilene. I sat with a wonderful group of ladies—all of whom were surprised to see this unusual vessel of First Ladies knowledge and information— we ate cute little finger sandwiches and drank flower flavored teas together. My mom and my Nana would've been over the moon about this. Thank you, Abilene. I look forward to coming back.

GETTYSBURG, PENNSYLVANIA

The Eisenhowers retired to their farm in Gettysburg, Pennsylvania when President Eisenhower left office in 1961. They lived there together quietly, and entertained as often as they could. They mostly enjoyed time there with each other and their family. Dwight D. Eisenhower died from congestive heart failure at Walter Reed Hospital outside of Washington, DC on March 28, 1969. Mamie lived on the farm and continued without her husband there for another ten years. C-SPAN traveled to the Eisenhower farm for the live Mamie show—just like we did for the Wilson show in DC. However, I was out on another location assignment at the time. I will make a trip to the Eisenhower farm as my travels continue, and expand this portion of the chapter accordingly. Stay tuned.

BOONE, IOWA

Mamie Eisenhower was born on November 14, 1896, in her family's home at 718 Carroll Street in Boone, Iowa. I spoke to the Director there about a visit during my travels for the series. Between the government shut down and the other trips and other First Ladies, and given the huge number of artifacts and resources available to us in Abilene, a trip to Boone didn't materialize. I will make this trip happen, as well, and report on my findings and adventures in future editions of this book. I promise.

SUMMARY

Mamie Eisenhower was the quintessential military wife. She was raised in privilege and affluence, but chose a life of love and adventure over family wealth and status. It seemed to work out just fine for her and Ike. Anywhere they lived or called home, she threw the best parties, and always dressed the part. Even if she didn't know it at the time, she was getting the perfect training for what would be her biggest public role. First Lady. Mrs. Eisenhower was not without loss and tragedy. The loss of their son Doud was devastating and almost cost the Eisenhowers their marriage. They were able to rebuild it and move on. The most successful of these couples were the ones who could move on after devastating life events—like the loss of a child. Mamie was unique. The country loved her, and she was very popular on the international stage, too. She had her own style and way of doing things. Some people might have been just fine to stay in bed three days a week at the request of their doctor. Not Mamie. She made her heart condition work for her, and even ritzed it up a bit with a beautiful collection of house coats. She honestly did have the largest collection of clothes of any First Lady I saw during my travels. She was a confident woman who helped bring philanthropy into a new era. She was always there for her husband and family and put them ahead of herself. Before this project, I didn't know much more about Mamie Eisenhower than her name. It was great to add another one of these amazing women to my growing archive of expanded knowledge. Like George Washington, her husband was a great military genius, but it's hard to imagine him being as successful and influential without his wife. She was definitely unusual for her time.

I have been to Abilene, Kansas exactly two times in my life. Both times I ate at Ike's Place Bar & Grill. Both times I got the Mamie Wrap. I guess you can now call it "my usual," and file it under "if it ain't broke don't fix it." It's a Ranch chicken wrap with bacon. I get it with lettuce and tomato and a side of waffle fries. The bar is always lively, the crowd is forever friendly, and I've never had a bad time or a bad meal there.

PHOTO ALBUM

All Photos By Andrew Och

Pulled pork bbq nachos in Daleville, VA on the way to the birthplace of Edith Wilson

Dinner with Kate Fuller (Billy Carter's daughter) at the Buffalo Café

Posing with Ike and Mamie at the Eisenhower Library in Abilene, KS

Blueberry ice cream pie at the Big Meadows Lodge at the Shenandoah National Park where the Hoover's Rapadan Camp is located

Beautiful day at the George H.W. Bush Presidential Library and Museum in College Station, TX

A rainy day in Plains, GA on the Carter family farm with Ranger Steve Theus

Enjoying the newest presidential library in the system, George W. Bush in Dallas, TX

Clinton cutouts in the Clinton House Museum in Fayetteville, AR

Carter cutouts in the antique mall in Historic Plains, GA

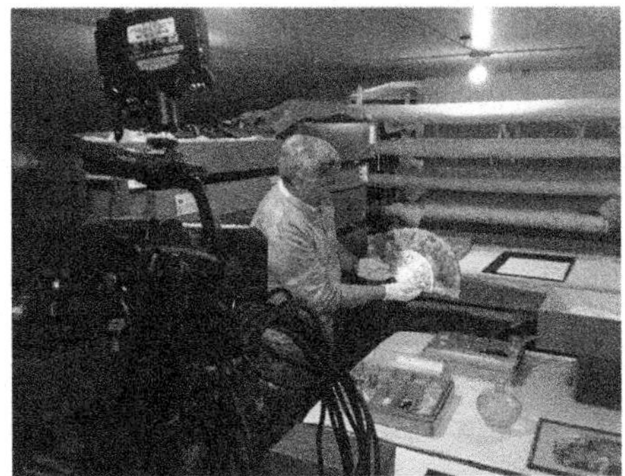
Grace Coolidge's fan at the Calvin Coolidge Historic Site in Plymouth Notch, VT with Director Bill Jenney

Looking at some of Grace Coolidge's purses at the Coolidge Museum in the Forbes Library in Northampton, MA with Julie Bartlett

The Coolidge family graves in Plymouth Notch, VT

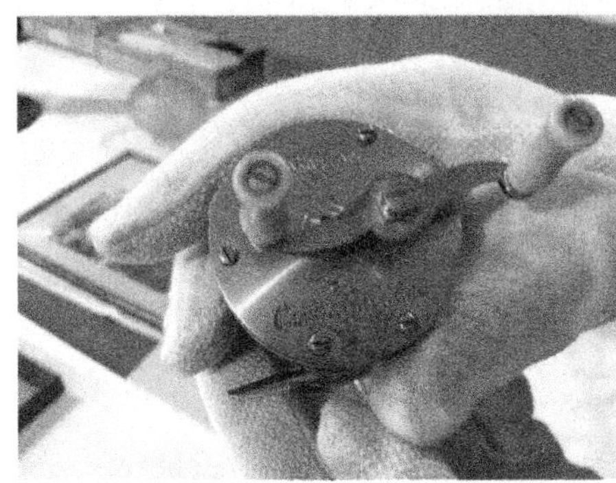
President Coolidge's fly fishing reel at the Coolidge Historic Site in Plymouth Notch, VT

The First Ladies Man at Coolidge family graves in Plymouth Notch, VT

The Edith Bowling Wilson birth room in Wythville, VA with Association President Farron Smith

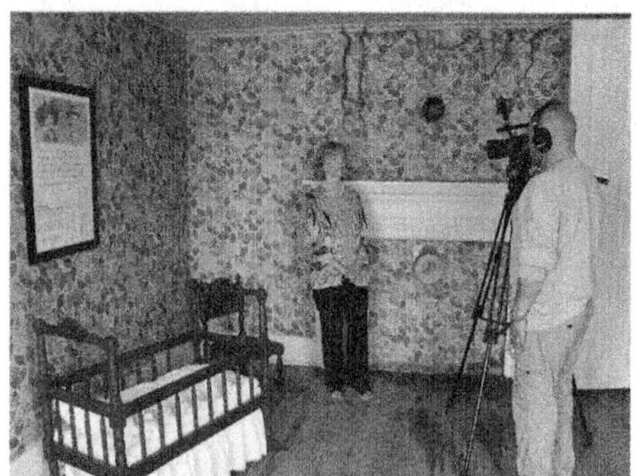

Lunch break for The First Ladies Mam while editing the Edith Roosevelt location pieces in Washington, DC C-SPAN offices

Filming Eleanor Roosevelt location pieces at her Val-Kill home in Hyde Park, NY with Ranger Victor Pennes

The First Ladies Man becomes a Razorback grid iron sensation in Fayetteville, AR

The Gerald R. Ford Presidential Museum in Grand Rapids, MI

The First Ladies Man editing Ellen Wilson location pieces at his home in Shady Side, MD

Boarding plane at Fort Benning Airport in Georgia after location shoot for Rosalynn Carter in Plains, GA

C-SPAN control room final wrap show
Washington, DC

The late, great musician Greg Allman in the Atlanta airport the day before Thanksgiving 2013, flying home to Maryland

Former First Lady Hillary Clinton speaking at Georgetown University in Washington, DC

The Lou Henry Hoover House at Stanford University in Palo Alto, CA

Grace Coolidge dresses in Northampton with Julie Bartlett

In Boston, MA with Jaqueline Kennedy's dresses at the John F. Kennedy Presidential Library and Museum

The First Ladies Man filming at the Lou Henry Hoover house at Stanford University in Palo Alto, CA

The First Ladies Man at the top of the Hoover Tower at Standard University

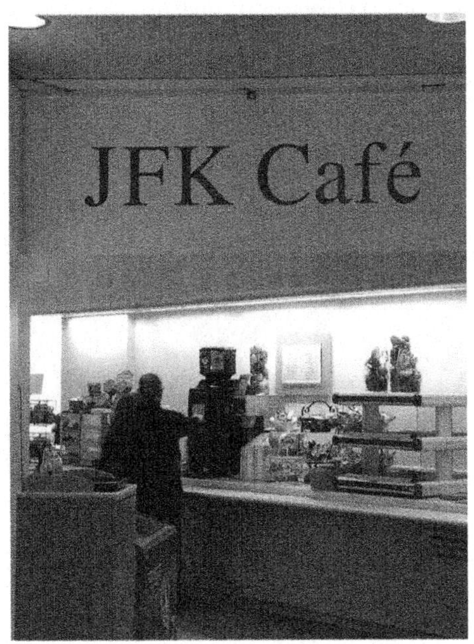

The JFK Café at the John F. Kennedy Presidential Library and Museum

Field office in Palo Alto, CA

The First Ladies Man on the LBJ ranch in Stonewall, TX. I call this picture "ranch hand."

The JFK Presidential Library and Museum in Boston, MA

The Johnson Suite at the LBJ Presidential Library and Museum

Lobster caesar created by The First Ladies Man in Boston, MA while filming Jackie Kennedy location pieces on the night the Red Sox won the 2013 World Series

First Ladies Man is interviewed by reporter Litsa Pappas about Lou Hoover and visiting Rapidan Camp in the Shenandoah Valley in Virginia

First Ladies Man engages in intense negotiations in the China Room at the Nixon Library and Museum in Yorba Linda, CA

The First Ladies Man stops to ponder the fate of the free world in the Oval Office photo op at the Carter Historic Site in Plains, GA

First Ladies Man at Nixon graves in Yorba Linda, CA

First Ladies Man with Lou Hoover cutout in West Branch, IA at the Hoover Presidential Library and Museum

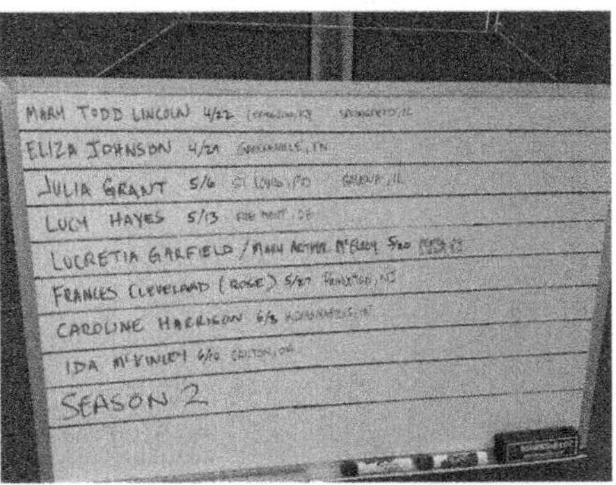

Dry erase board at The First Ladies Man's desk in the C-SPAN offices in Washington, DC. This board kept track of travels and locations for both seasons of "First Ladies: Influence and Image."

The Roosevelt's Pine Knot cabin in Keene, VA

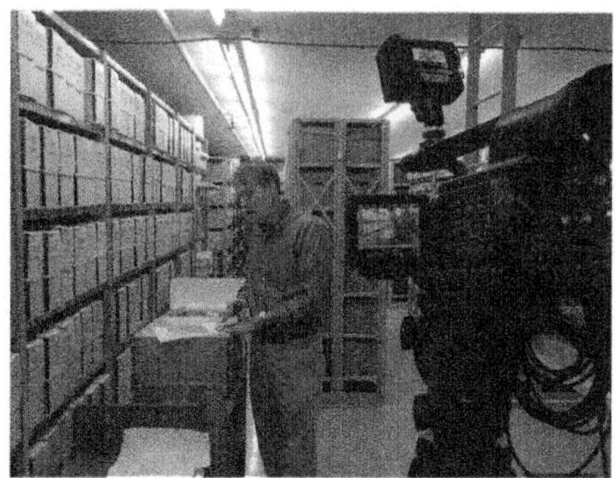

Reading the love letters of Woodrow and Ellen Wilson in the Samuel Mudd Library at Princeton University with Barksdale Maynard

The First Ladies Man with Paula Baezley at the Roosevelt Pine Knot cabin in Keene, VA

Boarding another plane for another destination along the nationwide trail of The First Ladies of the United States of America

Interviewing Paula Baezley at the Roosevelt Pine Knot cabin in Keene, VA

The family church of the Coolidge's in Plymouth Notch, VT

Calvin Coolidge's boyhood home in Plymouth Notch, VT

The Princeton Regional Airport terminal with gear waiting for a cab

Filming in the stacks of the Samuel Mudd Library at Princeton University with Barksdale Maynard

The gardens of the Prospect House designed by Ellen Wilson in Princeton University with Barksdale Maynard

The First Ladies Man in the gardens of the Prospect House designed by Ellen Wilson in Princeton University with Barksdale Maynard

The First Ladies Man with the Gipper in Simi, CA

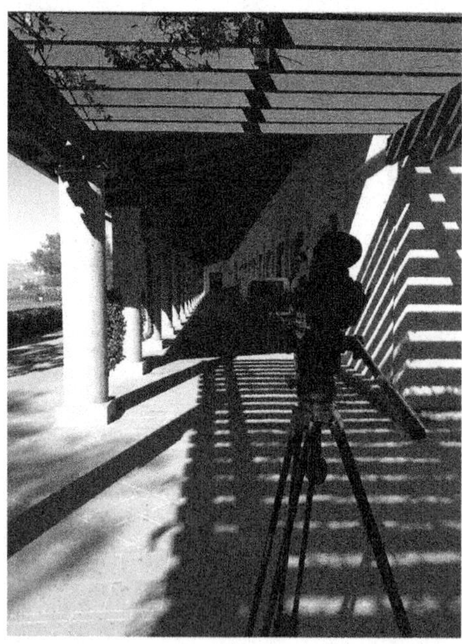

Filming exterior shots at the beautiful Ronald Reagan Presidential Library and Museum in Simi, CA

The First Ladies Man at the Reagan grave site in Simi, CA

Horse saddles in the Reagan Museum in Simi, CA

Picking up rental car in NYC and heading out to Oyster Bay, Long Island to film Edith Roosevelt pieces at Sagamore Hill

Fueling the research

The First Ladies Man gets briefed in the situation room (actual room from the White House before Bush 43 remodel) at the Reagan Library and Museum in Simi, CA

The First Ladies Man at Sagamore Hill the home of Theodore and Edith Roosevelt

Season 2 kickoff panel at the Newseum in Washington, DC with Cokie Roberts, Richard Norton Smith and others broadcast live on C-SPAN

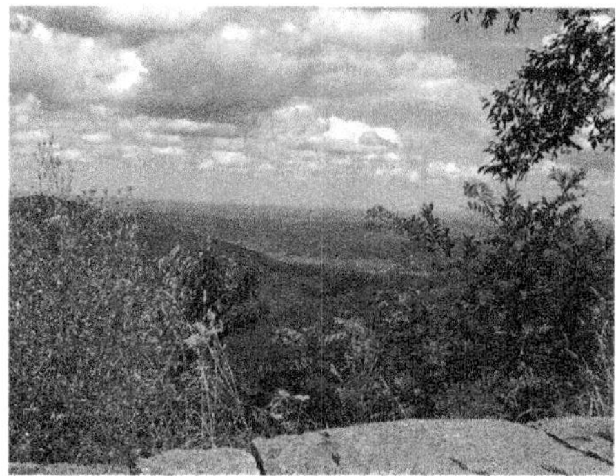

Skyline Drive outside of Shenandoah National Park for location shoot at Rapidan Camp for Lou Hoover episode

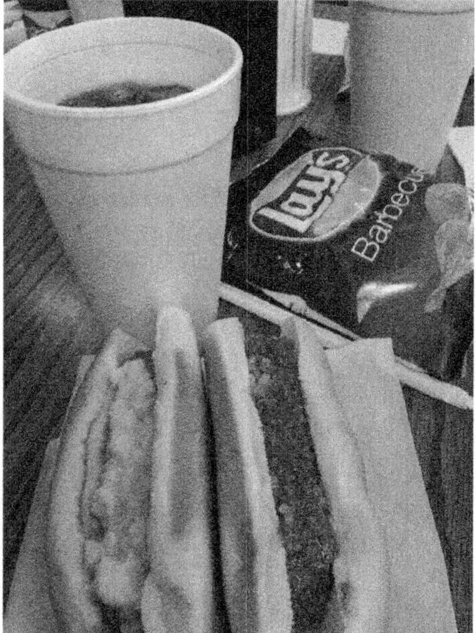

World famous Skeeter Dogs in Wytheville, VA

Skeeter's in Wytheville, VA birthplace of Edith Wilson

On the porch of the Truman House in Independence, MO. The First Ladies Man and his camera were the first allowed inside in over 30 years. The Truman's grandson (Clifton Truman Daniel far right)

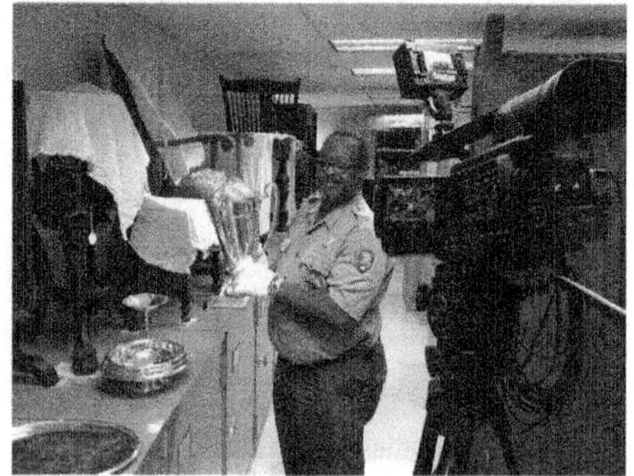

The Taft's sterling silver collection from their 25th wedding anniversary celebration in the White House with Superintendent Ray Henderson at the Taft historical site in Cincinnati, OH

The First Ladies Man on one of the many visits to the National Museum of American History to view artifacts on display and in the back storage rooms

The church in Independence where Harry met Bess Truman when they were 5 years old

The First Ladies Man enjoys a nice lunch with the Roosevelt's in Hyde Park, NY

On the road again - Amtrak North out of the BWI Station

The First Ladies Man with "Warren Harding" at the Harding home in Marion, OH

The Wilson house in Washington, DC

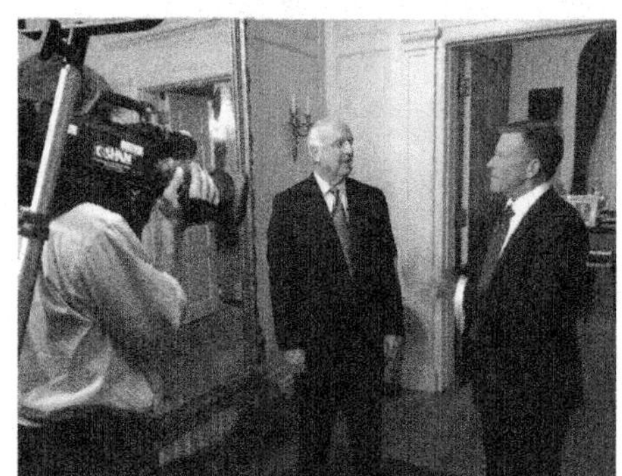

C-SPAN's Peter Slen interviews Director, Bob Enholm during the live Ellen and Edith Wilson Show

C-SPAN's Peter Slen interviews Edith Wilson's grandnephew Cary Fuller during the live Ellen and Edith Wilson Show

The First Ladies Man with Jacqueline Kennedy's personal secretary and author, Mary Gallagher

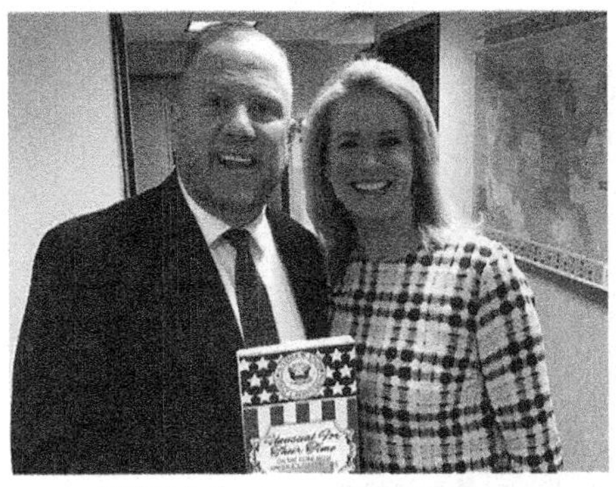

BBC interview with Katty Kay

That thing when your high school friend Debby gets you a giant Jackie paper doll

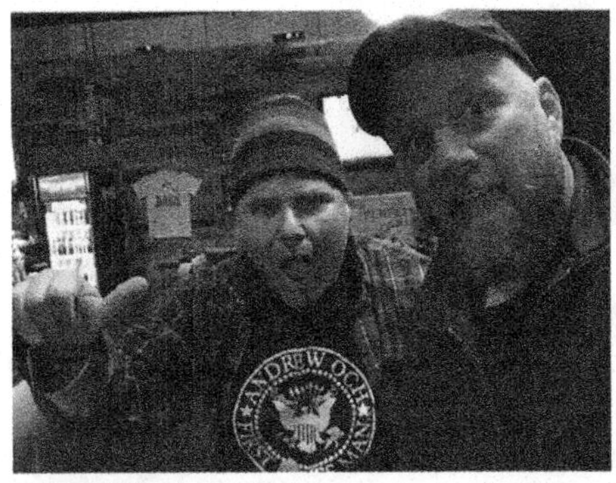

First Ladies Man with fraternity brother Steve West in Maine night before a speech. Thank, Steve!

Paul and Shirley Thacker are doing a lot in Chillicothe to preserve the legacy of First Lady Lucy Hayes

First Ladies Man at Dolley Madison birthplace in Greensboro, NC

First Ladies Man with Professor Jay L. Gordon (friend since elementary school) in Youngstown, OH

First Ladies Man's niece repping her uncle

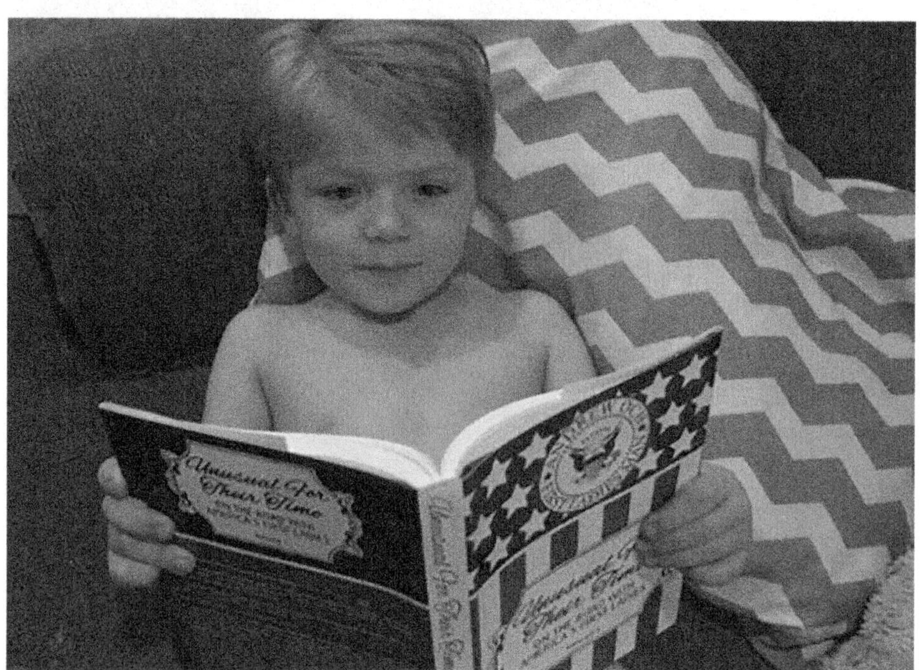

First Ladies Man's nephew doing some light reading

First Ladies Man with Miss Maryland 2016

First Ladies Man speaking at Maine State Library in Augusta, ME

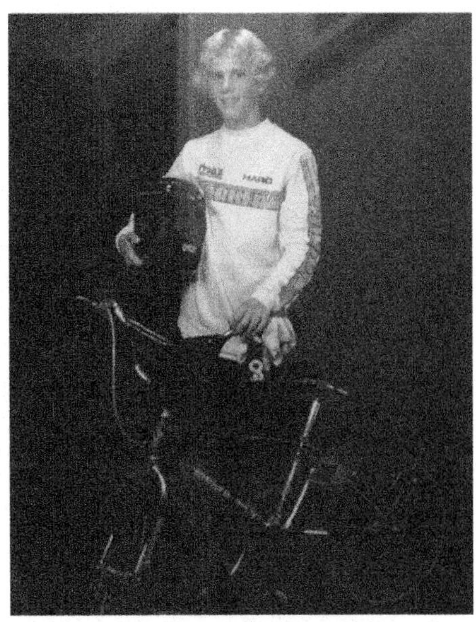

The First Ladies Man Olan Mills portrait with Toker BMX bike circa 1983.

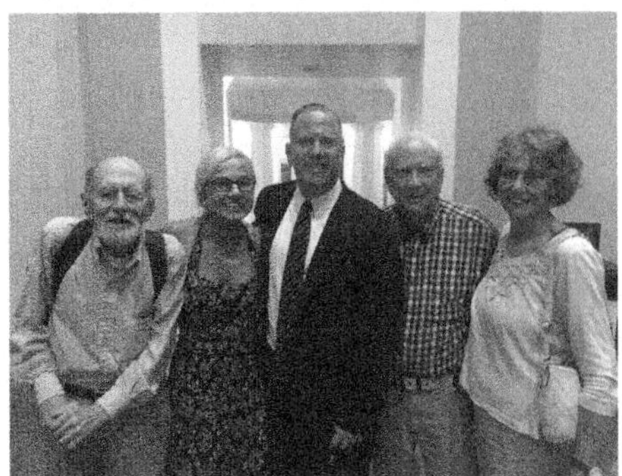

First Ladies Man with family after Smithsonian speech (l to r) Uncle Tiff, Heather, FLM, Dad and Marjie

First Ladies Man with his first lady, Heather out on F ST NW Washington, DC

CHAPTER ELEVEN

Jacqueline Kennedy

Boston, Massachusetts

Jacqueline Kennedy was born Jacqueline Lee Bouvier on July 28, 1929 in Southampton, New York. Her parents were John Vernon Bouvier III and Janet Norton Lee Bouvier. Jacqueline and John F. Kennedy were married on September 12, 1953. They had four children together. Jacqueline Kennedy died in New York, New York on May 19, 1994 at the age of 64.

BOSTON, MASSACHUSETTS

I arrived in Boston the day the Red Sox beat the St. Louis Cardinals (6-1) in game six to win the 2013 World Series. I watched (or more so listened) to the game from a very nice restaurant near my hotel. The restaurant staff cheered in front of the TV at the bar.

The place was quiet, as I'm sure most folks were at the game, watching at home or in a sports bar. I thought about how happy Grace Coolidge would have been to see her favorite team win the series. It was also the day before Halloween, and I pictured the streets being filled the next night with little ghouls, goblins and—no doubt—baseball players. At the John F. Kennedy Presidential Library and Museum, they feverishly prepared for the 50th anniversary of JFK's assassination (Nov 22, 1963). Because of the government shut down and all the anniversary preparations and events, it was a struggle to get my schedule and the museum's schedule to line up. This gave my colleagues back in DC a little over a week to get this new footage together for the live show on Jacqueline Kennedy which would be airing on Monday Nov 11th. It was a quick turnaround, for sure, but hadn't most of them been for one reason or another?! I also needed to think about getting to Texas for Lady Bird Johnson. I wanted to combine my Texas trip to visit the Barbara Bush and Laura Bush sites while I was there. November was going to be a busy month.

Jacqueline Kennedy was another Martha Washington…Mary Lincoln…or Eleanor Roosevelt. What hadn't been said or written about her already? How many television shows and movies were out there about the Kennedys? It was my job to find something new, and exciting. Or perhaps build on something that was already known, but approach it with a new angle. The artifacts, items and papers at the museum and in the library helped. They always did, and it was an amazing collection. But, Jacqueline Kennedy was different. She was (and still is) one of the most recognized faces and First Ladies in history. There was also the fact that, because of advances in technology, all of these modern First Ladies had more information and material already out there than many of the previous ones. We saw and heard them in their own words and voices in multiple forms of media. My location pieces were still a valuable asset to the shows and the series. They were far from unnecessary or obsolete, in fact quite the contrary. My work still uncovered new items, rare artifacts and untold stories. I still created the feeling of discovery and took the shows outside of the studio. My work just had to be more carefully thought out to get the best bang for our buck.

One of the first things I noticed when I walked into the building was the JFK Café. I thought to myself, "I guess it's too cheeky to call it the JFKafe?" and had a little chuckle while I waited for my host. Exhibit Specialist, James Wagner, was my partner in crime for this location, and he was very well-suited for the job. He knew everything there was to know about the exhibits, and showed me a wonderful collection of things not out on public display. He was also a natural on camera which always made for a more productive day together.

The C-SPAN series was called "First Ladies: Influence and Image," and Mrs. Kennedy was the embodiment of both—influence and image. She was on the cover of so many magazines, and the influence for so many different styles both nationally and internationally. The influence and impact she had on her husband's career, campaign and administration was remarkable. She was intelligent, attractive and understood her role in the world very well. When asked about her at my public speeches and events I say, "She got the role she was born to play." I don't think there can be too much said about her style and fashion. The museum had excellent examples of this both in the exhibits and behind the scenes.

The work and storage areas in these museums were always fascinating to me. For one thing, I felt privileged to be in them. Not only was it a backstage pass to these amazing collections, but it was where the work was done to preserve, restore, maintain and promote our history. This was not access I took lightly. From the very beginning of this project I felt (and continue to feel) a great responsibility to bring these artifacts and this access to the public through my camera and my stories. This particular work area at the Kennedy Museum had something unique. They had a larger than life black and white photograph from a recent art show and exhibit that celebrated Mrs. Kennedy's style and fashion. James had surrounded the picture with racks of dresses and outfits, and had others in their storage boxes on the tables along the walls of the room for me to see.

Author's Note – It's Official

James Wagner was kind enough to take my picture standing among the dresses in front of the giant black and white photograph of Jacqueline Kennedy. I have used this image as a profile picture on social media many times. The first time I used it was in November 2013 when I first referred to myself publicly as the FIRST LADIES MAN. I simply captioned the picture, "I am the First Ladies Man." It was (and still is) very effective.

Back in the storage room on one of the many racks, was the first dress she wore as First Lady on January 20, 1961, at her husband's inauguration. It was an interesting "greige" (grey and beige) colored dress and matching coat made by Oleg Cassini. The overcoat had two large buttons down the front and an oversized pocket on each side. The dress was simple in design and she looked great next to JFK in his tuxedo and top hat. She accented the dress with a brooch by Tiffany that JFK had given her to celebrate the birth of their son, John, Jr. The pin was two pine cones in a gold setting covered with rubies. At the top of the pine cones, two gold leaves and a twig finished off the piece. Like her outfit, the brooch was gorgeous, but understated and elegant. It was visible on her dress during the luncheon that followed the swearing in ceremony. This was one of Mrs. Kennedy's strengths when it came to fashion. She knew how to stand out without looking like she was trying too hard, while complementing the person she was with (usually her husband) or situation perfectly. She appeared to be able to do this effortlessly. The outfit included a matching pillbox hat made by Halston. It was a large round gray felt hat that would have typically been worn on top of the head. Mrs. Kennedy took a slightly different approach and had it pushed back on her head. This showed off her hairstyle and face a bit more, and started a new trend with how women wore their hats.

Jacqueline Kennedy was the only First Lady to win an Emmy Award. She received the award for her televised tour of the White House after her renovations were completed. The special aired on CBS on February 14, 1962. Charles Collingwood conducted the interview and accompanied Mrs. Kennedy on the tour, and it later aired on NBC and ABC, as well. The museum has her Emmy on display with a retro 1960's TV and living room set up. The TV showed footage from the televised tour. Back in storage—in the typical heavy cardboard gray box lined with tissue paper—was the dress she had worn in the televised White House tour. Even though television, and thus the broadcast, was black and white, Mrs. Kennedy's dress was a deep, vivid red. I was told the color always surprised visitors at the museum when the dress was on display, because everyone remembers the original black and white footage. The dress was made by Chez Ninon and was a very typical style for Mrs. Kennedy. It was wool and had a waist-length jacket that was worn over the shin-length skirt. The jacket had two large buttons on the left-hand side, and the skirt had a matching button on the left hip. It was an outfit that could easily be worn today. Mrs. Kennedy knew the program would air on Valentine's Day, and dressed accordingly. She always knew the right outfit for the occasion.

Another time when it was very appropriate for Mrs. Kennedy to wear red, was on her and JFK's first state visit to Canada in May 1961. She knew they would be greeted and accompanied by the Royal Canadian Mounted Police. Not only did Mrs. Kennedy want to match and complement the people she was with, she wanted to pay tribute and respect to the countries she visited. This made her wildly popular on the international stage. She made people feel comfortable with her at first sight. The bright red Pierre Cardin dress suit she wore on the trip was on display in the museum along with a picture of President and Mrs. Kennedy and details from the trip. The outfit consisted of a jacket with five buttons down the center of the front topped off with a wide folded down collar that went all the way around the neck. It had three quarter length sleeves that she finished off with long white gloves. The long wool skirt was smooth with a flat front. She added a matching red pillbox hat—worn to the back of her head—and a gold pin on the upper left shoulder of her jacket. The whole package was put together very nicely, and she fit right in next to the Canadian police.

Also, out on display in the museum was a light green, pistachio colored overcoat and hat Mrs. Kennedy wore in December 1961, during their trip to

Bogota, Columbia and throughout South America. She had a wide brim matching hat, to go with the coat, perched towards the back of her head—of course—framing her face nicely. The coat was double breasted with buttons that ran from top to bottom of the knee-length garment. It had a thin belt that tied just above the waist. A great picture of her and her husband standing at the top of the stairs to Air Force One emphasized what a good looking and well-matched couple they were. JFK wore a simple gray suit with a thin black tie. It was clear to see these two knew the power of a good appearance.

One case in the museum featured several gifts of state—mostly jewelry—Mrs. Kennedy received when she was First Lady. There were some exquisite gold pieces she was given on her trip through South America. One piece was a beautiful wide necklace with many bands of colors. It was accompanied by a matching set of bracelets. She was very tuned in when it came to items like this. She made sure to wear them to exactly the right event while she was in the country and presence of the leader or dignitary who gave her the gift. This was a simple thing to do that showed her appreciation, and further endeared her to her hosts and the people of whatever country she was visiting. When she did these little things, they were noticed and written about in the local papers. It was a subtle and respectful way for her to acknowledge the gift publicly.

Not only was Mrs. Kennedy aware of what her clothes said to the public and the people of the countries she visited, but her words were important, too. She took great care and attention to speak in the native languages of the foreign countries she visited whenever she could. Jacqueline Kennedy was a huge asset to her husband and the United States when it came to foreign relations. She came along at a good time for it, as well. Technology, fashion, style and pop culture seemed to be on her side. She was attractive, talented and intelligent. She was what Hollywood calls a "triple threat." She also wasn't afraid to use her resources and abilities in the public eye. She had no problem being the ambassador to America and her husband's administration. It was a role that came along with being First Lady. Some women accepted it. Some women ignored it. Some women ran from it. Jacqueline Kennedy, and those like her, gracefully gravitated towards it.

From an early age, Jacqueline displayed creativity and intelligence. She often wrote poems and stories for family members as Christmas or birthday gifts.

The museum had poems she wrote when she was as young as ten years old. One poem was called "Windy Song" and started like this:

> "Oh, I've a boat that's swift and trim
> The fastest in the bay
> I'll race her against that boat of yours
> And we'll sail on a windy day"

Another piece on display right next to it from about the same time was called "Sea Joy" opened like this:

> "When I go down by the sandy shore
> I can think of nothing I want more
> Than to live by the booming blue sea
> As the seagulls flutter round about me"

These were very well written and inspired pieces of work for a ten-year-old. I knew young Jacqueline Lee Bouvier was privileged, and there was a great deal to be said for that kind of wealth and upbringing. However, she had to have had a great deal of natural born intelligence, sensitivity, creativity, not to mention awareness of the world around her, to have written pieces like this at such a young age. Clearly these were not the works of an average ten-year-old—privileged or otherwise. She had a natural talent for writing, and her creativity did not stop there. She was also a talented illustrator. She drew objects and people around the poems to help tell and accent the stories.

"Sea Joy" had starfish, and seaweed that framed the verses. At the top of the poem above the title, she drew a young girl standing at the edge of frothy waves with her hands on her hips as she looked up at the sky and out towards the sea."Windy Song" had matching anchors with ropes, sea birds and boats that lined the outer edges of the paper. All her drawings were carefully done and fit the pieces very well. It was clear that a lot of thought and detail went into each one. I found it remarkable she thought to illustrate her pieces to get the most out of them and add to their impact.

Later, in high school, at Miss Porter's School in Connecticut, she wrote an essay called "Be Kind and Do Your Share." The first sentence of which was:

"Be kind and do your share, that's all there is to it."

The essay was all about doing your part to make the world a better place. She wrote about humanitarian efforts, and the importance of helping others. She continued about what a simple kind word did for another person, and how easy it was to make someone's day by being kind or saying something nice. It was a very forward thinking essay, and spoke to how she was raised to always think of other people and those less fortunate. It was an overall theme of leaving the world a better place than she found it, which continued throughout her life and her years in the White House.

When Jacqueline graduated from George Washington University in Washington, DC in 1951, her parents sent her and her sister, Lee—who had just graduated from high school—to Europe for a vacation. The two girls showed their gratitude by giving their parents a scrapbook of their adventures. They titled the scrapbook "One Special Summer," and it included photographs, hand-written stories, and illustrations from their trip. The illustrations were primarily of Jackie and her sister, and were all done by Jackie. She drew herself and her sister in various outfits and places, often with a camera in their hands. They even drew wooden frames and corner tacks around the photographs. It was cute. It was creative. And it, once again, showed Jackie's talent and imagination. I pictured Jacqueline and her sister as they sat of the floor of their bedroom with the photos, the glue and the tape, the pens and pencils, and perhaps notes from their trip, all laid out on the floor next to the blank pages of their scrapbook.

And there it was, again. The moment when a larger than life First Lady—one I had known, heard, read and learned so much about—became real. She was no longer Jacqueline Kennedy or Jackie O. She wasn't a picture in a magazine or a history book. She wasn't the woman in the White House tour documentary or the wife holding her husband on that awful day in Dallas. She was a person. A girl. A human. She and her sister were making a photo album scrapbook. I knew girls who did this. I still know girls who do this. I've helped my Godson's sisters and my niece do similar school projects. I had done similar projects as a kid. This was real. I looked at the scrapbook with a personal appreciation and real world experiences. I'm glad I saw this so early in the work day. It helped bring a figure like Jacqueline into perspective and I could apply that to the rest of my work there, as I got to know her better.

In Fall 1950, while she was at George Washington University, Jacqueline entered the Prix De Paris composition writing contest sponsored by Vogue magazine. The museum had her winning composition and her hand-written application. Her handwriting on the application was beautiful. It was always nice to see a First Lady's handwriting. It was one more thing that made a personal connection for me.

Historical Note - Letter By Letter

Elizabeth Monroe had the nicest and most beautiful handwriting of any First Lady. Mrs. Monroe was tiny – about 4'11" – and so was her handwriting, but it was perfect. She wrote in cursive. It was straight and legible and each letter was formed with remarkable detail, accuracy and clarity. There is only one letter known to exist in the world in her hand. It is in the Monroe collection at the University of Mary Washington. At the request of Elizabeth, James Monroe burned all her letters and writings when she died—which was typical for the time. Daniel Preston showed me the letter when I visited the James Monroe Museum in Fredericksburg, Virginia [see Volume One]. If I had permission to duplicate and patent her handwriting and sell it as a font, I'd be a millionaire.

The entrance application for the writing contest appeared to be fairly standard. She filled out her name and the name of her school along with all other pertinent information that was requested. It also had interesting questions like, "who are three people in history you wish you had known?" Her response was, French poet, Charles Baudelaire, author, Oscar Wilde, and Russian ballet impresario, Serge Diaghlieff. The essay itself was called "Self Portrait," and it revealed a very interesting perspective she had of herself. It was self-deprecating for a girl who later would be considered one of the most well-known and beautiful women of her time. Or maybe she just didn't take herself too seriously, and could make fun of herself. Either way, she wrote:

> "As to physical appearance, I am tall, 5'7," with brown hair, a square face, and eyes so unfortunately wide apart that it takes three weeks to get a pair of glasses with a bridge wide enough to fit over my nose."

She also wrote in the essay that she did not have a "sensational figure." After I read this, I couldn't help thinking about some of Mary Lincoln's teenage journals, diaries and letters. Mary's teenage writings lead people to think she had a miserable childhood and hated her stepmother. Now, this could have been true. Or, it could have been a teenage girl being just that. A teenage girl. Or a combination of the two. Walt Disney built a magic kingdom and made a fortune telling fairy tales about evil stepmothers. Mrs. Kennedy was a little hard on herself. Her opinion of her physical appearance and body image wasn't ideal. What young girl or woman hasn't thought or said these things about herself? And I don't limit that to women. What teenager—boy or girl—hasn't been at odds with their parents and thought they needed a makeover? My point here was that we shouldn't judge a teenage Mary Todd any differently than a teenage Jacqueline Bouvier. We need to take youthful writings with a grain of salt and an ounce of understanding.

These early writings were a wonderful way to get to know the young Jacqueline Bouvier. She loved writing, and knew the power of words. She continued to write throughout her life and she later become a very successful editor who worked with several authors in New York City.

One of Jacqueline's first jobs out of college was with the Washington Times Herald. She was the "Inquiring Camera Girl." Armed with a notepad, pen and camera, she roamed the streets of DC, interviewing people and creating newspaper columns. On display in the museum was her camera and an article from the early 1950's, along with numerous pictures of Jacqueline as the Inquiring Camera Girl. The specific article they featured had interviews with Vice President Richard M. Nixon, and a Massachusetts Senator named John F. Kennedy. The prophetic nature of the article was not lost on me.

Her intelligence and love of literature came in handy when her husband was running for President, too. They often appeared together at campaign events. One event they specifically highlighted in an exhibit at the museum was from June 1959 at a campaign dinner in Washington state. JFK was speaking at the dinner and the museum had a copy of his typed and prepared remarks. It was not uncommon for him to make changes and handwritten notes on the pages of his speeches. JFK wrote a note on the speech that said, "give me the last lines from Ulysses…come my friends," the Alfred, Lord Tennyson poem. Without hesitation Mrs. Kennedy jotted down the lines he was looking for from memory and JFK closed the speech to a great reaction from the crowd. Mrs. Kennedy was another woman who made her husband look good even before he got into the White House.

After James was done showing me around the public and behind the scenes areas, exhibits and artifacts inside the museum, I packed up my gear and went outside to get shots of the building and area around the facility. The facility is right on the shores of the Boston Harborwalk, on the Charles River at Columbia Point. It was a chilly, overcast day, but the building and its surroundings made for some excellent B-roll. JFK's 25-foot sailboat the Victura (Latin for "about to conquer") was outside the museum on the grounds facing the water. It got some really nice footage that was unlike any other museums I had, or would visit, and it was a pleasant and peaceful way to end my day of work.

Author's Note – The First Lady's First Lady

After I completed this chapter, and had moved on to Lady Bird, my friend, Terry, called me and invited me to meet Mary Barelli Gallagher. Mrs. Gallagher started working for JFK right out of high school in Massachusetts in 1952. She later became Jacqueline Kennedy's personal secretary during the campaign in 1960. She remained in that position until 1964, when Mrs. Kennedy and her children moved to New York City from their Georgetown home. Mrs. Gallagher knew Mrs. Kennedy like no other person. She took careful notes and kept a journal of their time and work together. Originally, it was just going to be a file for her two boys to have when they grew older. Mary wanter her children to have a greater understanding of what their mother did for a living. However, after JFK was assassinated and Jackie became even more of a public interest, Mrs. Gallagher saw a need to tell the real story of Jacqueline Kennedy from her perspective, as someone who knew and worked closely with her. Her exact quote was to show the world "THE HUMAN BEING BENEATH THE GODDESS FIGURE THE WORLD MADE HER INTO." Those words ran through me like a shot! It's EXACTLY how I feel about all these women, and what I'm trying to do here with my books and speeches. It's what The First Ladies Man and "Unusual for Their Time" is all about. Mary Gallagher published "My Life with Jacqueline Kennedy" in 1969. She just turned 90 in March 2017, and she is still going strong, and making public speeches and signing books [see picture section in middle]. Her stories are heartfelt, informative an interesting. To give you some perspective, in the infamous picture of LBJ getting sworn-in on Air Force One, after JFK was assassinated, Mary Gallagher can barely be seen just over Jackie's right shoulder. She told the story of that day and spoke specifically about that picture and the trip back to Washington, DC. I am getting chills just writing about it now. I not only urge, but implore you to read her book. Remarkable.

Historical Note – It's A Secret (Service)

I met a woman named Jane Ready at a speech I gave at the Mary Surratt House in Clinton, MD [Lincoln assassination conspirator] in September 2017. This book [Volume Two] had already been submitted to my publisher, Tactical 16. However, after I met Jane, I felt compelled to add this side note. Jane is another in a long list of interesting people I have had the good fortune of meeting at my live events and in my travels who have direct contacts and amazing stories that involve Presidents and First Ladies. Jane's father was John "Jack" Ready, special agent with the U. S. Secret Service. He died on February 24, 2014. On March 29, 2104 he was eulogized in a Washington Post Obituary article "Jack Ready, Secret Service Agent Who Guarded Kennedy in Dallas, Dies at 86." Jane said she was looking forward to Volume Two, especially the Jacqueline Kennedy chapter [for obvious reasons]. When I told her about my experience at the LBJ Ranch, and that I had learned more about the Kennedy assassination there than in Boston, she told me about her father. President Kennedy was Ready's first assignment as a new agent [he went on to serve under Johnson, and Nixon]. He was pictured right in front of

President Kennedy during his speech before the motorcade through Dallas. As Jane and I discussed her father and the events of the day, I told her about meeting Mary Barelli Gallagher, and how Mary could be seen standing next to Mrs. Kennedy on the plane as LBJ was sworn in. Jane told me her father was not in that picture, because he was in the back of the plane with the casket and Kennedy's body for the flight home. The Washington Post article reveals that Ready manned the hallway at Parkland Memorial Hospital where Mrs. Kennedy awaited the news from the doctors about her husband. It was incredible to add another piece to the puzzle of this story, and meet someone with this kind of connection to Mrs. Kennedy. It's people like Jane Ready and her father who make my job that much more interesting.

SUMMARY

Jacqueline Bouvier Kennedy was the first First Lady born in the 20th Century (thank you, Harriet). I rarely include her in my prepared remarks or speeches. I do this intentionally, because during the question and answer portion at the end, someone always asks, "why didn't you say anything about Jackie?" My answer is always, "because I knew someone in the audience would!" Typically, I tell people about women they don't know or wouldn't think to ask about. Mary Lincoln, Eleanor Roosevelt, Jacqueline Kennedy and Hillary Clinton always come up in the questions, answers and comments at the end. I've said many times before, this part of my live events is one of my favorite parts of getting out and speaking to folks. Jaqueline Kennedy is who many people think of when they hear the term "First Lady." She defined and expanded the role of First Lady as much as the role defined and expanded her.

She had "style for miles" and knew just the right thing to say at nearly every event she attended. She supported her husband in every aspect of his professional and political life. She made him a better man, and a more popular President. However, many First Ladies did this for their husbands. She came along at a time in the world when technology was on her side. She knew how to use the press and the television to her advantage. Americans—and people in general—like and are attracted to good looking people. That's just the way it is.

Either consciously or subconsciously, young, pretty, outgoing First Ladies start off on a more popular note than older, sickly and private ones. We saw this with Dolley Madison, Julia Tyler, Frances Cleveland, Grace Coolidge and many others. When there are young children in the mix, that popularity and interest only increases. Add intelligence and a worldly grace to the whole package, and you have all the elements of an exceptional First Lady. Mrs. Kennedy seemed to have it all. She was a national and international hit. These were the things I already knew. These were the things most people already knew. I wanted to know Mrs. Kennedy before she was Mrs. Kennedy.

In Boston, I found she had been a young, intelligent, creative woman. She wrote inspired poems when she was ten-years-old, she had a charitable and giving nature in high school and her unique perspective carried her into college and beyond. Her cute and interesting drawings went along with her stories, poems and scrapbooks, and added to the effectiveness and charm of each project. She was much more than a pretty face. She was a pretty face that didn't even think of herself as particularly pretty. She had an insight and an awareness of the world around her I found refreshing. She got a job right out of college that promoted and enhanced her natural strengths and talents. In these regards, she was very unusual for her time. She stood out. In a good way.

There is no doubt, Jacqueline Bouvier was born into a life of privilege. She had opportunities and resources most of us never had or knew. She could have rested on her laurels and her parent's wealth, but she didn't. She furthered her education, developed her skills and grew into a modern woman that could and would step out of traditional female roles and norms to help create a new world around her. She built on what other First Ladies had accomplished before her, and took the role to new levels and an ever-bigger presence in the public eye.

Fortunately, or unfortunately, Mrs. Kennedy got the role she was born to play. With that role, came a lot of attention and tragedy. She was known for the things she was known for because of her husband, yet, many times this seemed to lead to the bad things in her life, as well. During the interview with James, in front of the scrapbook detailing the summer travels in Europe with her sister, he said something I was already thinking. It was interesting to think about what Mrs. Kennedy (Miss Bouvier) would have become if she had not met and married JFK. She clearly could've pursued a writing or journalism career. She had a knack for fashion and public speaking. She was comfortable on camera. I really feel with her curious and adventurous nature and her natural abilities and talents the sky was the limit (her wealth and social connections didn't hurt her chances either). She chose JFK, and he chose to run for President. And I'm not suggesting she didn't know what was going on or went into the White House kicking and screaming. I am merely observing, that knowing what I know now about her, it is interesting to play "what if." It is also sad to think about the decisions she did make that—while presenting her with so much opportunity—caused her so much heartache, tragedy and loss.

A lot has been written about the less than ideal things in Mrs. Kennedy's life—affairs, assassinations, death, and other tragedies she endured. We know most—if not all—of them. Naturally, I came across much of it in my travels and research. However, I did not include any of that in this book. Why? Jacqueline Kennedy was not the first First Lady to deal with these incidents. I left these stories out of my books. When it comes to my speeches, projects and writing I want to celebrate, learn and teach the things about these women that show their selfless efforts to make the world around them a better place—outside of political interests. I know lines cross and it's not a black and white world in which we live when it comes to this. I also know that these women are not always saints or innocent of any wrong doing. Far from it. However, I am not interested in sensationalizing them. I am interested in quite the opposite. They are people. They are human. My intent and interest in them is to show them as the women who were unusual for their time.

Travelogue Food Tip

The first night when I got into Boston, I wanted to get a decent sit-down dinner. I knew the World Series was being played. I knew the Red Sox could lock it up and win over the Cardinals that night. I didn't want to eat my typical wings and a Caesar in a sports bar. I didn't want to get a pizza delivered, and I didn't want fast food. I was in Boston, I had been doing a lot of traveling and work, and I wanted a good meal. I wanted a lobster [LOBSTAH]. I asked the guy at the front desk of my modest hotel where I could go close by to accomplish this goal. He told me to go to Skipjacks. He did not steer me in the wrong direction.

Like I mentioned at the beginning of this chapter, I was alone in the restaurant—as far as customers were concerned. The staff was watching the game in the bar. The waiter that drew the short straw and got me as a table was very polite and gave great service. I told him, up front, I was low maintenance and didn't want him to miss the game.

My order was simple. I ordered a Caesar salad and a lobster. The lobster came with a side item, and I chose French fries. The waiter brought my salad first, even though I told him he could bring everything at once. The lobster and fries came, and he asked me if everything was okay with the salad, as I hadn't touched it. I told him everything was fine, and I had a plan [I always have a plan]. He looked at me a little strangely, but scurried off back to the bar to watch the game.

I picked my entire lobster clean of the meat setting it on my bread plate.

Author's Note - Peel & Eat

I also peel all my shrimp before I eat them.

I then dipped all the lobster meat in my butter, and put it on top of my Caesar salad. I squeezed fresh lemon over the top of the lobster that was now resting on the romaine lettuce [I had thought ahead, and asked for extra lemons…I usually do with seafood… always a plan]. I had created the world's first lobster Caesar. Well, in my world it was the first. I don't know about the rest of the world—and it was fantastic. Then I began to think, "what if I put this in a wrap or on a roll, and got a food truck?" That'll have to wait until after the First Ladies Man, but it'll happen someday. The waiter came back one more time to check on me, and nodded his approval at my creation. It was a great first night in Boston.

CHAPTER TWELVE

Lady Bird Johnson

Stonewall, Texas – Austin, Texas

Lady Bird Johnson was born Claudia Alta Taylor on December 22, 1912 in Karnack, Texas. Her parents were Thomas Jefferson Taylor and Minnie Lee Pattillo Taylor. Lady Bird and Lyndon B. Johnson were married on November 17, 1934. They had two children together. Lady Bird Johnson died in Austin, Texas on July 11, 2007 at the age of 94.

Texas is a big state. Let me rephrase that. Texas is a HUGE state. My first time to Austin, TX was the beginning of a long trek across the second largest state in the Union, and there would be a lot of driving, and I loved every mile of it. I landed and drove to my hotel in the rain. I got settled in and drove to the local Harley dealer to get myself a t-shirt. I was in town the night before my appointments and got to enjoy a little Austin nightlife before the work started. Another bonus to my Austin trip was I got to see my old buddy, Bircho. We hadn't seen each other in nearly 15 years—since our days of music and carousing in and around Washington, DC in the mid 90's. To say Bircho is connected is an understatement. He knew every cook/chef in every BBQ place and every bartender and doorman in every juke joint! We had a time! More on that later. I couldn't stay out and howl at the moon too late, because I had an early morning and a long drive through the hill country out to the LBJ Ranch in Stonewall, Texas.

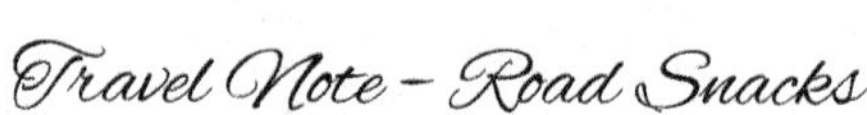

One of my staples during this whole adventure, which continues to be my favorite breakfast on the road is...a banana, two packages of cashews (one salted/one honey roasted), a monster size regular Slim Jim, and a Coke Zero. I guess you can call it... the breakfast of THIS champion. The drive out to the LBJ Ranch was fueled by this odd assortment, thanks to a gas station/convenience store on the way out of Austin.

STONEWALL, TEXAS

I had set up my visit to the LBJ Ranch with the superintendent, Russ Whitlock. Park Ranger Dave Schafer was going to show me around and do the on-camera interviews. Both men were very nice and there to greet me when I arrived. We had planned to do all the recording and official tour when the last public group finished later that afternoon. This left me the first half of the day to explore the vast property on my own and get B-roll. The ranch is over 1,500 acres, so I had a lot of ground to cover. This was a reverse order from what I was used to, but not completely out of the ordinary

The first place I visited was the Johnson graves. The family cemetery was nestled in under a large shade tree with a low, modest stone wall and gate. Both President and Mrs. Johnson are buried there, along with other family members. It was a quiet and pleasantly understated. Mrs. Johnson outlived her husband by almost 34 years, and lived a very active life on her own, right up to the end. It made complete sense that this became the Johnson's final resting place. It was one of their favorite places to be. They called it the Texas White House and they visited there 74 times during Johnson's Presidency. Mrs. Johnson loved to show off her home, and the Texas Hill Country. Lady Bird did a televised tour of their Texas home. She didn't win an Emmy for it, and it's not as well remembered as Mrs. Kennedy's White House tour from 1962. However, it did give the country a look into their President and his family's life at the ranch. I would get an even closer look into the home after I finished my self-guided tour of the grounds.

The Johnsons raised and kept Texas longhorn cattle on the ranch, and a large herd still exists to this day. I could get very close to a small group of them that was hanging out in the shade near the graves. The skies were big, open and clear the day I was there, and the fresh air was a nice change from stuffy airplanes and hotel rooms. Don't get me wrong, I love the musty smell of museums and history, but I could also get used to ranch life. It was easy to see why the Johnsons enjoyed this place and spent so much time here. I didn't have any formal guidance or knowledge of the ranch, so I just continued to work my way around the property. I explored the outbuildings, sheds, fields, garages and kept my camera rolling the entire time. This would be a personal record for most beautiful and most unnecessary (and unused) B-roll shot during the entire series.

One of the most unique features of the ranch was the runway and mini airport. I could park near the 6,300-foot asphalt strip, get out and walk up and down to get footage. The runway was not rated for the weight and size of Air Force One, however, the plane the Johnsons used when he was Vice President could land there. The runway would bring the Johnsons within 200 yards of their house, and records show Mrs. Johnson having been on the plane as First Lady numerous times. The 13 passenger Lockheed JetStar (tail number 612490) was often referred to as Air Force One Half, and it was one of the planes that brought them to the ranch during their time in the White House. Another lucky happenstance in the timing of the C-SPAN series and my travels was that about three years prior, in August 2010, this plane made its final flight here, and was now a permanent exhibit at the Ranch.

After a good long trek around the ranch I parked at the visitor center near the main residence, and took a walk around there. The two-story house was a big, but modest ranch style structure (naturally) with nice landscaping and an in-ground pool. Tall bushes and big shade trees provided a nice amount of privacy. The clapboard exterior was painted white with olive green shutters. There were comfortable sitting porches that surrounded most of the building. I could get nice footage of the home President and Mrs. Johnson were so proud of. The Johnsons hosted many personal and professional friends and family there. There were many dinner parties, luncheons and an annual BBQ was still held every year in the fall. There was another grove of trees below the house on the side with the pool, and there was no shortage of open fields and grass around the house. Large picture windows all around gave anyone inside a wide, and relatively unobstructed, view of the beautiful panoramic countryside.

Once the last tour group had departed, my gear and I were invited into the house. The first room I was shown was the kitchen. It had two parts. One side looked like a typical kitchen you might find in any home in America, the other side looked like more of an industrial or commercial kitchen. In the more commercial side stood a large, silver refrigerator with two huge doors. On top of that refrigerator was a small black and white television set. This was the TV where the ranch staff learned they were now working for the new President of the United States of America on November 22, 1963. The Johnsons and the Kennedys were both in Dallas that day. The Johnsons were hosting a picnic for the Kennedys at the ranch the next day. Some of the Secret Service were on the ranch preparing for the event, and securing the property. Part of this process shut down the phone lines for a period of time. One of the agents out on the grounds got word of the shooting in Dallas, and was trying to notify the people at the house, but couldn't get through on the phone. He ran up to the house and came into the kitchen, only to find the staff standing in the kitchen staring in awe at the little black and white television and crying. They had been watching the horrific events unfold live. In a split-second Vice President Lyndon B. Johnson became President Johnson, and Mrs. Johnson became First Lady.

Author's Note – Where Were You When Kennedy Was Shot?

Anyone who was alive and old enough when President Kennedy was assassinated knows exactly where they were when they heard the news. I was not alive when President Kennedy was shot. However, now I strangely feel as though I was. I have been to the grassy knoll, and the book depository. I (like nearly every other human on planet Earth) have seen archival footage from Dallas. I have seen movies about the assassination of President Kennedy. I have read books…both non-fiction and fiction…about the day and the events leading up to and after the shooting. This coupled with the fact that I have now stood in the kitchen and seen the television where the Johnsons' ranch staff watched the tragedy live, has put almost too many images in my head. I already knew so much about the day and the events, and I now have a physical place and real items to associate with the actual day. It's very odd. I'm getting goosebumps just writing this side note.

The main ranch house was built in the 1890's, and while the Johnsons made many changes, modernizations and upgrades, the living room was always called the "heart of the home." In this room, Lady Bird showcased her copper collection. There were teapots, urns, plates, bottles, lamps and various other objects displayed on shelves that surrounded the ceiling perimeter of the room, on tables, and in bookcases. Mrs. Johnson also had a lovely arrowhead collection displayed in a western-style shadowbox. She paid her daughters, Lynda and Lucy, one dollar for every arrowhead they found on the property. At one point, Mrs. Johnson wondered why Lynda was finding so many more than her sister. It turns out, she was paying her friends fifty cents per arrowhead which increased her numbers over her sister's dramatically. Mrs. Johnson thought it was important to highlight the history of the region in their home.

There were three TVs, side by side at the end of the room, and a large, red couch up against the wall to the left. Various other pale green chairs and a coffee table completed the room. There was still plenty of room on the light carpeted floor for the children and their friends to sit, play and watch TV. President Johnson liked to have all three news programs on (ABC, CBS and NBC) at the same time. Mrs. Johnson's favorite show was Gunsmoke. There were many old pictures of the family and their friends spending time and enjoying each other's company here. A large fireplace added to the coziness of the room. Minus the three TVs and all the copper, this room reminded me very much of my living room growing up. It was easy to imagine (even without the historical photographs) the Johnsons in this room. I only have one brother (Jeremy), and he and I spent time with my parents and our friends in our living room, and suddenly the Johnsons didn't feel like the President and First Lady, and I didn't feel like I was on a ranch. It just felt like home.

Park Ranger Schafer was really good at the whole "walk and talk" style of filming, and he knew the house as if it were his own. Our walking tour through the house was complete, and efficient. I could and would stay as long as it took (as I had at other locations), but the hour was getting late and I had a long drive back to Austin ahead of me. The den was next. This was typically where the Johnsons would have a cocktail hour or coffee and dessert after a meal (depending on the number of guests). They entertained Mexican President, Diaz Ordaz, Israeli Prime Minister, Levi Eshcolt, German Chancellor, Ludwig Erhard, and many others in this room during his Presidency. The room had a "clubhouse" vibe, with pictures of wildlife and game on the walls. Wild turkeys and other birds seemed to be a favorite. There were pillows on the long peach colored couch that shared the bird theme. The walls were covered with red flowered wallpaper, and yellow drapes (Lady Bird Johnson had a love of flowers that was almost unrivaled, which we will get to later in the chapter). Brass lamps were on the various end tables and it, too, was a very cozy room. This room also featured one of the large picture windows I mentioned earlier.

The dining room was one of Lady Bird's favorite rooms in the ranch house. The wallpaper was hand-picked by Mrs. Johnson, and showed outdoor country scenes with farm houses along streams with bridges and trees under open skies with big, puffy clouds. It reminded me of a modern version of the wallpaper Mrs. Jackson picked out for her Hermitage home in Nashville, Tennessee. This room had the largest window in the house, and the scenery outside was the real version of what depicted on the wallpaper. While each room was different, they all represented the Texas Hill Country Mrs. Johnson adored. The same china that was shown in Mrs. Johnson's 1968 television special was out on the large wooden dining room table. It was a blue based Mayan setting with red and yellow accents. I found it extremely unique and charming. The President's chair at the head of the table had a high back and was covered with a brown and white cowhide. It was very "Texas" and very "LBJ"—in a good way. There was a phone built into the dining room table next to the chair. The President loved to "work the telephones." Mrs. Johnson was not fond of her husband taking or making calls during meals.

As I mentioned earlier, Mrs. Johnson far outlived her husband. This gave her plenty of time to spend at the ranch, and consider her and her husband's legacy there. Her bedroom was a place she carefully designed and prepared for this purpose. Schafer shared a personal story in this room about the day he met Mrs. Johnson. He was working at the Truman Historic Site in Independence, Missouri, when Mrs. Johnson came in for a tour. She was very interested in history and how the Trumans' story was told there (I wonder what she thought when she saw Mrs. Truman's portrait over the fireplace, given the story Clifton Truman Daniel had told me about the painting). She knew that her home would be a national historic site one day. She took great care in arranging her bedroom with all this in mind. This room was part of the 1967 remodeling. She specified to the designers and architects she wanted this to be her "forever room."

Like most of the house, its primary color was white. She had modest, comfortable furnishings that one might expect in a bedroom. Her bed, nightstands and lamps were nice, but nothing special, and very functional. There was a comfortable sitting area with a few chairs and a love seat in front of a fireplace. She also had a small desk in her bedroom that faced a group of windows to the east. This was where she wrote personal letters and other correspondence at night. There were built-in bookcases that stretched along one entire wall. These held all kinds of items and memorabilia from her long and productive life. She displayed a few settings of her White House china and a number of bird sculptures on these shelves. President Johnson gave his wife a camera as a wedding present, and Mrs. Johnson become very interested in photography and home movies. There are many hours of Johnson family home movies because of her interest. Her cameras and pictures were kept on these shelves, as well. One very special item on these shelves (all behind protective clear plastic) was her tape recorder. Every night, while she and her husband were in the White House, she would record her daily observations. These recordings became the basis for the book, "A White House Diary." This followed in the footsteps of Julia Grant's memoirs, Caroline Harrison's diaries, and many other First Ladies who would come after Mrs. Johnson. A copy of Mrs. Johnson's book was on her desk. She also had numerous books about Texas, travel, politics and other interests there in her bedroom.

An interesting feature to have had access to in this room, was her walk-in closet. This gave yet another personal view into Mrs. Johnson's life. She had many examples of her colorful formal wear and business attire. There were casual ranch and gardening clothes, numerous hats, many racks of shoes and boots and stacks of blankets. One of the hats in the closet was one I had seen in a number of photographs. It was her straw hat with blue bonnets painted on it (Mrs. Johnson's love for wildflowers is something we'll get into in the next section at the LBJ Presidential Library and Museum…I haven't forgotten about it and I won't leave it out…I can't!). Beyond her walk-in closet was her private bathroom. Again, the walls were papered with a floral print. The most memorable thing in her bathroom were all the pictures of family that hung on every wall. I have never seen a bathroom decorated with photographs like this. It was a little odd, but cool. Somehow it worked. It told me a lot about what really mattered most in her life, and how she chose to decorate one of the most private places in her whole house.

Production Note - In The Still Of The Night

It was dark by the time we started filming in the LBJ Ranch house. This is the only filming I did at night during the entire series. I was worried that viewers would be able to tell it was night time in the final videos that aired in the Lady Bird show, so I avoided showing windows. I can still tell today when I watch the videos or show them during a speech or presentation. There's just something different about the lighting.

After we finished our work in the house, I packed up my gear, and headed down the road. Schafer's warning about wildlife on the road was warranted. I saw several creatures as I drove out through the night which included the giant long horns, raccoons, deer and many other sets of glimmering eyes in the night. I hadn't eaten since my convenience store breakfast, so I stopped at a little roadside joint with a crowded parking lot. The food wasn't bad, but the crowd wasn't there for the food. They were there for the karaoke...UNFORTUNATELY.

AUSTIN, TEXAS

The next day started off early with another fantastic—behind the scenes—tour of the LBJ Presidential Library and Museum in Austin at the University of Texas. Mrs. Johnson graduated from the university (with honors) in 1933, earning a Bachelor of Arts degree in History. She got a second degree in Journalism in 1934. The library was dedicated in May 1971. President Johnson died on January 22, 1973 from a heart attack. Mrs. Johnson lived to be 94. She died on July 11, 2007. It's almost fitting the library became a main office for Mrs. Johnson, and the work she continued after the White House and her husband's death would be conducted there. Lyndon Banes Johnson's political career was largely funded and successful due to Mrs. Johnson's financial help, moral support and sage political advice. She had turned a modest family inheritance into a successful communications company with a few radio stations and other holdings in Texas. This money and success helped her husband climb the political ladder all the way to the White House. The Johnsons are one of the best examples of a modern-day President who may not have been President had he not met and married the woman he did.

Before this trip, I did not know Presidents and First Ladies had apartment residences in most of the newer presidential libraries and museums. Mark Upgrove was the Director at LBJ, and gave me a private tour of the residence. It was on the top floor and even had a hidden door in a wall that I would've walked past a thousand times and not known it was there (even after I was shown where it was). I set up my gear and prepared to shoot the VIP tour of the residence. It was a large and open apartment with a dining room, bathroom, powder room, living room, kitchen and two bedrooms. Just outside of the living room was a large balcony that overlooked the university football stadium. It also had a great view of the city of Austin and the Texas capital building. The view was not accidental. The apartment location was hand-picked by the Johnsons. The whole place looked like a set from a late 60's/early 70's TV show (like Mary Tyler Moore or The Brady Bunch). Mrs. Johnson obviously favored yellow, because much of the furniture and artwork was that color or had bits of that color in it. She also had a lot of reds. These bright colors really popped with the white base of the decor. There was a large dining room table with bookshelves and artwork. Nice lamps and western art were on the coffee and end tables. It was very easy to imagine Lady Bird entertaining and meeting with people here. It was sophisticated and much more cosmopolitan than the ranch house. It was another side of Mrs. Johnson. The politician. The business woman. The work horse. I was also shown a photo album with pictures from events here in the residence. Many First Ladies visited here, including her Texas "sisters," Barbara and Laura Bush. This place allowed me to see the business side of Lady Bird. It still had an element of Texas, but the whole place had a formal evening feel to it, even in the day time.

Okay…FLOWERS!! One of her projects and her passions was the Highway Beautification Act, and she said, "where flowers bloom, so does hope." She had wildflowers planted along roads and highways across the United States. Many of the areas she established still bloom. The Lady Bird Johnson Grove is a section along the George Washington Parkway in Washington, DC, and a direct result of her beautification project. I saw her love of flowers in all her homes, and the country saw it in her White House china. Some of the china was on display in the bookcases in her ranch bedroom, but those were behind protective plastic panels. Here at the library, they brought out some of Lady Bird's fine flowered china for me to examine. We had to use white museum gloves to hold it, of course. It was remarkable to hold the plates and feel the weight, as if I were actually going to eat a meal off it in the Johnsons' White House. I got to study the intricate floral patterns and gold leaf accents. This was among some of the most tasteful and celebrated china in the whole White House collection. It was a very thoughtful way to represent a cause with an image that is so recognizably hers. The Johnson china has been used many times by other administrations since the Johnsons moved out of the White House.

Travel Note – Flowers For Lady Bird

There wasn't time in the schedule to visit The Lady Bird Wildflower Center while I was in Austin. The center is a public botanical garden, research and education facility. They have walking trails and many exhibits featuring sculptures and other visual arts. It is a place I will visit in the future.

My next stop in the museum was to see Mrs. Johnson's private office. This was an open exhibit in the museum, but I was going to get special access to the area and exhibit from Mrs. Johnson's former Social Secretary. Marjorie Morton worked with Lady Bird Johnson from 1976 through 1990. She was the perfect person to show me exactly what went on in the office, because she was there. They had three people working in Mrs. Johnson's office during this time. One person kept her calendar, another came from the White House as her press secretary, and helped her work on speeches, and Marjorie handled everything else. Mrs. Johnson kept a very busy post-White House schedule. She kept up with her Highway Beautification Act, and was very involved with the University of Texas in Austin, National Geographic, the Smithsonian, one of the local banks and many other organizations. She conducted much of her daily work from her office here.

The office (now behind a chest-high glass enclosure) had white cabinets and shelves behind a reddish-orange desk. A love seat that matched the desk was on the left wall with tan pillows. Family pictures, awards and other mementos covered the white painted walls and shelves behind her desk. There was a small swiveling arm chair in front of the desk for whomever happened to be working or visiting with Mrs. Johnson at the time. A small television was also on top of the low cabinets that lined the wall behind her desk. White lamps with white shades were on each of the end tables. A large, white area rug was under the desk and covered much of the dark, hard wood floor. A large picture window provided the same fantastic view of Austin that she enjoyed from the apartment on the same top floor.

Her work day would start at 9am when she came in carrying her straw bags full of papers, documents and files. She would say she felt like a "little burro," because of the heavy load in each hand like saddle bags. She kept a very orderly desk with her pens, paper weights, letter opener, her calendar and her daybook. Details and files for things she was working on, or trips she was going to take were kept on her desk. When she completed that work, it would go on the floor to her right. She kept large envelopes on her couch with titles and dates on them so she could work on the individual projects and keep everything together. If she wasn't currently working on something, the envelopes and files remained closed. She would stay and work at the office most of the day and make her phone calls from her desk. This was her routine Monday through Friday, unless she was having guests, then she would head out to the ranch a few days early to get the house ready. She would spend time in each of the rooms to make sure everything—from the lights and water to the televisions—was in working order. Each trip out to the ranch also involved a stop at the store to pick up magazines and books that were guest-specific. She was very thoughtful and meticulous in hosting guests at the ranch. She wanted to make sure everyone felt at home and had everything they needed no matter how particular or unusual. That went for clothes, food, reading material and activities. Each Friday when there were no guests staying with her at the ranch (which she called home) she was ready to leave by three thirty in the afternoon. If there was nothing left to do, she would clap her hands, rub them together and say, "tell the Secret Service I'm ready to go." The staff would pack up her two big straw satchels and she would head out to the ranch for the weekend.

Mrs. Morton shared one particular story with me about a guest off-camera. It seems one gentleman who visited from an East Coast city really wanted the Texas cowboy experience. So, Mrs. Johnson got him a new wardrobe complete with Wrangler blue jeans, a checkered shirt, boots, a big ole cowboy hat and a bandana. She served up hearty breakfasts and had a horse for him to ride the range. The man had the time of his life. Morton went on to tell me how much she learned from working with Mrs. Johnson about entertaining and making people feel at home and welcome. She told me all this with a slight tear in her eyes. It was a very heartfelt and touching experience, and a wonderful way to get to know Lady Bird Johnson from someone with whom she worked so closely, and spent so much time.

Production Note – Slip Sliding Away

Marjorie was a firecracker, and a lot of fun to work with and interview. I'm sure she and Lady Bird had a great time working together, and it showed in the way she spoke so fondly of her former boss. We definitely clicked and had a fun afternoon together, which is why I'm sure she won't mind me telling you this little story. I mentioned the private office was behind a small glass wall and had wood floors. Well, Marjorie had on slick soled flats that turned into virtual ice skates when she hit the inside of the glass wall on the wood floor. She tried walking around, but I almost lost her a couple of times. It was so slippery I had to walk her over onto the rug and tell her to stay there behind the desk for the entire interview. We even tried having her hold onto the glass wall for one take, but that just looked like she was on an actual ice rink holding onto the wall for dear life. She was a great sport about it, and sincerely grateful for my arm and support. I kept her from having an embarrassing fall in a crowded museum. I hope she reads this and gets a kick out the memory and our afternoon together. She was great.

SUMMARY

Lady Bird Johnson reminded me just how much these men…these Presidents…needed their wives to succeed, and to become the men they became. They truly were the greater women behind great men. This is not to take anything away from President Johnson or his achievements and abilities. It is only to remind people (as it reminded me) just how influential these women were, and what a big part of the story they were. In most cases, they were not just the women who married a man who became President of the United States. They were the women, the wives, that helped them become the President of the United States.

Mrs. Johnson was smart, educated and politically tuned in. She helped her husband with speeches and policy. She critiqued his public appearances and performances, told him to speak more clearly or to stand up straighter, and he always responded with a "yes, ma'am." As a public speaker who is frequently on television or in front of large crowds and audiences, I have my own "Lady Bird" looking out for me. We even jokingly call her a "Quirky Bird"—very affectionately…of course. I, too, always respond with a "yes, ma'am" or a "thank you, ma'am" when she gives me pointers, proofreads my work, critiques a TV interview or helps me pick out ties.

Many First Ladies long outlived their Presidential husbands. Dolley Madison, Julia Tyler, Sarah Polk, Mary Lincoln, Lucretia Garfield, Frances Cleveland, Ida McKinley, Edith Roosevelt, Edith Wilson, Helen Taft, Florence Harding, Eleanor Roosevelt, Bess Truman, Mamie Eisenhower, Jacqueline Kennedy, Nancy Reagan all come to mind. Mrs. Johnson is right up there at the top of the list with all the First Ladies who not only preserved and protected their husband's legacy, but also continued her work for the greater good of humanity. She worked tirelessly almost to her dying day, and the age of 94, to promote and advance the causes and organizations in which she believed. She was a woman who was unusual for her time.

I also always feel a special bond and closeness to the women with whom I have spoken to their friends or colleagues, relatives or staff. It's important to connect in those ways every chance I get. It's a combination of being in the place, holding the item and being told the story by the person that was there when it happened. It's better than anything you can read in any book. It's real life. It's intense. And it's unforgettable.

Travelogue Food Tip

If you've read Volume One, and now Volume Two...you know I'm serious about my BBQ. I've been through the Carolinas, Tennessee, Virginia, Kansas City and now Texas. I've traveled around enough in other projects and adventures to know that nearly every Irish pub I've ever eaten in has fantastic pulled pork BBQ and slaw (why? I don't know, but they do...trust me on this one). I know that the best baby back ribs I've ever eaten are served at Adam's Ribs in Maryland (of all places). HOWEVER. The best overall BBQ meal and experience happened for me at Sam's BBQ in East Austin. The whole meal from start to finish was so incredible that I will relate it from beginning to end right now...

I was hanging out with my buddy (and fellow drummer) Bircho, who hails from Little Rock, Arkansas. We were shooting pool at a bar when I told him I was hungry for some BBQ. Bircho said, "let me make a call!" Next thing I know, Bircho is on the phone with some guy named Sam asking him if he has anything left this late. Well, Sam said to bring me over and he'd take care of me. Bircho then asked me if I was still adventurous, and didn't mind sketchier parts of town. I laughed and said, "the sketchier the better sometimes, as long as the food is good!" We both laughed and hopped into my rental... just like old times...almost. Remember, I had an early morning and work to do, so I wasn't up for anything too much wilder than a late dinner and a Coke Zero.

We got to Sam's and it looked like a house. Only on the front of the house it said in big red letters, "YOU DON'T NEED TEETH TO EAT MY BEEF!" I knew we'd hit pay dirt. We parked the car, walked past all the fellas hanging out in Barcaloungers under the carport in the driveway (said our "hellos and howdys"), and went in to see Sam. It was like we had walked into his living room. Only in Sam's living room, there was a meat counter, steam trays, a cash register and a soda machine.

Bircho introduced me as his "TV and music buddy from Washington, DC." Sam said "hello" and got right down to business. He said, "You like beef?" and handed me a piece of beef..."you like chicken?" and handed me a piece of chicken..."you like pork?"

and handed me a piece of pork…"sausage?" and handed me a piece of sausage. All of it was fantastic, and they weren't small samples. He nodded. I nodded. I asked if I could get coleslaw. He said, "potato salad." I nodded again, and Sam loaded up my meal in a Styrofoam to-go box, slapped a couple slices of white bread on top, set it on the counter, studied it for about 10 seconds and said, "eleven bucks…soda's in the machine and beer's across the street." I gave him $11, and stuffed a few more dollars into his tip jar and got myself a soda.

Sam proceeds to show us the way to the screened in porch laid out with picnic tables and a TV. Another large group was eating in the corner and Sam said, "New friends from Sweden…" the grouped responded 'SWITZERLAND!!" Sam said, "Same thing! Meet my new friend, Andy, from New York City!" I said, "Washington, DC" Sam said, "Same thing!" And we all sat and ate while Sam showed me a photo album of a movie he was in with Al Pacino called "Manglehron." I had never seen or heard of the movie (I didn't tell Sam that). But, I will tell you this…again…it was the some of the BEST DAGGONE BBQ I HAVE EVER TASTED!! Now, I have all my original teeth, but I did not need them to eat this meal. I have since recommended this to anyone traveling to or through Austin. Let's just say this. . . Sam doesn't have a comment or suggestion box on the premises. Doesn't need one.

CHAPTER THIRTEEN

Pat Nixon

Yorba Linda, California

Pat Nixon was born Thelma Catherine Ryan on March 16, 1912 in Ely, Nevada. Her parents were William Ryan and Katherine Halberstadt Bender Ryan. Pat and Richard Nixon were married on June 21, 1940. They had two children together. Pat Nixon died in Yorba Linda, California on June 22, 1993 at the age of 81.

Pat Nixon was a quiet, but active First Lady. She was the quintessential politician's wife. She was dedicated and supportive to all her husband's endeavors. She was the most traveled First Lady (and Second Lady as wife of the Vice President) until Hillary Clinton surpassed her many years later. She was not terribly outspoken, but she was very effective and productive. Her travels accomplished great things for American diplomacy and her husband's administration.

She did all of this while striking and maintaining a refined and distinguished image.

In June 1970, there was a horrible earthquake in Peru. Mrs. Nixon decided on her own that she should gather supplies and travel with some U. S. forces to help the citizens of Peru on behalf of the American people. The supplies and troops were all loaded onto planes and Mrs. Nixon went with them to Peru. She went into very remote, dangerous and damaged areas with the President of Peru. All of this was done without many cameras or photo-ops. This was the kind of quiet, effective and productive woman First Lady Pat Nixon was. Like those before her—Lucy Hayes, Harriet Lane, Eleanor Roosevelt— she did it because it was the right thing to do.

Even though her father worked in a silver mine when she was born, Thelma Catherine Ryan was not born with a silver spoon in her mouth. In fact, her father was working in Utah the day she was born. She was born on March 16th, but he didn't find out until the next day…St. Patrick's Day. The Ryans were an Irish family, and she was nicknamed "Pat." Her father always thought of her as his little St. Patty's Day baby. When mining didn't work out, William Ryan moved his family to California, and took up farming. Pat's mother died when she 14, and her father died three years later. Pat took care of her two younger brothers and the failing family farm for most her teen and young adult years. She graduated from high school in 1929 and went on to attend Fullerton Community College and University of Southern California. She worked her way through college as the manager of a pharmacy, a typist, a retail clerk, Hollywood extra, radiographer, and other odd jobs. She was the first First Lady to get a post-graduate degree. She earned a Master's Degree in teaching. A former teacher noted Pat "stood out from the empty-headed, overdressed little sorority girls of that era like a good piece of literature on a shelf of cheap paperbacks."

YORBA LINDA, CALIFORNIA

The Richard M. Nixon Presidential Library and Museum in Yorba Linda, California surrounds his small boyhood home, just like the Hoover and Eisenhower Museums. I had never been to Yorba Linda before and the Nixon campus and town had that same understated, yet effective and accomplished vibe

Mrs. Nixon had. In fact, the whole library and museum was very modest looking from the outside. The buildings were low and built into the side of a hill, they were classic and tastefully designed. They were effective without being overstated or flashy. Just like Mrs. Nixon. The only thing that really stood out was the giant helicopter (Marine One) that brought the Nixons home to California after President Nixon resigned in 1974. During my work in Yorba Linda, I had the unique experience of working with the Nixon Foundation staff and the Nixon Library and Museum staff. In other locations, it had typically just been NARA (National Archives and Records Administration) folks, but here the foundation wanted to show me through the actual museum. This was cool by me, and an interesting way to get a different perspective and voice into my video pieces and research. I started on the library side with Jim Bryon from the Nixon Foundation.

Production Note – Young Blood

Jim Byron was a young guy. I would guess him to have been in his 20's. I couldn't help but think about some of the other young professionals and historians I had worked with during the series. There was Amanda Matthews who was incredibly well-read on Louisa Catherine Adams at the Massachusetts Historical Society, Jennifer Walton knew everything there was to know about Harriet Lane at James Buchanan's Wheatland and Nick Sierkierski, from the Hoover Institution, was extremely helpful on Lou Hoover's time at Stanford. The importance of these young minds when it comes to the next generation of history and what we pass on to the generation after them is beyond crucial. I was out to dinner recently with my friends the Kemps and the Fillers, and we were discussing the relevance of Graceland and Elvis to kids growing up these days. I have not made my love of Elvis, his music and Graceland a secret in the pages of this book. The future of our history lies in the hands of our younger generations. This has always been the case. I know that. Maybe it's my age, certainly it's my First Ladies Man project, but I also feel it's a change in the way we gain and preserve our information with modern technology, the invention of the internet, and our "virtual" lifestyles. Sometimes there is no substitute for going to a place and seeing and learning and hearing about things first hand. This project reinforced that need for me on multiple levels.

In yet another example of fortunate timing, when I arrived at the Nixon Library in the middle of November 2013, they had just published the Nixon love letters in 2012. Richard Nixon met Pat Ryan in a small community theater group in California in 1938. He apparently asked her to marry him on their first date. He said something to the effect of, "I'm going to marry you some day," and she laughed it off later saying, "I thought he was nuts or something!" This was interesting to me, because LBJ had the same reaction to Lady Bird on their first date, and many other men who became President were very impulsive, quick to fall in love and very romantic. It's just something to mention here, and probably the topic for a whole different book.

The Nixon love letters began in 1938 when they started dating. Nixon addresses Pat as "Dearest Heart" and refers to long drives on Sundays. He wrote about books they read and trips sightseeing in the mountains. And possibly most significantly, he said, "let's really grow together and find the happiness we know is ours." In a letter Pat wrote back, she flirted with him about coming over for dinner "early at 6" and says she'll see if she can burn a hamburger for him. She often included little clovers and Irish references, as he called her his "wild Irish gypsy." She also mentions a clock that Nixon gave her as a gift she called "Sir Ric," and said he had such a nice face and she liked him "so very much." These letters, along with family pictures of the Nixons on a beach vacation with their two young daughters and other moments in their young life really opened my eyes to a side of the Nixons I had never known, and feel most of the world never saw. There it was. That moment. In the first piece of the day. The Nixons were another Presidential couple I thought I knew, but didn't. I grew up just outside of Washington, DC, and it's hard to be a human being in the 20th Century and not know or have an opinion about the Nixons and his Presidency. But, just like all the others before them, they came alive. They became real. These letters showed a side of both President and Mrs. Nixon I had never seen or heard of before. They were two young adults who fell in love and started a family. They dreamed of a happiness they knew to be theirs.

The Nixon Library also had documents and artifacts that represented Mrs. Nixon's extensive travel. Her diplomatic passports from when she was the Second Lady (wife of the Vice President), were brought out for me. Mr. and

Mrs. Nixon shared one passport, and they were both pictured in black and white on the first page. Vice President and Mrs. Nixon visited 53 countries from 1953 through 1961, and all the stamps were in these passports. Jim patiently thumbed through the pages so I could get incredibly detailed footage of the colorful, and often, intricate stamps. Pat Nixon was not afraid to get her hands dirty here at home or when she traveled. She did much more than wear fancy dresses and go to ritzy parties, dinners and receptions in these foreign countries. She visited orphanages, hospitals, poor and hurting people in tiny villages on the outskirts of towns and cities. She went to a leper colony in Panama. Mrs. Nixon was genuinely concerned for the greater well-being of people and it showed in her causes and her actions.

One of the more unique items related to her travels were luggage tags from her second to last trip as First Lady. She visited Austria, Egypt, Saudi Arabia, Syria, Israel and Jordan in June 1974. The tags were laminated and had an American flag on them. Another tag specifically for Mrs. Nixon's personal bags was all red with "Mrs. Richard Nixon" printed across the bottom in bold, black letters. All this travel resulted in a lot of gifts, mementos, souvenirs and artifacts that were mostly housed and on display in the museum. So, I packed up my gear and went over to the museum side, and was greeted by the curator, Olivia Anastasiadis.

There were almost too many objects on display from Mrs. Nixon's travels to talk about and get on camera. Olivia knew the collection well, and could navigate through the exhibits, pointing out the most unique artifacts. One of the rarest objects in the collection was a Carnelian necklace that dated back to the 11th or 12th century. B. C. It was made up of primarily small round beads with several, larger vase-like beads in the middle. It was given to her by Israeli Prime Minister, Golda Meir in November 1969. The only thing I'd seen in my travels that came close to its color, were some of the coral pieces in Ida McKinley's collection. This piece was magnificent. There were many examples of Belgian lace on display, too. A table cloth from King Baudouin of Belgium was in a case, high on a wall. He gave it to Mrs. Nixon in February 1969. It was similar to the Belgian lace in the Hoover museum in West Branch, Iowa. A brilliant gold watch pin was a gift from Prime Minister Columbo of Italy in September 1970.

The pin was in the shape of a bow, and the watch hung from the bow. The whole thing was covered in diamonds and rubies. It was a delicate and beautiful piece.

One of the Nixon administration's crowning achievements was the trip to China in February 1972. It was the first time a sitting U. S. President (and First Lady) had visited the country. The photographs from the trip were remarkable. The Nixons walked along the Great Wall, and toured the capital city of Beijing. Mrs. Nixon wore a beautiful red winter overcoat, that she sometimes complemented with a large fur collar. This trip did wonderful things for the relationship between the two countries. It also gave Pat Nixon one of her greatest accomplishments as First Lady (in my opinion). This was the trip that brought the Giant Pandas (Ling-Ling and Hsing-Hsing) to the National Zoo in Washington, DC.

The Nixons visited the Peking Zoo, and saw the panda exhibit. Later that night at a state dinner in their honor, Mrs. Nixon was sitting next to a Chinese dignitary who happened to be smoking "Panda" brand cigarettes. Mrs. Nixon mentioned how much she like the pandas at the zoo earlier that day. By the end of the conversation, arrangements were made for two Giant Pandas to be sent to the United States. The story alone was fantastic enough, but they had one of the crates on display that had been used to ship the pandas overseas. It was olive green with black bars and writing. It was remarkably small considering the size of a panda and the distance it had to travel. Clearly the pandas made it to Washington safely. Ling-Ling lived until 1992, and Hsing-Hsing lived until 1999.

Author's Note - Friends Of The National Zoo

Anyone who grew up in or around Washington, DC in the late 60's – early 70's knows what a big deal these two pandas were. Everyone had PANDA FEVER! I can't even tell you how many times I've been to the National Zoo or how many times I saw those two pandas, and continue to visit and be interested in the current pandas. Panda babies are an even bigger deal than the adults. I know that once the internet came along, and the Panda Cam soon after, whenever there was a pregnant panda or a looming panda birth,

I could expect 'round the clock updates from my mom, who was glued to her computer screen. When you become a "Friend of the National Zoo," they call you a FONZ. Again, for a kid growing up in or around DC, who also watched Happy Days, this was all you wanted to be. I didn't even know what it meant or what you got with your membership, but the strategically place television commercials (right in the middle of cartoons and dinner time) had me begging my parents to "be a FONZ." It was a brilliant marketing campaign, and it continues to be a success today. I get it, too. Pandas are cute and fun. They make great stuffed animals and cartoon characters. In fact, I was just at the Memphis Zoo two weeks prior to writing this chapter, and everyone down there was going crazy (myself included) about the newly refurbished Giant Panda exhibit. People love pandas, and we have Pat Nixon to thank for having them here in America.

The crate and a few photographs were not the only artifacts on display to represent the China trip, and the acquisition of the pandas. They also had a package of the Panda Brand cigarettes. This was a great way to complete the story, and made me feel as though I were there at the dinner. I could see the package, the logo, the writing, and imagine it sitting next to a dinner plate at the head table. I could connect the images and put Mrs. Nixon in the room talking about her day. I had grown up with the pandas in the Zoo, and now I knew what the crate looked like that brought them here. This story may have had more of an impact on me, because of where I grew up, but it was a national story, and it was well told at the Nixon Museum in Yorba Linda. There was also a beautiful diamond and black jeweled (onyx, maybe) panda pin that was given to Mrs. Nixon by the World Wildlife Foundation. The Nixon administration (and Pat Nixon specifically) did a lot for endangered species. The Endangered Species Act of 1973 was signed by Nixon. The pin was given to Mrs. Nixon to show the WWF's appreciation for her work when it came to the protection of animals in America and around the world.

The C-SPAN series was called "Influence and Image," and there was no shortage of clothes and images in Yorba Linda. One of the most interesting facts I found out about Pat Nixon's clothes was that she had her dressmaker put pockets in all her formal gowns and dresses. She said it was necessary, because so many people passed her notes (both for her and for her husband) in receiving lines she couldn't hold them all and still shake guests' hands. This was something I had never thought of or considered. Not only did this make sense, but it was a fantastic solution to her predicament.

The selection of dresses and clothes on display were fantastic and well representative of Mrs. Nixon's love of trim, clean and sparse design. The first piece that caught my eye was the iconic double breasted red coat from her and President Nixon's 1972 trip to China. The large, wide fur collar was on the coat, but what I didn't know and couldn't tell from the pictures, was the coat was also lined with the same fur. The trip was in February, and sightseeing in China in February would have been quite chilly. This was just one of those great pieces of clothing that you've seen in so many pictures it was fantastic to see it in person. This was another artifact that made the China trip and the panda story that much better in my mind. The museum was very proud of the fact they had Mrs. Nixon's 1973 inaugural gown on display. Typically, inaugural gowns got to the Smithsonian (see the Helen Taft chapter in Volume One) to be in the First Ladies exhibit in the National Museum of American History. However, women whose husbands have two terms get two inaugurations, and thus, two dresses. The second dress is often kept by the Presidential museums. This 1973 dress was designed by one of Mrs. Nixon's favorite designers, Adele Simpson. It was an aqua blue (light blue) with silver beads, sparkles and sequins.

The Nixon's youngest daughter, Tricia, got married while her parents lived in the White House. The ceremony took place in the Rose Garden on June 12, 1971. The Mother-of-the-Bride dress Mrs. Nixon wore was on display at the museum. It was made by Priscilla of Boston, a very famous dressmaker known for her wedding dresses. It was a simple dress with a white background, covered in beautiful pastel flowers and light green leaves, all sewn on, and made from different materials, which gave them a textured style. She wore small white wrist length gloves to top off her look for this special day. There was a wedding gazebo built and brought in for the ceremony which was also on display in the garden at the museum and library. Mrs. Nixon was also known to buy and wear Geoffrey Beene off the rack for her every day and casual wear. They had examples of these styles, too. All of the dresses were on mannequins that were carefully designed with the Nixon daughters to make sure their mother was proportional and accurately represented here in the exhibits to scale.

The museum had a few items that related to Mrs. Nixon's younger years, so I did a little backtracking there with Olivia. They had accounting tape and bookkeeping papers from 1931, when she helped run the family farm at the age of 19. The figures weren't very good, and it was easy to see the family was struggling. At the end of the tape she wrote "total deposits…none made since January." It was also interesting to see Pat's handwriting and all that went into her efforts to help keep the family business afloat. Her many odd jobs over the years included modeling, personal shopper, and the extra and walk-on acting I mentioned earlier in the chapter. She got a call back from Paramount Pictures and RKO that was published in an industry periodical, of which they had a copy. She was also cast in a speaking role in the 1935 film called "Becky Sharp." She can be seen dancing in the movie, but her speaking role was cut out. This display case had several letters, envelopes and stage passes from movie and casting companies. Her hard work resulted in her degree from University of Southern California, and they had her diploma on display, as well. It was another well-told story that showed how Pat Ryan became the woman she was who would meet a young Dick Nixon in the small theater group.

There was still quite a bit of California sun left, so I met back up with Jim Bryan to look around the grounds and Mrs. Nixon's rose garden. There was a beautiful pond in the middle courtyard next to Mrs. Nixon's rose garden, the childhood home of President Nixon, and their graves and final resting place. There are two rose gardens on the premises, and Mrs. Nixon's personal garden had over 80 varieties of her favorite roses. It is one of the largest rose gardens in Orange County, and among the top five largest in Southern California. The Pat Nixon Rose was a special rose developed in 1972 from a black floribunda bloom, and can only be purchased at the museum gift shop. There are many other special roses in the garden named for First Ladies, special groups, events, people and causes. Mrs. Nixon always loved the outdoors, farming and gardening, and it made sense she wanted that represented and remembered here.

As with any grave I visited during my travels, this place held special reverence. Maybe even more so here, because it was where Pat Nixon's funeral was held and televised. The world watched as an inconsolable President Nixon said goodbye to his wife surrounded by friends, family and world leaders past and present on June 26, 1993. This was another image and footage I had seen numerous times, and I stood where it all took place. It made the scene unfold in a much more real way, right before my eyes. It was a fitting way to watch the sun go down on the day, as I remembered and documented the way Pat Nixon lived her life and was remembered here.

SUMMARY

Pat Nixon was a quietly remarkable First Lady. She was the last to toot her own horn, and she didn't have much interest in having others toot it for her either. She was a strong, loving, and confident supporter of her husband's career and administration and she was dedicated to her own causes. Much like Abigail Adams or Lucy Hayes, she saw a problem and both quietly and effectively addressed and fixed it. If she saw people in need or in trouble, she helped them. She shared Mrs. Kennedy's love of, and respect for, preserving history. Instead of hosting a TV special or a public White House tour (which was fine and more suited for Mrs. Johnson or Mrs. Kennedy) she humbly assembled and collected more than 600 historical pieces and artifacts for the White House (more than any other First Lady before or since). Her style matched her personality. It was classy, elegant and often understated…simple, but effective.

An interesting thing happened during the live Pat Nixon show on C-SPAN. A man called in who was a member of the Camp David house staff during the Nixon Administration and the Watergate scandal. I was watching from my hotel room in Plains, GA, and I was riveted by this call. The man related how hurt the family was. He talked about Mrs. Nixon specifically being beaten down and troubled by the whole affair. It gave me yet another chance to look at this woman as a human being, and not the First Lady of the United States of America. I could take right and wrong out of the equation, and think about how something like that would affect a family member embroiled in the political scandal.

Her difficult upbringing made her strong. She stood out from other students in her class to teachers, and she worked her way through life and into the White House. From there she became the most traveled Second and First Lady of her time and beyond. Her travels around the world were well documented, but not over-publicized. She promoted and encouraged people with a quiet grace that comes from within and often can't be taught or learned. Pat Nixon was a class act, and she was certainly unusual for her time.

Travelogue Food Tip

As I have mentioned, many times, my travels allow me to visit and catch up with friends and family across the country and around the world. A lot of friends from college and professional colleagues are in California. Some childhood friends have even moved and settled there. After my day at the Nixon Library and Museum, I braved the traffic and drove down the coast to the pier at San Clemente. I met my college buddies, Joel Bailey and Ryan Vener at the Fisherman's Restaurant and Bar where I had my first taste of Dungeness Crab. I had it in a cold cocktail salad with a Caesar salad (of course). Ryan and I had seen each other recently in Maryland, but it had been many years since I had seen Joel, and even longer since the three of us had been in the same room. It was a great meal and a fun evening. We walked out onto the pier and talked to the fishermen. One guy had a really cool video of a small Pacific Octopus he had caught the previous night. After hanging out watching the people fish for a while, we walked up the hill to a little joint and watch a female singer songwriter for a while. It was a quiet night, and we were the only ones there with a few of her friends. Not only did we buy her CD, but we got up and sang with her. Joel even did a couple solo songs, and tunes we played together in a band back in college. It was a great way to end another very productive and fun trip to California. I rarely have a bad time anywhere I go, but I've never had a bad time in California

CHAPTER FOURTEEN

Betty Ford

Grand Rapids, Michigan

Betty Ford was born Elizabeth Ann Bloomer on April 8, 1918 in Chicago, Il. Her parents were William Stephenson Bloomer and Hortense Neahr Bloomer. Gerald and Betty Ford were married on October 15, 1948. They had four children together. Betty Ford died in Rancho Mirage, California on July 8, 2011 at the age of 93.

Betty Ford was the first First Lady I remember being in office during my lifetime. I was out with my family in DC one afternoon, when a long black limousine pulled up in front of us. The door opened, and Mrs. Ford stepped out. My mom said, "Andy take a picture, that's the President's wife…the First Lady." Luckily, I had my trusty Kodak 110 camera with me and I snapped a picture of Mrs. Ford through the crowd. My mom took another picture of me in front of

Mrs. Ford's car. I was seven at the time. Not only do I still have the memory, but I still have the pictures. On the back of them, in my mom's handwriting, it says "Apr. 14, 1976 Mrs. Ford's Limo." (see photo section in this book) Growing up in the Washington, DC area had many advantages. One of which was access to the White House, and the people who lived and worked there.

The Gerald R. Ford Presidential Library and Museum has something very unique about it, unlike any other of the NARA run facilities. It's not an "it," … they're a "they." They are two different buildings in two different cities. The Ford Library is in Ann Arbor, Michigan, and the Ford Museum is in Grand Rapids, Michigan. We chose to go to the museum to see more items and artifacts, because there was already so much material on and from Mrs. Ford on camera and in video.

GRAND RAPIDS, MICHIGAN

It was a cold November day when I touched the ground in Grand Rapids. I remember it very clearly, because I didn't pack a proper Winter jacket. Why, you may ask? Well, remember I traveled with seven cases, which included my suitcase and backpack, and I took any chance I got to lighten my load. According to my contact there, and my Google searches, my hotel was right across the street from the museum. They were right. It was. I still should have brought a better coat.

The building was a beautiful, white, rectangular structure with large plate-glass windows and a nice man-made pond and fountain. The Fords are both buried there in a grave and memorial like the Reagans' in Simi Valley, CA (which we will get to in the Reagan chapter). I didn't spend much time at their graves (no jacket), but it was peaceful and well done. The lobby had large vaulted ceilings, grand staircases, hallways, and exhibits shooting off in every direction, and a nice little gift shop. The Ford Museum had everything I had come to expect from the NARA operated facilities. It was well run, full of great items and artifacts, and told tons of great stories. I was ready to get to know the woman behind the title, the woman who I thought I already knew so well.

Mrs. Ford changed the entire image, function and role of the First Lady. As she did this, she also changed the image, role and function of women in America.

Many First Ladies before her had causes, and helped people. This was not a new thing. However, Mrs. Ford taught people it was okay to help themselves. In 1974, soon after becoming First Lady, Betty Ford went through breast cancer diagnosis, surgery and recovery. She spoke to America, and the world about an issue that had been kept locked and hidden behind doctors' doors for centuries. One of John and Abigail Adams' daughters (Nabby) had a mastectomy after her cancer was discovered in 1811, and died two years later at the age of 48. Everyone knew about the disease. Mrs. Ford decided to talk openly and publicly about it. She was openly pro-choice and supported the Equal Rights Amendment. This went against her husband's Republican Party, and caused some political backlash for President Ford. However, she believed in these causes and positions, and supported them in a respectful way that earned her the title of "Fighting First Lady" and Time magazine's "Woman of the Year" in 1975. After the White House, in 1978, her family staged an intervention, and forced her to deal with her alcohol and substance abuse problems. In the early 80's as a part of her sobriety, she opened the Betty Ford Center (originally called the Betty Ford Clinic) to help others with substance abuse. Betty Ford was unusual for her time, and the whole world knew it.

The Fords came into the White House, and specifically the Presidency, under less than ideal circumstances. Dan Holloway was the curator at the Ford Museum. He would be the one to show me around the facility. The museum had Mrs. Ford's dress from the swearing-in in ceremony on display. It was a light blue dress with white trim, and a light jacket. Mrs. Ford was not thrilled to be the new First Lady, but she said if she was going to be the First Lady, she was going to have fun doing it. Ten days into office, the Fords held a State Dinner for King Hussein of Jordan. Betty Ford had a background in dance, and loved to entertain. Mrs. Ford had the distinct pleasure of being First Lady during the United States Bicentennial celebrations in 1976. There were many exhibits that highlighted these celebrations. Valery Giscard d'Estaing, the President of France, and his wife attended a dinner on May 17, 1976. An invitation indicated the dinner started at 8pm at the White House. Emperor Hirohito and his wife came to visit the Fords and celebrate the Bicentennial. This marked the first time a Japanese Emperor had ever left Japan. There was a letter of appreciation written in Japanese, and translated in English in the exhibit.

Perhaps the most remarkable and largest Bicentennial visit came from Queen Elizabeth and Prince Philip. In July 1976, the Fords hosted a State Dinner for the royal couple at the White House. The dinner menu listed New England Lobster in Bellvue, Saddle of Veal, Garden Salad and Peach Ice Cream with Fresh Raspberries. The Queen gave the Fords (and the American people) a gilded and enameled soup tureen. It was red, white and blue with gold eagles and other designs. A hand painted image of the White House was in the center, on the front. The Queen also sent a hand-written letter in which she wrote:

> "It was the greatest pleasure for us to visit the United States and to be able to join in the Bicentennial celebrations."

She signed it, "Your Sincere Friend, Elizabeth"

Her handwriting was surprisingly regular, if that makes any sense. It was very clear and legible. It was large and confident, but still feminine. I'm not sure what I expected a queen's handwriting to look like, because I had never considered it before I saw this letter. This was the only handwritten letter from a queen I have seen before or since.

Social Media Note – Muskrat Love

Just above this note, I typed my 100,000th word in this book. It was the word "dinner," referring to the Queen's event hosted by the Fords. I took a picture of myself holding a 100,000 sign and posted it [to great response] on social media. A friend and follower on Facebook made the following comment:

William Kresse: The Queen and POTUS danced to "The Lady is a Tramp." Also, Captain & Tenille performed "Muskrat Love." I kid you not. I remember watching the live coverage of it on TV.

He then provided a link to a story about the Captain & Tenille's performance that night. It seems Mrs. Ford had requested they play "The Way I Want to Touch You," saying it was one of her and "Gerry's" favorites. So, The Captain & Tenille performed "The Way I Want to Touch You" and "Muskrat Love," and said it was a "fun group."

What a fun world we live in, where I can post something about my 100,000th word typed in my second book on social media, and another person can add to the story and make it into the book I was posting about. I really enjoy this kind of interaction and storytelling online and face to face.

Betty Ford was thought of as a stylish First Lady. She kept up with current fashion trends, dressed appropriately for her age, she kept it fun, and supported American companies and dressmakers (like many First Ladies before her). Holloway brought out several her dresses and outfits on a rack, and set them up in a very 'Presidential" looking conference room in the museum. The first dress was made by one of her favorite dressmakers. Frankie Welch had a boutique in Alexandria, Virginia, and made many of Mrs. Ford's formal dresses and gowns. She had a beautiful long white gown with a wide, feathered collar and matching cuffs. Mrs. Ford wore this to her first official State Dinner as First Lady for King Hussein of Jordan. Also on the rack was another white dress with sheer sleeves and lace accents along the edges and the button-up middle. She wore this on the cover of Time magazine. The cover read "Ford's First Year – At Ease in the White House." It was made by Cuban-American designer, Luis Estevez. There were several casual outfits she got from Albert Capraro of New York. They were in beiges and purples with flowers. They were simple designs, but looked comfortable and functional while still having an appropriate amount of flair.

The next dress was the red-orange one she wore in her official White House photograph, where she is leaning on the railing next to the yellow flowers. She also wore this dress when her husband was sworn in on the House floor as the new Vice President under President Nixon when Spiro Agnew resigned. In fact, these dresses and outfits all came alive with pictures to back them up. Just as it had been with the earlier First Ladies, photographs of Mrs. Ford wearing these clothes helped put me in the time and space when she would have worn them. It was the combination of having actual real-life memories of Betty Ford, the photographs and the outfits right there in front of me that gave me an unusual sense of having been there and solidified my recollections. All of this was only further reinforced by the secretary cards Mrs. Ford kept. The museum had a file box full of note cards that listed all of Mrs. Ford's clothes and outfits with details about each outfit. The cards were in both Mrs. Ford and her secretary's handwriting. The notes included a description of the article of clothing, the designer's name and where it was purchased or made and where and when she wore it. She wore a lot of clothes listed during and after the White House. She also wore many of the outfits multiple times, which shows she was both practical and down-to-earth.

Holloway then showed me a very important dress in the collection. It wasn't important because of its design or designer. It wasn't important because of the dinner she wore it to, or the world leader she entertained while wearing it. This was the beige dress with wide white collar she wore in her 1975 interview with Morely Safer. It had a matching beige scarf that was worn over the shoulder with a tastefully ornate gold brooch pin holding it in place. The Ford Museum had the interview running on display. This interview changed everything a First Lady was and could be.

President Ford was elected to Congress in 1948, weeks after he and Betty were married. He rose through the ranks and became the House Minority Leader. He stepped up after Spiro Agnew resigned and Nixon needed a Vice President, and then stepped up, again, when Nixon resigned and the country needed a President. Ford was an intelligent and capable politician. However, it was no secret that he lucked into and was appointed to some of his top political seats rather than elected to them. All while his wife quietly raised their four children in Northern Virginia. She was not openly excited about the move to the White House nor did she have political aspirations of her own. She openly said in the Safer interview:

> "I'm going in as myself, and it's too late to change my pattern…if they don't like it, then they'll just have to throw me out."

The 60 Minutes interview was like no other the world had heard or read from a previous First Lady. Mrs. Ford was unlike any First Lady before her. She openly disagreed with her husband's party and politics when it came to women's rights and the ERA. She said the legalization of abortion in America was a huge step for women, and brought the procedure out of the back alleys and dark ages and into the hospitals where it belonged. She spoke about the possibility of her 18-year-old daughter having pre-marital sex, and how it just made her human. Mrs. Ford said, if she were a teenager in the 70's, she would have most likely tried marijuana. These were all hot button topics in politics and polite society, and probably not the best thing for her husband's political career. She even made a casual reference to her and her husband's private life, and said President Ford didn't have time for affairs or other women, because she kept him very busy. It was a vague enough comment not to set off too many alarms, but she made sure everyone got her meaning. She said all of this with honesty and conviction, and the public response was mostly positive.

Betty Ford was also outspoken about her breast cancer and mastectomy. She told Safer:

> "There are women all over the country like me. If I don't make this public, their lives will be gone. They're in jeopardy."

This was yet another topic that, before Betty Ford, was not openly discussed. She talked about her diagnosis, treatment and recovery in the 60 Minutes interview, and at women's health forums and cancer awareness events all over the country. Because of Mrs. Ford hundreds of thousands of women went to their doctors and got checked. President Ford supported her in this awareness, and spoke to the country about her operation and recovery. The museum had a whole exhibit on her breast cancer. They had the original get well card signed by every member of Congress, and the picture of her and President Ford reading the card in the hospital. There was a football signed by the Washington Redskins wishing her a speedy recovery. Cards from foreign dignitaries and their wives were in the display. The whole world was on Betty Ford's side and watched her recover from this disease. Interestingly enough, Mrs. Ford said the hardest part about her whole ordeal was coming out into public at her first State dinner after her surgery. She said she felt as though everyone was staring at her chest and trying to figure out or remember "which one." Mrs. Ford was unusual for her time.

After the White House, the world watched as Betty Ford recovered from another disease. Addiction. Her family had an intervention with her in 1978, and let her know that they knew she had a problem with alcohol and pain killers. She got help, and conquered, yet another problem that typically went undiscussed. She did this, again, with the whole world watching. Now her living legacy helps those addicted, by way of the Betty Ford Clinic in Rancho Mirage, California. The museum had countless certificates, medal, honors and speeches (both written and on video) of Mrs. Ford and her work in this arena.

Later, in 1997, the Fords sat down with Leslie Stahl for another interview, in which, President Ford was asked about his wife's openness, even when it wasn't advantageous to his political party or his career. The former President had long said his views were more in line with his wife's than the Republican party's. He went on to say in the interview, even if he had disagreed with his wife, she was an independent woman and thinker, and it wouldn't have much mattered. President Ford's use of the term "independent thinker," made me think of Lou Hoover—another independent woman—and her school essay, "Independent Girl."

Gerald Ford was also not Mrs. Ford's first husband. She was the second lady to be divorced before marrying their Presidential husband (Florence Harding being the first). Betty Bloomer married William Warren in 1942, and they were divorced in 1947. Mrs. Ford was asked about her first husband when she was First Lady. A reporter asked her why she didn't talk about her first marriage? Her answer was that no one ever had asked about it until then.

Before Mrs. Ford was Mrs. Ford she was Betty Bloomer, and all Betty Bloomer wanted was to be was a dancer. Betty always had a interest in performing and fashion. She worked from an early age (especially for a girl at that time), as a clothes model, at the age of 11. She studied dance during the summers at Bennington School of Dance in Bennington, Vermont. After high school, she moved to New York City to study and become a dancer in Martha Graham's dance company. Graham was considered the "high priestess of modern dance" at the time, and young Betty considered herself fortunate to be among such an accomplished set of performers, studying her passion under one of the greats. While in New York she did more modeling, and eventually performed at Carnegie Hall. However, her mother talked her into coming back home to Grand Rapids where Betty formed and performed in her own dance group while she taught dance on the side, and became a fashion coordinator at a local department store called

Herpolsheimer's. Her former life as a dancer was not a secret during her White House years, as many will remember a well-known picture of her dancing on a large conference table in the Cabinet Room.

To get a better understanding of her love and passion for dance, I was taken into the back storage and work rooms of the museum. This was the part I loved. The public displays and exhibits were always informative and well put together. They highlight some of the rarest and most interesting artifacts and stories of these people's lives. They often explain why these people are important, why we care about them or focus on their greatest achievements. But, with someone as public as Betty Ford, who lived her life (ups, downs and in-betweens) on the world stage, in the public eye, and often on camera, in her own words at events giving speeches…I wanted something the public hadn't seen and didn't know. It was my personal focus for all my work at each of the locations for every woman I studied, and this was that moment. So, I gathered my gear, wires and cables and went "backstage."

Like all these facilities, the storage and work rooms were where it was at! And what I was about to see had a personal connection and relevance I couldn't have predicted or imagined. They showed me a young Betty Bloomer's record collection. As a musician who has not only released his own music on vinyl, but also still has all his and his parent's old records and 45's, this was something special. Her record collection was extensive and primarily 78's.

Author's Note – You Spin Me Right 'Round, Baby

Music is in my blood, my bones and my DNA. Some of my earliest childhood memories are jumping up and down on my parent's bed singing Elvis tunes while I stayed home from school, pretending to be sick [sorry Dad]. Music was all around me growing up, and I'm thankful for it. My first introduction to 78 records came from my Uncle Max. Growing up he bought and reworked a refurbished 1941 780-E model Wurlitzer jukebox designed by David Rockola [who also designed guns]. This jukebox was made the same year Betty Bloomer moved home to Grand Rapids from New York City. Max had a great record collection. A family favorite was always Spike Jones and His City Slickers. First of all, just having a jukebox in your house was cool. The fact that it lit up and worked and you could punch in all the numbers and hear the records made it that much cooler. It was always a highlight of visiting Uncle Max, Aunt Marge and my two cousins, Cathy and Sharon, on any holiday or family gathering.

Betty had all the hits of her day. She had Count Bassie, Gene Autry, Glenn Miller, Duke Ellington, Charlie Burnett and the Dorsey Brothers. Her collection was kept in book-like albums leather bound with embossed and gilded covers and brown paper sleeve as pages that held the records. It was easy to see she took great pride in her collection by the careful organization and storage of the records (like her secretary cards and her clothes). The best part of the whole collection was the hand-written notes in the books and on some of the pages and sleeves. It seems young Betty lived with other girls as roommates and shared her collection, but was concerned and strict about their use and proper return. Many of the notations were not only about the record, song or artists, but about people putting the discs back in the proper order and the condition in which they were found. The relatability factor here was so high I almost couldn't contain myself. The number of beach houses, cars, college roommates, group and band houses in which I have lived over the years is an entirely different book (or movie) for another time in my life. However, seeing the handwritten notes in Mrs. Ford's record collection not only made her that much more real to me, it made her in-dispensably relatable to me on a personal level.

I have a wicked mix tape collection. I also used to put all my albums on cassette tape using my parents' stereo. This was so I could listen to them in the car or in my room and on my Walkman. I would sit for HOURS and decorate the tape box labels writing the exact band logo on the front and on each of the labels on both sides of the tape. I would use colored felt tip markers and fine tip pens to get every detail. I remember being particularly proud when I had mastered the KISS and IRON MAIDEN logos and font (although it wasn't called font back then to my knowledge). I know I would get extremely frustrated with longer song titles like "I Still Haven't Found What I'm Looking For" by U2, and "When the World is Running Down You Make the Best of What's Still Around" By The Police. They wouldn't fit on a single line, and it would mess up the whole "look" of the cassette label.

SUMMARY

Betty Ford was the first truly liberated First Lady. She shared her life, her problems, her faults and her family with the world. She didn't hide behind politics or the watchful eye of her husband's political party. She held the position of First Lady with style, poise and grace, even when she and President Ford were the unlikeliest of candidates who weren't even elected into the White House. And most of the American public loved her for it. What she did for women, breast cancer, equal rights and civil rights is unparalleled. Her candid openness brought so many issues to the front page and headlines, issues that had been previously buried and all but ignored. The treatment of substance abuse and addiction the world over would not be where it is today had it not been for Betty Ford's public discussions and treatment of the disease. I would dare say there is not a human being on planet Earth who has not been directly or indirectly affected by cancer, addiction or both. To think that any good or resolution or healing or treatment that was experienced by any person dealing with cancer or addiction (which we've already established is every human being on Earth) can directly or indirectly thank Betty Ford in some way, shape of form is pretty remarkable. I don't think I'm being dramatic or overstating the facts, either. She was extremely unusual for her time, and the perfect example of someone without political goals or aspirations who was not seeking the role, or elected to the role or paid for the role of First Lady, who took the ball and ran with it. She did it not because it was cool, or because she was supposed to. She did it because she wanted to, and it was the right thing for her to do at that point and time in her life.

All that being said, to see her as a real person who loved her family, loved to dance and loved her record collection is truly something special. It made her a better First Lady, knowing she struggled to get into Carnegie Hall, and worked as a model at the age of 11, and went through a divorce from an alcoholic and abusive husband (who she stuck with and saw through a coma even with the abuse and other factors—again…another book for another time). She was truly one of the most unusual women in this book I had the pleasure of learning about and getting to know.

Travelogue Food Tip

Tip #1, in general, when in Grand Rapids, Michigan [especially, in the Winter] ...BRING A COAT! The walk from the hotel to the restaurant was BRISK, to say the least. But, the food at The Bull's Head Tavern was so fantastic, I risked life, limb and hypothermia to visit there twice. Once, for dinner after dark when it was particularly frigid. The décor was very "Nat Geo/Teddy Roosevelt/world hunter's club," with big game trophies all around. I'm not sure they were real, as it appeared to be a fairly new establishment. They had a great Caesar [shocking], and fantastic burgers. Their appetizer menu was interesting, as well, though I can't seem to recall any one specific item. You'll just have to go yourself and let me know.

CHAPTER FIFTEEN

Rosalynn Carter

Plains, Georgia

Rosalynn Carter was born Eleanor Rosalynn Smith on August 18, 1927 in Plains, GA. Her parents were Wilburn Edgar Smith and Frances Allethra Murray Smith. Jimmy and Rosalynn Carter were married on July 7, 1946. They had four children together. Rosalynn Carter is living in Plains, Georgia with her husband, President Jimmy Carter.

Rosalynn Carter was the first living First Lady I had the opportunity to study during this whole adventure. I found it strange that I didn't realize this or even think about it until about halfway through my visit to her home town of Plains, Georgia. This was the first woman who was going to or had the opportunity to watch this C-SPAN version of "This Is Your Life." I guess as a public figure and spouse of a world leader and American President you're used to that kind of thing, but this was the first project and show I had been a part of that told the story of a person's life while they were still living. I can't lie, I felt some additional pressure. I wanted to do a good job telling the world about Mrs. Carter, and all the first Ladies from here on out. This had always been my goal, and I feel I accomplished that. However, this would be the first time I might hear about it if I didn't—straight from the source.

I had the option of going to the Carter Center in Atlanta to do my filming and research in the presidential library and museum, but opted to get the stories for the series in Plains. Plus, other members of the C-SPAN production team were going to interview Mrs. Carter at the Carter Center. So, we had that location covered. It was very important for me to feel we had covered all angles, locations and aspects of these women's lives. This interview with Mrs. Carter was a first for the series, as well. This new factor in our shows of having the actual First Lady in the show was a game changer for me. Michelle Obama was First Lady when the series launched in February 2013, and she contributed a pre-taped interview to the live event that started to series (more on that in the Michelle Obama Chapter). However, this was the first First Lady to be interviewed for her own episode. The whole team was very excited. This may have overshadowed my trip to Plains, but it didn't make my visit or my footage any less important to telling her whole story. However, it gave the actual First Lady the opportunity to speak about her life and times, especially in the White House, on her own terms and in her own words. So, I was left to dig into the pre-White House and post-White House years even deeper. There were even fewer gaps for me to fill in when it came to policies, initiatives, and travel. I could really focus on the location and the stories it told. Which was exactly what I did in Plains.

PLAINS, GEORGIA

It was a sunny day (that wouldn't last) when I flew into Fort Benning airport, picked up my rental car and drove to Plains. I arrived late in the afternoon and checked into my hotel. I stayed in the center of town at the Plains Historic Inn, which had been renovated by Mrs. Carter. The innkeeper welcomed me to Plains, as I checked in with all my gear. The town's sheriff was even hanging out there, which gave Plains a real "Mayberry" feel. Everyone was expecting me, and interested in the series and my work. They were very friendly, and couldn't do enough for me. Each room at the Inn was themed and decorated according to a decade from the Carters' lives between 1920 and 1980. I stayed in the 1980 room, but had a chance to peek in the other rooms which weren't occupied at the time. They were all fairly accurate to their decades. My room had magazines, books and decor I recognized and remembered from growing up in the 80's. There was a TV Guide with Mr. T on the cover, right on top of my television and VCR (yes, there were even old VHS tapes in a basket under the television, including Jane Fonda workout tapes). The whole downtown area was a National Historic Site, and you couldn't go very far in any direction without seeing something that related to President and Mrs. Carter.

The Inn was part of a small two-story strip mall in the center of town called the Antiques Mall. I was later shown a picture of the same mall from 1925. Downtown Plains looked then as it did when I was there, and when President and Mrs. Carter grew up there in the late 1920's and 30's. The whole town looked virtually unchanged. Mrs. Carter had overseen restoring the mall and downtown area, and it was named the Jimmy Carter National Historic Site. There was a really cool flea market style shop in one of the spaces on the first floor of the mall, and the Old Bank Café was where I had all of my meals (including a generous serving of homemade peanut butter ice cream). The Old Bank Café was also where I met and chatted with Billy Carter's daughter, Kim Fuller, and her husband. The sheriff popped back up in the café, too, and I'll tell that story a bit later in the chapter. The Carters' family peanut business offices were right next door to the mall, as was Mrs. Carter's butterfly trail, and the original train station which served as campaign headquarters during Carter's successful Presidential campaign in 1976. This was also where Rosalynn Carter lead the Peanut Brigade during the same campaign. Mrs. Carter's childhood home was not far off, and neither was the school where she and a young Jimmy Carter would meet in the 1930's. After a good night's sleep in the 1980's room at the Inn, I would start my work at the school first thing in the morning with National Park Ranger, Steve Theus.

Steve greeted me on the steps of Plains High School where both Jimmy Carter and Rosalynn Smith attended first through eleventh grades. Plains was not a large town when the Carters were growing up and one school held all the students in all the grades. The population in Plains during the late 20's and early 30's was under 600, and everyone knew each other and their families. The school had been converted into the National Park Service offices for the Jimmy Carter National Historic Site. The hallways and many of the classrooms have been preserved and restored to look as they did when young Rosalynn was a student there. One of Mrs. Carter's earliest memories of school was getting straight A's her first quarter. Her parents, Edgar and Allie gave her a dollar for her achievement. Her academic achievements didn't stop there. When she was in the seventh grade, a local businessman held a contest for the student with the best GPA. The bulletin board by the former school office had a small display with Rosalynn Smith's seventh grade picture and a notice which read "Awarded $5 by the M and M store for making the highest average in the 7th grade." At one point, she was assigned to tutor some of the younger students in math. She went on to be her graduating class's valedictorian. Rosalynn was also on the girls' varsity basketball team. There were pictures on display of her in her team uniform. She wore dark shorts and a short sleeved, collared satin shirt, that looked more like a bowling shirt, but, hey…it was the 1930's, and she was a girl playing basketball. This was when it dawned on me…or more accurately, became more apparent…these First Ladies all did things that were uncharacteristic or unusual for girls and women of their time. Maybe it was learning different languages, or finance, money, or business…they were privy to political discussions or reading certain books, a love of art, theater or sports…most of the women who became First Ladies had some talent, interest or ability that was unusual for females of the times. Mrs. Carter was no exception. The series and my travels had taught me this very early on, however, it was this more modern picture of a First Lady I could vividly remember from her time in the White House (because I was alive for it) as a school girl in her basketball uniform that brought it all together for me. It made the fact that all these women had been this kind of unusual female, doing typically non-female things, crystal clear.

It was fascinating to be walking the halls and in the classrooms where all of this took place for Rosalynn Carter. It was also incredible to think about her being friends with Jimmy's sisters, Ruth and Gloria. She was particularly close to Ruth. It was easy to imagine the girls sitting together in class or at lunch, or maybe playing ball out in the schoolyard. There's no doubt their older brother Jimmy would have seen Rosalynn in the hall or with his sisters, and the two would have talked or interacted throughout their school years.

Mrs. Carter's childhood home was not far away from the school (nothing is very far away from anything in Plains), and we went there next to learn more about Rosalynn Carter's childhood and her lifelong ties to the Carter family. She was the oldest child of Edgar and Allie Smith. She had two younger brothers and a younger sister. The Smiths were not wealthy people, and farming was their main income. Rosalynn helped with household chores and even made clothes for her and her brothers and sister. Their house was a modest little cottage with a front sitting porch, and she has fond memories of her father coming home and swinging her mother around in the kitchen and giving her a big kiss after a long day of work. They were a happy family, until her father fell ill while Rosalynn was thirteen. It was Jimmy Carter's mother who took care of Mr. Smith. Lillian (most commonly known as Miss Lillian) was a nurse in Plains, and was with Rosalynn's father when he died. The night Edgar Smith died, Miss Lillian took Rosalynn to the Carter family farm outside of town to be with her friend, Ruth.

Production Note – When The Rain Comes

It had been sprinkling for most of the morning, but it was really starting to come down when we moved outside to go to Mrs. Carter's childhood home, and the Carter family farm. We had umbrellas and raincoats, etc. , but working outside in the rain is always less than ideal for numerous reasons. I don't care if I get wet, but I was concerned about the gear and the footage being compromised. This also meant that stand ups in front of the houses and footage of the locations had to be shot and reshot and reshot. It's bad enough when a vehicle drives through your shot, it's even worse when you're on a noisy water covered street, and worse yet when the vehicle is a dump truck of semi (all of which passed us at the Smith house). The other thing to consider is the folks on camera. None of the people I spoke to were television professionals or reporters, and they were all pulling long hours and letting me drag them around making them repeat themselves take after take in place after place after place to make sure I got the information and footage I needed. Doing this in the rain made it even more tricky. But, Steve was a trooper! He trudged and drove me and my gear around in the rain, helped me carry and set up gear, and laughed right along with me when it seemed like it was never going to let up. So, thank you, Steve for being one of the tough ones!

The Carter family farm was outside of town, and we drove out there to see where Rosalynn and Jimmy would have definitely crossed paths when she was visiting with his sisters. This house was small, too. Jimmy's sisters, Ruth and Gloria shared the front bedroom. It was easy to imagine the girls in here listening to records, doing homework, playing games or gossiping, and just being teenage girls. Unfortunately, the rain made it difficult to see too much of the farm itself, but I got to see the house, and this was where Rosalynn spent most of her time here, with Jimmy's sisters. So, I did get to put an important puzzle piece into place. Seeing all these places first hand, and getting the footage really helped me (and the viewer, I hope) see what life for Rosalynn and Jimmy Carter was like, and how they were raised and where they interacted as kids. So, where and when did Jimmy and Rosalynn Carter get together and become a couple? Like most young people in the south at that time…in the church. And, that's exactly where we were off to next.

The rain let up a little by the time we got to the Plains United Methodist Church (divine intervention? Maybe). And, it's right on the steps of the side entrance where Jimmy Carter asked Rosalynn Smith out on their first date. They continued dating throughout college and President Carter's time at the Naval Academy in Annapolis, Maryland. They got married in the same United Methodist Church in Plains after Carter graduated from the academy.

Author's Note - In The Navy

I live about 10 miles south of the Naval Academy in a town called Shady Side. I have been to the Naval Academy and surrounding Annapolis area many times. The campus is great, and there's a Naval and maritime museum that is open to the public. You could even call Annapolis a fairly regular hangout of mine. It's the state Capital, and the streets and houses are very quaint and pretty with lots of interesting shops and boutiques. The restaurants are great and seafood is always a favorite of mine. They have great live music, pubs and clubs. I've even done a Halloween ghost tour there with former C-SPAN producer and friend Lauren Torlone Mahoney and her husband Jack, and we went to dinner at Middleton's Tavern to celebrate their marriage. In the nice weather, it's a great motorcycle ride and parking is easy right up front and center at the City Dock. The city even has some First Lady history that dates back to Louisa Catherine Adams's family. Her father was born into a wealthy family in Maryland, and her uncle, Thomas Johnson, was the first Governor of Maryland. In loosely related news, one of my father's favorite Christmas presents in recent years is a Navy sweatshirt I bought in the museum gift shop at the Naval Academy. Nothing but the best for my Pop!

It was right outside the Methodist Church where I had the revelation (no pun intended) about Mrs. Carter still being alive which I mentioned in the first paragraph of this chapter. Steve and I were talking about all the places I had been up to this point, and the cool stuff I had seen and the great access, etc. I happened to mention, as I have many times in these books, how I always went to the graves when time and location permitted, and how that had been the case with most of the Presidents and First Ladies. Steve made mention he knew where the Carter's final resting place was going to be. He didn't, and couldn't tell me, but it put a lot of perspective on things. How far I had come in this journey. How many places I had seen, how many years and decades and centuries I had covered. I was definitely over the hump, as I now am with Volume Two. It was bitter sweet. It was also kind of creepy and morbid, so we moved on to our next stop. Campaign

Headquarters 1976. The train station.

The train station was back across town, and it was interesting to crisscross through town as we zigzagged through Rosalynn Carter's life. The unique thing here in Plains was that her and President Carter's lives were so closely linked and intertwined. In most cases, I had asked my hosts to stay away from the stories about the Presidents and just focus on their wives. This was still the case with Rosalynn Carter, but many of her stories, friends, and experiences included Jimmy Carter or members of his family there in Plains. It was something very unique and memorable to the Carters. It was also fun to be exploring another one of the true love stories in the White House. This was almost like the Hoovers relationship and true partnership, accept the Hoovers weren't from the same town, and they didn't grow up together, knowing each other's families.

The platform and building that had been the Plains train station was converted into Governor Jimmy Carter's campaign headquarters for his successful 1976 run for the White House. It was made of dark brown wood and had a barn-like feel to it with an open floor plan and high ceilings. It was centrally located in town within walking distance to the Antique Mall and Historic Inn, and it was easy to see how it made a perfect location for a campaign office. Its high platform made a natural kind of stage for the street and people below on the side, away from the tracks. I had seen buildings and front porches transformed into these facilities before in Ohio for Harding, McKinley and Garfield and later in Arkansas for President Clinton. In all these cases, their wives played significant roles, and here in Plains, Mrs. Carter's role was just as important, if not more so. These days the converted train station is a museum and testament to that successful campaign. The walls were covered with campaign banners, pennants, and posters. Display cases mounted to the walls held buttons, flyers and all kinds of memorabilia. Enlarged photographs and newspaper articles were also hung on the walls. It had the true feeling of exactly what it was…a grassroots, hardworking successful political campaign headquarters.

By the time we got there, the rain had really started coming down hard (again…or, more so). Most of our work was done inside or under the overhang, so we were fine to hold up there for an hour or so. The first thing I learned during my research here was President and Mrs. Carter had three sons. WHAT

THE HECK? Seriously, you could have knocked me over with a feather. I was very young (elementary school) when Carter ran and was elected. I remember their daughter, Amy, very clearly. She grew up in the White House. She played the violin. She was seen walking with her parents across the South Lawn to Marine One, and at various public events. I can't remember a single mention of, nor recollection seeing any, of their three sons. EVER. To repeat, I was in Elementary School in 1976, and even though I grew up outside of Washington, DC, and knew who the Carters and the Fords were, I had no idea about many of the specifics of the campaign and their families. But, there in Plains, I learned the Carters' sons were very active in their father's campaign and played a significant role in the Peanut Brigade lead by their mother. President Carter's mother, Miss Lillian, also played an important role in the campaign. The Peanut Brigade and Carter's family were both high-profile groups at the train station.

Jimmy Carter was not a well-known political figure on the national or world stage when he ran for President. This has been the case for many Governors in the past, and has been a very successful "non-Washington" strategy of getting elected. Obviously, he won. The catch was, you must make yourself known at some point to win. That's where the Peanut Brigade came in. The Peanut Brigade was started during Jimmy Carter's first run for Georgia Senate in the early 60's. They were a group of regular folks who traveled around the state at their own expense in support of Jimmy Carter's political career. They canvassed door to door talking to anyone who would listen about their candidate. They stayed with him and helped him win the Georgia Governor's seat. When Jimmy Carter announced his candidacy for the White House, the Peanut Brigade went national with their candidate, and Rosalynn Carter went with them. She often referred to them as her "home folks." It was this down-home appeal and "every day" man and woman vibe the Carter's possessed that got them elected. The Peanut Gallery demographic was a huge part of that image. Numbers estimate the Peanut Brigade to be more than five hundred strong at their largest numbers.

My soggy day came to an end shooting B-roll in and around the converted train station. The rain let up long enough for me to get a little footage of the butterfly trail as well, just in case. My rule was always to get as much footage of everything possible while I was there, because you never knew what would come in handy for the show or what you would need after you get the material back to DC and into the editing process. We loaded up the gear in Steve's truck, and he drove me back across the street to my hotel. I got showered up and dried off and set out to the Old Bank Café (also known as the Buffalo Café) for one last meal on this leg of the adventure. I ordered two chili dogs with fries. Just as I ordered my homemade peanut butter ice cream cone, my "old friend," the sheriff, came in and I really started thinking I was in a TV show of my own instead of making one for C-SPAN. He said, "Hey there Mister Television Producer. You get everything you need for your show?" I told him I had, and that Steve was an excellent ambassador to their town and a patient tour guide, especially with all the rain. We had a good laugh over that. I continued to tell him I had seen the Baptist Church where President Carter asked Mrs. Carter out on their first date, the Methodist Church where they still teach Bible class on Sundays when they're in town, and everything in between. Then I heard a voice from the corner table where a couple had been quietly enjoying their dinner while I was enjoying mine say, "it's the other way around." I responded with a "beg your pardon" or "pardon me" to which the sheriff stepped in and said, "I'd listen to her, son, she's in the family. That's Billy Carter's daughter!" I'm not exaggerating when I say, I almost dropped my ice cream cone. My response and the first words out of my mouth (I think) were, "I still have your dad's beer in my beer can collection at my parents' house!"

Her name was Kim Carter Fuller, she was eating dinner with her husband, and she was Billy Carter's daughter. They invited me over to their table and she explained her initial comment. I had it backwards, the Carters still taught Bible class at the Baptist Church and Jimmy asked Rosalynn out on their first date at the Methodist Church. I then told them about my day, what I had learned and what the whole series was about. Her husband then took over the conversation with story after story after story about being Billy Carter's assistant or "handler" back in the days of the White House. I was sworn to secrecy, and the stories would be a whole other book, trust me. Suffice to say I laughed and laughed and laughed. They were great. Everyone finished up their meals and desserts, I got a few pictures with them, and we parted ways hoping to cross paths again somewhere down the road. I glanced at my watch and saw it was show time back in

DC and the Nixon show was on live. Good thing they had TV's in the 80's so I was all set up to watch it from my room.

Production Note - Race Against Time

I want everyone reading this right now to think about this, as I've mentioned it several times in these books, and at speeches. BUT, it bears repeating. This schedule and my travel and work was so tight, I was watching the Nixon show live having just finished shooting the material for the Carter show, and I was still in Georgia. That's a one administration buffer...which is NOT much. Especially, considering the new Carter material had to be brought back to DC and edited. Again, TV people will understand exactly the amount of work that goes into turning this material around, but everyone can imagine it's A LOT. It was a marathon and a sprint all at the same time.

Author's Note - More Than 99 Cans Of Beer On My Wall

While I'm repeating myself, I should mention my father and my beer can collection again here, since it came up at dinner with my new friend Kim Carter Fuller and her husband. As a kid growing up in Rockville, Maryland, my beer can collection started in 1976 with a Bicentennial can of Narragansett Lager my father drank while he was doing the cinderblock foundation which extended the driveway of our Myer Terrace home. The Billy Beer cans were soon to follow, given Jimmy Carter was inaugurated in January 1977. Not only did my dad drink the majority...like 95%. . . of the cans in my collection over the years (his proudest—or darkest—moments were his ability to finish Hop'N Gator and Champale), but we also built the display shelves that went up one wall and around the perimeter of my room against the ceiling. I still have the cans stored at his house in Rockville, and might just build some shelves in my house one day to proudly display them again. Thanks, Pop!

SUMMARY

Rosalynn Carter has been, and still is, one of the most active First Ladies our country has ever known. Like many First Ladies before her, she helped preserve and secure her husband's legacy with her work establishing the Carter Center in Atlanta, Georgia. Like many First Ladies, she took an active and informed interest in her husband's political career. Like many First Ladies, she helped get her husband elected in the first place with her work in the Peanut Brigade. Like many First Ladies, she continued her philanthropic work after moving out of the White House. However, Rosalynn Carter took all these things to the next level. She built upon the work and reputations of all the First Ladies before her. The most significant example of this is her and President Carter's work with Habitat for Humanity. She is still swinging a hammer after all these years, building and repairing homes for those who can't afford it or need the help the most, and so is he.

She and President Carter also still teach Bible School on Sundays at their church in Plains, when they are in town. This is a remarkable continuation of a need to serve and help people right here at home, specifically, in their home town. They are a unique Presidential couple in that they have both lived and continue to live such long and productive lives together. As I mentioned, Plains was a unique trip for me, because they both were from the same town. It was a small town. Rosalynn Smith was best friends with Jimmy Carter's sister, Ruth. Jimmy Carter's mother, Miss Lillian, was Rosalynn's father's home nurse in his dying days. They went to the same church growing up. There were only about 600 people in their town, and everyone knew each other. Studying this couple together was the only way to study them, like no other couple that lived in the White House. These two have spent most their lives not twenty feet from each other, and most that time they've been in love. The Carters' story is a remarkable one, even if you take the White House and the Presidency out of it. They successfully raised a family in the public eye, and in the world of politics, which is never an easy feat. And I learned all of this in a day, driving around in the pouring down rain, in a tiny little town in Georgia.

It was a great privilege to learn so much more about a couple I knew, but knew so little about. They had been in my memory bank, and to a certain extent my cognitive adult knowledge all along, but I really didn't know much about them. I was too young when they were most politically active, and in the news. I will be making a trip to the Carter Center in the future to continue my research, make new friends, and expand this chapter. I would also like to find out more about their three sons, who all but seemed to disappear after the campaign and the election. Their daughter Amy still has ties to and is active with the Carter Center. Again, their story together throughout their lives outside of politics make both Jimmy and Rosalynn Carter unusual for their time.

Travelogue Food Tip

The Old Bank Café or Buffalo Café in Plains, Georgia is a solid place to eat. And, it's a good thing, as it's pretty much the only place in the center of town to eat when you're staying at the Plains Historic Inn in the Jimmy Carter National Historic Site. I suggest the chili cheese dogs, although their burgers and soups are excellent, as well. The one thing you can't leave without trying, is the homemade peanut butter ice cream. Admittedly, I'm a sucker for ice cream, but this stuff really is the real deal. If you're lucky, Billy Carter's daughter, Kim might be in there with her husband having dinner, and you might catch a couple of those Billy Carter stories I glossed over earlier. Be sure and ask him about Las Vegas.

CHAPTER SIXTEEN:

Nancy Reagan

Simi Valley, California

Nancy Reagan was born Anne Frances Robbins on July 6, 1921 in New York, New York. Her parents were Kenneth Seymour Robbins and Edith Luckett Robbins. Nancy and Ronald Reagan were married on March 4, 1952. They had two children together, and Nancy was stepmother to two other children from President Reagan's first marriage. Nancy Reagan died in Bel Air, California on March 6, 2016 at the age of 94.

The way I researched Nancy Reagan, and the way we covered and handled her show in the series changed many times over the course of this project. Even now, as I am writing her chapter, it has changed considerably from what I first imagined it would be. When my work on the series began in 2012—the first show aired in 2013, and the Reagan episode aired in 2014—Mrs. Reagan was alive. We had already interviewed Rosalynn Carter, and had plans to interview every living First Lady. We knew that Mrs. Reagan was not a sure thing, because of her age, but we were hopeful. Once again, with C-SPAN's amazing reputation and connections, almost anything was possible. When the time came, Mrs. Reagan respectfully declined our interview invitation. Her staff said she wasn't making any more public appearances, and was still more interested in her husband's legacy than her own. We obviously understood.

Between the completion of the television series, Volume One, and now Volume Two, Nancy Reagan had passed away. She died on Sunday March 6, 2016, and I know exactly where I was. I was on the phone with my girlfriend, Heather, sitting on a couch in my living room (which I call the Jungle Room. What? Elvis had one, why can't I? BE YOUR OWN KING, I always say) We were both watching the Sunday political talk shows when I saw the news. I stopped in the middle of a sentence, and said, "Oh, no. Nancy Reagan died." As we discussed Mrs. Reagan, her life and my work with the First Ladies, my phone started blowing up. I was getting text messages, phone calls, voicemails, emails, texts, Facebook posts and messages. I was still processing the loss, and formulating my own thoughts. I didn't realize that other people and the public would want to hear those thoughts. The news and multimedia world were going into "BREAKING NEWS" mode. They wanted the FIRST LADIES MAN to be a part of it. Heather and I said "goodbye" …I jumped in the shower…threw on a suit and tie…and headed into DC. My work, television appearances, radio interviews and writing didn't stop until after her funeral.

Ronald Reagan was essentially taken from Nancy around 1994, when he announced he had Alzheimer's. In his statement, he wrote:

> Unfortunately, as Alzheimer's progresses, the family often bears a heavy burden. I only wish there was a way to spare Nancy from the painful experience."

Mrs. Reagan and other family members became instant advocates for research and a cure for the disease. In a "60 Minutes" interview that aired on Sept 25, 2002, Mrs. Reagan was very candid about how the disease had "stolen her husband" and "took [their] golden years from [them]." President Reagan died on

June 5, 2004, at the age of 93. Mrs. Reagan put her hands on her husband's flag covered casket, kissed him goodbye one last time, laid her head down and closed her eyes. President Reagan was flown back to California, and taken up the hill to be entombed in the memorial at the Ronald Reagan Presidential Library and Museum in Simi Valley.

The Reagans were not quiet or shy about their love and devotion for one another. It's in their books, their letters and their comments. They are a true American and Hollywood love story. The Reagans are one of the best love stories to come through the White House (the Trumans and the Carters come to mind here, too). So, when Nancy Reagan died, I was not sad. She lived a full life in her 94 years. Much of the happiness she expected to share with her husband in their later years was robbed from them by a terrible disease. Many of us, including myself, can relate to that in one form or another. Ronald Reagan and Nancy Reagan were the Paul and Linda McCartney of politics. I don't think anyone was happier than Nancy Reagan to lay down one final time to rest, and have her spirit make the journey up the mountain to the memorial in Simi Valley to be beside her "Ronnie" once again.

Originally, I was going to start the chapter with this personal story. When I was 12, my mom checked me out of school and took me to President and Mrs. Reagan's first inaugural parade. For a 12-year-old kid, any day off school for any reason was awesome. My mom and I were always close and my brother was only 5 at the time, so this was just another fun adventure with my mom. I had no idea it would turn into pages in a book I would write later in life, but here we are. For many (or most) of us in or near Washington, DC, politics is our sports. We follow it closely, see it nightly on our local and national news, it's right out our windows and on this day, it was walking right down our street. Growing up I had a political bumper sticker collection on my metal "Planet of the Apes" trashcan, and a political button collection on my bulletin board. During election years, my parents had signs in the yard and I even remember a boat-like sign with white plastic cords and clips on the top of our 1966 white Ford station wagon and the blue 1969 Camero with a white vinyl top (which embarrassed me to no end as a kid). Every Election Day, I would ride my BMX bike up to the Bauer Rec Center to ask my mom for snack money while she worked the polls. My dad was adamant about me registering for the draft when I turned 18, and getting the right to vote. We were a fairly typical, and politically active family for the DC metropolitan area. It's hard not to get caught up in the fanfare of it all, especially when you're right there in the thick of it. The inaugural parade was a blast. I hadn't seen that many people in the Nation's Capital since the Johnny Cash concert in 1976. I was excited to add a few more stickers and buttons to my collection, but the part of the day that sticks out most to me may surprise you. Remember, 1981 was a simpler time and it was 36 years ago (at the time of writing this book).

I was not a tall kid when I was 12, not that it really would've helped all that much with the massive crowds that day, but I couldn't see much from eight or more rows deep on the sidewalk. I was trying to get pictures of the parade with my little Kodak 110 camera (same one I snapped the picture of Betty Ford with). I was climbing up on steps, streetlight poles, parking meters, mailboxes...anything I could get a good grip on really. My mom was even trying to hold me up, and help me jump high enough to see something and get a good shot, but nothing was working. A man was standing next to us watching our efforts and came over. He was dressed in jeans, and navy blue hoodie, and had a 35mm camera with big, fancy lenses and a camera bag around his neck. I remember he was also scruffy and unshaven with sliver framed glasses (kinda like John Lennon). He said something like "come on, kid, we'll get you a shot." He told my mom and me he worked for "The Washington Post," and got her approval to assist. He grabbed my hand and said, "Let's go!" The next thing I know he's dragging me through the crowd towards the street yelling, "SICK BABY...SICK BABY... GOTTA GET THROUGH...SICK BABY COMING THROUGH!" and next thing I know we were right up front. This was one of the slickest moves I'd ever seen.

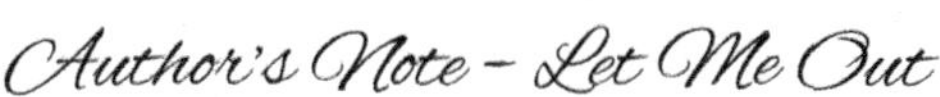

Author's Note - Let Me Out

I also used a similar "SICK BABY" trick to get out of a mosh pit during the fourth Lollapalooza at Charlestown Race Track in West Virginia during the Smashing Pumpkins set in 1994.

So, we got up front, and I got my pictures (which, sadly, I can't find for the life of me). He also showed me how to hold my camera up over my head and shoot in the general direction of the subject, and hope for the best shot. He also explained that method could get a little expensive with the cost of film and developing, but he was being paid to take the pictures, and I was just a kid. I tried his way for a couple shots and don't really recall if they turned out or not. He was cool though, and it's a memory I will always have that involves Nancy Reagan. It's also a story that involves my mom, who was one of the most fun people I've ever been around.

When I began researching Nancy Reagan, and the possible locations I could hit, I found out she was born in New York City, but no remaining house, museum, historic site or landmark existed there. Her parents divorced when she was an infant. Her father abandoned the family, her mother resumed her silent film career, and left her daughter (now nicknamed, Nancy) in the care of her sister, Virginia, who lived in Bethesda, Maryland (very close to where I grew up). However, no museum, house or even plaque existed in relation to her early life in Maryland either. The natural choice was the library and museum in Simi Valley, but the Reagan Ranch north of Santa Barbara was a possibility, as well. It was December 2013 by the time I was setting up these trips for the shows that would be airing in January and February 2014, the Carter show being the last live show that aired in 2013. The series ended on Presidents' Day 2014, and I still needed to do another run through Texas for both the Bushes, and get myself over to Arkansas for Hillary Clinton. We took a short break from broadcasting for the holidays, which I thought would give me a chance to catch up on my work and my breath. However, the Executive Producer and I had just gotten word that all my travel and work had to be wrapped up by the end of 2013. That's when my contract was up, and there wasn't any money left in the budget to extend it. So, instead of coasting to the finish line, it was an all-out sprint. I had come this far, I wasn't going to skip or miss one of the ladies, and hard choices needed to be made. For these reasons, I kept my Nancy Reagan trip to one location. The Ronald Reagan Presidential Library and Museum in Simi Valley, California. I packed up my seven cases and bags, booked a plane, rented a car, and headed out to the West Coast. Again.

SIMI VALLEY, CALIFORNIA

It was a beautiful sunny California day when I drove up the long, mountain road driveway to the Reagan Library and Museum to meet my contact, Kirby Hanson, who was a special project consultant there. I barely had all my gear in the door, when she told me how lucky I was that some new items were brought in and donated recently by Mrs. Reagan. They hadn't even gone on display, and I was going to be the first person outside of the staff there to see them. So, that's where we started.

The items Kirby was so excited about were very personal to Mrs. Reagan, and she kept them in a small wooden box, about four inches long, three inches wide and two inches deep the size of a small paperback book). It was painted with a white glossy lacquer, and had a needle point piece on the top surrounded by a gold painted chain design. The needlepoint piece was of a brown-haired boy, and a blonde girl holding hands, and said, "LOVE IS THE WHOLE WORLD" in brown block letters. In the box were a few items that Mrs. Reagan held near and dear to her heart, and said the museum should have them, because they meant so much to her and her husband.

Ronald Reagan met Nancy Davis in 1949, when he was President of the Screen Actors Guild (SAG). She had the same name as a person on the Communist blacklist, was having trouble getting work, and needed his help. The two went out to lunch to discuss the matter. Later in life, Mrs. Reagan was asked if it was love at first sight. She said if it wasn't, then it was "pretty darn close." The two began dating and were married a few years later in 1952. In 1950, Nancy had signed a contract with MGM Studios and got her own dressing room. Reagan had a custom gold key to her dressing room with the thespian "Comedy and Tragedy" masks made for her at a Beverly Hills jeweler. That key was in the box.

Later in 1952, after they were married and bought their first house together, Nancy went to that same jeweler in Beverly Hills and had two more gold keys made for their new home. These keys were in the shape of a little house (like one a kid might draw…very square) with jeweled hearts for windows. Her initials "N. D. R." were engraved on the back of her key, and "R. W. R." were on the back of his. Mrs. Reagan added "Our First" engraved in her handwriting above the initials on his key as a little something special. Both of these keys were in the box, as well. All three keys were very heart-warming, and added to the love story of the Reagans. The box and all its contents were also a very "real" thing to me that made Nancy Reagan very human. These were two larger than life figures, when you combine their political and Hollywood celebrity. The little keepsake box was both endearing and relatable. Most people I know keep such jewelry boxes and similar items. It was like the feeling I got when I was shown Harriet Lane and Florence Harding's jewelry boxes. A lot of very personal and special items in there that gave me a closer connection to each of these women.

There were a lot of things on display that told stories about the Reagans' relationship. Mrs. Reagan was a very sentimental woman and kept a great number of mementoes from their wedding. They filled up a whole wall-full of cases in the museum. They had the wedding cake top, an invitation, photo albums, various books and documents, and her bouquet. The most significant item in the exhibit about their personal relationship was a letter Ronald Reagan wrote to Nancy dated July 15, 1953. He was staying at the Sherry Netherland Hotel on 5th Avenue in New York City, and wrote the letter on hotel stationery. The letter opens with "Dear Nancy Pants" (remember John Adams's letter from 1762 in which he calls Abigail "Miss Adorable," and the Richard Nixon letter to Pat from 1938 that began "Dearest Heart"). This letter was written as if Nancy were there with him at the dinner table that evening. He described the meal, what she would have liked and disliked. He discussed other people there in the restaurant, and how they may have laughed together at one woman's hat. This, again, made them real people. They became more than people on TV or in the White House. They were a young married couple in love. I often liken this letter in public speeches to things I (and other people) do when I travel and am away from my significant other. Only now, we text, take pictures of our food and all the other things modern technologies afford us. The fourth and final page of Reagan's letter concluded with this:

> "I suppose some people would find it unusual that you and I can so easily span three thousand miles, but in truth, it comes very naturally. Man can't live without a heart, and you are my heart. By very far the nicest thing about me, and so very necessary. There would be no life without you, nor would I want any.
>
> I Love You,
> The Eastern Half of Us"

The handwritten letter on the hotel stationery gave the whole display a classic, "Hollywood love story" vibe. There were a ton of black and white photographs of the couple's early life together in Hollywood, which added to the glitz and glamour. It was very romantic and impressive. The centerpiece to this part of the museum was a television monitor that played her 2002 "60 Minutes" interview I referenced earlier. She was so clear and honest about losing her husband to Alzheimer's disease and how it made her feel and what it did to her husband, herself and her family. It was very heavy.

This California lifestyle and her prior career as an actress carried over into her life as the wife of a politician. The series was called "Influence and Image," and Nancy Reagan had style and image for days. The exhibits that featured her gowns, dresses and outfits was fantastic. The first dress I was shown represented that transition from movie star to First Lady of California. It was a gold lame' gown made by one of her favorite designers, James Galanos. She wore it to Governor Ronald Reagan's second inauguration. It was floor length with a high, wide neck adorned with a large, bright, clear gemstone brooch. The entire dress had crystals and beads that sparkled and shimmered. The next dress was peach with a tied bow collar and horizontal pleats that alternated with the same smooth fabric in between. It had long sleeves that were slightly puffed at the cuffs, which were secured by two large buttons. This was said to be Mrs. Reagan's lucky dress. She most famously wore it to the 1980 Republican National Convention in Detroit when Reagan was nominated as the Presidential candidate for his party.

In 1985, President and Mrs. Reagan flew to Geneva for the first summit with Mikhail Gorbachev. Mrs. Reagan wore a very dignified and business-like navy blue skirt that fell just below the knees with a matching navy and gray houndstooth double breasted jacket. This ensemble was also designed by James Galanos. There was a picture of Nancy Reagan wearing the outfit at a lunch with Raisa Gorbacheva. The two women were seated in plush, pink chairs with a floral pattern and matching pillows. They were about to have tea served from an elegant sterling silver tea service. There was also a very ornate fireplace and mantel in the room.

Red was Mrs. Reagan's favorite color (remember Dolley Madison and her red rooms both in the White House and in her Montpelier home). She wore it often and most memorably in her official White House portrait. Her portrait dress, also a James Galanos, was on display in the case with several her other gowns. It was a sleek, long sleeved gown with a high, tight collar accented with multiple strands of pearls. She wore this gown on many occasions. It was a very flattering and elegant on her petite and slender frame. Nancy Reagan was in her 60's when she was First Lady. She very appropriately wore a lot of high tight necklines with stylish modesty. Most of the gowns on display there had this design.

One last outfit which could not go unnoticed, and without mention, was the one she wore to the March 27, 1982 Gridiron Club Dinner in Washington, DC. Mrs. Reagan publicly stated she wanted to restore a "Jacqueline Kennedy" style image of class to the position of First Lady and to the White House. This combined with her Hollywood past was often met with criticism. She decided to make fun of herself and wore a mish mash of clashing clothes comprised of bright yellow, rubber rain boots, a light blue floral print skirt that clashed with her loud red floral print blouse. She accessorized the outfit with a long double string of costume pearls, a white feather boa, and topped it all off with a red straw hat with pink, white and black feathers and a wide black ribbon that tied under her chin. She then gave a prepared speech…or rather song…called "My Second Hand Clothes" to the tune of "Second Hand Rose." Mrs. Reagan had quite a sense of humor, and was not opposed to laughing at herself.

It was impossible to talk about Nancy Reagan without discussing her "JUST SAY NO" anti-drug campaign. This was the focus of her philanthropic work as First Lady. She was not the first First Lady to take on drugs and addiction. We've seen First Ladies and Presidents of the past take vows of temperance and limit the amounts and kinds of alcohols served in the White House (Sarah Polk, Lucy Hayes and Frances Cleveland come to mind). We know President Lincoln was concerned about alcohol abuse in America before he was assassinated. And, of course, Betty Ford's ground breaking work in this area when she battled her own addictions after the White House and founded the Betty Ford Clinic. However, Nancy Reagan took this kind of work to a new level. She used her celebrity and her Hollywood friends and connections to reach a much wider (and younger) audience. She made appearances on popular television shows of the day like "Diff'rent Strokes." She used pop culture stars like Mr. T to help spread the word and deliver her message. She used marketing tools like commercials, PSA's, bumper stickers, t-shirts and board games to get the word out. She appeared at professional sporting events to speak to the crowds, and tell them it was okay to "JUST SAY NO." On February 4, 1988, Nancy Reagan was physically picked up by Indiana Pacer, Wayman Tisdale, and Philadelphia 76er, Charles Barkley, at an NBA game in Indianapolis, so she could slam dunk a "JUST SAY NO" basketball. The museum had these items and all the events represented in an exhibit. They even had the basketball she slam dunked in Indianapolis. It was her legacy as First Lady, and work she would continue after the White House. She changed the playing field when it came to the power, scope and level of outreach and impact a First Lady could make for a good cause.

On my way out, I passed through a room that showcased President and Mrs. Reagan's life on their Rancho del Cielo (or Sky's Ranch or Heaven's Ranch). Photographs, clothes and items used on the ranch were all on display. There were old cowboy hats and pairs of boots to show the down-home and casual nature of their time there. The photographs showed a genuinely happy couple living a lifestyle where they were most comfortable. The coolest thing, in my opinion, the museum had on display in this room, were their horse saddles. They had them set up with a backdrop that would make it look like you were riding the range with the former President in a photograph (you KNOW I got one…see photos in center of book). It was a great way to capture some images and get an idea about a place that was so special to them both. This made not going to the ranch seem more okay. I will get there one day and expand this chapter on Nancy Reagan about their life on the ranch.

I had one final stop to make before I left. I went to see and film the memorial and grave occupied by President Reagan. I was told that the Reagans had initially looked at Stanford University as the location for his library and museum, but they were turned away. Stanford already had a President associated with them in Herbert Hoover (not to mention a Republican President), and it seemed like overkill to them. A friend took the Reagans up the mountain to its current location to show them a piece of land he knew was for sale and available. They fell in love with the spot and the decision was made. I would have to say, it was a good choice. The view was spectacular, and on the clear day I was there, you could see the coast on one side, and for miles into the Valley on the other. It was a beautiful final resting spot (one of the more majestic I had seen throughout my whole adventure). As you all know, it's important to me to visit these Presidential couples and spend some time with them to thank them for all the information and sharing their lives with me, but this one was a little different. At the time, I knew Nancy Reagan was closer to the end of her life than the beginning. Her husband was already gone and waiting for her. I gave myself some extra time there to mark the significance of this moment. The next time I go there, I will be visiting President and Mrs. Reagan.

Travel Note – The Long And Winding Road

After my work, and before my dinner plans, I had time to ask Siri where the closest Harley Davidson dealer was. The closest one was Simi Valley Harley Davidson. YES! How far could that be? Well, you know the phrase "getting there is half the fun?" Well, I think whoever came up with that did so after driving from the Reagan Library and Museum to the Simi Valley Harley Davidson. These roads (or more accurately...trails or paths) that twisted and turned up and over the mountains even had a well-traveled daredevil like myself on the edge of my driver's seat. I know I said a few choice words, that could be misconstrued as off-color prayers, as I skirted the side of the road in my rental car. I also got to see some of the coolest and most unusual homes, yards and landscaping I've ever seen in the Continental United States. The homes prompted questions in my mind like, "how do they have water and plumbing way up here" ... "how do they get their trash taken away," and "where do they work that they commute from here every day?" I'm telling you, it was wild. Now, every time I fly into California, I look at the homes on the tops of all the mountains and ask myself those same questions. I did make it to the Harley dealer well before they closed and snagged a pretty cool shirt to remember Nancy Reagan and this leg of my adventure.

SUMMARY

Ronald Reagan once said something to the effect that he never made any decision in life or the White House without running it by his wife, Nancy. He got roasted in the press for his comments. The funny thing here was that when George Washington wrote similar comments about not being able to clear his mind and think straight during the Revolutionary War without Martha at his side no one seemed to care. There are a few reasons for this. The first being... not many, if anyone, knew Washington made these comments or thought these things, because there was no TV, not many people read his private letters at the time, and no one knew about them until long after he was dead, gone and on the one dollar bill and Mount Rushmore. My point here is, Presidents, leaders, men and women, husbands and wives have been sharing and taking and giving professional and personal advice since the beginning of time. It should not have surprised anyone when President Reagan came out and said it. Sarah Polk did it for President Polk, Lucy Hayes did it for President Hayes, Ellen Wilson and Bess Truman did it for their husbands, and on and on and on and on. This is not a political statement. This is a life statement about men and women. Humans. Significant others. And in most cases, we should be glad it is this way.

Nancy Reagan was a glamorous Hollywood star who made her way to Washington, DC hand in hand with her partner and the love of her life. She did this after very difficult and humble beginnings. She was abandoned and pawned off by her birth parents, and made her way across America to California and the silver screen. She then married a man who became the Governor of one of the largest states in America and then the President of the United States. She lived the American dream. She learned grace and style along the way and brought that back into the White House under much criticism, even though she was emulating one of the most stylish and celebrated First Ladies of all time. When she bought new White House china, the public complained about the cost and frivolous spending of tax-payer dollars. There are two things wrong with this complaint. Okay, maybe three. First of all, nearly every administration since the Monroe Administration has designed and purchased new White House china. Second, it was paid for by Reagan supporters and not the American taxpayers. Finally, Nancy Reagan would have gotten blasted for not getting new china and reusing old beaten up or out of style china if she hadn't gotten a new set (I know this because it's happened to other First Ladies). The American public, as a whole, can be very hypocritical with extremely short and poor memories. Again, this is not a political statement. It's about what's good or bad for one First Lady, should be the same good or bad for the next. It's not that way, and it will never be that way, but it should be that way. Nancy Reagan is the best example to point this out in modern times, and why I do so here and in my speeches and public events.

Climbing down off my soapbox (or china cabinet), and getting back to the specifics of the First Lady at hand. Mrs. Reagan changed the face and marketing technique of a First Lady's causes and philanthropic endeavors. Like Jacqueline

Kennedy, she used her style, grace, and the technology available to her to expand her reach and thus, her effectiveness. She brought the issues and problems of drug use and addiction further out of the shadows, and simplified it to "JUST SAY NO."

She could and did laugh at herself, which is important, in my book. She remained active and visible in American politics and her causes until she wasn't physically able to do so. But, above and beyond anything else, she stood by her man…even when he couldn't stand by himself. She was indeed unusual for her time.

Article By Andrew Och March 2016 On The Death Of Nancy Reagan And Her Relationship With Her Husband:

FROM MARCH 2016: A bittersweet ending has come to the Hollywood romance that is one of America's greatest love stories. Nancy Reagan began to lose her husband, President Ronald Reagan, in 1994 when he was diagnosed with Alzheimer's disease.

She then put him to rest in a grave on top of a mountain in Simi Valley, California, at the Ronald Reagan Presidential Library and Museum after he died on June 5, 2004.

Now, with her passing on Sunday, March 6, 2016, Nancy Reagan's spirit has climbed the mountain in Simi Valley to be by her husband's side once again.

During my research and filming as one of the producers of the C-SPAN series "First Ladies: Influence and Image," I visited the Reagan Library in November 2013. Just days before I got there, Mrs. Reagan had given the museum a little white box with some of her treasured keepsakes and mementos. Among the items were three gold keys.

Ronald Reagan had given the first key to Mrs. Reagan in 1950 when he was president of the Screen Actors Guild. They were dating at the time, and Mrs. Reagan — then Nancy Davis — had just been given her own private dressing room under her new contract with MGM. The gold key was shaped with the theater masks of tragedy and comedy at the top, and it went to her new dressing room.

Clearly, she thought enough of the token to keep it safe for 63 years until she turned it over to the museum.

Two years later, after they were married and bought their first house together, Nancy returned the gesture in the form of two gold house keys. The tops of the keys were shaped like little houses and had red heart-shaped gemstones. Mrs. Reagan's key has her initials engraved on the back and President Reagan's has his. In addition, his key has something special that his wife included for him. Above his initials, inscribed in Mrs. Reagan's handwriting, are the words: "Our First."

When asked if this was love at first sight, Mrs. Reagan always answered, "It might not have been, but it was pretty darn close." The couple often spent time away from each other because of his business travel. Reagan was out of town a lot as president of the Screen Actors Guild, as governor of California, and later as president of the United States.

One of the most personal and remarkable items at the Reagan Library and Museum is a letter that Ronald Reagan wrote to Nancy Reagan in 1953 shortly after they were married. He had been in New York on business, while she stayed behind in California.

The letter starts off very affectionately, addressed to "Nancy Pants." He goes onto have a conversation with her, as if she were there with him at dinner. He writes about the meal, and what she would have liked or disliked. He holds a written conversation with her about other diners in the restaurant, and laughs about jokes they would have told each other.

I was told that they used this style of letter writing quite often in these situations. The Reagans had a bond so strong and so special that even when they were apart, they were still together.

After the president's Alzheimer's had progressed, Mrs. Reagan did an interview on CBS's "60 Minutes" in which she talked about the "long good-bye" to her husband. She was very open about the loneliness that the disease had created in her life. She said that her partner, the man with whom she had spent almost her entire life, the man with whom she was looking forward to sharing her golden years, was taken away from her. Her pain was clear.

Now, Nancy Reagan's pain is gone. She will be laid to rest next to her husband, President Ronald Reagan, in the grave on top of the mountain in Simi Valley, California, at the Ronald Reagan Presidential Library and Museum.

She has been reunited with her "Ronnie." They are together once again.

I got into LA early enough the night before that I could meet up with some old friends, associates and even a former roommate from Washington, DC. It seems a lot of people I know went west, loved it and stayed there. I often wonder why music or television and film didn't pull me to that side of the country. Who knows, maybe it will someday. Here I'd like to give a shout out to Corbett Riner, Lee Ross, Shannon Prasad, Jenn Katz, and Disco Dan "The Dragon" Gallo. We had a blast catching up and eating sushi and frozen yogurt in Santa Monica. I will add here; The Dragon's new Polo and faux leather biker look was on point!

The second night of my trip I was fortunate to also head over to Los Feliz (pronounced incorrectly as FELL-IS) and see my old friend Jeff Tremaine. Jeff and I built our first quarter-pipe ramp together with Nick Rigopoulos, and Joey Cavanaugh (which I know I have mentioned earlier in this book). Jeff is also the Director and co-creator of "Jackass," "Wild Boys," "The Birth of Big Air," "Bad Grandpa," "Angry Sky" and many others. I'm very proud of him and the work he's done, and we've been fortunate enough to work on a few things together.

When I pulled up to Jeff's house in the hills of Los Feliz, he was standing in the street with another guy in a "Wild Boys" hoodie trying to jump start a woman's car. My rental car (which I failed to mention earlier) was a beautiful, bright, robin's egg blue 2012 Dodge Dart. I stopped my car next to their operation, rolled down the window and said, "can I help you boys with something?" Jeff's response was, "Sweet ride, dude!" I told them the rental car guy had told me it was "totally a rad LA color, man!" and that I had told him, "don't feed me that line of horse business, and just give me the keys, if this is the only thing you've got." All of which was true and quite a scene of its own.

Anyway, I jumped the woman's car with my Dart, and we went out to dinner at a local Irish Pub called The Morrison. The guy in the "Wild Boys" hoodie ended up being BMX super star Matt "The Condor" Hoffman, and we spent the night talking about ramps, tricks, BMX injuries (Matt totally dominated that portion of the conversation), First Ladies, favorite movies, talk shows and my plans to become the First Ladies Man. They had great burgers, and we were doubled over laughing the entire meal. Catching up with old friends and meeting new ones was the greatest side effect to this entire project, and I was grateful every time I got to do so.

CHAPTER SEVENTEEN

Barbara Bush

College Station, Texas

Barabara Bush was born Barbara Pierce on June 8, 1925 in New York, New York. Her parents were Marvin Pierce and Pauline Robinson Pierce. Barbara and George H. W. Bush were married on January 6, 1945. They have six children together. Barbara Bush is living in the River Oaks community of Houston, Texas, and Kennebunkport, Maine with her husband, President George H. W. Bush.

I leave politics at the door when it comes to these women. This is difficult sometimes in the Q&A portion of my speeches. People always want me to pick a side or talk about current news or opinion (especially in an election year), and bring politics into it. I may not be the sharpest knife in the drawer, but I'm not the village idiot, either. I get it. I know these are political people. However, my interest in them is personal. I want to know about the women behind the title and the position. I care about their husbands, children and families as they relate to them as wives, mothers, daughters, aunts, grandmothers, sisters, etc. Over the course of this project, I have had the opportunity and good fortune to speak to many people who are related these women, have worked for and with these women or their husbands, and some who are even still working in the White House and on Capitol Hill. Without question, the answer I get when I ask, "who was the best to work for or with?" is… "George H. W. and Barbara Bush." This says a lot about their character. The word I hear most from people that know or worked for or with Barbara Bush is "thoughtful." I also hear "genuine" and "tough" a lot, too.

In 2013, when Mrs. Bush was interviewed at their Houston home for the C-SPAN series, two significant things happened. She said she found it hard to believe that Americans couldn't come up with Presidential candidates whose names weren't Bush or Clinton. She went on to explain these families had served, and it was time for some new blood. This was before her son, Jeb, announced his campaign for the 2016 election. When Jeb did decide to run, she did what any good mother would do. She supported her son when she was needed. She has always supported her family, and served her country when she was asked (or required, because of her husband's work). Then, after the interview, she noticed one of the dogs had had a small accident in the corner of the room. She asked when that had happened, as she pulled a tissue out of her pocket and picked it up. Authenticity is another word often associated with Barbara Bush. She has always seemed to be a real person, and reports from people who know and work with her support that statement.

When I think of Barbara Bush, I get an image of a grandmother, and I know I'm not the only one. This was not unique to Mrs. Bush. Many First Ladies have given off a "Grandmotherly" image. Martha Washington, Abigail Adams, Eliza Johnson, Caroline Harrison, Florence Harding, Lou Hoover, Bess Truman have all been older ladies, and I think that look has worked out well for them. It's a trusting look. The only woman I can think of who this didn't work out so well for, was Rachel Jackson (story in Volume One).

Barbara Bush has looked the same since the first time I ever saw her. She has always been a pleasant, no nonsense, white-haired older lady wearing pearls.

However, she was not without her critics and detractors. She dealt with the negatives just like she dealt with everything else. She was typically upfront with refreshing and self-deprecating candor and humor. She was interviewed in the Ladies Home Journal during the early years of her husband's Presidency. She commented on things people had said about the way she dressed. She mentioned there was a myth "out there" that she didn't dress very well. She countered by saying she dressed very well, but just didn't "look very good." She was also very open about the fact that her trademark pearls were to conceal the wrinkles in her neck.

COLLEGE STATION, TEXAS

After two days in Austin for Lady Bird, I had all my bags and gear packed up and was headed for the George H. W. Bush Presidential Library and Museum in College Station, Texas on the Texas A&M campus. Like everything in Texas, it was big and spread out under beautiful clear, blue skies. I was meeting up with Director, Warren Finch, and his wife Mary, who was an archivist at the library. Warren worked at the National Archives in Washington, DC before he signed on at the Bush Library, so we had a lot to talk about, and much in common, when it came to living and hanging out in the Nation's Capital. As an archivist, Mary knew the facility and the collection very well, so my work here was going to be relatively easy lifting, as far as putting the missing pieces in between what already existed and what we got out of the recent interview with Mrs. Bush.

Because of the long face-to-face interview, and the significant amount of original material that existed from when Mrs. Bush was First Lady, only one of my video pieces was used in the live show, but it was a significant one. It was different than any other piece that had aired for any other First Lady. Mrs. Bush started making and keeping scrapbooks around the time she and George got engaged. They met at a Christmas dance in Andover, Massachusetts in 1941. They were engaged for a year and a half, and eventually married in 1945. There were hundreds of these scrapbooks in the library. There were hundreds of pages in the hundreds of scrapbooks. There were hundreds of photos on the hundreds of pages in the hundreds of scrapbooks. The Bush's entire life together was preserved in these books. They were displayed in a way and laid out in chronological order unlike anything I had ever seen for any prior (or future) First Lady. At the time of writing this book, President and Mrs. Bush had raised six children of their own (one daughter, Robin, died from leukemia at the age of three in 1953), had fourteen grandchildren, and seven great grandchildren. That's a lot of family to scrapbook. She was still adding new pages and books in 2013.

If Andover, Massachusetts sounds familiar...GOOD! It means two things. One, you read Volume One, and two, you remembered Volume One! Andover is where Jane Pierce's sister lived, and where her son Benny lost his life on the train tracks. Unfortunately, when I was in Andover for Jane Pierce, Barbara Bush was so far out of my line of vision, I didn't even realize the connection. I have a few thoughts about how Barbara Bush and Abigail Adams are similar, but I'll save those for the summary. There's not much point to this side note, other than to remind you Andover has a significant part in the lives of two First Ladies.

I was permitted to walk and film the library archive shelves that held the boxes that held the scrapbooks, and photo albums assembled by Mrs. Bush. To say it was vast and visually remarkable was an understatement. It was borderline overwhelming. I knew there wasn't nearly enough time to talk about even a fraction of the books. So, I did the next best thing. I got footage of them all. The shelves, the boxes, the books inside the boxes, and the books out on a work table The library had every book Mrs. Bush had ever made except for the ones she was working at the time of my visit, and maybe a few other select ones she was reviewing or keeping for any number of reasons. The point being, at least 95% of the books were right there in front of me.

As I walked the aisles, and looked at the labels on the boxes and all the years, 1941 through 2013, there was remarkable perspective that these books represented the lives of a lot of people. A large and active family with an extensive history.

It represented two Presidents and 3 presidential terms, which was 12 years. It showed two Vice Presidential terms, a CIA career, a stint at the RNC, the United Nations, a Congressional seat, World War II, and a lifetime together since they were teenagers. Where should I began, and what should I include?

I flipped through the pages of a number of random albums and books looking for pay dirt. In them I saw articles on a local, national and global level from every year and decade related to the Bushes' life together. Those hundreds of pictures per album came to life, and I almost felt as if I were looking at one of my own family albums. I recognized many of the faces, and the events, holidays, celebrations. Some of the poses were even like those of my own family's. Brothers and sisters were at sporting events and gathered around Thanksgiving tables with dads and uncles carving turkeys and making funny faces. Moms carried birthday cakes adorned with candles in to rooms full of people, balloons and presents. Weddings, picnics, graduations and just everyday life. It was all there.

This was when I got that weird sense of intrusion I had felt so many times before during this journey. I felt like my eyes were prying where they shouldn't be, and I had severely invaded someone's personal space. How would I feel if someone I didn't know was looking at all my pictures and letters and life the way I was theirs? It was odd to think that I now knew so much about these women, their lives and those of their families, too. I was lost in the pages and shelves and it was a very surreal experience. But, reality snapped me back into place, and I remembered these people were public figures who, for the most part, entered into their public lives willingly, and we did own a bit of their lives by nature of their positions. So, now, where was I going to start, and how would I bring something to the series that we didn't already know about Barbara Bush? Warren solved that problem for me, as he pulled one of his favorite albums which documented one of Mrs. Bush's favorite times and assignments of her life. China.

When President Ford reopened the lines of communication with China, George Bush was looking for a new position on the heels of his year at Republican National Committee. President Ford asked Bush what he wanted to do, and he said he wanted to go to China. So, Mrs. Bush packed her bags once again, and they boarded a plane for China. By 1974, the Bush's youngest child, Dorothy, was 18, and it looked like the Bushes were going to get to spend some time alone together for the first time since they were newlyweds. The U. S. did not have a full embassy in China at the time, nor did we have an actual Ambassador. So, Bush's title and position was Chief of the U. S. Liaison Office to the People's Republic of China. This also meant a smaller office, and virtually no staff. At least, not nearly the same numbers as that of an embassy and an Ambassador. This turned out to be an added bonus for Mrs. Bush, in that all of their interactions with the Chinese people and government were on a much more intimate and personal level. They could see and enjoy more of the country and its people, and they took every opportunity to do so.

From page one, the China scrapbook read and viewed like a vacation photo album. A very long year and a half vacation photo album. All the photos were black and white, and it appeared as though the Bushes saw nearly every part of the country. They took pictures of the house where they lived, and the surrounding area and neighborhood. The Bushes went most places by bicycle, and there were pictures of them with their bikes. They rode through squares and parks and visited numerous temples. There are pictures of them at dinner parties, having tea, shopping in an open-air fish market, and playing tennis. President Bush even learned a good bit of the language. There were also the obligatory photos from their day at the Great Wall.

A few pictures stood out to me as clear favorites. One was of their dog Fred, who was a cocker spaniel looking breed. Fred appeared throughout the whole album in various pictures, but the best one was captioned "Fred with bone." The Bushes were already very real and human to me. I remembered the Vice Presidency and Presidency very well, but animals made them more human for me, because of my own personal experiences and memories with my pets. The other clear favorites were a couple pictures of Mrs. Bush. Everything about these pictures was so different from every perception and image I had of her. Barbara Bush was doing Tai Chi, or some form of martial arts exercise, in a larger room surrounded by other people. She was wearing a white turtleneck under a dark sweater. She had on casual slacks with a block plaid-like pattern that were light in color…and SNEAKERS. She had a huge smile on her face in one of the pictures, and it looked as if she was having the time of her life. These pictures backed up everything Warren had told me about this being one of Mrs. Bush's favorite assignments and times of her life. This also achieved my goal of sorting through the mountains of scrapbooks to bring the viewer something they hadn't seen or known about Mrs. Bush.

Their third child, Neil, was dyslexic, and because of this, Barbara Bush has always held reading and literacy very near and dear to her heart. She is still very involved as the head of the Barbara Bush Foundation for Family Literacy, and it's impossible to walk through the George H. W. Bush Presidential Library and Museum without understanding how important this cause is to Mrs. Bush. In fact, it's one of the larger sections of a Presidential Library and Museum dedicated this cause. They had books, photographs, banners, cards, plaques and just about every kind of award, representation and recognition of reading and literacy known to man there in the museum. Mrs. Bush also still holds events and book fairs there at the library and museum in support of her foundation.

SUMMARY

In a recent interview, I saw with President and Mrs. Bush that was conducted by their granddaughter, Jenna, Mrs. Bush was the only one who didn't cry. Some people think Mrs. Bush is cold or stern. I would offer this counterpoint, she is confident and in control. She is the matriarch of a political dynasty that had the potential to do what no family has ever done in the history of our country. She could have been the wife of one President and mother of two others. Like it, don't like it, vote for them or don't vote for them…it could've happened. Instead she is just tied with Abigail Adams by being the wife of one President and the mother of another. She is quite different than Mrs. Adams in the fact that Abigail Adams didn't live long enough to see her son become President. John Quincy Adams was elected President in 1825, and his mother died in 1818. Adams' father did get to see his son elected President. He died the year after in 1826. However, Mrs. Adams and Mrs. Bush do have other things in common. Both women were the backbones of their families. Both women were very involved in their husband's professional and political lives. Both women were outspoken when it came to their political and personal views. Both women were fierce protectors and supporters of their children and husbands.

Most recently (in 2017), the world saw President and Mrs. Bush at the coin toss during Super Bowl XXXIII when the New England Patriots defeated the Atlanta Falcons 34-28 (sorry Falcons fans and Atlanta friends for bringing this back up). We have also seen the couple together in recent years on President Bush's birthdays when he has made skydiving jumps with the Army's Golden Nights. Mrs. Bush was always patiently waiting on the ground at the landing area for her husband to come back to her, safely. When those folks I mentioned in the introduction told me why they liked the Bushes so much, they were usually speaking of their kindness, and the personal touch they always put into conversations, remembering birthdays and special dates, and the nice cards and gifts that they always gave in recognition of these dates and holidays. Mrs. Bush has always seemed to be true to herself. This is represented in her clothes and her style. Like Lucy Hayes, Washington didn't change Mrs. Bush. She left as she came in. There's a lot to be said for that. She runs her family while supporting her husband, children, grandchildren and great grandchildren. She has done so in every instance of her husband's lifelong commitment to public service.

Mrs. Bush's candor and openness in her interview for the C-SPAN series gave us a real and unobstructed view into her life and the office of the First Lady in ways we had never seen or heard before. She explained her views and thoughts completely, honestly and with conviction. There is a lot to be said for that, as well. Her scrapbooks gave us an in depth look into one of the most well-known political dynasties of the modern world. The backstage pass into her and her family's lives was unprecedented as far as the series, my adventures and all the other First Ladies. And that says a lot about Mrs. Bush. There's a lot to say about Barbara Bush, and from where I stand, it's all good. According to my tally, Mrs. Bush has three primary schools and two middle schools named after her in Texas, an elementary school in Mesa, Arizona, a library in Texas and the Barbara Bush Children's Hospital at the Maine Medical Center in Portland. She is clearly unusual for her time.

Travelogue Food Tip

If it isn't wings and Caesar...it's BBQ! And when in Texas...I don't order salads. J. Cody's Steaks and BBQ was highly recommended by the clerk at my hotel, and I can say with certainty that my food choice streak continued through Texas. I had almost everything on the menu at it was all excellent. The cornbread, ribs and beans were particularly good, but seriously, you can't order anything bad there. As an added bonus, Mondays must've been open mic or open stage night when I was there. A pick-up group of what had to be some of the best pickers and grinners College Station and surrounding area had to offer was set up in the middle of the lower dining room kicking out old standards like "Folsom Prison Blues," "Always On My Mind" and "Move It On Over" for as long as I was there. And I was there for a while. If I didn't have an early start time the next day, I would've closed the place down. No doubt. And you can bet your brisket I'll go back some day. Great music and even better food is always a win win in my book. And it's actually IN my book!

CHAPTER EIGHTEEN

Hillary Clinton

Fayetteville, Arkansas

Hillary Clinton was born Hillary Diane Rodham on October 26, 1947 in Chicago, Illinois. Her parents were Hugh Ellsworth Rodham and Dorothy Howell Rodham. Hillary and William Jefferson Clinton were married on October 11, 1975. They have one child together. Hillary Clinton is living in Chappaqua, New York with her husband, President Bill Clinton.

From the moment Hillary Clinton hit the national stage and entered the White House, America knew they would be getting a different kind of First Lady. Even on the campaign trail, Bill Clinton said voters would be getting "two for one." This strategy hadn't worked out for other Presidents in the past (Ronald and Nancy Reagan come to mind), but seemed to do well for the Clintons. From the beginning of our Nation's history, these First Ladies had taken an active role in their husband's careers and politics (Adams, Madison, Polk, McKinley, Wilson, Roosevelt, Truman, Kennedy, Johnson, Ford, Carter and Reagan all come to mind). However, Hillary was about to take things to another level. She was a highly-educated woman for any time, and the two were a power couple right from the start. However, it was a start that almost didn't get started.

Bill Clinton met Hillary Rodham at Yale Law School in 1971. Their schooling and careers (both political and legal) took each of them all over the country. The couple lived and worked in Connecticut, California, Massachusetts, Washington, DC and Arkansas. Throughout the early 70's as they studied, worked and moved, Bill proposed multiple times to Hillary. Each time she refused, but they stayed together. Hillary wasn't sure if she wanted to give up her own promising and developing career for his. She finally gave up, and in her own words "chose to follow my heart instead of my head." She moved to Fayetteville where she and Bill had jobs teaching in the School of Law at the University of Arkansas.

When it came to researching Hillary Clinton, I had many options. Almost too many. Like Rosalynn Carter and Barbara Bush, the plan was to conduct a sit-down, face-to-face interview with Mrs. Clinton for the series. She was still involved in the Obama Administration, and was wrapping things up as the former Secretary of State at the time and we couldn't get our schedules to match up. So, the interview never happened. I should mention here…she was the first (and only) First Lady to become Secretary of State. I was going to go to the William J. Clinton Presidential Library and Museum in Little Rock, Arkansas, as I had done for many other First Ladies. However, they couldn't get their board together in time to approve and plan my visit. The Clinton campaign machine was in the process of battening down the hatches for the 2016 campaign, so I understood. She was also the first First Lady to run for President. She was the first woman to secure the nomination for President from a major U. S. political party, and she was the first First Lady to be elected to the U. S. Senate. If there's a glass ceiling in Hillary Clinton's way she will, more times than not, break through it, and you will hear her coming. There was more than enough footage, interviews, speeches, hearings, books, articles and information for the Clinton show without me even leaving taking one step outside of DC. Like the other locations I didn't have time or budget to visit during the C-SPAN series, I will visit the Clinton Library and Museum in Little Rock, and expand on this chapter for future editions.

Museum Note - Loud And Proud

I recently visited the National Civil Rights Museum at the Lorraine Motel in Memphis, Tennessee. It was a fantastic facility and extremely educational. It was a remarkable experience—almost beyond words—to stand in the room and walk on the balcony where Martin Luther King, Jr. was shot and killed. It was equaly remarkable–and even more beyond words—to stand in the room across the road where the assassin stood and pulled the trigger. It was one of the most solemn, and moving places I've been. To know the story so well, then read about it and all the theories in such great detail, only to stand exactly where it all happened from both sides, was life changing. I highly recommend a visit. In any event, there was a t-shirt in the museum gift shop that had, "Well Behaved Women Seldom Make History," and having recently completed and released Volume One, it gave me pause for thought. From my very first speech, I have been saying "behind every great man was an even greater woman," in reference to these First Ladies, but now I had another catch phrase to consider. Hillary Clinton was one of the first names that popped into my head. As sad as it is to say, or write here in this book, women have had to work extra hard to get noticed for certain accomplishments. This was something I learned from trip and First Lady number one.

But, if I never took a step outside of DC, we wouldn't have had any new or unknown material to bring to the Clinton show. So, with Little Rock unable to help me for the series, I had to look elsewhere in Arkansas. One of the many books which came in handy during my research was "Homes of the First Ladies" by William Clotworthy. It was great to learn more about the collections and locations of the presidential libraries and museums, but it was nice to have this resource to find alternative places, should the need arise, as the case was with Hillary Clinton. So, I contacted the Clinton House Museum in Fayetteville, and scheduled my final trip of the series.

Travel Note - A Light At The End Of The Tunnel

As was the case in season one, travel did not always go in order of administration and presidency. My long run through Texas took care of Barbara Bush and Laura Bush, and then I hopped a plane over to Fayetteville to wrap things up. It was a bitter sweet trip.

FAYETTEVILLE, ARKANSAS

It was a cold night when I landed in Fayetteville, and the whole town was decked out for the holidays. Fayetteville has a beautiful town square, and college towns are always active and fun. I checked into my hotel just off the square, and got settled. It was very nice and comfortable, and I had afforded myself a two-night stay in Fayetteville as a reward to myself for a road well-traveled. My host, and Director of the Clinton Home Museum, Kate Johnson, was going to pick me up in her Jeep, take me to dinner to plan our next day together. We ate at a nice place called Theo's with a lounge vibe right in the hipster section of town. I had fish tacos and they were excellent. At dinner, I discovered Kate had quite a family history in Fayetteville, and knew both Clintons personally. Her mother, Marilyn, was the former Mayor, and President and Mrs. Clinton had both visited her at the museum. Mrs. Clinton's first trip back to her old home was in 2007, when she first ran for President. We called it an early night, and I headed back to my hotel for a good night's sleep.

Author's Note – He Be Illin'...Again

Little did I know, but a 24-hour bug was about to creep up, and punch me in the gut HARD. It happened the next day, just after lunch. Hit me like a Mack truck outta nowhere. BLAM!! I guess the long and winding road had taken its toll once again. Lack of sleep, changing beds and venues every day, plus all the air travel was building up and having its ill-effects on me, but I wouldn't change it for the world. It really was a blast, and now looking back, it happened in a flash. Albeit, a flash of fever, exhaustion and sickness, but a flash none the less.

We met at the museum, and got to work bright and early. It wasn't a big house, and wouldn't take long, but I also wanted to get a tour of the town for B-roll, and hear about what the Clintons did there over the years, and what the town meant to them. It was especially cool to hear these stories from someone who knew them. The house sits up on a small hill near the university on what used to be called California Boulevard. The road is now called Clinton Drive. Kate had it changed by the city in 2010 when she was at the museum. It was a small shaker style house with brick and stone construction and a large matching chimney. A brick porch with a few steps and an iron railing lead the way up to the front door. It was very quaint, homey and kind of fairytale-looking. It gave off a Hansel and Gretel vibe (but, maybe that's just me). I got my usual tour of the house, and exhibits, loaded my gear in, and got rolling. This house told the story of the humble beginnings of two larger than life people.

I asked Kate to start outside as she told me the story of how the Clintons came to live here. The year was 1975, Bill was teaching at the university, and Hillary lived and worked in Washington, DC as a member of the impeachment inquiry staff advising the House Judiciary Committee during the Watergate scandal. One day when Bill was driving Hillary back to the airport after a weekend together, they passed the little house on the hill. She mentioned what a cute house it was, and noted the fact it was for sale. By the time she came back to Fayetteville, he had bought the house and prepared for yet another (fourth) proposal. He told her he bought her the house, and she would have to marry him, because he couldn't live there by himself. It was at this point, Hillary decided to "follow her heart and not her head." She accepted the proposal and moved to Fayetteville.

The move was not without its issues, and even temporary "buyer's remorse." Hillary and a friend packed up all her belongings in DC, and started driving south. Along the way, the two stopped at nearly every National Park. At each stop, Hillary tried to talk her friend into talking her out of moving to a state which she could barely bring herself to say out loud…for a man. Hillary loved Bill, and the two had been together for quite some time, but she was all about the Women's Liberation movement. The idea of giving up her promising career was giving her second thoughts. I couldn't help but think Mrs. Clinton must have been a big fan of Betty Ford (at some point), given the fact that Mrs. Ford was such a big proponent of the ERA, and women's rights, and went against her husband's Republican party to do so. Mrs. Ford also blazed new trails in the role of First Lady. In any event, she made it to Fayetteville, got a job teaching law at the university with Bill, and the two got married on October 11, 1975 right in the living room of the house on California Boulevard.

The wedding was held in the living room, and only nine people were invited. The invitations made it clear Hillary would be keeping her maiden name. While this didn't seem to bother Bill, reports from the event said Bill's mother, Virginia, "gasped" and Hillary's mother, Dorothy, "cried." Hillary and her mother had picked out her wedding dress the night before. They bought it off the rack at Dillard's, and they had a replica on display at the museum right in the living room accompanied by pictures from the ceremony. The dress was white with a high laced collar that plunged into a low neck line with a bow string. The sleeves were long and cuffed at the wrists and elbows with more lace that matched the collar. It was floor length with a tight waist, and very attractive. It may sound strange, but it matched the house, in my opinion. The rest of the living room was appropriately decorated with Clinton campaign banners, signs and memorabilia from both the Clintons.

One of the first things Hillary did after they were married was to convert the formal dining room into a campaign headquarters, resurrect her new husband's political career, and stage his successful 1976 run for the State's Attorney General of Arkansas. She referred to the room as the "War Room," and there was a desk with a map of Arkansas on it which had all the counties outlined. Her plan was to visit each county three times to form the base of their grassroots campaign efforts. This strategy would prove successful in future campaigns, as well. There was also some pop art of the Clintons hanging in the dining room. This, along with a life size, color, cardboard cutout of the Clintons for photo ops made for a fun experience for visitors (and me) at the museum.

Author's Note - Say Cheese

I have had my picture taken with a number Presidents and First Ladies (cutouts)...and seated at a few mock Oval Offices at various libraries and museums. I have posed with Bill and Hillary Clinton, Ronald Reagan, Jimmy and Rosalynn Carter, Dwight and Mamie Eisenhower, Lou Hoover, Warren Harding, and Millard Fillmore cutouts. I've also had my picture taken with reenactors who played Martha Washington, Dolley Madison, James Monroe, and Andrew Jackson. The Oval Office pictures took place at the Carter Historic Site, and the Reagan and Bush libraries. I looked quite Presidential in all these photos, if I do say so myself.

The next room was the kitchen. Apparently, not much went on in there, as Mrs. Clinton didn't cook. It was only mentioned that Bill used to cook fried food in here on occasion. It was average size, and nothing special. It had been restored to the original tomato red walls and counters with yellow and white shelves and cabinets like when the Clintons lived there. All the appliances were harvest gold. There was some cream ceramic tile work, as well. It was very 70's, and Mrs. Clinton always felt it needed to be remodeled.

The Clintons both made about $14,000 a year as law professors back then, and there wasn't much luxury or anything terribly fancy in their home. The back porch (which was later closed in) was where they slept during the warmer nights in the summer. This reminded me of the sleeping porch at Julia Grant's White Haven house in St. Louis, Missouri. They also entertained friends there. Their favorite games were Scrabble and Clue. This was when Hillary Clinton became a real person for me. I've been in the same room with her, and even shaken hands with her and President Clinton at a press picnic on the South Lawn of the White House. I knew they were real. However, a power couple with as much combined political clout and achievement as Bill and Hillary Clinton put them on a whole different level for me. It wasn't as historical as a George and Martha Washington, but more of a Franklin and Eleanor Roosevelt. It was even somehow stranger for the Clintons, because so many of my memories, and so much of my knowledge of them came from seeing them on TV in real time, as the events, his presidency and her political career were happening. They weren't TV "stars" per se, but they were definitely larger than life figures with a pop culture aspect to them. Seeing this back porch area, and knowing they had to sleep there, because they had no air conditioning, it all made them very real. They had a salary, and a budget. They played board games, and had friends over, just like my family. We were even playing the same games at the same time. I still have both of those games at the Deep Creek Lake house, and I'm sure most of you reading this have them, too.

We wrapped things up at the house, and I got some footage of the exterior, the road and the surrounding area, before we packed up my gear, and headed to lunch. We spent the afternoon wandering around the campus, seeing the town square, and posing with Razorback mascots and wooden cheerleader cutouts that you stick your head through for pictures. Kate explained more about Hillary Clinton, and how she adjusted to life in Fayetteville. Mrs. Clinton wasn't a fan of the city or the move in the beginning, as I mentioned. However, she quickly settled in, got to work, and became active in the community. Her work with children and civic groups began here, and she was accepted almost right off the bat by the people and students in Arkansas. The town square was a great place to get a feel for the city she had moved to and became a part of. It was also good to walk around the campus, and see the buildings in which she taught, the halls in which she walked and the offices like those she had at the school. I often say at my speeches, "I've walked tens of thousands of miles in the shoes of these ladies, and man, are my feet killing me!" I say this, of course for the comedic value, but it's also true. There really was no way better to get to know somebody. Hillary Clinton is such a well-known public figure it was hard to get to know a side of her that wasn't already known. I was able to do that in Fayetteville.

Political Note – What If?

What if Hillary won? I've been asked since speech number one at the Herbert Hoover Presidential Library and Museum in West Branch, Iowa. . ."What will we call Bill, if Hillary wins?" My answer has always been, "President Clinton." My answer meets with mixed looks of realization (that "ah ha" moment), confusion, bewilderment, confirmation (that "yup, I knew that" moment), and thoughtfulness. Until we conceive a title or position in the United States higher than President, and President Clinton wins it, he will always be referred to as President Clinton. All the looks I get are interesting and amusing to me. It's even more interesting and amusing that THIS was one of the first questions on people's minds when considering President Hillary Clinton. So much so, President Clinton was asked this by Stephen Colbert on the "Late Show." And do you know what one of the suggestions on the show was? You guessed it...THE FIRST LADIES MAN (too bad, Mr. President, I already own it)! I Tweeted the Colbert folks, and told them they should get the REAL First Ladies Man on (or at least do a Google search when they write the show), to get the real story on the possibilities that lay ahead for the spouse of the first female President elected in the United States. They never tweeted back. So, you get to hear my thoughts in this book now.

Keep in mind, Martha Washington was called Lady Washington, and she didn't even live in the White House, because it wasn't finished being built until the John Adams Administration. The first woman to be called First Lady was Dolley Madison, but she wasn't First Lady at the time. It was at her funeral when she was eulogized by President Zachary Taylor. The next woman was Harriet Lane, and she wasn't technically a First Lady, because she wasn't married to a President. She was the hostess for her uncle, President James Buchanan. The first sitting or active First Lady to be called First Lady is credited to Lucy Hayes, but there's even some debate about that, too. Everyone wants to be the first or the best or the most, don't they? When it came to titles and procedure and form, America didn't have everything figured out quite as quickly as we might like to think. However, if we are to follow the format of the television show "24," the title would be the First Gentleman. I think that's most likely where we will land, when it does happen. But, that doesn't answer the Clinton question. He would still be President Clinton, and that would have been an issue for President Hillary Clinton. So, here's my theory on how that would've played out.

President Clinton would be called President Clinton even in the role of First Gentleman in President Hillary Clinton's administration. This would create an issue (conscious or subconscious...overt or subdued) for any world leader or official who came to meet with President Clinton...if the other President Clinton were also in the room. Think back to how many times we saw Secretary of State Clinton or Senator Clinton with President Clinton in the same room or at the same event together. Not many. And, it would be the same—even more so—in a President Hillary Clinton White House. Hillary is intelligent and a very capable strategist, diplomat and politician. She knows her husband possibly better than anyone. He is no shrinking violet and everyone who is in the room with him leaves thinking they're Bill Clinton's best friend and favorite person. That's one of his super powers. Therefore, a genuine power struggle would arise between President Hillary Clinton and President Bill Clinton to control the room. It's in their DNA, it's just an inescapable fact. So, Hillary Clinton, being the intelligent person she is, would have her husband out and away from the White House. He would be "on assignment" any and every chance she got. This would avoid having any guest or visitor from having to choose which President Clinton he or she was going to deal with or speak to first. This would leave Bill Clinton as a de facto Deputy or Assistant Secretary of State (for lack of an official title) and out on the global stage where, quite frankly, he would do more good, and be more effective. He's still a very popular and effective figure in that arena. And let's be honest. The man is a former President, and a man. He would most likely not be doing the typical First Lady duties or roles, and by his very nature would have to be carving his own spot and blazing his own new trails. So then, who is the First Lady or official White House hostess, in a Hillary Clinton Administration?

Chelsea Clinton. Mrs. Clinton's daughter would, no doubt, step up to help her mother out with this role. She has White House experience. She grew up in the White House, and was trained to be in the public eye from an early age. Her parents knew what politics was about, and they taught her to brush things off and not take things personally when it came to the press. When Chelsea was young, and attended Sidwell Friends School in Bethesda, Maryland, she would often do her homework in the library at the Blair House (which is the President's guest house on Pennsylvania Avenue across from, and within walking distance to the White House). The Clintons are big readers, and would read in the evenings as Chelsea did her homework there. A daughter stepping up to help her presidential parent is not unprecedented. She would know the ropes, the events, the protocols, and her way around the role very well from her time there. And she wouldn't be the first.

Many female relatives have served in this capacity over the years. The third administration of our country had no official First Lady. Not that she would've even been called that at the time, but President Jefferson's oldest daughter, Martha "Patsy" Jefferson Randolph, was his official White House hostess. His wife, Martha, had been gone 20 years or so before he was elected President. The Monroe daughters filled in for their mother when she was ill with what we guess to have been epilepsy. Emily Donelson filled in for her Uncle Andrew Jackson when his wife Rachel died a month before he was inaugurated. Like Jefferson, Martin Van Buren was a long-time widower before he became President, and his daughter-in-law, Angelica Singleton Van Buren performed the hostessing duties for him. President Harrison's wife never had time to move to Washington, because her husband died a little more than 30 days into office. One of his daughters represented her mother at the inauguration. The very next administration was not without its First Lady issues, when the first Mrs. Tyler (Letitia) died in the White House, one of President Tyler's daughters filled in until he married the second Mrs. Tyler (Julia). Margaret Taylor's daughters helped their mother in poor health, as did the oldest Fillmore daughter for the same reasons. President Buchanan was the only President never to marry, and his niece Harriet Lane was one of the most popular and accomplished non-spouse hostesses in the history of our country. Eliza Johnson had consumption, and her two daughters handled most of the entertaining in their father's White House. Mary Anne McElroy would move to DC from upstate New York to help her brother, President Chester Arthur, during the Washington social season, because his wife had died very young before he was even elected Vice President, under James Garfield. Another Presidential sister, Rose Cleveland, served as official White House hostess for her brother, President Grover Cleveland until he could marry Frances Folsom Cleveland (the youngest First Lady at 21 years old). And, finally...President Woodrow

Wilson's oldest daughter, Margaret, filled the role when her mother died in the White House in 1914. So, it would seem Chelsea Clinton would have been in fine company should her mother have won, and she had been tapped to help her family out. It should also be noted, currently Ivanka Trump, in any capacity she may be assisting her father or First Lady Melania Trump, is also in that same fine company. While it may be unusual in modern times and recent history, it is certainly not unprecedented or unheard of for a female family member to help with the duties and role of the First Lady.

SUMMARY

Hillary Clinton was the most politically active and successful First Lady in the history of America. Period. She was the first and only First Lady to be elected a U. S. Senator. She's the first First Lady to be appointed a U. S. Secretary of State. She was the first First Lady (or woman) to be nominated as a major political party Presidential candidate. These are facts. Some folks may be surprised, disappointed or outraged I did not discuss any issues, scandals or troubles Mrs. Clinton has had or been involved (directly or indirectly) here in this chapter. My answer is simple. We've heard and read about them and continue to do so in other books, and in the news. This book is about where I went, and what I learned about these women during my travels for the C-SPAN series, "FIRST LADIES: Influence and Image." That's it. I am not personally or professionally interested in the salacious or the unseemly. I write about what interests me about these women and what makes them unusual for their time. Nearly every accomplishment she made as First Lady was unusual for her time and our country's time in that role. She redefined the office of the First Lady.

Mrs. Clinton has been a champion for children her entire adult life. She broke the First Lady role by getting directly and openly involved in policy during her husband's Presidency, in trying to reform health care in America. It didn't work for various reasons, but she tried. Many First Ladies before her were active in their husband's careers and in politics, but not when it came to dealing with Congress and developing policy. This was a game changer. She spoke before Congress in 1993 as the Chairperson of the Task Force for Health Care, and has done many interviews (including one for C-SPAN in 1997) about her role. In doing this she opened the door for criticism, and to make political friends and enemies. It paved the way for a successful career in politics, and it provided the ammunition to keep her from being President twice. Well behaved women seldom make history.

Hillary Clinton was like Martha Washington, Mary Lincoln, Eleanor Roosevelt, Jacqueline Kennedy, Nancy Reagan or any of the First Ladies of recent years. She was well known. She was arguably more well-known than any of the other women, because of the times and the news cycle, and the political career and the Presidential campaigns. What was I going to bring to the table. . . to the show…to the viewers, they already didn't know? With the help of Kate Johnson, I brought them Fayetteville. This was a side of Hillary Clinton, maybe even the Clinton campaign machine didn't want people to know. This side exposed her as a woman who followed her heart instead of her head. This was something that could have hurt her, in some people's eyes, during the election. This made her a human. And the country might not be ready for a woman who is also a human to be President. Hillary Clinton has broken through a lot of glass ceilings. However, the glass was still too think on the one she may have wanted to break through most. The one she had been waiting for all her life. Even if she couldn't break through to the Presidency, that doesn't make her any less unusual for her time, in fact it only makes her more unusual in that she tried.

Travelogue Food Tip

Every college town worth its salt has a solid burger joint, dive bar, greasy spoon. Fayetteville and the University of Arkansas are no exception. I must thank my good friend and video editor extraordinaire, Fetcher Bransford for telling me about Hugo's. From what he told me, and the burger I had while I was there, it was just as good as he remembered, from back in the day. There are a ton of great places to eat in Fayetteville, as I mentioned earlier, and will revisit in a few chapters when I conclude this book, and mention a few very special things about this last trip of the series. If you find yourself in Fayetteville, just make sure one of your stops is Hugo's for a burger. May I also suggest the onion rings as a side. You can thank Fletcher and me later.

CHAPTER NINETEEN
Laura Bush

Dallas, Texas

Laura Bush was born Laura Welch on November 4, 1946 in Midland, Texas. Her parents were Harold Bruce Welch and Jenna Hawkins Welch. Laura and George Bush were married on November 5, 1977. They have two children together. Laura Bush is living in Dallas, Texas and Crawford, Texas with her husband, President George W. Bush.

Laura Bush has always been a very real person to me. For whatever reason, I didn't need that "moment" when she became a real human being at a location… or because of an item or artifact. It was just a feeling I've had about her from the very beginning. Maybe it's because she reminds me of a cross between my mother (born in 1943) and my Nana (Mom's mom born in 1903). My mom was a teacher, and my Nana had a similar quiet grace and style. I met Laura Bush a few years before I even signed on for the C-SPAN project. In December 2006, I went on another amazing adventure to South Africa and Mozambique. This was also a work assignment. I was producing news for Channel One (a junior and senior high school daily national broadcast that went into subscribing schools all over the country). We (a team of three) went to Mozambique to do a short series on malaria. President and Mrs. Bush were holding the first White House Summit on Malaria in Washington, DC that December. Our work won a first-place Tele Award, and got us an interview with Mrs. Bush. She and her staff were delightful to work with, and the interview helped get our news pieces a lot of national attention.

Author's Note – A Picture Is Worth A Thousand Words

When you interview a President or a First Lady, their staff gathers your whole crew together for a group picture. They get your office address and ship everyone a picture as a souvenir of the event. It's a very nice courtesy [paid for, I'm sure by our tax dollars]. A few weeks after the interview, there was a white envelope on my desk with an image of the White House in the upper left-hand corner. I opened it, and there we all were, just as we had been photographed on the day of the interview. I was in my navy blue suit and white shirt with a red, white and blue tie, standing right next to the First Lady. I thought, "cool," and slid the picture back into the envelope and took it home. When I got home, I took the 8x10 photograph out, and proudly put in on my refrigerator. Quite honestly, I had forgotten about taking the picture altogether, and it was a pleasant surprise. I was admittedly and rightfully proud of myself and the work we had all done together in Africa and back here in DC. I took a step back to better appreciate the whole thing, and to my horror, I noticed a hand on Mrs. Bush's shoulder. It looked as if I had put my arm around her, like we were in a bar...or on vacation together...or at some college fraternity party! I was mortified. What would I tell my mother? Why hadn't Secret Service tackled me when I touched her? Why hadn't she slapped or punched me? I was so confused, and just stood there—mouth agape—staring. Then, I noticed something. Both of my hands were properly clasped in front of me at parade rest, as they should have been. So, who was groping the First Lady? Whose hand was on her shoulder? It was one of our cameramen, who [quite frankly] was older and been doing this kind of work a lot longer than I had, and should've known better than to touch the First Lady at all, let alone without some kind of invitation or appropriate reciprocating gesture initiated by her. At first I was relieved, and still am. It's the only way I was going to keep the picture up on the fridge [where it still is to this day 10 years later]. However, every time I see the picture, I can't help but think, "I hope Mrs. Bush didn't think it was me!" Out of respect for the guilty party, I will not reveal the cameraman's name here. Decorum. But, others in the picture reading this can go and look at their copy, and figure out who it was.

I knew we were going to have a sit-down interview with Laura Bush specifically for the series, as we had with Barbara Bush and Rosalynn Carter. We also had miles and miles of original footage, interviews and events, as we did with all the First Ladies from 1980 on. With the advent of CNN, and other 24-hour news channels this material was in abundance. There was also video of her at the White House during her father-in-law's (Bush 41) terms as Vice President and President. In addition to all this, the George W. Bush Presidential Library and Museum had just opened in April 2013. C-SPAN (and just about every other news agency) had already covered the construction and the grand opening. Laura Bush had given C-SPAN a guided tour of the facility and all its exhibits. What could I possibly bring to the table? How could I get any new information out of this location, and this First Lady? I planned a trip to the George W. Bush Presidential Library and Museum in Dallas, Texas to see what I could dig up and get on film that would be different than anything nearly everyone had already seen.

DALLAS, TEXAS

I got into Dallas very late after driving from College Station and a full day of work at the George H. W. Bush Presidential Library and Museum. It was a beautiful clear day for my 3-hour drive north. The Texas roads were long and straight, and it was a very pleasant ride, and gave me time to decompress, and switch gears from Barbara Bush to Laura Bush in my mind. I had a room at the Lumen Hotel, right across the street from the George W. Bush Presidential Library and Museum. It was a very comfortable sight for sore eyes, legs, feet and brain. The hotel had really decked their halls for the holidays, and everyone was in a very festive mood. There wasn't any time for me to celebrate with the other guests, though. The hour was getting late, and I had an unusually early start time in the morning. We were going to try and knock out most of our work before the museum opened at 9am.

Travel Note - Give A Man A Fish

As I checked into my hotel, I noticed a small decorative bowl with a goldfish on display at the front desk. As the clerk entered my information and programmed my room key, I was saying "hello" to the fish. The guy says, "Would you like one in your room, sir?" I said, "One what?" He replied, "A fish! We can have one sent up to your room!" I laughed and thanked him, but explained I had fish at home, and wouldn't even be in the room 24 hours. I didn't need a pet for the short stay. He said he understood, but to let him know if I changed my mind. It was "no trouble at all," and he could have it "taken care of at a moment's notice!" After I unpacked, I didn't have the time or feel the need to leave the hotel for dinner, so I ate at The Front Room Tavern, beside the lobby. I had steak tartare and tomato soup. It was excellent. After my quick dinner, I walked back through the lobby to the elevators (the decorations were really spectacular). As I passed the front desk, I stopped to talk to the goldfish, again (it gets lonely on the road). The clerk heard me and popped his head out from the back room and said, "Seriously, sir, it's not a problem...we can have a fish in your room by the time you get there!" I laughed again, and said, "No thank you" as I entered the elevator, and went up to bed.

It was a short commute across the street to the George W. Bush Presidential Library and Museum the next morning. It was also dark. John Orrell was the Public Relations Director, and I was meeting him at the loading dock at 5am. John was right on time, and there was no way I could've gotten lost driving across the street, but the new Bush facility was second in size and square footage only to the Reagan Library and Museum in Simi Valley, so finding the loading dock could've set me back, but it didn't. We loaded in my gear and got to work. I was quickly introduced to Director, Alan Lowe, who would be my on-camera guy for the day. Alan and I had a lot in common. He was a drummer, and his favorite band was the Foo Fighters. We were gonna get along just fine.

From my initial walk through and tour of the building and its exhibits, it was clear that a reoccurring theme was 9/11. It made sense. It defined the George W. Bush Administration and changed America and the world forever. It was also the impetus for many of my conclusions, opinions and overarching thoughts about Laura Bush, and her place in history as a First Lady. The museum had an entire room dedicated to the terrorist attacks of 9/11. There was a giant piece of twisted steel in the center of the room. It was a remarkable piece from one of the World Trade Center towers. It represented the horror, and destruction, but it also represented the healing and rebuilding in an artful way. They carefully and tastefully laid out a timeline, and explained where everyone was and how the events unfolded. This included First Lady Laura Bush. Alan took me into a conference in the back of the museum, where he had a very specific item he wanted to show me that was not on display.

On the morning of September 11, 2001, Mrs. Bush was on Capitol Hill in Senator Ted Kennedy's office about to speak before a Senate Hearing about education, and the "No Child Left Behind" program. Senator Kennedy had just given Mrs. Bush a painting he had done himself, as a gift. The next thing they knew the attacks were under way, and Mrs. Bush, Senator Kennedy and everyone in the Capitol building and surrounding areas were being evacuated. It was complete chaos, and no one knew what was really happening at the time. The museum had the painting. It was a green and yellow design with a hint of blue in a swirling pattern possibly inspired by clouds or the ocean in a simple, brown, wooden frame. The piece was about three feet by two feet. Alan explained that the colors had faded and changed after the painting was tested and treated for potential exposure to anthrax or other elements of chemical warfare surrounding the attacks. When Kennedy originally gave it to Mrs. Bush, it had been a gesture of friendship, and a symbol of hope in working together for better education for young Americans. The events of the day changed its meaning forever. I was amazed that in all the chaos of the evacuation and the day, the painting still existed and they had it there in Dallas.

The country was still confused and in a great deal of turmoil and uncertainty during the holiday season in December 2001. Typically, a First Lady chooses a theme for her Christmas tree decorations, and that year Mrs. Bush's theme was "Home for the Holidays." Her ornaments featured Presidential homes such as Mount Vernon and Monticello. She also had childhood homes represented with Lincoln's log cabin. There were many White House ornaments, as well. They were primarily white with different colored ribbons and gold accents. This tree and these ornaments were never on display for the public. Security risks were still too high. The U. S. Government and Intelligence Agencies were still unsure of the enemy and what to do about them. The tree and ornaments from Mrs. Bush's 2001 Christmas tree were on display in Dallas, and they were gorgeous. It was a beautiful tree, and a poignant exhibit. Being there in December made it all that much more special.

Historical Note – Oh Christmas Tree... Oh, Christmas Tree

Jacqueline Kennedy had the first "themed" Christmas tree in the White House in 1961. Her tree was in the Blue Room and had ornaments with toys, birds, and angels designed after Tchaikovsky's "Nutcracker" ballet. All First Ladies since have followed Mrs. Kennedy's lead and had a themed tree. Before her, however, Caroline Harrison had the first decorated tree in the White House, but it was only for the First Family and kept in the upstairs, second story residence of the White House. Lou Hoover had the first Christmas tree on display for the public, but it did not have a theme.

Laura Bush changed after 9/11. We all did. We had to. But, we all weren't First Lady. When her husband took office, he was not a foreign policy President.

He was not interested in nation building. Like her husband, Mrs. Bush was a domestic First Lady. Her interests were with education, children and reading. She was a librarian, who happened to fall in love and marry a man who became President of the United States. Her's was a story like many First Ladies. They don't teach FIRST LADY 101 in college. The only training for the unelected and unpaid job of First Lady was life. So, after the dust of the attacks settled down, and the country got its feet back on the ground. Mrs. Bush changed gears for the world that had changed around her. She became a well-traveled champion of women's rights and women's education around the world with a focus on war-torn countries, and the countries of our enemies and our attackers. Laura Bush traveled to over 70 countries during her time in the White House, and became a global ambassador for women everywhere. She did all this very quietly, too. Her post 9/11 travels reminded me of Mrs. Nixon's goodwill travels and foreign aid trips. Her trips were not a PR mission or photo op. Sure, there were pictures, footage, events and news coverage. A President and First Lady can barely make a move these days without a news crews covering it, but Mrs. Bush traveled with dignity, grace and humility. She had a purpose, and it was genuine. The museum did what Mrs. Bush didn't do while she was First Lady. They highlighted her work and travels. There were several cases and displays with maps and pictures from many of Mrs. Bush's foreign trips. There were gifts she had been given, like traditional ceremonial gowns and outfits. She was given a lot of jewelry, and colored beads, scarves, sashes and robes. The colors and craftsmanship of these pieces were amazing. It was like looking at the U. N. General Assembly or a United Colors of Benetton ad (for those old enough to remember). It really was remarkable to see the culmination and collective efforts of so many miles and so much work there all together in one room. And as Allen reinforced, she did it all fairly quietly and without much fanfare.

There was also a section in the museum that focused on President and Mrs. Bush's work in Africa with HIV/AIDS and malaria. That December I went to Mozambique in 2006, the Bushes had donated a huge amount of time, efforts, U. S. funds, research, and mosquito nets to help the people of Africa (specifically Sub-Saharan Africa) who suffered so greatly. A large number of treated sleeping nets were gifted in the Bush family names as Christmas presents to towns and villages there. The museum had actual nets on display, and pictures of the people they helped, illuminating the good they were doing. Having been there on the ground and seeing the suffering first hand made this a particularly moving exhibit for me.

One exhibit still under development, was the situation room, and Alan was more than willing to give me the grand tour of the work in progress. The set up consisted of three rooms. They had an Oval Office, a situation room and a briefing room. The oval office had actual wood panels, carpet, and furniture from the George W. Bush White House. Some of President Bush's Oval Office items were given to the Reagan Library and Museum. The whole set up was to create mock emergencies and situations for school children to understand a little bit about life in the White House as a member of an administration, and as a member of the press corps. The Reagan and Bush facilities could communicate back and forth to work on the same situation together. As a librarian with her great interest in education in America, Mrs. Bush's fingerprints and influence were all over this interactive exhibit. The George W. Bush Library and Museum was the newest in the fleet, the shining example of what a Presidential Library and Museum could be, and they had all the bells and whistles. It was a massive foot print in the facility and an exciting new way to teach children about their government and the free press.

As I finished my behind the scenes work and preview of things to come, the museum was opening to the public. There was one more thing Alan wanted me to see. The main lobby. Speaking of "shining" example…this was the "crowning jewel" of that shining example. By law—the Foreign Gifts and Declarations Act of 1966—a President and First Lady can only accept gifts of a certain value. All others must be turned over to NARA. As of January 2014, the amount was $375. Anything valued more than that was property of the U. S. Government and its people. The main lobby had square display cases built right into the white marble walls about three feet by three feet by three feet. There were about ten on each of the two outside walls, twenty altogether. Each case had a display of gifts of state that had been given to the Bushes while they were President and First Lady. There were swords, daggers, vases, watches, clocks, masks, tea services, and carvings in every color, shape, size, and material you could think of.

There was even a golden oasis sculpture that had been a gift from Saudi Arabia. It looked kind of like a little cedar nativity scene I remember being out at my house growing up around Christmas—only this one was much bigger and made of gold. It shined like something out of "Raiders of the Lost Ark." In fact, the Executive Producer for the C-SPAN series (Mark Farkas) and I had always talked about those "moments of discovery" or feeling like Indiana Jones going into these storage facilities, and collections. Here it all was right in front of me. Every case had something in it that looked like it came from King Solomon's mine, Blackbeard's treasure chest or King Tut's tomb. It was unreal. It really was as unique a collection as anything I had seen (and remember, I had seen some impressive collections). There was a jeweled gold stirrup set which had been given to them by the Moroccan government and people. The one item that stood out to me was directly across from the main desk in the center of the lobby. It was a diamond and sapphire necklace. I'm guessing the setting was platinum. It was silver in color and the whole piece was like nothing I'd ever seen. The case that probably meant the most to both President and Mrs. Bush contained memorial bracelets from the families of captured and killed U. S. service members. You really couldn't go anywhere in the museum without understanding the gravity and impact of 9/11 and the subsequent conflicts.

SUMMARY

When it came time for the live Laura Bush show, none of my video pieces made it to air. I wasn't upset or disappointed. We had all the bases covered, and my rule of thumb for success was met. If after all the reading, all the studying, all the exhibits, all the interviews, and all the footage I learned something new during the show? We had (or I had…as it was my personal mark for my own satisfaction) succeeded. Laura Bush has always been a kind and compassionate person. We can see that in her efforts for better education for young Americans. We can see that in the love, support, and respect she gives her family, friends, colleagues and the American public. She's what my mother called a "class act." The big accomplishment for me, in going to the George W. Bush Presidential Library and Museum, was that I had learned something new about Laura Bush. I knew how life had changed in America, and I knew how life had changed for me personally. I now knew how life changed for this First Lady. As I have mentioned before in these two books, I am often asked who my favorite First Lady is. A cheap answer is all of them, and it's not entirely incorrect. However, my "better" answer is to break them down into some of my favorite Ladies by century. It lets me answer the question without answering the question, because it's a question I can't honestly or definitively answer. The first time I spoke about this in prepared remarks was with a private women's club in Dallas, Texas. It was met with great approval (no surprise), but I wouldn't have said it if I didn't mean it. My favorite First Lady of the 21st century is Laura Bush, and here's why. The terrorist attacks on September 11, 2001 were like nothing else I, we, the world, had ever seen, and hopefully we never see anything like it again. It was life changing for our world. Laura Bush had to change everything about her role and focus as First Lady, and she did this with the eyes of the world upon her. She had to represent the United States of America in this new world as First Lady. It happened while her husband was President. She was the first First Lady to have to do this in this way and she did it without training, without specific education, without being elected, and without being paid. It played out in every medium available, including television and radio, domestically and abroad. She carried herself with confidence, humility, style, grace and purpose. This is a woman who was truly unusual for her time. We all changed after 9/11. We had to. Laura Bush did it as the First Lady of the United States of America.

Travelogue Food Tip

The only real meal I had that I can mention or pass along here, is the dinner I had at The Front Room Tavern. If I was only going to have one sit down meal in Dallas on this trip, that was a great place to have it. It was a lovely restaurant, and the holiday decorations and cheer only added to the success and ambience of the whole scene. The place was busy, which made the people watching better, too. The tomato basil soup was fantastic. It was creamy enough without being too heavy. The basil wasn't overpowering, either. Just a hint. The steak tartare was amazing. Cooked to perfection, as any steak tartare should be. You don't want to get the outside too crispy or well done. It was served with a nice cracker-like flat bread which complemented the steak, and the soup. So, that was a win-win, too. It was a quick trip to Dallas, and what I ordered wasn't necessarily what I would call "local" cuisine or my regular, but it was a light and pleasant change on a late night in Texas.

CHAPTER TWENTY
Michelle Obama

Washington, D. C.

Michelle Obama was born Michelle LaVaughn Robinson on January 17, 1964 in Chicago, Illinois. Her parents were Fraser Robinson and Marian Shields Robinson. Michelle and Barack Obama were married on October 18, 1992. They have two children together. Michelle Obama is living in Washington, DC with her husband, President Barack Obama.

WASHINGTON, DC

There is a difference between intelligent and well-educated. Michelle Obama is both. In her exit interview with Oprah Winfrey, Mrs. Obama said she had no interest in a future political career. If she ever changes her mind, I think she will do very well. She is a highly-educated person, with an Ivy League education and a law degree. She was intelligent enough to play the role of wife, mother and First Lady very well. I feel as though it came very naturally to her, because she was always so genuine. Even in uncomfortable moments, she seemed unflappable. In an interview for the C-SPAN series she even said she tried to bring enough of herself into the role while still respecting the tradition of the role and the women who came before her. When she spoke about the unique perspective each woman brought to the position and her surprise at any comfort level she had living in the White House as First Lady, she said something that reminded me of a sentiment Lucy Hayes had shared about being First Lady. Lucy Hayes said she could never compare to the great women who had come before her. This mirrored Mrs. Obama's sentiment about each woman inserting enough of herself into the role to make it her own, and being able to connect with those women in her own attempts. The respect both Michelle Obama and Lucy Hayes gave to the women who came before them was admirable and humbling. When Mrs. Obama first moved into the White House she met and spoke with former First Ladies Laura Bush and Nancy Reagan. She wanted their perspectives. She wanted their advice. By the time she had one term under her belt, she began to sound a little like Martha Washington who had compared being First Lady to being in a prison. Mrs. Obama said in one interview that her new bangs were her midlife crisis, "because they wouldn't let [her] bungee jump or get a sports car." She said she often daydreamed about walking out the door of the White House, past the Secret Service only to just continue walking.

Michelle Obama, having a similar educational background as Hillary Clinton, could have easily taken the same road that Clinton did, and gotten into policy and politics. Instead, she raised her children, supported her husband, our troops, and the nation's children. She took a more traditional approach to being First Lady. She did this all with a genuine interest and sincerity that worked very well for her and the causes and people she supported. This also made it very difficult for her to create enemies (especially political ones). She lived in the White House for eight years. She knows the deal, and she learned the ropes without getting too tangled up in them.

During the C-SPAN interview that aired in the introduction show for the series, Michelle Obama gave her thoughts about the role of the First Lady, and how she fit into the picture. She mentioned she could connect with modern "ground floor" First Ladies like Eleanor Roosevelt and Jacqueline Kennedy. She knew their stories and they were "real people" to her. I got that, and felt the same way about the women who had been alive and active in my lifetime. So much so, I wrote about it in nearly every chapter of these two books. She said the "second story" First Ladies, and more historical First Ladies were harder to identify with, because they were characters from "wonderful stories" in history books. I could relate to this, too. They were faces on paintings, and lessons in classes. It was exactly what I had been feeling or thinking about all these women before I began this journey. My travels, the locations, the letters, the pictures, the stories, the rooms, the buildings, the artifacts, and collections made these women come alive for me. I knew exactly what Mrs. Obama meant when she said the historical women were not as easy to identify with, because I was right there with her, until I walked all the miles, and became the FIRST LADIES MAN.

There was no museum or library to visit for Michelle Obama. There was no plaque at a birthplace home or collection of artifacts at a university or college. I have been to Chicago many times, but never specifically for Michelle Obama. She did have an inauguration gown and shoes in the First Ladies exhibit at the National Museum of American History. I've seen it as many times as I've been in the museum (which is quite a few). Her gown was a beautiful single-shouldered white silk chiffon creation by Jason Wu. His inspiration behind the dress, which was also accented with organza flowers and Swarovski crystals, was hope (a theme of the 2008 Obama campaign). She wore matching open-toed shoes designed by Jimmy Choo with a modest heel. Her diamond earrings, bracelet and ring were designed by Loree Rodkin. The whole ensemble was stunning. She and President Obama looked like they stepped out of an early 1930's or 40's Hollywood movie. She was ready to take Washington, DC and the world, by storm as First Lady, and she was dressed for it.

I didn't do any travel or hit any specific locations for Michelle Obama, nor did we think I would need to. The loose plan, and expectation was to have Mrs. Obama on her own show live, as the current First Lady. At the very least, we would do a new sit down interview for her show, as we had done with Rosalynn Carter, Barbara Bush and Laura Bush. We even kicked around the idea of doing the last show from the White House, as we had done location broadcasts from the Wilson House in Washington, DC and the Eisenhower Farm in Gettysburg, Pennsylvania. All these options sounded great to me. At the very least, I could pop back over and visit my friends at the National Museum of American History, and put together something on her dresses, and any other artifacts they might have from the Obamas. Well, none of that happened. Not a huge problem, because we had two very capable guests, an excellent host, countless viewer calls and endless video from campaigns, speeches, past interviews and events. There really was (as was the case with all the "modern day" First Ladies) too much material. So, when it comes to Michelle Obama, I can only share with you my current thoughts, as I am writing Volume Two, and assure you I will add to this chapter down the road as the Obama Administration, and Michelle Obama's contributions as First Lady transition from current news to the pages of our country's history books.

The Barack Obama Presidential Library and Museum is scheduled to open in 2021 in Chicago. This facility will be the first Presidential Library and Museum not to be operated by NARA, instead it will be run entirely by a non-profit foundation (the Barack Obama Foundation). Other Presidential Foundations play a significant role in their libraries and museums, but all the others (Herbert Hoover to George W. Bush) work with NARA in doing so.

In her eight years as First Lady, she was on the cover of almost every magazine out there—multiple times. I can hardly remember being in line at the grocery store and not seeing her face on "Redbook," "Good Housekeeping" or any number of other magazines. She did several interviews on daytime television, like "Ellen" and "The View," and she was a fairly regular guest on "The Tonight Show with Jimmy Fallon." She did funny skits with Ellen and Fallon, and proved herself to have a very good sense of humor, and always came off as a naturally appealing individual. She had a kindness, and genuine quality in interviews, like Laura Bush. She wasn't stuffy. She was young, attractive, stylish, had young children, and was raising them in the White House. This was the formula for success for Julia Tyler, Lucy Hayes, Frances Cleveland, Edith Roosevelt and Jacqueline Kennedy, Rosalynn Carter and Laura Bush. There was one thing about Michelle Obama no previous First Lady could claim. She was, and always will be, the first African American First Lady in America. There's no changing that, disputing that, or taking that away from her.

Author's Note – I Love A Parade (aka The Coldest I've Ever Been In My Life)

Remember when President Reagan cancelled his second inaugural parade because of the cold temperatures? No? Well, apparently, neither did President Obama. When President Obama was elected, I was working for Sky News and teamed up with one of their Washington correspondents, Robert Nisbet, and cameraman, Jeff Martino. Both are some of the best in the business, real pros who continue to be fantastic to work with. Sky News was in the process of switching to HD. All the major networks and news organizations were in the middle of it, and working hard to figure it all out. It was a big deal on top of an even bigger deal. We had reporters, producers, crews and technical teams in from all over the world. The Nation's Capital was a circus (more so than usual). Roads were closed off and things were shut down all over the city. Hotels in DC and surrounding Maryland and Virginia were booked solid. It seemed as though the world was coming to Washington, and anyone that wasn't already here would be watching it on TV, and we had to make that happen.

We went out for a big meal the night before with most of the team. We ate well, shared stories, and had a great time. I parked my truck on a safe street and crashed on a colleague's couch to make for an easier commute in the morning. We had to get started and in our assigned position along the parade route in the wee hours of the morning, before it was even light out, due to the incredible amounts of security that surrounded this type of event. So, I dozed off under a throw blanket, ready to brave the elements and the challenges of the next day.

I woke up early the next morning, and something was off. I wasn't quite sure what was wrong, but something was physically wrong with me. It wasn't that I slept funny or didn't sleep enough. Maybe I was coming down with something, or the calamari didn't sit quite right, but I didn't have time to worry about it. I suited and bundled up, and started walking down to the parade route. I was instantly frozen from the time I stepped outside, but the brisk walk kept my blood pumping and the hypothermia at bay. I got to our location without incident, and met the rest of my team there. We started running cables and getting our spot sorted out on the bleachers with the throngs of other news crews when we hit our first snag. A Secret Service agent told Robert we couldn't be down along the metal fences where I had taped down some cables. I asked which agent had told him we couldn't set up where we wanted to. I had quite a bit of experience with Secret Service during my White House Transmission Pool days during the George W. Bush Administration. I knew in most cases, if you politely talked it out with Secret Service and found out what you could do, as opposed to what you couldn't do, both parties got what they wanted. I spoke to the agent and explained that once every other hour or so we wanted to walk down to the fence, plug into our cables and get some interviews and reactions from the people in the crowd. He said that was fine if our camera stayed up where it was supposed to be on the bleachers, and we didn't stay plugged in down by the fence while we weren't broadcasting live. I didn't even hesitate or ask why he needed us to do what he had asked (Secret Service ALWAYS has a reason). We got what we wanted, and the agent got what he wanted. Later in a Sky News documentary about switching over to HD, Robert credited me with "saving the day and the live shot" during our inaugural coverage, and I remain flattered he said so.

So, as I continued to run our microphone cables down to the metal fence it hit. The sickness. Whatever I had, hit me like a ton of bricks and I almost blacked out. I seriously lost my vision for a moment as I was down on my hands and knees securing the cable. I was only roused back to reality by Jeff yelling down to me something like, "Hey, Andy… you got that cable locked down?" I shook off the haze, and replied something I hope made sense, but don't even remotely recall. All I thought was "not today…I can't be sick…I can't go home…not today." So, I gathered myself and walked back up to our spot on the bleachers, and sat down. Finally, after a few live reports, and a complete inability to eat or drink anything, I confessed to Robert and Jeff that I felt on the edge of death, but would persevere. I had to. There was no other choice. There was no one to fill in for me, even if we could get them through the crowd to where we were in a timely fashion. Which we couldn't.

So, our work continued and the morning turned into afternoon. I had high points and low points, and the only thing that made the high points high was that they were slightly better than the worst I've ever felt in my life. Fortunately, at some point, I got so cold that everything (including the misery) reached a plateau, and I just got used to it. When the day turned into night, and the Obamas were safely in their new home getting ready for all their inaugural ball and celebrations, it was time for us to pack up. Robert and Jeff took mercy on me and the whole process was as painless as possible. Then, we had to wait for our ride to come pick us and our gear up. The van showed up, and we piled in with a couple other crews, and headed back to the bureau. My next challenge was getting back to my car. On any other night, it wouldn't have been a problem. However, I had no idea if there was a Metro (subway) stop near my truck, I couldn't get a cab to (almost literally) save my life, and my brain was so fogged up, I wasn't exactly sure where I had parked my truck. After a walk that seemed ten times longer than it had been that very morning, I found my truck. I was like a guy in a movie stranded in a desert, who just stumbled onto an oasis complete with a harem of belly dancers and a buffet of fresh fruits and vegetables. My truck never looked so good. I got in, turned it on, and cranked the heat. I felt like a cartoon character (Elmer Fudd, or Pepe Le Pew) who was being thawed out, and I could imagine a line of color scroll down my body from head to toe, as I thawed. The only problem was the cold temperatures that had plagued us all day were also keeping the sickness from fully attacking my body. The warmer I got, the worse I felt. The virus was also thawing inside me. I barely made it home, and into bed. I drank copious amounts of tea, Nyquil, and Theraflu. Enough to knock me out, and keep me in bed for a full 24 hours until it passed. It seemed to exit my body as quickly as it entered. One minute it was there, the next it was gone.

Here's what I took away from that day. I did get to see, and clearly remember the newly elected President and First Lady pass by on their way to the White House. The peaceful transfer of power we pride ourselves on in America, the rights that men and women have fought and died for walked right in front of me. I was proud to be an American, and even through the sickness and the cold I was harboring, that pride warmed my heart.

It was also interesting to hear the thoughts of my colleague's from other countries. For a country as diverse as the United States of America, they were rather shocked we were just catching up and melting into our own pot, as far as our leadership was concerned. This fact lead me to the most remarkable happening and memory of the day. We interviewed a man who had traveled, on what may have been one of his last dimes, to Washington, DC. He was not a young man. He stood along the parade route all day long in the freezing elements, so he could see a man who looked like him enter the White House as President of the United States. He cried as he told Robert his parents and grandparents wouldn't have believed it, if they had lived to see it. He could hardly believe it himself. As he told us all this, I felt a warm tear roll down my frozen cheek.

One more positive check mark on the clipboard of Michelle Obama's likability was that she was the mother of two young daughters during her time in the White House. I have mentioned in both volumes of this book how hard it is to be a mother and a First Lady. This was especially hard when the children are young and going to school while their father was President. The Tylers, Lincolns, Hayeses, Garfields, Clevelands, Roosevelts, Coolidges, Kennedys, Carters, Clintons and Bushes (George W. and Laura) all went through this. There's a whole other series to do on the children of the White House. But, their parents, and specifically their mothers, had to raise them there, as the world watched. The Obamas did a remarkable job of keeping a close eye on their daughters, letting the public feel like they had appropriate access to and information about them, while letting them be as normal as possible…given the circumstances. As far as child rearing in the Executive Mansion goes, I give President and Mrs. Obama an "A+." The only thing they really caught grief over was when Mrs. Obama moved her mother into the White House to help raise the girls. I have three things to say about this. One, children need their grandparents, if they are fortunate enough to have them in their lives. Two, you can't tell a mother how to raise her children (especially, when you didn't elect her and you don't pay her). Three, if you knew (and you do now from Volume One) how many family members and friends the Jacksons and the Grants (and many others) moved to Washington, into the White House and onto the tax payer's payroll, you wouldn't mind one little old lady from Chicago coming to town to be with her two granddaughters.

SUMMARY

Mrs. Obama has written the story of her time as First Lady. We watched her do it live on TV for eight years. She is working on a book that will, no doubt, tell even more of her story. Then, it's up to the American people, the world, the Barack Obama Presidential Library and Museum, and history to show us her legacy. As I have mentioned, I will be doing a lot more research on this woman in the years to come. I found her to be a highly intelligent, well-educated and likable person. She was dedicated and genuine in her work as First Lady. She gave respect and credit to the women who came before her. Lucy Hayes supported causes, veterans and philanthropies before it was expected or cool. Michelle Obama made the whole job of First Lady cool. She embraced it. She took charge of it. She made it her own. She blazed her own trails without covering the ones made by other First Ladies, and that's not an easy thing to do. She was both traditional and non-traditional. She knew when to let her hair down, and even better, she wasn't afraid to do it. She has a lot in common with Betty Ford in that area. If she wanted to do something, or thought it was important, she did it. She did it all with class, and, from where I sat, it looked like she had a blast doing it. From the first day of her husband's first term, to the last day of his second term—Michelle Obama was unusual for her time.

Perhaps her greatest accomplishment as First Lady was to not get wrapped up in politics and policy, creating enemies who could keep her from pursuing a future political career. There are some that think she still will (and want her to), even though she says it's out of the question. Michelle Obama is a young woman with a bright future ahead of her. She kept her children, and the children of America as a priority in her life the entire time she was First Lady, and that priority will continue outside of the White House. She says she wants to get her daughters through college, and out into the world on their own, and what good mother wouldn't. I believe she will do that. The Obamas have purchased a house in Northwest Washington, DC, and we will wait to see what the future holds for them and their family. A lot of things have happened in and around Washington, DC since 2008. As I write this book in the middle of 2017 (almost 10 years after

President Obama was sworn into office) there are a lot of things better in the world, and there are a lot of things worse in the world. Just as President and Mrs. Hoover could not have fixed, nor did they create the Great Depression on their own, President and Mrs. Obama could not have fixed or broken the United States of America by themselves. Like every other couple that has lived as President and First Lady, they are only human.

Travelogue Food Tip

Because I live in Maryland, and have spent my entire life going out to eat in and around Washington, DC, it is almost impossible to pick a favorite restaurant or recommendation for this town and this chapter. I have already mentioned my friends at Perry's in Adams Morgan for sushi and other interesting menu items. I always go to the Original Big Slice for a giant slice of pepperoni pizza, before or after a live show when I'm in town. The area over by the 930 Club along U St. NW always seems to have some cool new restaurant to try, and I've never gone wrong dining out around there. But, one area I have noticed that's changing quite a bit for the better, is the Southeast area of Washington. The Nationals baseball team came to DC during the Bush Administration, but the new baseball stadium had its first game in 2008, at the beginning of the Obama Administration. The area around the stadium has continued to develop and flourish ever since. I went out to dinner at a newer restaurant not too long ago called Osteria Morini. They feature fresh homemade and unique recipes from Northern Italy with a beautiful view of the Anacostia River. Folks who know DC, and haven't been back in a while will laugh when they read this, because back in the day, you wouldn't want to be caught in this area during the daylight, even if you were driving a tank, let alone have dinner there. Let me tell you, times have changed, and this was, by far, the best Italian meal I've ever had. Period.

CHAPTER TWENTY-ONE

Melania Trump

Washington, D. C.

Melania Trump was born Melanija Knvas on April 26, 1970 in Novo Mesto, Slovenia, Yugoslavia. Her parents were Viktor and Amalija Knavs. Melania and Donald Trump were married on January 22, 2005. They have one child together. Melania Trump is living in Washington, DC in the White House with her husband, President Donald Trump.

WASHINGTON, DC

When Donald Trump first pulled ahead in the polls, and it looked like he had a shot at becoming the Republican Presidential Candidate, I said Melania Trump would be a huge asset. As the field narrowed, I said she could be the next Jacqueline Kennedy. This upset some people, and I knew it would. One person who agreed with me was Donald Trump. I'm not saying I gave him this idea, or he got the idea from me. However, the timing on my statement and his statement was very interesting. Here's what I meant when I said Melania Trump could be the next Jacqueline Kennedy.

Article By Andrew Och June 2016 On Melania Trump Being The Next Jacqueline Kennedy:

Americans have always fallen in love with first ladies who are young and attractive. Melania Trump, 46, is both.

If Donald Trump is elected president of the United States in November, his wife has all of the elements to be as popular on the national and international stage as a Jacqueline Kennedy or a Laura Bush.

First ladies serve many purposes on both the public stage and behind the scenes. They typically poll higher than their husbands — and history has shown that those who poll extremely well can even help their husbands' numbers and popularity.

The youngest first lady in history was Frances Cleveland. At just 21 years old, Frances Folsom married a 49-year-old bachelor president, Grover Cleveland. They are the only presidential couple ever to get married in the White House.

The Cleveland team immediately got to work using Frances' image and popularity to help secure Cleveland a second (and non-consecutive) term in the White House. The Clevelands were the only couple to do this as well. Mrs. Cleveland's image appeared on posters, ad campaigns, and every kind of souvenir imaginable. She was definitely a hot commodity — in fact, she was Jacqueline Kennedy before Jacqueline Kennedy.

In 2016, Melania Trump could do the same thing. She could become as much a part of the Trump campaign as Mamie Eisenhower was for her husband, Dwight D. Eisenhower, in 1952 and 1956.

Mrs. Trump is also smart. She speaks five languages: Slovenian, English, French, Serbian, and German. The only other first lady who knew more languages was Lou Hoover — Mrs. Hoover spoke seven, including Mandarin Chinese. She is confident and seemingly unflappable by the press. She has her own ideas and sticks to her convictions.

Melania Trump has dabbled in philanthropic endeavors, as well. She has worked with the Red Cross, and been involved with breast cancer awareness work. Causes like this play very well both nationally and internationally in the public eye, and thus would reflect well on her husband. She has even said in interviews that she would be a more traditional first lady, like Betty Ford or Jacqueline Kennedy.

And what of her nationality? Melania Trump would be only the country's second foreign-born first lady. John Quincy Adams' wife, Louisa Catherine Adams, was the first — born in London, England. Mrs. Trump was born in the war-torn Eastern European country of Slovenia, then part of Yugoslavia. This could also play very well for her. If Mrs. Trump were to take on international causes, such as refugee orphans or global women's rights and freedoms — similar to a post-9/11 Laura Bush — this would push her popularity up even higher. She also supports her husband's immigration policies, which could pull people in Washington and across the country over to his way of thinking.

She could even grease the skids of foreign relations with Vladimir Putin and the Russians, if she played her heritage correctly.

Melania Trump is a former model and fashion designer who is poised to grace the cover of almost every major magazine out there.

She is also the mother of a 10-year-old boy, Barron William Trump, the youngest of Donald Trump's five children. The only thing that plays better than a young, attractive first lady in a first family is young children.

Melania Trump really does have it all when it comes to the elements that make a popular first lady.

One of the first times most of the world saw Melania Trump was at the Republican National Convention in Cleveland, Ohio on July 18, 2016. Everything was going very well, and she was well-received, until it was discovered that some lines in her speech came directly or almost directly from Michelle Obama's DNC speech in 2008. Mrs. Trump (or her people) had cited Mrs. Obama as someone Mrs. Trump admired in the past, and they claimed Mrs. Trump offered previous speeches made by Michelle Obama to her staff as inspiration and example when writing her 2016 RNC speech. Fine. Anyone who thinks any of these people (Presidents or First Ladies) write their own speeches by themselves is living in a world of make believe and unicorns. Sure, they write, contribute, influence, and approve their speeches, but they have large staffs of people, consultants and speechwriters who handle these things. The bottom line is someone messed up, but worse things have happened. Here's what happened on the back end, or in the fallout that could have been avoided, in my opinion.

After the RNC speech, Melania Trump all but disappeared. She pulled back from the public, the news, the interviews and campaign events, and made things worse when the Trump campaign could have used her or needed her most. In the even grander scheme of things, none of this matters, because Donald Trump is now President Trump. However, if Melania Trump had handled things a little differently, she might be having an easier time with some of her critics today. If I were advising the Trumps at the time of the speech or currently (which I wasn't and am not), I would have put her right out the next day at every event I could get her to. She could've explained for herself her appreciation and respect for Michelle Obama, and how much she was inspired by her as a First Lady and wife. This would have reinforced her intent, the mistake, the use of Mrs. Obama's words, and her admiration for the previous First Lady. More importantly, it would have taken the fuel out of the fire for the news agencies. If you admit to the mistake or take ownership of the accusation, the media has no interest in it. Trust me on this one. More importantly, it would have let Melania Trump be the campaign asset she could have been for her husband, and created a more user friendly and positive public image for herself.

One of the greatest things a First Lady does for her husband is make him a more likable person (Dolley Madison and Grace Coolidge come to mind). They make him more human. They make him a family man. Donald Trump was a controversial and divisive individual before he ever ran for office or was elected President. First Ladies always poll higher than their husbands, and have a better reputation than their husbands. This is in part, because we don't elect them or pay their salaries. We don't officially own or control them in the way we feel we do with our Presidents. This is because they are not politicians. This is where Hillary Clinton gambled and won some, but lost the big one (but, I digress). Melania Trump could, and still may, help her husband and his administration in the PR Department. As I said in the article above and at countless speeches... younger, more attractive First Ladies with a good sense of style, and young children, are historically very popular and effective.

When Melania took a step back, Donald Trump's children stepped further into the spotlight. Trump incorporated his adult children into his campaign, and now his presidency, in a way that other Presidents (Jefferson, Monroe, Jackson, Van Buren, Taylor, Fillmore, Buchanan, A. Johnson, Wilson, Ford and Carter) have been doing since the 1800's. Adult children can also be a huge asset to a President and First Lady. One of the greatest assets for a presidential candidate is his or her family - this has long been the case.

Article By Andrew Och August 2016 On The Role Of The Family In Presidential Campaigns:

Ever since the days of George Washington, candidates of all parties have been using their spouses and their family members to help drive home their points, show a more personal side, and win over voters. During the American Revolution, Martha Washington made speeches on behalf of then-General Washington from her coach while on the road to and from winter encampments.

From the winter of 1775 through the winter of 1778, Mrs. Washington traveled at great personal risk to be with her husband during the war. There she was, bundled up to protect herself against the elements - and she would have no problem stopping to address the crowds that would gather along the way to hear news about the general and the fighting. She also entertained visiting dignitaries and military officials at Valley Forge and other encampments to help promote her husband's views and policies with a softer touch.

Flash forward to the conventions in Cleveland and Philadelphia these past two weeks - and the world watched as the spouses of the candidates, as well as the Trump children and Chelsea Clinton, delivered carefully crafted speeches in support of their loved ones. None of this is an accident.

In America's past, some candidates kept their children and families as far out of the public eye as possible. The Cleveland, Garfield, and Theodore Roosevelt campaigns come to mind as examples of this. Why, you may ask, in light of the positives just mentioned? For starters, security back then wasn't what it is today. Public access to the candidates and their families was virtually unobstructed, and in some corners there was genuine concern for the safety of the candidates' young children and the families' privacy.

The press and the public can be cruel - and raising children in the white-hot political spotlight can be difficult.

But children and spouses usually make a candidate seem more user-friendly and congenial, even as using them effectively and responsibly in a campaign can be a tough line to walk.

A gregarious and affable wife - such as a Dolley Madison or a Grace Cleveland - can put gruffer husbands in a better public light. A clever candidate can use his politically savvy spouse and adult children to reach an entirely different audience and send important messages to benefit the campaign. These family members become surrogates and can even find Cabinet or administration positions in the event their family member wins the election (think of Robert F. Kennedy, who served as U. S. attorney general in the administration of his brother, John F. Kennedy).

This plan was used effectively by the Jimmy Carter campaign in the 1976 election, as one example. Rosalynn Carter organized and mobilized a group called the "Peanut Brigade," which employed the Carters' three adult sons - Jack, James, and Donnel - as well as Jimmy Carter's mother, Miss Lillian. Their grassroots efforts and sheer numbers covered a lot of ground and helped introduce a relatively unknown Georgia governor to the masses.

The Bush family has campaigned tirelessly for three different Bush men up to this point. And while it didn't work out so well for Jeb, earlier on for the Bushes, their work did show the power of family and the ability to get a candidate's message out there.

The Clintons are a known factor. With two presidential terms, a Senate career, and four years as secretary of state between them, the public knows Bill and Hillary Clinton pretty well. Chelsea Clinton grew up in the public eye. Then she all but disappeared for a little while, and now she's emerged again as an adult with a husband, two children, and a voice that could prove effective on the campaign trail. Chances are, if you like the Clintons, you will like Chelsea - and she could take some of the negative attention of controversy and scandal off Hillary - and perhaps even minimize Bill Clinton's past indiscretions.

When it comes to children, the Trumps seem to have the best of both worlds. Donald Trump has adult children who can campaign on their own and deliver serious policy and issue speeches. He also has a young son, Barron, age 10, who can travel with either of his parents and bring the family vibe that Americans love so much. Donald Jr. , Ivanka, and Eric are all highly educated and have proven themselves more than capable of delivering a clear and effective message for their father.

Both Donald Jr. and Ivanka made very well-received speeches at the RNC, as did Tiffany Trump, and if that kind of clarity and positive reception continues on the road, the Trump children will prove to be huge assets to their father.

What the candidates need to remember is this: As soon as those family members are brought to the national stage, they become fair game for the public and the press. This is hardly the kindest platform - and having thick skin is a must. Candidates' children and family members need to ignore the criticisms, stay on message, and keep the ultimate goal - the White House - in their sights.

Most of the folks involved know the risks before they enter the game of politics. Like all games, there are winners and losers. The election in November will write the next pages of history - and tell us which political family played the better game.

When President Trump first took office, Melania Trump and their son Barron stayed in New York City. She endured considerable criticism for this. She said she wanted to let her son finish his school year, and they would move into the White House over the summer. People doubted her, but she and her son moved to DC, as she said she would in June 2017. I don't have any children of my own, but I hear raising them can be difficult. Raising them in the White House compounds that difficulty significantly. I also hear if you try and tell a woman how to raise her children you are not a very wise person. First Ladies have been struggling with raising children in the White House for centuries. Melania Trump was only doing what she felt was best for her son at the time.

Article By Andrew Och May 2016 On Raising Children In The White House:

The unique sorority of women known as America's first ladies have been (and are) many things to many people. They have been ambassadors. They have been confidants. They have been advisers, friends, partners, campaign managers, and sounding boards for their presidential spouses.

They were also many things before they ever occupied the White House. These flesh-and-blood women were little girls, young women, daughters, sisters, cousins, brides, aunts, and girlfriends - and most of them were mothers. Only one first lady never had any children and that was Sarah Polk. She and James Polk were a political power couple for the ages, but that's a different article for another day. This weekend we celebrate Mother's Day, and so we recognized the first ladies of our country who were and are mothers.

It's hard enough being a mother under what we might consider "normal" circumstances. Mothering children while living in the White House fishbowl is quite another story. In most cases, this becomes an issue early, on the presidential campaign trail. With today's smartphones, 24-hour-news and the Internet, it's hard for first ladies to protect their children and their everyday activities from the prying eyes of the outside world. It makes their jobs as mothers even harder - and that challenge is something these women have shared for centuries.

When Congressman James A. Garfield went off to the Republican National

Convention in Chicago in 1880, it was to nominate a presidential candidate, not to become one. However, he returned to his wife, Lucretia, and their family in Mentor, Ohio, as just that. Garfield then proceeded to conduct the country's first presidential front-porch campaign. The Garfields had extensively renovated their Lawnfield estate, and the last thing Mrs. Garfield expected or wanted was some 20,000 people roaming across her pristine yard - but that's what happened.

She also had her five children to think about. She did not want them bothered or drawn into the ever-growing media circus.

During the campaign, Mrs. Garfield would stand at the front door and wait for her husband to come downstairs from his second-floor office, where he would then walk out the front door to greet the masses. She would promptly shut the door behind him. She did allow some people into the house. There were important supporters, military members, and party officials who needed to be entertained on a more personal level, and they were welcomed into the front foyer - but only the front foyer.

There, she served "standing" refreshments such as water, tea, or lemonade, maybe some cookies to the privileged supporters - but she provided no seating. This was all part of an effort - a successful one - to keep her children out of the public eye. Sadly, President Garfield was assassinated less than a year into his presidency, so there is little to go on in terms of how she raised her children as first lady.

Grover Cleveland was the second bachelor to be elected president (James Buchanan was first). But Cleveland didn't stay single for long. He married Frances Folsom - he was 49, she was only 21 - on June 2, 1886. She remains the youngest first lady to date and they're the only presidential couple to be married in the White House. The young and attractive Frances Cleveland took Washington, D. C. by storm. She was Jacqueline Kennedy before Jacqueline Kennedy. She was stylish and charming, and before long, there were babies in the White House.

During the Cleveland administration, the White House and its grounds were still fairly open and accessible to the public. People would come right up to the Cleveland children and pick them up out of their strollers and out of the hands of their nannies. The public back then (as it does now, in some respects) believed the White House and everything in it belonged to the people - and that included the president and the first lady's children. But this was completely unacceptable to Mrs. Cleveland, who took measures to put an end to this kind of behavior.

The Clevelands chose to spend less time at the White House. They were there for the social season, but during the summer months and off months they took up residence near what is now Meridian Hill Park in Washington, D. C. The public felt snubbed. Many thought the Clevelands had become reclusive and snobbish as they tried to hide their once-celebrated children from the public.

Yet Mrs. Cleveland cared not a whit. She put her children's well-being ahead of her own popularity and her husband's. As it turned out, the negative opinions weren't enough to keep the Clevelands out of the White House for a second term. They were the only president and first lady to serve two nonconsecutive terms.

After President Willian McKinley was shot by an anarchist named Leon Czolgosz in Buffalo, New York, on September 6, 1901 - and died eight days later - the country had a new president in Theodore Roosevelt and a new first lady in his wife, Edith. After the Roosevelts moved their six children from New York to Washington, D. C. , the White House was once again alive with youthful, bustling activity.

If you count President Roosevelt, Mrs. Roosevelt now had seven children to look after in the White House. The Roosevelts were responsible for one of the largest structural renovations there, and Edith Roosevelt worked tirelessly with a well-known architect to redesign the executive mansion. They moved the family quarters upstairs and built the East and West Wings of the White House.

Given the size of the family and all of the pets that went with them (including a pony, a lizard, a barn owl, a hyena, numerous guinea pigs, and a blue macaw named Eli Yale) - the renovations were a necessity. The public couldn't get enough of this amazingly interesting family.

Ultimately, Edith Roosevelt decided to give the public what it wanted - the children. She, however, would control the access. She very wisely hired a professional photographer, Frances Johnston, to shoot a series of portraits of the family to give to the press. These photographs remain some of the best-known pictures of any presidential children.

There is a picture of son Quentin on Algonquin, the pony, as a police officer stands watch. (Algonquin was the only pony ever to have ridden in the White House elevator.) Another picture shows Archie on his favorite bicycle. Kermit is in a picture with one of the family's beloved dogs, Jack. Theodore Jr. proudly holds the famous blue macaw in another photo. The girls, Alice and Ethel, wore lovely dresses and stood under trees. These pictures were famously compiled and published in The Ladies' Home Journal and seemed to satisfy the public's vast appetite for images of the Roosevelt children.

In more modern times, we've seen such presidential children as Amy Carter and Chelsea Clinton struggle through their teenage years. We saw the Reagan children go through some rough patches with their parents, and, very recently, mourn them deeply in public. The Obamas have kept a watchful eye over their daughters and restricted media access to them. Now, during the 2016 presidential campaign, we've seen a new group of political offspring make their way across campaign stages, eat ice cream sundaes in public, give speeches at some events, and share their lives with the world while standing beside their aspiring parents.

The White House is the people's house. Presidents and their families are "hired" by "we the people," and they represent us in many ways. They are, of course, just people, striving to do their best in sometimes trying circumstances. But from Martha Washington to Michelle Obama, America's first ladies have always worked to protect their families and their children, come what may - and for this they can be applauded.

Another function of the First Lady, which also helps in the PR department of her husband's administration, is in her charity work, the causes she supports and the philanthropies she endorses. Mrs. Trump first claimed cyber bullying as a cause she would like to support and combating it is an area in which she would like to work. She has since broadened that to include the overall wellness of children. Advocating for children is very good place for a First Lady to focus her efforts. Dolley Madison, Harriet Lane, Lucy Hayes and many other early First Ladies worked with children's causes, especially after the Civil War. Other more modern First Ladies like Grace Coolidge, Lou Hoover, Nancy Reagan, Barbara

Bush, Hillary Clinton, Laura Bush and Michelle Obama have also made children their main focus when it came to their support and philanthropic efforts. In her first six months as First Lady, Melania Trump has visited schools, read to children, and participated in holiday events at the White House. During President Trump's first international trip, Mrs. Trump went to see children in hospitals, schools and orphanages in Brussels, Italy, and Jerusalem. Time will tell where she puts her priorities, and what groups and organizations will get more of her attention. If I were advising Mrs. Trump (and, again, I'm not), I would encourage her to use her (and her husband's) star power and celebrity. It worked out very well for the Reagans and Obamas. Both Presidential couples were very popular with Hollywood, and in pop culture. Star power and celebrities have always been an integral part of the White House and the philanthropic work that comes out of it. Here's a free idea or suggestion for Melania Trump. Lady Gaga is a strong voice in the world of anti-bullying. She was also a big supporter of Hillary Clinton. If the Trump people and the Gaga people could put political differences aside for the sake of the children, I think it would send a powerful message to world.

SUMMARY

It's difficult to summarize something or someone that hasn't really started or began their work in the role for which you a summarizing, so this will be brief. What Melania Trump has done, so far…in life, on the campaign trail, and as First Lady is not neither unheard of nor unprecedented. We've even had a couple First Ladies who were models. Julia Tyler was called "The Rose of Long Island" after she appeared in a newspaper advertisement for a local dry goods company, and Frances Cleveland appeared in an ad for a Merrick Thread. Melania put her child first, and allowed him to finish out his school year in New York, before moving to Washington, DC. Her husband's other (adult) children played a large roll in his campaign, and now his daughter, Ivanka, has taken on a visible advisory role in her father's administration, and occupies office space in the White House. All of this has been done. The unusual thing here, is Melania is young enough, intelligent enough and in good health, so we expect her to take on a more active and public role as First Lady. Technically, she doesn't have to do anything. I've said it more than enough times in these two volumes, but I'll say it again. We do not elect or pay these women. They are women who happened to marry men who got elected to be President of the United States. There is no job description or rules for the First Lady…only public opinion and expectation. So, when it comes to Melania Trump, let's wait and see. We barely know how history is going to portray Michelle Obama, and the Obama Presidential Library and Museum hasn't even opened yet. We're still learning things about Martha Washington, Dolley Madison, Mary Lincoln, Nancy Reagan and Hillary Clinton. There's plenty to keep us busy over the next four, eight, sixteen years and beyond, before we start worrying about the current First Lady and what history will say about her.

Travelogue Food Tip

I don't know anything about Slovenian cuisine, but I can promise you this…I WILL before all this FIRST LADIES MAN business is over. I'm still waiting for the Obama Museum to open in Chicago so I can go get a couple of good hot dogs, and a Lou Malnati's Pizza. I hear Hawaii is nice this time of year, too. Stay tuned!!

CONCLUSION

Behind every great man is an even greater woman...or in this case...lady.

If George Washington had never met and married Martha Dandridge Custis, this book would be called something quite different. It may have been written in a different language, or perhaps never written at all.

If George and Martha Washington had never married, America would be a very different place... or quite possibly... not America at all.

Martha Washington was unusual for her time.

Each chapter in Volume One and Volume Two has started out with the same format. This volume started with Edith Roosevelt. The first First Lady of the 20th Century.

Edith Roosevelt was born Edith Kermit Carow on August 6, 1861 in Norwich, Connecticut. Her parents were Charles Carow and Gertrude Tyler. Edith and Theodore Roosevelt were married on December 2, 1886. They had five children together. They raised Theodore's daughter (Alice) from his first marriage to Alice Lee in 1880. Alice Lee died giving birth to daughter Alice in 1884. Edith Roosevelt died in Oyster Bay, New York on September 30, 1948 at the age of 87.

This format was not accidental. It took me a long time to figure out, and settle on the information I wanted to include there. It introduces you to a woman, but also to a concept each of you already knows. We all know what a First Lady is. We all have a face and name that pops into our head when we hear the term "First Lady." Mine might be Lucy Hayes. Yours could be Jacqueline Kennedy, Abigail Adams, Nancy Reagan or Michelle Obama. The First Lady is not a new title or concept for any of us. However, they were not born a First Lady. Their last name was not Washington, Taft, Hoover or Clinton (but, it might have been Roosevelt!). They had parents, brothers, sisters, aunts, uncles, and families. They met and married men who became President. They had children with these men who became President, and in most cases, they had these children before they were First Ladies. They were more than just First Ladies, they were, and are, real people who lived, died, laughed, cried, won, lost, and loved. They were and are human beings, and I wanted to make that point at the beginning of each of their chapters.

When I joined the team at C-SPAN, we had a meeting. We didn't have the entire staff in place or a final blueprint for the individual shows yet. We had historians, the White House Historical Association, a studio, a host, a concept, and we had the First Ladies. I told myself not to say anything during the meeting. Everyone in the room knew much more about the First Ladies than I did. I was the new kid on the block. Anyone who knows me, knows this is an impossible thing to ask of me, but I had a pep talk with myself before the meeting. I said out loud, "just sit there, listen and learn. Don't say anything. Listen and take notes." It was a good plan…on paper (or in my mind), and I followed the plan for most of the meeting. But, something was missing from the conversation, as we outlined the contents of each show. So, I held my breath, waited for a pause in the conversation, deviated from the plan, and raised my hand to speak. I said we were missing or hadn't brought up the importance of these women outside of, or before the White House. They were wives and mothers before they were First Ladies. When I finished my point, I physically winced. I was waiting for the laughter, the "well, DUHHHHHHHH" or, "That goes without saying!" I was quickly validated by one of the historians for the series, William Seale, who was seated to my left. He turned and gave me a thoughtful look. I think I may have even ducked as he looked my way, but I tried to remain confident. Bill then turned back to the group assembled and said, "He's right." I WAS RIGHT! I guess it DID need mentioning. I mean, it wasn't on the dry erase board or any of the basic outlines of the show, so I said something. And I'm glad I did. It was added to the dry erase board and the show outline. It was also the genesis of my thoughts, focus and research that developed into the FIRST LADIES MAN.

When I started this adventure, I was not a historian, or an author. Thanks to these women and their amazing stories, I am now both. I was a television producer working on a televisions series. I was just doing my job. Telling good stories, and making TV programs. I had no idea what was ahead of me, or how big a part of my life these women would become. I got to know this unique sorority of women, and learned how each one of them was and is unusual for their time. I accomplished this by visiting their homes, reading their letters and having access to their collective lives in a way no one ever had before. They were and are First Ladies, and because there is only one (in most cases) every four to eight years, that makes them unusual at face value alone. But, they were all more than a face. They helped form, develop, organize, maintain and continue the ideas and values of our country...the United States of America. They were unusual for every man, woman and child of their time...before their time...and after their time. For that, all of them deserve our gratitude and continued interest, research and respect.

It has always been my goal to represent these women, and tell their stories as real people. I have done countless shows, stories, documentaries, travels and work during my life. I have only written books about one subject. I only speak about one topic. First Ladies. I will continue this work as long as there are First Ladies, and eventually (hopefully soon) a First Gentleman. No matter who is the elected leader in the White House, I will do my best to tell the personal story of their spouse. That's my job. My name is Andrew Och, and I'm THE FIRST LADIES MAN.

ADDENDUM

Many People ask me why I like the First Ladies so much, or how I first got interested in them. My initial answer is always, "I fell backwards right into them, and was in the right place at the right time." I wasn't particularly or outwardly interested in them until after I started the work on the C-SPAN series. Before the series, or at the beginning of the series it was just another job. However, now that the series is long over, and I have finished two books about these amazing women, I am thinking about the woman to whom this whole FIRST LADIES MAN project is dedicated, and I am reminded of her image and influence over me. Here are the words I spoke at Julie Carroll Och's memorial service on November 22, 2010.

Today I wear all black. I clearly remember July 4th, 1976. My mom pointed through a crowd of tens if not hundreds of thousands of people on the national mall in Washington, DC as the opening notes of Folsom Prison Blues echoed over the bicentennial celebration. . . and my mom said. . . there he is. . . the man in black. . . that's Johnny Cash. So, today I wear black. Not because I'm sad and not because I'm at a funeral. I wear black because the man in black is cool. . . and I know this is cool…because that's what my mom taught me.

Who here today remembers where they were the day Elvis died? Show of hands? It was August 16th, 1977. I was eight and my brother Jeremy was one and a half. I remember looking through the bay window in the kitchen of Myer Terrace. . . crying. My mom taught me about Elvis. The story gets better when I found out my dad…who was out of town in Camp Perry, Ohio…was really worried that my mother had packed my brother and me up in the white Ford station wagon and headed south to Graceland. And for me…that story has better over the years. . . as I have realized how cool it was to have a mom crazy enough that my father thought she would have done something like that…that it was an option. . . but she was sensible enough not to go. Truth be told. . . I wish we had gone.

My mom taught me how to order things from TV commercials. Things like the double record gate fold album Elvis Goes Hollywood... she then taught me how to use the U. S. Postal Service. . . and thus had to teach me patience as I waited for my package to arrive. And when it finally came in the mail she taught me how to enjoy the fruits of my labor and reap the rewards of my patience...we made the full color collector's edition photo booklet into a mobile for my room. It was an Andy and Mom original and I was the only kid on my block who had one.

My mom was a teacher. During her life, she taught some of us as a mother. . . some of us as a den mother. . . she taught as a wife, a sister, an aunt, a daughter, a school trip chaperone, a part time librarian. . . and as a friend.

In my Halloween costumes and school play get ups my mom taught me that a Leggs pantyhose egg container could become frog eyes. . . and in her crown jewel of creativity...that a radio shack catalog could be transformed into Darth Vader's chest plate control panel...the greatest Darth Vader costume a kid could ever ask or hope for. She handmade corsages for many of you sitting here in the crowd today so you would be the only girl at the dance with those flowers. She taught me creativity and imagination. Thinking outside the box and beyond the norm.

When I stuck a piece of blue rubber from a zips sneaker in my ear and forgot about it. . . wondering much later why my ear hurt so badly. . . she taught me that hydrogen peroxide makes things float! She taught me to talk to people in line at the grocery store. . . she taught me to honk at people driving similar cars. . . she taught me that ketchup, mayonnaise and lemon juice made a pretty good substitute for French dressing. . . and she taught me that when you see stars in the sky that don't twinkle or flicker...they aren't stars at all they are planets.

And in one of her final moments of clarity she reinforced something that she had been teaching me all my life. . . loyalty. On Monday November 15th. . . just two days before she died...my mother said she wanted to watch the Redskins vs Eagles Monday Night Football game. . . barely able to speak. . . not even really able to focus enough to watch television. . . she wanted me to put the skins game on. For the purpose of this conversation we won't go into the details of the game. . . but it got me thinking...life has kinda been like the Redskins. . . I've had good seasons and bad seasons. . . good plays and bad plays...I've had teammates that I've been lucky enough to keep. . . and teammates that I've been better off trading. However. . . no matter what kind of season or game I was having. . . my mom was always watching and cheering me on. I can easily remember more than one halftime pep talk. . . get yourself together. . . get back out there. . . pull yourself up by your bootstraps!!!! She was always there coaching. . . teaching and cheering.

One final thing my mom only recently taught me about a month ago. She told me that funerals are for learning things you didn't know about people. So today. . . let's all learn something about her. I know what I remember about her. . . but what do you remember about her? Tell me…I'd like to know. You can easily find me. . . . just look through the crowd. . . today. . . I am the man in black.

LOCATIONS

Thank You

THE FIRST LADIES MAN would like to thank all of the locations that shared their people, places, collections, information and time.

Volume 1

COLONIAL WILLIAMSBURG

VALLEY FORGE NATIONAL HISTORIC PARK

INDEPENDENCE NATIONAL HISTORIC PARK

GEORGE WASHINGTON'S MOUNT VERNON

ADAMS NATIONAL HISTORIC PARK

UNITED FIRST PARISH CHURCH

ABIGAIL ADAMS HISTORICAL SOCIETY

MASSACHUSETTS HISTORICAL SOCIETY

THOMAS JEFFERSON'S MONTICELLO

JAMES MADISON'S MONTPELIER

THE OCTAGON HOUSE

THE DUMBARTON HOUSE

THE JAMES MONROE MUSEUM AND MEMORIAL LIBRARY

ASH LAWN-HIGHLAND

OAK HILL ESTATE

ANDREW JACKSON'S HERMITAGE

MARTIN VAN BUREN NATIONAL HISTORIC SITE

CEDAR GROVE PLANTATION

SHERWOOD FOREST

JAMES K. POLK ANCESTRAL HOME

MILLARD FILLMORE HOUSE

THE PIERCE MANSE

NEW HAMPSHIRE HISTORICAL SOCIETY

ANDOVER HISTORICAL SOCIETY

THE AIKEN HOUSE

FENDRICK LIBRARY

JAME'S BUCHANAN'S WHEATLAND

HARRIET LANE BIRTHPLACE HOME

MARY TODD LINCOLN HOUSE

LINCOLN HOME NATIONAL HISTORIC SITE

ABRAHAM LINCOLN PRESIDENTIAL LIBRARY AND MUSEM

PRESIDENT LINCOLN'S COTTAGE

ANDREW JOHNSON NATIONAL HISTORIC SITE

ULYSSES S. GRANT NATIONAL HISTORIC SITE

GRANT'S FARM

ULYSSES S. GRANT HOME

RUTHERFORD B. HAYES PRESIDENTIAL CENTER

JAMES A. GARFIELD NATIONAL HISTORIC SITE

ST. JOHN'S EPISCOPAL CHURCH

SMITHSONIAN INSTITUTION

NATIONAL MUSEM OF AMERICAN HISTORY

GARRETT COUNTY HISTORICAL SOCIETY MUSEUM

BENJAMIN HARRISON PRESIDENTIAL SITE

SAXTON MCKINLEY HOUSE

NATIONAL FIRST LADIES LIBRARY

WILLIAM MCKINLEY PRESIDENTIAL LIBRARY AND MUSEUM

Volume 2

GREENSBORO HISTORICAL MUSEM

LUCY WEBB HAYES HERITAGE CENTER

SAGAMORE HILL NATIONAL HISTORIC SITE

WILLIAM HOWARD TAFT NATIONAL HISTORIC SITE

WOODROW WILSON PRESIDENTIAL LIBRARY AND MUSEM

EDITH BOLLING WILSON BIRTHPLACE MUSEUM

PRINCETON UNIVERSITY

THE PRESIDENT WOODROW WILSON HOUSE

HARDING HOME PRESIDENTIAL SITE

PRESIDENT CALVIN COOLIDGE STATE HISTORIC SITE
CALVIN COOLIDGE FOUNDATION
CALVIN COOLIDGE PRESIDENTIAL LIBRARY AND MUSEUM
THE FORBES LIBRARY
HISTORIC NORTHAMPTON MUSEUM
OPAL DEVELOPMENT
HERBERT HOOVER PRESIDENTIAL LIBRARY AND MUSEUM
STANFORD UNIVERSITY
THE HOOVER INSTITUTION
SHENANDOAH NATIONAL PARK
FRANKLIN D. ROOSEVELT PRESIDENTIAL LIBRARY AND MUSEUM
HOME OF FRANKLIN D. ROOSEVELT NATIONAL HISTORIC SITE
HARRY S. TRUMAN PRESIDENTIAL LIBRARY AND MUSEUM
HARRY S TRUMAN NATIONAL HISTORIC SITE
DWIGHT D. EISENHOWER PRESIDENTIAL LIBRARY MUSEUM AND BOYHOOD HOME
JOHN F. KENNEDY PRESIDENTIAL LIBRARY AND MUSEUM
LBJ PRESIDENTIAL LIBRARY
LYNDON B. JOHNSON NATIONAL HISTORIC PARK
RICHARD M. NIXON PRESIDENTIAL LIBRARY AND MUSEUM
RICHARD NIXON FOUNDATION
RICHARD M. NIXON PRESIDENTIAL LIBRARY AND MUSEUM
GERALD R. FORD PRESIDENTIAL MUSEUM
JIMMY CARTER NATIONAL HISTORIC SITE
RONALD REAGAN PRESIDENTIAL LIBRARY AND MUSEUM
GEORGE BUSH PRESIDENTIAL LIBRARY AND MUSEUM
CLINTON HOUSE MUSEUM
GEORGE W. BUSH LIBRARY AND MUSEUM

RECOMMENDED *Reading*

Books used during the series, travels and writing of this book:

VOLUME ONE

The First Ladies Fact Book

by Bill Harris Revised by Laura Ross

Homes of the First Ladies

by William G. Clotworthy

Loves, Lies and Tears: An Intimate Look at America's First Ladies

Volume 1 by Jacqueline Berger

The First Ladies: An Intimate Portrait of the Women Who Shaped America by Feather Schwartz Foster

Rating the First Ladies: The Women Who Influenced the Presidency

by John B. Roberts II

Martha Washington: An American Life

by Patricia Brady

Abigail & John: A Portrait of Marriage

by Edith B. Gelles

Abigail Adams: A Writing Life

by Edith B. Gelles

My Dearest Friend: Letters of Abigail and John Adams

Edited by Margaret A. Hogan and C. James Taylor

The Adams Papers: Adams Family Correspondence *Volume 10*

Edited by Margaret Hogan, C. James Taylor, Sara Martin, Hobson Woodward, Sara B. Sikes, Gregg L. Lint and Sara Georgini

A Perfect Union: Dolley Madison and the Creation of the American Nation

by Catherine Allgor

The Adams Papers: Diary and Autobiographical Writings of Louisa Catherine Adams *Volumes 1 & 2*

Edited by Judith S. Graham, Beth Luey, Margaret A. Hogan and C. James Taylor

A Being So Gentle: The Frontier Love Story of Rachel and Andrew Jackson by Patricia Brady

First Lady: The Life of Lucy Webb Hayes
by Emily Apt Geer

Harriet Lane Johnson
by Joan C. McCulloh

Destiny of the Republic: A Tale of Madness, Medicine and the Murder of a President by Candice Millard

VOLUME TWO

Frank: The Story of Frances Folsom Cleveland, America's Youngest First Lady by Annette Dunlap

Loves, Lies and Tears: An Intimate Look at America's First Ladies Volume 2 by Jacqueline Berger

The First Ladies: An Intimate Portrait of the Women Who Shaped America by Feather Schwartz Foster

Helen Taft: Our Musical First Lady
by Lewis Gould

Ellen and Edith: Woodrow Wilson's First Ladies
by Kristie Miller

Woodrow Wilson: Princeton to the Presidency
by W. Barksdale Maynard

First Lady Florence Harding: Behind the Tragedy and Controversy
by Katherine A. S. Sibley

Young Mister Roosevelt: FDR's Introduction to War, Politics, and Life
by Stanley Weintraub

My Life with Jacqueline Kennedy
by Mary Barelli Gallagher

ABOUT
THE FIRST LADIES MAN

Andrew Och

ANDREW OCH (age 7) - April 14, 1976 in front of First Lady Betty Ford's limo

Andrew Och is an award winning television and multi-media producer who has traveled the world with his pen, paper and camera. A Radio, Television and Film graduate from the University of Maryland, Andrew started his production career in music, recording and touring with his band in the 1980's and 1990's. Soon after that he added his camera to the mix and all the pieces fell into place. A storyteller from a young age, Andrew enjoys the art of communication, and will go anywhere in the world for more knowledge, greater understanding and a good story. He is a true documentarian of life.

Most recently, for the C-SPAN series – "First Ladies: Influence and Image," Andrew spent over a year traveling to nearly every location that helped tell the stories of every First Lady of the United States of America. He covered Martha Washington through Michelle Obama and visited with people and places all across the country. From Colonial Williamsburg to Stanford University he was given an ALL ACCESS – BACKSTAGE PASS to some of the nation's most treasured collections and historical landmarks. He spent time in libraries and museums, homes and schools, birthplaces and cemeteries, train stations and churches. No stone was left unturned nor door left unlocked in his unique and historical journey to learn everything he could about these women before, during and after their time in the White House.

Historians, archivists and enthusiasts agree "Andrew's recent project and travels put him in a small and rare group of people." He is responsible for one of the most vast and complete collections of material and information about this unique sorority of women ever assembled. He is the First Ladies Man and he is excited to share the stories of his adventures.

Credits and Contributors

Publishing: Tactical 16, LLC
CEO, Tactical 16: Erik Shaw
President, Tactical 16: Jeremy Farnes
Cover Design: Kristen Shaw
Author Photo: Austin Polasky
FLM Logo: Joe Wilk and Andrew Och
Web design - www.firstladiesman.com: Joe Wilk at Shadowfire Web Development

ABOUT THE PUBLISHER

Tactical 16, LLC

Tactical 16 is a Veteran owned and operated publishing company based in the beautiful mountain city of Colorado Springs, Colorado. What started as an idea among like-minded people has grown into reality.

Tactical 16 believes strongly in the healing power of writing, and provides opportunities for Veterans, Police, Firefighters, and EMTs to share their stories; striving to provide accessible and affordable publishing solutions that get the works of true American Heroes out to the world. We strive to make the writing and publication process as enjoyable and stress-free as possible.

As part of the process of healing and helping true American Heroes, we are honored to hear stories from all Veterans, Police Officers, Firefighters, EMTs and their spouses. Regardless of whether it's carrying a badge, fighting in a war zone or family at home keeping everything going, we know many have a story to tell.

At Tactical 16, we truly stand behind our mission to be "The Premier Publishing Resource for Guardians of Freedom."

We are a proud supporter of Our Country and its People, without which we would not be able to make Tactical 16 a reality.

How did Tactical 16 get its name? There are two parts to the name, "Tactical" and "16". Each has a different meaning. Tactical refers to the Armed Forces, Police, Fire, and Rescue communities or any group who loves, believes in, and supports Our Country. The "16" is the number of acres of the World Trade Center complex that was destroyed on that harrowing day of September 11, 2001. That day will be forever ingrained in the memories of many generations of Americans. But that day is also a reminder of the resolve of this Country's People and the courage, dedication, honor, and integrity of our Armed Forces, Police, Fire, and Rescue communities. Without Americans willing to risk their lives to defend and protect Our Country, we would not have the opportunities we have before us today.

Giant Squid Creations

Washington, DC

GIANT SQUID CREATIONS is the brainchild of Senior Executive Producer and President, Andrew Och. Andrew is an award winning television, music and multimedia producer who has been working in the United States and around the world for nearly 30 years. Giant Squid is a creative service that provides your projects an open-minded way of thinking that customizes and creates every project to fit the personal a professional wants, needs and desires of the client. Everything began for Andrew with musical rhythms, notes and the sound of drums. A lifetime of music and drumming has opened Andrew's eyes, ears and mind to the limitless world of multimedia. Anything and everything is possible with Giant Squid Creations.

www.giantsquid.us

CPSIA information can be obtained
at www.ICGtesting.com
Printed in the USA
BVOW09*0926031117
498909BV00004B/4/P